Food, Scarcity and Power in Southeastern Europe during the Second World War

Food, Scarcity and Power in Southeastern Europe during the Second World War

Edited by
Paolo Fonzi, Sabine Rutar and
Xavier Bougarel

BLOOMSBURY ACADEMIC
LONDON • NEW YORK • OXFORD • NEW DELHI • SYDNEY

BLOOMSBURY ACADEMIC
Bloomsbury Publishing Plc
50 Bedford Square, London, WC1B 3DP, UK
1385 Broadway, New York, NY 10018, USA
29 Earlsfort Terrace, Dublin 2, Ireland

First published in Great Britain 2024

Cover image: Youth conference in Majkic Japra (Western Bosnia), date unknown.
© History Museum of Bosnia Herzegovina.

A catalogue record for this book is available from the British Library.

A catalog record for this book is available from the Library of Congress.

ISBN: HB: 978-1-3503-3391-8
ePDF: 978-1-3503-3392-5
eBook: 978-1-3503-3393-2

Typeset by Integra Software Services Pvt. Ltd.

To find out more about our authors and books visit www.bloomsbury.com
and sign up for our newsletters.

Food, Scarcity and Power in Southeastern Europe during the Second World War

Edited by
Paolo Fonzi, Sabine Rutar and
Xavier Bougarel

BLOOMSBURY ACADEMIC
LONDON • NEW YORK • OXFORD • NEW DELHI • SYDNEY

BLOOMSBURY ACADEMIC
Bloomsbury Publishing Plc
50 Bedford Square, London, WC1B 3DP, UK
1385 Broadway, New York, NY 10018, USA
29 Earlsfort Terrace, Dublin 2, Ireland

BLOOMSBURY, BLOOMSBURY ACADEMIC and the Diana logo
are trademarks of Bloomsbury Publishing Plc

First published in Great Britain 2024

A catalogue record for this book is available from the British Library.

A catalog record for this book is available from the Library of Congress.

ISBN: HB: 978-1-3503-3391-8
ePDF: 978-1-3503-3392-5
eBook: 978-1-3503-3393-2

Typeset by Integra Software Services Pvt. Ltd.

To find out more about our authors and books visit www.bloomsbury.com
and sign up for our newsletters.

Contents

Figures

Maps

Contributors

Nikica Barić is Scientific Advisor at the Croatian Institute of History in Zagreb. He obtained his PhD from the Department of History of the Faculty of Philosophy in Zagreb in 2004. He has written several monographs and numerous scientific papers dealing with various aspects of twentieth-century Croatian history, including topics around the Second World War, as well as the era of communist Yugoslavia and the country's subsequent disintegration during the 1990s. From 2007 to 2016, he was Editor-in-Chief of *Časopis za suvremenu povijest* (*Journal of Contemporary History*) published by the Croatian Institute of History.

Alberto Basciani is Professor of East European History at Roma Tre University, where he heads the Interdepartmental Research Centre on Central and Eastern Europe, Russia and Eurasia (CRIERE). His research interests include ethnic and national conflicts and processes of modernization in the Balkan countries in the interwar period and fascist imperialism in Southeastern Europe, with a special focus on Albania. His latest books include *L'illusione della modernità. Il sud-est dell'Europa tra le due guerre mondiali* (2016) and *L'impero nei Balcani. L'occupazione italiana dell'Albania 1939–1943* (2022).

Xavier Bougarel is Senior Researcher at the Centre d'études turques, ottomanes, balkaniques et centrasiatiques (CETOBaC) at the École des hautes études en sciences sociales (EHESS) in Paris. He is the author of *La division Handschar. Waffen-SS en Bosnie 1943–1945* and *Chez les partisans de Tito. Communistes et paysans dans la Yougoslavie en guerre 1941–1945*, as well as a co-editor of *Local Dimensions of the Second World War in Southeastern Europe* and *Far from Jihad. Combatants of Muslim Origin in European Armies in the 20th Century*. He is currently working on a history of the Second World War in Southeastern Europe.

Paolo Fonzi is Associate Professor of Contemporary History at the University Federico II, Naples. He was a postdoc fellow at several institutions, including the Harvard Ukrainian Institute (Cambridge, MA), the Istituto Nazionale per la Storia del Movimento di Liberazione in Italia (Milan) and the Gerda Henkel Foundation (Düsseldorf). He has authored three monographs addressing different aspects of the history of the German and Italian occupations during the Second World War. His book *Fame di guerra. L'occupazione italiana della guerra 1941–1943* (2019) examines the Italian occupation of Greece during the Second World War through a social history approach.

Markenc Lorenci is a Teaching Fellow at Roma Tre University and an associate member of the Centre d'études turques, ottomanes, balkaniques et centrasiatiques

(CETOBaC) at the École des hautes études en sciences sociales (EHESS) in Paris. In 2021, he obtained his PhD with a dissertation on the Albanian Communist Party from its foundation to the seizure of power (1941–44).

Sabine Rutar is Senior Researcher at the Leibniz Institute for East and Southeast European Studies in Regensburg, Germany, where she works as Editor-in-Chief and Managing Editor of *Comparative Southeast European Studies*. In 2022–23 she was acting Professor of Global History at the University of Potsdam. She recently edited, with Anna Wylegała and Małgorzata Łukianow, *No Neighbors' Lands in Postwar Europe. Vanishing Others* (2023). In her forthcoming monograph *Resistance at Work under Hitler and Tito. Mining and Maritime Industries in Yugoslavia, 1940s–1970s*, she compares microhistories of industrial labour during the Second World War and the early Cold War.

Mojca Šorn holds a PhD in History and is a Research Fellow at the Institute of Contemporary History in Ljubljana, Slovenia. Her research focuses on Slovenian social history in the first half of the twentieth century. Among her prolific publishing endeavours are the monographs *Življenje Ljubljančanov med drugo svetovno vojno* (2007) and *Pomanjkanje in lakota v Ljubljani med véliko vojno* (2021). She is Editor-in-Chief of Založba INZ (the publishing house of the Institute of Contemporary History).

Spyros Tsoutsoumpis is a Lecturer at Lancaster University. His research interests are centred on the history of paramilitary violence, nationalism and irregular warfare in the Ottoman and post-Ottoman Balkans. His first monograph, *A History of the Greek Resistance in the Second World War: The People's Armies*, was published in 2016. He previously worked and taught at the Universities of Manchester, Wolverhampton and Manchester Metropolitan, and has been awarded fellowships by the School for Advanced Studies in Sofia, the New Europe College in Bucharest and the Harry Frank Guggenheim Foundation in New York City.

Marija Vulesica is Alfred Landecker Lecturer at the Humboldt University of Berlin. In her current research she examines the history of the Holocaust in the Independent State of Croatia through a biographical approach. She received her PhD in 2011 from the Technical University of Berlin with a dissertation on the formation of political antisemitism in the Habsburg Crown Lands of Croatia and Slavonia. She is the author and editor of numerous articles and books on Jewish history, the history of antisemitism and the Holocaust in Southeastern Europe.

Mirna Zakić is Associate Professor of History at Ohio University in Athens, Ohio, USA. She holds a PhD in History from the University of Maryland, College Park. She is the author of *Ethnic Germans and National Socialism in Yugoslavia in World War II* (2017) and the co-editor, with Christopher A. Molnar, of *German-Balkan Entangled Histories in the Twentieth Century* (2020). Her research articles have appeared in the *Journal of Contemporary History* and *Holocaust and Genocide Studies*.

Abbreviations

AVNOJ	*Antifašističko v(ij)eće narodnog oslobođenja Jugoslavije* (Antifascist Council for the People's Liberation of Yugoslavia)
BK	*Balli Kombëtar* (National Front)
CIOM	*Compagnia Italiana per l'Oriente Mediterraneo* (Italian Company for the Mediterranean Orient)
EDES	*Ethnikos Dimokratikos Ellinikos Syndesmos* (National Republican Greek League)
EAIS	*Ente Approvvigionamento per gli Impiegati dello Stato* (Procurement Agency for State Employees)
EAM	*Ethniko Apeleftherotiko Metopo* (National Liberation Front)
ELAS	*Ellinikos Laikos Apeleftherotikos Stratos* (National Popular Liberation Army)
GBW	*Generalbevollmächtigter für die Wirtschaft* (General Plenipotentiary for the Economy)
HCK	*Hrvatski crveni križ* (Croatian Red Cross)
JDC	American Jewish Joint Distribution Committee
KEDES	*Kentrikes Epitropes Dianomon Erythrou Stavrou* (Central Committees for the Distribution of the Red Cross)
KNÇ	*Këshillat Nacional-Çlirimtar* (National Liberation Council)
KPH	*Komunistička partija Hrvatske* (Communist Party of Croatia)
KPJ	*Komunistička partija Jugoslavije* (Communist Party of Yugoslavia)
KPNÇ	*Këshilli Përgjithshëm Nacional-Çlirimtar* (General National Liberation Council)
LNÇ	*Lëvizja Nacional-Çlirimtare* (National Liberation Movement)
NDH	*Nezavisna Država Hrvatska* (Independent State of Croatia)
NKOJ	*Nacionalni komitet oslobođenja Jugoslavije* (National Committee for the Liberation of Yugoslavia)
NOB	*Narodnooslobodilačka borba* (People's Liberation Struggle)

NOF	*Narodnooslobodilački fondovi* (People's Liberation Funds)
NOP	*Narodnooslobodilački pokret* (People's Liberation Movement)
NOO	*Narodnooslobodilački odbor* (People's Liberation Committee)
PEEA	*Politiki Epitropi Ethnikis Apeleftherosis* (Political Committee for National Liberation)
PFSh	*Partia Fashiste e Shqipërisë* (Albanian Fascist Party)
PKSh	*Partia Komuniste Shqiptare* (Albanian Communist Party)
SACIG	*Società Anonima per il Commercio Italo-Greco* (Public Limited Company for Italo-Greek Trade)
SASTEB	*Società Albanese Commerciale Agricola / Shoqi Anonime Shqiptare Tregtare Bujqësore* (Albanian Society for Agricultural Trade)
SITA	*Società Anonima Commerciale e Industriale* (Public Limited Company for Trade and Industry)
SKOJ	*Savez komunističke omladine Jugoslavije* (League of Communist Youth of Yugoslavia)
SSAA	*Sottosegretariato agli Affari Albanesi* (Undersecretariat for Albanian Affairs)
SOE	Special Operations Executive
UNÇSh	*Ushtria Nacional-Çlirimtare Shqiptare* (Albanian National Liberation Army)
UNRRA	United Nations Relief and Rehabilitation Administration
VOMI	*Volksdeutsche Mittelstelle* (Ethnic German Liaison Office)
ZAVNOBiH	*Zemaljsko antifašističko vijeće narodnog oslobođenja Bosne i Hercegovine* (Provincial Anti-Fascist Council for the People's Liberation of Bosnia-Herzegovina)

Map 1 The partition of Southeastern Europe in 1941.

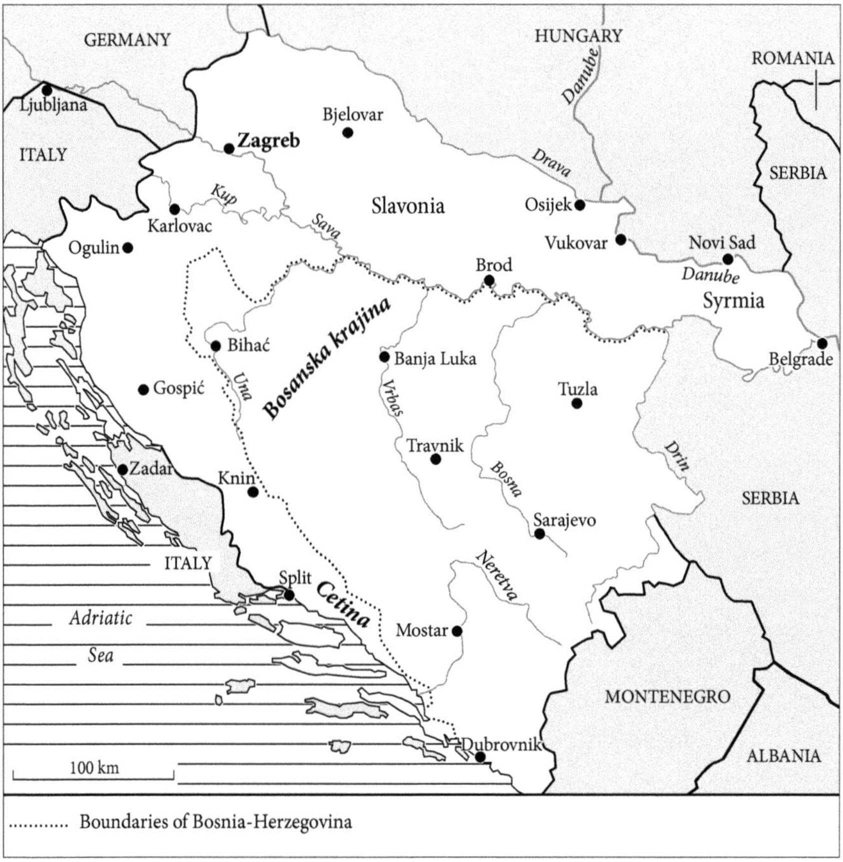

Map 2 The Independent State of Croatia in 1941.

Map 3 Occupied Serbia in 1941.

Map 4 The partition of the Drava Banate (Slovenia) in 1941.

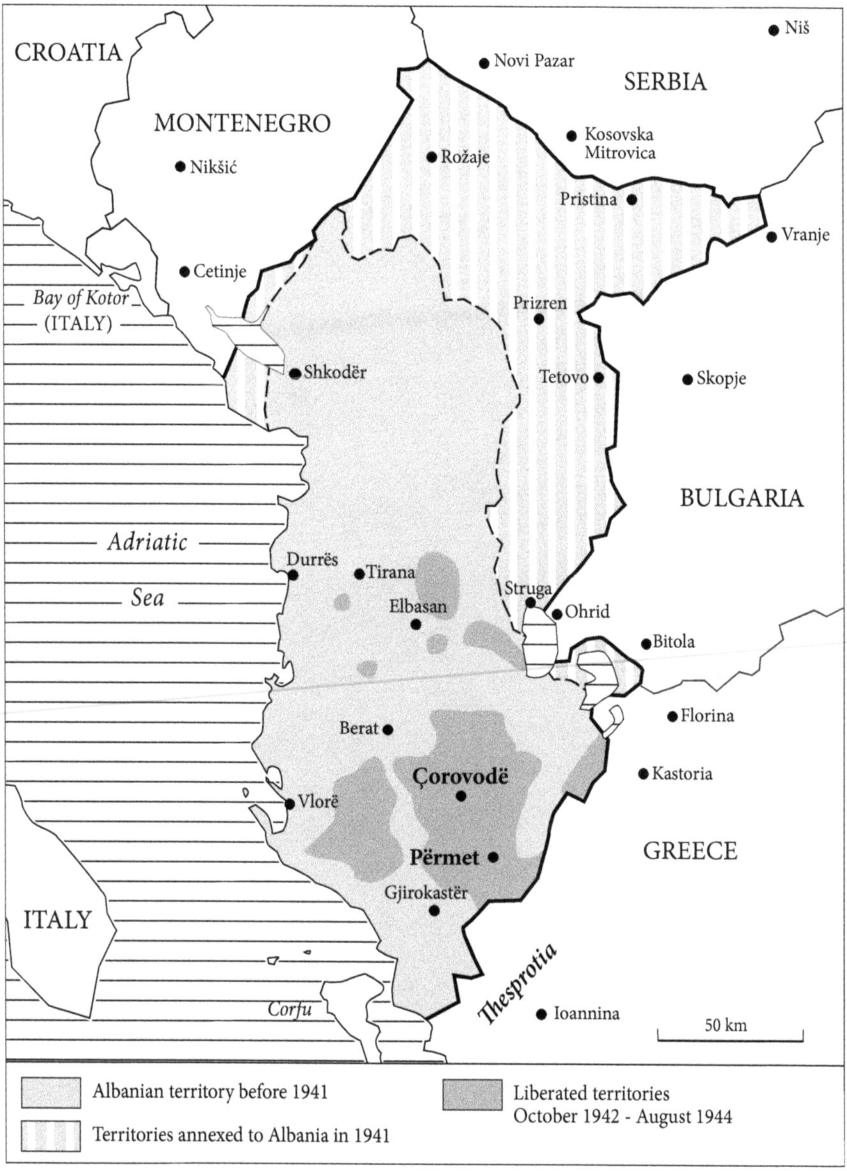

Map 5 Greater Albania (occupied by Italy 1941–43; occupied by Germany 1943–44).

Map 6 The partition of Greece in 1941.

Introduction

Paolo Fonzi, Sabine Rutar and Xavier Bougarel

One of the many aspects of everyday life impacted by the Second World War was the way people produced, accessed and consumed food. The war disrupted patterns of production and distribution throughout the world, while at the same time requiring increased physical activity and thus raising the demand for food consumption. This is reflected in the large number of deaths due to hunger or hunger-related diseases across the globe. The death toll from starvation during the Second World War amounted to 20–25 million people, the situation being particularly dire in Asia.[1] In terms of production, as noted by Adam Tooze, the war 'unleashed more profound change in the social order of the agrarian world than in any other area of society'.[2] The mobilization of large sectors of the rural population for recruitment into insurgent armies, partly a product of the transformation of rural economies, is probably the most glaring manifestation of such change. Even more than the countryside itself, however, it was its relationship with the urban world that was affected by the war. The overhaul of existing food systems increased insecurity for many groups of the population, making food resources a highly politicized matter. This politicization was linked to and, at the same time, reflected in the introduction of food rationing in all belligerent countries.

This book emerged from a series of projects promoted by a core group of scholars based in Italy, Germany and France. The work of this group has spanned ten years, creating a network of historians in many European countries and resulting in several publications.[3] The main idea behind the overall project is that the history of the Second World War in Southeastern Europe, if compared to other parts of the continent, can contribute to developing new approaches that look at the way war and occupation were connected to social phenomena. The title we used for our first project ('New Approaches to the History of the Second World War in Southeastern Europe') expressed our then still imprecise ideas about how to reframe and reconstruct the history of the region during this period. However, we then explored different ways to implement our endeavour, analysing the existing historiography and its development, the local dimensions of war and occupation and, finally, the circulation of goods, people and ideas throughout the region during the war. This book grew out of the idea that the issue of food can serve as a lens through which to analyse the social history of the Second World War in Southeastern Europe, one capable of putting into relief many of the angles we wanted to explore. The authors discussed their chapters in two workshops held at the Humboldt University of Berlin in October 2021 and at the University of Eastern Piedmont, Vercelli, in October 2022.

In this introduction, we first briefly review the scholarly literature on which we base our project and explain how we position ourselves in relation to this literature. We then provide an overview of the history of war and occupation in the three countries that are at the centre of our book. Finally, we analyse the main content of the chapters highlighting how they contribute to a better understanding of the linkage between food and power in war-torn Southeastern Europe.

The issue: Food in the Second World War

The initial idea for this book stemmed from the observation that, despite its relevance, food has remained an under-represented topic in the scholarship of the Second World War. As early as the 1950s, studies of food systems in wartime Europe were published by the Stanford Food Research Institute in its series 'Studies on Food, Agriculture and World War II'.[4] Yet, it would take another forty years for the issue of food to be integrated in studies addressing key aspects of the war such as occupation regimes and extermination policies. The now classic 1993 study by Götz Aly and Susanne Heim, *Architects of Annihilation*, revealed how the Third Reich's quest for food self-sufficiency, along with ideas of population resettlement and modernization, strongly influenced its extermination policies throughout Europe.[5] Drawing on Aly's and Heim's seminal insights, a host of studies have investigated how Nazi Germany's food policies in the occupied regions were influenced by and also shaped its racial policy and military goals. Christian Gerlach's voluminous study on the German occupation of Belarus provided a detailed analysis of the links between the exploitation of agricultural resources and the use of violence by the Nazi authorities in this region.[6] Following in Gerlach's footsteps, Alex J. Kay and Gesine Gerhard addressed the Nazi 'hunger plan' which aimed to starve millions in the occupied Soviet regions and the role of agricultural experts in the implementation of German occupation policies in the East.[7] Thanks to these studies the multiple interconnections between warfare and hunger in Eastern Europe have now become an established field of inquiry.[8] Building on this literature, Lizzie Collingham provided the first global account of how the countries drawn into the Second World War incorporated the quest for food into their war strategy.[9] While these approaches have introduced a fresh viewpoint to the studies of violence and occupation, questioning intentionalist and merely race-based perspectives, the idea for this book was prompted by the realization that this body of literature limits itself to a top-down approach. We, therefore, felt the need to investigate how food and power intersected within the social reality created by war and occupation.

A different strand of literature, more focused on everyday life, has helped us develop the approach adopted in this book. Historians have investigated how food insecurity affected the home front in European societies, with a host of studies devoted to single instances of famine, such as the Dutch hunger winter of 1944.[10] A volume edited by Wendy Goldman and Donald Filzer on wartime food provisioning in the

Soviet Union, the European country with the largest number of hunger-related deaths, includes contributions ranging from the analysis of state policies to inquiries into popular reactions to hunger.[11] Two other projects are particularly indicative of a trend away from top-down approaches to the issue of food. The first has resulted in a book with a markedly transnational approach, published in 2006, with the title *Surviving Hitler and Mussolini*. The book includes a long chapter by Polymeris Voglis devoted to food, and a series of other chapters by various authors on work, resistance and reprisals under occupation, which also touch on the topic of food.[12] More recently a collective research project on daily life in 'occupied societies' (*Besatzungsgesellschaften*)[13] has placed particular emphasis on food-related issues.[14] Concentrating on the strategies that ordinary people employed to survive food shortages, this project has been underpinned by a number of contributions by Tatjana Tönsmeyer, who addresses 'hunger economies', namely the way people navigated a complex system of rationing schemes, black markets and, more generally, the far-reaching transformation of existing food systems.[15] Finally, a further set of studies that inspired this book investigated how food was handled by other actors, such as the Partisans.[16]

Another observation that prompted the project that led to this book was that Southeastern Europe is under-represented in all the strands of studies outlined thus far. This is all the more surprising since at the time of the war this area was still predominantly rural, with about 80 per cent of the population directly dependent on agriculture. The history of food systems during the war and occupation remains almost entirely unexplored in the case of Albania and has received only scant attention when it comes to Yugoslavia. What is more, the break-up of the country in the 1990s led to the consolidation of national(ized) historiographies that for a long time showed little interest in each other. A few regional studies on food supply or food smuggling have appeared in Croatian[17] and Slovenian journals and collective volumes,[18] with close to no reciprocal referencing, along with some articles on food aid to Yugoslavia at the end of the war.[19]

Greece is a slight exception here, as food-related issues drew the attention of scholars early on. Following the first social history approaches to the Greek resistance, Giorgos Margaritis's book *From Defeat to Revolt*, published in 1993, argued that food insecurity and the ensuing conflicts between the state and the peasants over the control of food resources changed the latter's attitude towards the former, spurring them to join the resistance.[20] Following in Margaritis's footsteps, Yannis Skalidakis investigated the Political Committee for National Liberation (*Politiki Epitropi Ethnikis Apeleftherosis* – PEEA), created by the Greek resistance movement in 1944, stressing the importance of its food policies in helping establish a state-like institution in the liberated areas.[21] Yet, although the famine has always featured prominently in the Greek memory of the war, no single study explicitly dedicated to this subject appeared until Violetta Hionidou's monograph on the Greek famine was published in 2006. As well as addressing the different causes of the food crisis, from the agricultural output to the collapse of the food market, Hionidou details how food became a politicized matter under the Italian and German occupation.[22] As Greece was the only occupied country in which a large-scale relief operation was carried out under the aegis of the International Committee of the Red Cross, historians have also addressed humanitarian aid as a political issue. Therefore, both the wartime relief scheme and the programme implemented by the United Nations Relief and Rehabilitation Administration (UNRRA), which fed the country after the liberation, have been the subject of intensive research.[23]

While taking stock of the results of the literature presented so far, this book's goal is to overcome a clear-cut distinction between the macro- and the micro-level by looking at a space of social action that lies in between. Its main interest is to bring into focus the different ways in which the management of food was entangled with different political agendas and strategies of survival and to investigate the interplay between power – both political and social – and food in wartime societies. In order to do this, the book does not primarily examine a single actor and the way this actor managed food according to their priorities, but rather, centring on food in individual social settings, it looks at how various actors interacted in their attempt to gain control over this key resource. The protagonists of the studies contained in this book are Southeast European state institutions, collaborationist movements, resistance movements, stakeholders in the war economy, local and international humanitarian organizations, as well as various social groups and individuals. The authors are interested not only in food insecurity, scarcity and famine, but also – and indeed rather – in the ways in which social and political actors wielded their power to adapt to and, at the same time, shape the new entitlement structures created by the war and occupation. These structures were conditioned by racist ideologies as well as changes in legislation, supply chains, food distribution regimes and, last but not least, moral economies.

The setting: Southeastern Europe during the Second World War

Although April 1941 is often seen as marking the beginning of the Second World War in Southeastern Europe, its early stages actually date back to April 1939, when Italy occupied Albania, and to October 1940, when it attacked Greece (starting from Albania). It was on 6 April 1941 that the war spread to the rest of the region, with the German, Italian, Bulgarian and Hungarian armies attacking Yugoslavia, and the German army attacking Greece (starting from Bulgaria). The swift defeat of the Yugoslav and Greek armies allowed the Axis powers to undertake a vast geopolitical reshaping of Southeastern Europe (see Map 1). Yugoslavia was divided into nine different political entities, the largest of which was the Independent State of Croatia (*Nezavisna Država Hrvatska* – NDH), which roughly covered present-day Croatia and Bosnia-Herzegovina, but was deprived of part of its coastline, which was annexed by Italy (see Map 2). Serbia was essentially reduced to its 1912 borders and placed under German occupation. In the province of Banat in Vojvodina, also occupied by the German army, the local German minority exerted a decisive influence (see Map 3). Slovenia was divided between Germany, Italy and Hungary: while the Italians created the Province of Ljubljana, the Germans administered Upper Carnolia and Lower Styria from the *Reichsgaue* of Carinthia and Styria (see Map 4). At the same time, Hungary annexed the provinces of Prekmurje in Slovenia, Međimurje in Croatia (see Map 4) and Bačka in Vojvodina (see Map 3). Further south, Montenegro became an Italian protectorate, and most of Kosovo was attached to an Italian-occupied Greater Albania, while much of Yugoslav Macedonia was annexed by Bulgaria (see Map 5). Greece was also divided between the Axis powers: Italy occupied most of the Greek territory, while Germany took control of several strategic positions, such as the greatest part of the island of Crete, the port of Piraeus (south of Athens) and Greek Macedonia including the city of Thessalonica. Bulgaria, for its part, annexed Western Thrace (see Map 6).

In most of these political entities, the occupiers collaborated with part of the local political and military elites, as was the case in Serbia with the regime of General Milan Nedić, in Greece with that of General Georgios Tsolakoglu and in Albania with Prime Minister Shefqet Vërlaci, who was a powerful landowner. In Montenegro, Italy first attempted to establish a local monarchy linked to the Italian crown, but later abandoned this project and allied with the Chetniks (Serbian royalists). In the occupied Slovene territories, the break with the past in terms of removing, annihilating or deporting the elite was more radical, at least in the German-occupied area, much like in the Independent State of Croatia, which was under the control of the Ustashas, a minority fascist movement led by Ante Pavelić. Here, the pre-existing elites were largely replaced by new ones. This did not prevent Germany and Italy from dividing the NDH into two separate occupation zones, a situation that led to permanent competition between the Germans and the Italians, and to growing tensions between Italy and the NDH. On the one hand, the Ustashas sought to emancipate themselves from Italian tutelage, rejecting, among other things, Rome's plans for a custom and monetary union with Italy. At the same time, however, they had to tolerate the development of the German police apparatus and the privileged status of the German minority, concentrated north of the Sava, in Slavonia and Syrmia (see Map 2). Similar rifts and conflicts evolved in Kosovo and Macedonia, where the Germans, Italians and Bulgarians never really settled their border disputes.

The geopolitical reshaping of Southeastern Europe was followed by the implementation of brutal racial and ethnic policies. The Jewish communities of the region were decimated by the extermination policies of the Third Reich and the Ustasha regime, despite the fact that the Italian occupation zones constituted a precarious refuge until September 1943. Similarly, the Roma community also suffered severe discrimination, which rapidly turned into outright genocide. The NDH also saw the implementation in 1941 of a genocidal policy against its large Serbian minority. Serbs (rather than Jews) constituted the majority of victims among the prisoners of the Jasenovac extermination camp, which operated from August 1941 to April 1945. Due to the uprising of the Serbian population as well as pressure from Germany and Italy, the Ustashas' anti-Serb policy was attenuated from 1942 onwards.

In Kosovo, Macedonia and Bačka, Serbs were the victims of discrimination and violence, which especially affected the colonists installed here between the two world wars. German-occupied Serbia was therefore confronted with large flows of refugees, their total number being estimated at 400,000 at the end of 1941. Finally, the Third Reich implemented a brutal policy of Germanization in Slovenia, which resulted in the deportation of tens of thousands of Slovenes and the classification of the population into several allegedly more or less 'Germanizable' (*eindeutschungsfähig*) categories.

The capitulation of Italy in September 1943 led to another geopolitical reshaping. German forces took control of Albania and Montenegro, and the parts of Slovenia, the NDH and Greece that had been under Italian occupation until then. A year later, in September 1944, faced with the advance of the Red Army, Bulgaria changed sides. A month later, German troops began their withdrawal from Southeastern Europe, dragging in their wake a good part of the German minorities from Vojvodina, Croatia and Slovenia, and tens of thousands of local collaborators.

The economic dimensions of the German and Italian occupation in Southeastern Europe were largely influenced by the occupiers' goals in this region. Control of economic resources and endeavours to create an integrated economic area under Italian control were crucial in the fascist project for a Mediterranean empire. As a consequence, plans to seize major assets and establish a monetary and customs union with the occupied countries were devised by several Italian institutions. For the Nazi leaders, Southeastern Europe was a 'supplementary space' (*Ergänzungsraum*) that had to be integrated into the Reich's 'great economic space' (*Großwirtschaftsraum*). However, short-term exploitation largely prevailed over the enactment of any long-term economic penetration plans. On the other hand, the integration of Southeastern Europe into the German economy relied on a high degree of continuity with the past, since the Reich's economic penetration in this region had already begun in the last years of the Weimar Republic, intensifying after 1934, when Germany significantly shifted its trade relations towards Southeastern Europe, competing with French and British economic interests there.

After April 1941, and due to its military superiority over its allies, the Third Reich was able to seize most of the economic resources of the region. In the weeks following its offensive, the German army plundered the resources of the occupied countries and organized, for example, the transfer to Germany of Serbian arms factories. At the same time, Germany took control of the mines of Bor (copper) and Trepça (lead, zinc) in German-occupied Serbia. It also wrested the bauxite mines in Herzegovina and the Ljuboten mine (chrome) in Macedonia from the Italians and Bulgarians, respectively. In the first weeks after the capitulation of Greece and before the Italians took over their area of occupation, the Germans were also able to seize much of the Greek mineral production. The exploitation of various ores was indeed one of the priorities of the German authorities in Southeastern Europe. The other priority was the export of agricultural produce to the Reich, facilitated by the control of the fertile lands located north of the Sava (Slavonia, Syrmia) and the Danube (Banat), or in Greek Macedonia. On the other hand, the zone of Italian occupation mainly covered areas that were known as 'passive' (dependent on food imports), such as Dalmatia, Montenegro, northern Albania, central Greece or the Greek islands. Finally, with Western Thrace, Bulgaria annexed one of the most fertile regions of Greece. More generally, Germany was able to extract resources from Southeastern Europe through a clearing system which permitted large quantities of unpaid imports, for which, through the high occupation costs, the occupied countries, and especially Greece, were forced to pay. Finally, Southeastern Europe was an important source of labour. Nearly half of the 180,000 prisoners of war from Yugoslavia held in Germany were employed in agriculture and, during the war,

270,000 workers from the NDH, 70,000 from Serbia and 40,000 from Greece were sent to Germany either voluntarily or by force.

At the same time that the mining industry was partly militarized and also employed thousands of forced labourers, the peasantry was subjected to a regime of regulated prices and forced requisitions that became increasingly harsh as the war progressed. But in seeking to exploit the economic resources of Southeastern Europe, the occupiers came up against several obstacles. The first was the structural weakness of the region's economies, and in particular their transport infrastructure, which hampered the export of ores and agricultural products. In addition, the proliferation of state entities and occupation zones resulted in new customs and administrative barriers, and the occupation authorities were competing among themselves or with the local collaborators for control of the economic resources. Moreover, the armed resistance movements sabotaged railways and electricity cables, destroyed crops and agricultural machinery, encouraged farmers to hide their produce, and thus contributed to the economic depletion of the occupied cities and territories.

This begs the question as to whether the Axis powers succeeded in exploiting the economic resources of Southeastern Europe. The historian Holm Sundhaussen even claimed that Germany had to subsidize the NDH economy to prevent its total collapse. Whichever the case, the fact is that the countries of the region had to bear the brunt of the occupation costs. Everywhere, the result was rapid growth of money supply and rampant inflation that exacerbated the economic chaos, incited the peasants to reduce their production or to sell their products on the black market and contributed to the plight of the urban population. The supply of agricultural products to the occupying and collaborationist troops also contributed greatly to the growing shortage of food in the region.

From this point of view, the harshest conditions were those experienced by Greece during the winter of (1941–42). Before the war, this country had imported 40 per cent of its food. Consequently, the naval blockade established by Great Britain, the cessation of food shipments from Thrace and eastern Macedonia under Bulgarian occupation, and the poor transport infrastructure, which was strongly impacted by wartime destruction, created a food shortage in many parts of the country. This situation was further aggravated by the requisitions of the occupying armies and the generalized administrative disorganization. The result was, during the winter of (1941–42), a famine that mainly affected Athens and the Greek islands, and caused between 100,000 and 300,000 deaths. This humanitarian catastrophe led, on the initiative of Sweden, Switzerland and the International Committee of the Red Cross, to the implementation of a plan to import Canadian wheat with the agreement of Great Britain, Germany and Italy. This humanitarian operation lasted until the autumn of 1944. In other parts of Southeastern Europe, the situation was less dramatic, although isolated cases of starvation were reported in the mountainous regions of Dalmatia, Herzegovina and Montenegro, and in the Dalmatian islands. More generally, the cities of Southeastern Europe endured strict food rationing and skyrocketing prices on the black market, and the search for food occupied much of the time, energy and material resources of their inhabitants. The rural population was less affected by this food shortage, but they too found themselves in conditions of great destitution and were the first to suffer from the offensives and reprisals of the occupying armies and their local collaborators.

Besides the co-existence of several occupying powers, each with their own political agendas – a peculiarity of Southeastern Europe within the wider context of the Axis occupation – another of the region's specific features was the early development of armed resistance movements, which, along with their local allies, took up arms against the occupiers.[24] These can be divided into two categories, namely the resistance movements led by the communist parties of the region, also called Partisan movements, and those with nationalist and anti-communist leanings, such as the Chetniks (Serbian royalists) in Yugoslavia, the National Republican Greek League (*Ethnikos Dimokratikos Ellinikos Syndesmos* – EDES) in Greece and the National Front (*Balli Kombëtar*) in Albania. In Yugoslavia, fighting broke out at the end of 1941 between Yugoslav Partisans and Serbian Chetniks, leading the latter to collaborate more and more with the Italian army and subsequently with the German army. Later, a similar type of military confrontation took place in Greece and Albania, resulting in unstable and complex configurations at the local level. In all these cases, the communist resistance movements gradually succeeded in setting up real armies, whereas the nationalist resistance tended to be made up of armed bands gathered around local notables or former officers of the interwar armies.

In parallel with the expansion of territories under their control, the communist Partisans established their own political institutions. In Yugoslavia, an Antifascist Council for the People's Liberation of Yugoslavia (*Antifašističko v(ij)eće narodnog oslobođenja Jugoslavije* – AVNOJ) was formed in November 1942, and a year later became the sole holder of legislative power in the liberated territories. At the same time, a National Committee for the Liberation of Yugoslavia (*Nacionalni komitet oslobođenja Jugoslavije* – NKOJ) was created, which served as a kind of provisional government and was headed by the General Secretary of the Communist Party, Josip Broz Tito. The Greek and Albanian Partisans followed suit some time later. In Greece, a National Liberation Front (*Ethniko Apeleftherotiko Metopo* – EAM) brought together the Communist Party and several other small parties in as early as September 1941, but a provisional government, namely the above-mentioned Political Committee for National Liberation (PEEA), was not formed until March 1944. In Albania, a National Liberation Movement (*Lëvizja Nacional-Çlirimtare* – LNÇ), dominated by the Communist Party, was created in September 1942, but the same party did not convene a General Council for National Liberation (*Këshilli Përgjithshëm Nacional-Çlirimtar* – KPNÇ) until May 1944. These different state-like institutions fought for international recognition and therefore confronted the royalist governments in exile. Whereas the Yugoslav and Albanian Partisans gradually succeeded in asserting themselves on the international scene, this was not the case for their Greek counterparts, who confronted the British troops in Athens in December 1944 and had to lay down their arms a month later, following the Varkiza agreement. These latter events marked the defeat of the Greek communists and the comeback of the prewar political elites.

In the liberated territories, a parallel society developed, with local institutions responsible for the organization of the economy, justice, education and health services. The political mobilization of the population, and in particular of previously marginalized groups, namely the peasantry, women and youth, also took place at the local level. Against this background, the issue of food remained crucial. Partisans and occupiers fought a genuine 'harvest war' for the control of agricultural production, whereas the collection, concealment and distribution of food were one of the main tasks of the local institutions, and one of the main sources of legitimacy for the Partisan movements. During the course of the war, the needs of the Partisan armies became more and more important, but resources were running out. Therefore, the support of the Allies became essential to feed the civilian population after the war, as shown by the creation of the UNRRA in November 1943 and its role in delivering international food aid to Southeastern Europe from 1945 onwards.

The book: Food, scarcity and power in Southeastern Europe

The contributors to this volume address, in six parts, the interconnections between food, scarcity and power in Southeastern Europe during the Second World War. As laid out above, there were significant disparities in the availability of food in different locations as well as between different groups, especially those discriminated against by extreme racist, often genocidal, policies, such as the Jews, but also the Slavs and the Roma. Territories marked by borders drawn between the occupational regimes were contested among the latter; borderlands existing since prewar times were often marked by a multi-ethnic population whose members were not always at ease with each other, by volatile (state) boundaries, by weak statehoods, and thus generally by a particularly vulnerable and fragile social fabric. These regionally idiosyncratic complexities are at the heart of the authors' research foci, while their comprehensive take on questions of food, scarcity and power in Yugoslavia, Greece and Albania makes for a meaningful and methodologically comprehensive whole.

The first part of the book, 'Germany: Extracting food and labour', focuses on the interplay between food extraction and labour deployment in German-occupied Yugoslavia. Mirna Zakić analyses how the ethnic German minority in the Serbian (western) Banat, occupied by Germany between spring 1941 and autumn 1944, administered the region on the Nazis' behalf and played a key role as food producers and suppliers for the German war effort. Their agricultural cooperatives and trade networks had drawn them into the Nazi orbit even before the invasion of Yugoslavia, so that agriculture and food production became a key feature of Banat German identity and propaganda. The German occupiers expected their local ethnic co-nationals to make sure that the Banat lived up to its 'breadbasket' (*Kornkammer*) reputation, while at the same time treating them as second-class, peasant Germans. Zakić pays particular attention to the propaganda portraying the hard-working ethnic German peasant, the Banat's agrarian output and the realities of German-German relations during the occupation years.

Sabine Rutar focuses on food and labour supply regimes in the exploitation of the Bor copper mine in eastern Serbia and of the coalfields in the Zasavje region of Slovenia. She demonstrates how, in the supply regimes, the miners held a position that was equal or even superior to the army. Nevertheless, experiences of violence, hunger and (forced) labour prevailed everywhere. Efforts to establish viable food and labour supply regimes were entangled, but significantly impeded by Nazi racist ideology and violence. On the one hand, policies to provide the war economy with a labour force struggled in the face of the increasing scarcity of both workers and food. On the other, the occupiers continued to mistreat, even kill, certain groups of labourers, actions which completely ignored the goal of a functioning war economy.

The second part of the book, 'Italy: Instrumentalizing food', focuses on the Italian occupation of Albania and Greece. Alberto Basciani outlines how the Italians managed food supplies in Albania between 1939 and 1943 once they discovered that the country was anything but self-sufficient. With the arrival of thousands of workers from Italy, the Albanian economy faced significant population growth as well as an increase in money circulation due to Italian investments. This, in turn, resulted in increased demand for and a rise in the prices of consumer goods, especially foodstuffs. As Basciani shows, the Italian authorities proved incapable of establishing an adequate food distribution system, nor could they counter phenomena such as hoarding and the black market. These growing difficulties were an important factor in fascist Italy losing control over Albania, substantially contributing to the country's capitulation in September 1943.

Paolo Fonzi investigates Italy's food deliveries to Greece between 1941 and 1943, the aim of which was to help stem the famine that ravaged the country. Drawing on recent literature on other world regions, Fonzi highlights the connection between humanitarianism and modern imperialism, taking Italy's policy in Greece as a case in point. He shows how, despite supplying Greece with foodstuffs, Italy exploited the resources of a number of Greek regions to feed the Italian population. In addition, Italy was hostile towards the International Red Cross relief scheme, which in the summer of 1942 started feeding the Greek population with food procured by international organizations and Allied governments. Lastly, Italy's food assistance needs to be seen in the context of its overall economic policy in Greece: food provisioning was intentionally employed as a tool of Italy's plan for long-term economic penetration.

The third part of the book, 'Cities: Searching for food', shifts the perspective away from the occupiers towards the plight of the civilian population. It also transcends the threshold of the Italian capitulation on 8 September 1943, i.e. it covers both the Italian and the subsequent German occupation. The two chapters highlight case studies in Yugoslavia, looking specifically at the capital of Slovenia, Ljubljana and the capital of Croatia, Zagreb. Mojca Šorn explores food policies in the Province of Ljubljana, which was annexed to the Kingdom of Italy after the Italian occupation and, after the Italian capitulation, incorporated into the German Operational Zone of the Adriatic Littoral. Šorn focuses on the system of rationed food supply and on the reasons for the chronic shortages of basic foodstuffs in the city, then going on to outline the strategies employed by both the local municipal authorities and the citizens to deal with scarcity.

Marija Vulesica takes a biographical approach to explore the role of food provisioning in the face of terror against the Zagreb Jewish Community after the Ustashas rose to power in April 1941. In the Independent State of Croatia, Jews were arrested, disfranchised, expropriated and deported to camps. The remaining members of the Jewish Communities were placed at the bottom of the hierarchy when it came to getting access to food, and Jewish camp inmates were even lower down the pecking order. And yet, leading members of the Jewish Community – first and foremost Aleksa Klein (1898–1974) and Drago Rosenberg (1898–1946) – mobilized all their connections to provide camp inmates with food. Vulesica focuses on the agency of these two men when their lives were at stake, in particular on their efforts to supply female camp inmates with food. She also reveals Jewish women's experiences of hunger in the camps, and the existential importance of the food they received.

The fourth part of the book, 'Contested territories: Fighting for food', focuses on Dalmatia in Yugoslavia and on Thesprotia/Chameria in Greece, thereby providing a transnational perspective. In both regions, various groups fought bitterly for control, and food played a substantial part in this. Nikica Barić shows how in central Dalmatia, which in April 1941 became an Italian-controlled part of the Independent State of Croatia, all political and military actors endeavoured to come to terms with the region's meagre domestic agricultural resources. Soon after the establishment of the NDH, Partisan units assembled, led by the Communist Party of Yugoslavia. The authorities of the NDH proved unable to secure sufficient supplies, which was one of the reasons for their lack of credibility among the population. Italian counter-insurgency and reprisals against civilians included the destruction and plunder of the region's scant agrarian resources. The Partisan movement, on the other hand, aimed to win the hearts and minds of the population, but also to harness civilian resources for its struggle.

Spyros Tsoutsoumpis explores the impact of economic and material shortages on inter- and intra-communal relations, focusing on the ethnic conflict between the Greek and Albanian communities in the border region of Thesprotia/Chameria in Greece. Tsoutsoumpis analyses how food scarcity and insecurity impacted ethnic conflict and political mobilization, and, conversely, how and to what extent ethnic violence contributed to food insecurity. The social transformations caused by scarcity were a key factor behind the rise of the resistance in occupied Greece, as well as a defining moment for the local ethnic conflict. As Tsoutsoumpis shows, food, or the lack of it, was a driver and motivator of interethnic violence.

The fifth part of the book focuses on 'Liberated territories: Feeding the partisans', providing case studies to illustrate the connection between food and power in Yugoslav and Albanian liberated territories. Xavier Bougarel depicts the harsh material conditions in the liberated territories of western Bosnia, in the Independent State of Croatia. The production and distribution of food were primarily the task of the local and regional People's Liberation Committees. These groups were in charge of collecting 'voluntary contributions' from the peasants. As Bougarel shows, a 'moral economy' regulated the relationship between the Partisan movement and the population, based on the survival of the greatest number and on strict equity and reciprocity. Any small injustice committed by the Liberation Committees or excessive behaviour by the army could threaten this fragile equilibrium, as became clear towards the end of the war, when the increased use of forced requisitions marked a break with the compromise established between the Partisan movement and the rural population.

Markenc Lorenci comes to similar conclusions in his case study of the district of Skrapar in the prefecture of Berat and the district of Përmet in the prefecture of Gjirokastër, both in southern Albania. After the National Liberation Movement (*Lëvizja Nacional-Çlirimtare*) had liberated these territories, the Albanian Partisan movement took charge of the food policies for both military and civilian purposes. Lorenci analyses the extent to which the food policies implemented by the National

Liberation Movement in the liberated territories contributed to its support and credibility in these locations and to swelling the Partisan ranks during the war.

The authors provide important insights into the entanglements between food, scarcity and power in Yugoslavia, Greece and Albania during the Second World War, shifting from the German and Italian occupation of the Balkans to German-only occupation regimes after the Italian capitulation in September 1943. In so doing, they produce a solid body of research, while also identifying how little we still know about the social history of the Second World War in Southeastern Europe, especially regarding its local dimensions. Our book is also an invitation to delve further, taking a transnational and comparative approach, into the war experiences of Southeast European societies. Last but by no means least, the history of the Yugoslav, Greek and Albanian 'occupied societies' (*Besatzungsgesellschaften*) on a more general European level offer compelling arguments for diversifying the analysis of the socio-political history of the Second World War. As elsewhere, the violence of the extreme times people faced during the war forced them to develop 'strategies to adjust to the state of confusion',[25] and searching for food as well as living with the lack thereof was the existential materiality of this radical 'confusion'. During the war, social norms and structures were volatile and under constant stress, which called for a very flexible adaptation of actions, decisions and choices in all realms of life. Food was necessary to make sure such adaptation remained viable and its lack radically reduced the ability to adjust to other types of hardship, including the very question of survival. At the same time, the ephemeral and radicalized situation fostered a yearning for a normal, somehow comforting, everyday life. Access to food meant a glimpse of normality, all the more so when people were able to eat food resembling their normal diet and nutritional rituals. Scarcity, in all its variations, whether structural or more directly imposed by the occupiers, was part and parcel of people being faced with 'no option of non-involvement'.[26]

Acknowledgements

The contributions contained in this volume were discussed in two authors' workshops held at the Humboldt University of Berlin in October 2021, organized by Hannes Grandits, Chair of Southeast European History, and Xavier Bougarel, and at the University of Eastern Piedmont, Vercelli, in October 2022, organized by Paolo Fonzi. We are sincerely grateful to Hannes Grandits for his many excellent ideas and advice. In addition, we would like to express our thanks to the Chair of Southeast European History at Humboldt University, along with the Department of Humanities at the University of Eastern Piedmont, in particular Edoardo Tortarolo, and the Leibniz Institute of East and Southeast European Studies, Regensburg, for providing financial support for these events. Our gratitude also goes to the Centre d'études turques, ottomanes, balkaniques et centrasiatiques (CETOBAC), Paris, and the Chair of Global History at the University of Potsdam for generously funding the copy-editing. Carla Hammes-Welch diligently copy-edited the entire volume; Ivana Dinić, Lasse Maerz and Jakob Weizman provided meticulous editorial assistance in preparing the manuscript as well as compiling the index and the list of abbreviations. Last but not least, a heartfelt thank you is due to Gabriella Cox, Rhodri Mogford and Shamli Priya Vijayan at Bloomsbury for providing such excellent guidance in the production process. To all involved we extend our sincere gratitude.

Notes

1 Cormac Ó Gráda, 'The Famines of WWII', *VoxEU Debate CEPR*, 2 September 2019, https://cepr.org/voxeu/columns/famines-wwii (accessed 27 July 2023).

2 Adam Tooze, 'The War of the Villages. The Interwar Agrarian Crisis and the Second World War', in *The Cambridge History of the Second World War*, ed. Michael Geyer and Adam Tooze (Cambridge: Cambridge University Press, 2015), 385–412, 386.

3 *The Second World War in Historiography and Public Debate*, ed. Sabine Rutar, thematic issue of *Südosteuropa. Journal of Politics and Society* 65, no. 2 (2017); *Local Dimensions of the Second World War in Southeastern Europe*, ed. Xavier Bougarel, Hannes Grandits and Marija Vulesica (Abingdon: Routledge, 2019).

4 The series included, for example, a study by Karl Brandt, a German émigré who served as Chief of Food and Agriculture of the US Military Government in Germany, together with German experts who had worked within the Nazi administration of Europe, such as Otto Schiller and Franz Ahlgrimm, *Management of Agriculture and Food in the German-Occupied and Other Areas of Fortress Europe: A Study in Military Government* (Stanford: Stanford University Press, 1953). See also Bruce F. Johnston, *Japanese Food Management in World War II* (Stanford: Stanford University Press, 1953), which is largely based on the records of the Allied occupation authorities of Japan.

5 Götz Aly and Susanne Heim, *Vordenker der Vernichtung: Auschwitz und die deutschen Pläne für eine neue europäische Ordnung* (Frankfurt: Fischer, 1993; English translation, London: Weidenfeld and Nicolson, 2002).

6 Christian Gerlach, *Kalkulierte Morde: Die deutsche Wirtschafts- und Vernichtungspolitik in Weißrußland 1941 bis 1944* (Hamburg: Hamburger Edition, 1999). See also Christian Gerlach, *Krieg, Ernährung, Völkermord. Deutsche Vernichtungspolitik im Zweiten Weltkrieg* (Zurich: Pendo, 2001).

7 Alex J. Kay, *Exploitation, Resettlement, Mass Murder: Political and Economic Planning for German Occupation Policy in the Soviet Union, 1940–1941* (New York: Berghahn Books, 2006); Gesine Gerhard, 'Food and Genocide: Nazi Agrarian Politics in the Occupied Territories of the Soviet Union', *Contemporary European History* 18, no. 1 (2009): 45–65; Gesine Gerhard, 'Food as a Weapon: Agricultural Sciences and the Building of a Greater German Empire', *Food, Culture and Society* 14, no. 3 (2011): 335–51. See also the final report of the historical commission for the history of the Federal Ministry of Food and Agriculture, *Agrarpolitik im 20. Jahrhundert. Das Bundesministerium für Ernährung und Landwirtschaft und seine Vorgänger*, ed. Horst Möller et al. (Berlin: De Gruyter Oldenbourg, 2020), 206–31.

8 *Kriegführung und Hunger 1939–1945. Zum Verhältnis von militärischen, wirtschaftlichen und politischen Interessen*, ed. Christoph Dieckmann and Babette Quinkert (Göttingen: Wallstein, 2015).

9 Lizzie Collingham, *The Taste of War: World War II and the Battle for Food* (New York: Penguin Press, 2011).

10 See, among others, Henri van der Zee, *The Hunger Winter: Occupied Holland 1944–1945* (Lincoln: University of Nebraska Press, 1988).

11 *Food Provisioning in the Soviet Union during World War II*, ed. Wendy Z. Goldman and Donald Filtzer (Bloomington: Indiana University Press, 2015).

12 *Surviving Hitler and Mussolini. Daily Life in Occupied Europe*, ed. Robert Gildea, Olivier Wieviorka and Anette Warring (Oxford/New York: Berg, 2006).

13 Tatjana Tönsmeyer, 'Besatzungsgesellschaften. Begriffliche und konzeptionelle Überlegungen zur Erfahrungsgeschichte des Alltags unter deutscher Besatzung im Zweiten Weltkrieg', *Dokupedia-Zeitgeschichte* (18 December 2015). Available online: https://docupedia.de/zg/Besatzungsgesellschaften

14 See the description at http://www.societies-under-german-occupation.com/ and the publication resulting from the project *Fighting Hunger, Dealing with Shortage. Everyday Life under Occupation in World War II Europe: A Source Edition*, ed. Tatjana Tönsmeyer et al. (Boston: Brill, 2021).

15 See also Tatjana Tönsmeyer, 'Hungerökonomien. Vom Umgang mit der Mangelversorgung im besetzten Europa des Zweiten Weltkrieges', *Historische Zeitschrift* 301, no. 3 (2015): 662–704; *Coping with Hunger and Shortage under German Occupation in World War II*, ed. Tatjana Tönsmeyer, Peter Haslinger and Agnes Laba (Basingstoke: Palgrave, 2018).

16 Kenneth Slepyan, *Stalin's Guerillas: Soviet Partisans in World War II* (Lawrence: University Press of Kansas, 2006), 60–103; Masha Cerovic, *Les enfants de Staline: la guerre des partisans soviétiques 1941–1944* (Paris: Seuil, 2018), 165–92; A. Brakel, '"Das allergefährlichste ist die Wut der Bauern." Die Versorgung der Partisanen und ihr Verhältnis zur Zivilbevölkerung. Eine Fallstudie zum Gebiet Baranowicze 1941–1944', *Vierteljahresschrift für Zeitgeschichte* 55, no. 3 (2007): 393–424.

17 See Nikica Barić, 'Brod na Savi i krijumčarenje hrane na željeznicama za vrijeme Nezavisne Države Hrvatske', in *Prilozi za povijest Broda i okolice – knjiga 2*, ed. Marija Karbić (Slavonski Brod: HIP, 2013), 163–96; the series of three articles written by Franko Mirošević on food supply in the region of Dubrava, published in *Radovi zavoda za povijesne znanosti HAZU u Zadru*: 'Prehrana stanovništva u Velikoj župi Dubrava od lipnja 1941. do prosinca 1942', no. 55 (2013): 148–73; 'Prehrana stanovništva Velike župe Dubrava u 1943. godini', no. 56 (2014): 289–321; 'Prehrana stanovništva Velike župe Dubrava u 1944. godini', no. 57 (2015): 317–58; as well as Marica Karakaš Obradov, 'On Nutrition, Harvest and Purchase of Food in the Second World War: Examples from Slavonia and Srijem', *Review of Croatian History* 17, no. 1 (2021): 331–54.

18 See Žarko Lazarević, 'Kmetovanje v vojni vihri na podlagi dnevniških zapisov', in *Mikro in makro: pristopi in prispevki k humanističnim vedam ob dvajsetletnici UP Fakultete za humanistične študije*, ed. Irena Lazar, Aleksander Panjek and Jonatan Vinkler (Koper: Založba Univerze na Primorskem, 2020), 227–40; Bojan Himmelreich, 'Organizacija preskrbe na osvobojenih ozemljih Slovenije in priprave na povojno obdobje (1944–1945)', *Prispevki za novejšo zgodovino* 49, no. 2 (2009): 109–24; Bojan Himmelreich, *Namesto žemlje črni kruh – organizacija preskrbe z živili v Celju v času obeh vojn* (Celje: Zgodovinski arhiv, 2001); Tone Ferenc, 'Landwirtschaft und Ernährung in Slowenien (1941–1945)', in *Tone Ferenc, Izbrana dela, Okupacijski sistemi med drugo svetovno vojno, vol. 3: Nasilje in izkoriščanje gmotnih sil za potrebe okupatorskih držav*, ed. Mitja Ferenc (Ljubljana: Oddelek za zgodovino Filozofske fakultete Univerze v Ljubljani, 2009), 379–402.

19 Vera Kržišnik-Bukić, 'Hrana kao glavni vid UNRRA-ine pomoći Jugoslaviji 1943–1948', *Časopis za suvremenu povijest* 20, no. 3 (1998): 59–76; Kornelija Ajlec,

'UNRRA v Jugoslaviji in Sloveniji', *Prispevki za novejšo zgodovino* 53, no. 2 (2013): 79–99.

20 Giorgos Margaritis, *Apo tin itta stin exegersi: Ellada anoixi 1941 – fthinoporo 1942* (Athens: Politis, 1993).

21 Yannis Skalidakis, *I Eleftheri Ellada. I exousia tou EAM sta hronia tis Katohis 1943–1944* (Athens: Asini, 2015). On the same subject, see, in English, Yannis Skalidakis, 'From Resistance to Counterstate: The Making of Revolutionary Power in the Liberated Zones of Occupied Greece, 1943–1944', *Journal of Modern Greek Studies* 33, no. 1 (2015): 155–84.

22 Violetta Hionidou, *Famine and Death in Occupied Greece, 1941–1944* (Cambridge: Cambridge University Press, 2006). On this see also Violetta Hionidou, 'Relief and Politics in Occupied Greece, 1941–1944', *Journal of Contemporary History* 48, no. 4 (2013): 761–83.

23 *Bearing Gifts to Greece. Humanitarian Aid to Greece in the 1940s*, ed. Richard Clogg (Basingstoke: Palgrave, 2008). See also George Kazamias, *Allied Policy towards Occupied Greece: The 1941–1944 Famine* (PhD diss., Department for European Studies, University of Bradford, 1990); Flora Tsilaga, *The UNRRA Mission to Greece. The Politics of International Relief, October 1944 – June 1947* (PhD diss., Department of Byzantine and Modem Greek Studies, University of London, 2007); Flora Tsilaga, '"The Mountain Laboured and Brought Forth a Mouse": UNRRA's Operations in the Cyclades Islands, c. 1945–46', *Journal of Contemporary History* 43, no. 3 (2008): 527–45.

24 For a recent study of the resistance movements in Southeastern Europe, see John Paul Newman, Ljubinka Škodrić and Rade Ristanović, eds, *Anti-Axis Resistance in Southeastern Europe 1940–1944* (Leiden: Brill, 2023).

25 Jan Philipp Reemtsma, *Vertrauen und Gewalt. Versuch über eine besondere Konstellation der Moderne* (Hamburg: Hamburger Edition, 2008), 66–7.

26 Doris Bergen, 'What Do Studies of Women, Gender, and Sexuality Contribute to Understanding the Holocaust?', in *Different Horrors, Same Hell. Gender and the Holocaust*, ed. Myrna Goldenberg and Amy Shapiro (Washington: University of Washington, 2013), 16–37, 21.

Part One

Germany: Extracting food and labour

1

The western Banat as Germany's breadbasket and the role of the Banat Germans in agricultural extraction

Mirna Zakić

The Vojvodina region in today's northern Serbia comprises the western Banat, the Batschka/Bačka and Syrmien/Srem/Syrmia (see Map 3). The western Banat itself is one half of the historical Banat region, which until 1918 formed the southern part of the Kingdom of Hungary and was then divided between Romania and Serbia. The whole of Vojvodina consists predominantly of fertile flatlands watered by the Danube and the Theiss/Tisa and has long been a locus of intensive farming. Due to their status as borderlands (between the Ottoman and the Habsburg Empires, then between Serbia/Yugoslavia and Hungary), the Banat and the whole of Vojvodina have experienced multiple waves of migration and have always had an ethnically diverse population, including a significant German presence until shortly after the Second World War.[1]

In April 1941, the Third Reich and its allies Hungary, Italy and Bulgaria attacked, defeated and partitioned the Kingdom of Yugoslavia. The western Banat and Serbia proper (south of the Danube) became a single occupation zone under the *Wehrmacht*'s control. Between April 1941 and October 1944, the ethnic German (*Volksdeutsche*) minority administered the western Banat on the Nazis' behalf. The Banat Germans' position – as Germans, as Banat Germans and as members of an officially nazified community – remained precarious and, in the eyes of the Reich Germans (*Reichsdeutsche*), always in need of shoring up, which served as an incentive for collaboration. The Banat Germans' main role within Hitler's New Order was triune: they alleviated the Nazis' lack of manpower by taking on many bureaucratic and security tasks in their home region; they participated in Nazi anti-partisan warfare in the Balkans; and they provided the occupying forces with substantial food provisions.[2]

Since the settlement of German speakers in the Banat in the eighteenth century, the economy had been intertwined with politics. In the interwar period, it was the economy and foreign trade that helped pull the Yugoslav Germans into the Nazi orbit, increasing their mental separation from their home country and their corresponding attachment to Germany. Under occupation, the extraction of agrarian surpluses from the fertile and relatively pacified western Banat became crucial for the Reich's food supply; it also became an arena in which tensions between Reich and Banat German identities and priorities played out. The Reich's superior attitude towards ethnic Germans, the chronic imbalance between the Banat's wartime exports and imports, and Banat Germans' desire to strengthen their ties to the Reich and their separation from Serbia proper all served to affirm the unequal relationship between the Reich and the Banat Germans acting as its collaborators.

Although they did not have the ability to craft independent economic policy, the Banat German leadership could nevertheless facilitate the economic exploitation of its home region, while also replicating the Reich's attitude that this economic collaboration was a key prerequisite for the Banat Germans' claim to belong to the nazified community of all 'racial' Germans, the *Volksgemeinschaft*. This claim remained contingent on constant affirmation through Banat German compliance with the Reich's demands. Moreover, the desired volume of agricultural extraction from the Banat depended on the participation of the Banat's other ethnic groups, not just the Germans. In vain did Banat German propaganda invoke the image of the Banat as the 'breadbasket [*Kornkammer*] of Europe', made such solely through the hard work of German peasants over the generations.[3] If anything, the metaphor only heightened Nazi expectations that the Banat would live up to its *Kornkammer* reputation.

The Banat Germans and agriculture before the Second World War

German speakers migrated to and settled permanently in Southeastern Europe from the early eighteenth century onwards, on the heels of a string of border wars between the Austrian and the Ottoman Empires. For the Habsburg court in the era of enlightened absolutism, planned settlement was a means to repopulate areas that had been depopulated due to war and the Ottoman withdrawal, and to make those areas economically productive again; to extend and assert the spread of Habsburg political power; and to help tie the newly conquered areas to the imperial centre. Alongside ostensible Germans (mostly from the southern and western German states), Hungarians, Romanians, Serbs and Jews participated in the colonization of what was then southern Hungary. Into the early twentieth century, German speakers in the Banat tended to live in ethnically homogeneous villages – alongside majority Serbian, Romanian and Hungarian villages, as well as ethnically mixed towns like Temeschburg/Temišvar and Grossbetschkerek/Veliki Bečkerek – and while the landowning aristocracy remained Hungarian, the German settlers included rich peasants, landless peasants, tradespeople and craftspeople. Among the German settlers, there were also Ashkenazi Jews, whose business networks facilitated trade in agricultural produce and banking transactions, and who sometimes owned agricultural land, too.[4]

Following the collapse of the Austro-Hungarian Monarchy at the end of the First World War, the Banat was partitioned between Romania (which got the eastern half of the region, including Temeschburg) and the Kingdom of Serbs, Croats and Slovenes (from 1929 the Kingdom of Yugoslavia, which got the western Banat including Grossbetschkerek). The western Banat covered an area of 9,300 square kilometres (930,000 hectares or 2,298,000 acres), and Yugoslav agricultural, population and trade policy had an impact on its economy. According to the 1931 Yugoslav census, 84 per cent of Banat German households were involved in agriculture, while 65 per cent engaged in agriculture to the exclusion of other economic pursuits. Numbering some 120,000 people, the Banat Germans represented about one-fifth of the Banat's population. Collectively they owned 11 per cent of the Banat's arable land, mostly divided into smallholdings (around one-fifth of the 'German' share of land belonged to Jews, of whom some 4,000 lived in the Banat). There were very few industrial workers among the Banat Germans, in part because the western Banat was the historical region's less industrialized half. What industry existed was geared towards agriculture and dominated in the interwar period by Hungarian, German and Jewish owners. Banat Germans owned grain mills, slaughterhouses and meat-packing facilities, breweries, sugar factories, vineyards, brickyards, and glass, textile and rope manufacturing businesses. Cattle-raising was of far lesser economic importance than the growing of grains and vegetables, though Banat-bred horses were greatly esteemed, and raising pigs and poultry was widespread.[5] Agriculture thus remained the main occupation and source of income of the Banat Germans as well as a major identity marker for this minority community.

After the western Banat was incorporated into Yugoslavia, the new state's economic and social problems had an impact on the Banat's economy. The state attempted various policy solutions, including an ambitious interwar land reform in Vojvodina and the gradual reorientation of Yugoslav trade towards Germany in the 1930s.

Interwar Yugoslavia tried to solve several pressing demographic and economic problems through the aforementioned land reform. It had a large peasant population of mixed ethnic background, with the poor Slavic peasants concentrated in underdeveloped areas such as southern Serbia, Montenegro, Macedonia and Herzegovina. Many had served in the Serbian army in the First World War. They had borne great sacrifices, and expected to be rewarded by the new state, dominated as it was by the Serbian bureaucracy and royal house. The key to peasant poverty was that so many were landless peasants and agricultural labourers or owned 'dwarf' landholdings that could not support a family. Finally, by turning their sights on large landholdings in Vojvodina, the Yugoslav authorities intended to shift the ethnic balance in this newly annexed region away from the economic and political influence of the resident Hungarians and, to a lesser extent, Germans, and towards South Slav colonists who would serve as living exponents of the new state's authority. Land ownership and economic policy thus intersected with population policy and the struggle of post-1918 successor states to assert their authority and legitimacy in their new borderlands.[6]

As an exercise in elite policymaking and social engineering, the interwar land reform was, at best, a partial success, and even ended up benefitting those whose economic power it was intended to undercut. The reform began in 1919 and was concluded in 1930–31, during which time some 20,000 families totalling 100,000 people migrated to and settled in Vojvodina, usually on small landholdings carved out of the large estates expropriated from the Hungarian nobility, most of whom had been absentee landlords or had moved to post-Trianon Hungary.[7] Since the Banat Germans tended to own small- or medium-sized landholdings, the reform affected only 1.5 per cent of their land, leaving them about as well-off as they had been before the war.

The Banat Germans who suffered the most due to the land reform were the landless peasants who had eked out a living as day labourers on the great estates and were outnumbered by landless Hungarian peasants.[8]

Despite this, the interwar land reform began to loom large in the Banat Germans' understanding of their position within the Yugoslav state. Creating an idealized, orderly and fruitful homeland (*Heimat*) away from the German heartland through hard work was a long-standing trope, which justified Germans' eastward expansion. For ethnic Germans, this idealization of peasant migration overlapped with other markers of ethnic distinction and superiority (thrift, cleanliness) which were supposedly unique to Germans.[9] Within the context of the interwar land reform, both ownership of arable land and the difficulties associated with obtaining and cultivating it became a 'distinguishing cultural characteristic'.[10] Thus complaints of unfairness – because the land reform was intended to privilege Serb and other Slav settlers and buyers over Germans and other minorities interested in acquiring more land – became rote in the Banat Germans' public pronouncements and interwar politicking. Yet by the end of the 1930s, due to government corruption, subterfuge (e.g. using intermediaries in land transactions in order to conceal the buyers' ethnic identity), and in 1940, the lifting of a ban on selling land to ethnic Germans, the Banat Germans, too, benefitted from the land reform. By 1940, while still only accounting for 20 per cent of the population, economically the Banat Germans punched far above their weight, controlling 31 per cent of the Banat's arable land as well as 30 per cent of its trade, 40 per cent of its handicrafts and 49 per cent of its (scant) industry.[11]

The role of the Banat Germans in interwar Yugoslavia's trade relations was another example of the intersection between the economy and politics. Extensive scholarship exists on how Southeastern Europe's agricultural economies were drawn into Germany's economic sphere as early as the 1920s and then more intensively in the 1930s, when Nazi Germany sought to secure supplies of coal and oil, metals, food and animal fodder as part of its preparations for the Second World War.[12] With regard to Yugoslav exports, Vojvodina played a key role – covering 7 per cent of Yugoslavia's land surface, it accounted for 50 per cent of the state's agrarian exports, especially of wheat, corn, sunflower oil, sugar beets and hemp. In the Banat alone, 91 per cent of the ground surface was under cultivation, four-fifths of that as arable land (which a Reich report from December 1941 claimed yielded more tonnage of grain per hectare than comparable land in the Reich itself) and the rest as pasturage, vineyards and forests.[13]

Beginning in 1922, with the founding of the economic cooperative *Agraria*, the Yugoslav Germans developed an extensive network of cooperatives (*Genossenschaften*) to help peasant producers sell their goods on both domestic and international markets. These cooperatives were concentrated predominantly in Vojvodina. *Agraria* served as the hub organization and clearing house for cooperatives exporting pigs and cattle, poultry and eggs, grains and hemp, as well as for the import of agricultural machinery from Germany. The cooperatives also helped their members purchase land.[14] In addition, the cooperatives served a political purpose, instilling a sense of ethnic self-sufficiency[15] as well as suspicion towards other ethnicities, nurturing the Germans' self-image as more diligent and therefore also more prosperous than other ethnic groups, and generally reinforcing the perception that to be an ethnic German in Southeastern Europe was to stand apart from one's environment and home state and to look both to one's own insular community and to the distant 'motherland' in Germany – now the Third Reich.

The Banat Germans and agriculture under occupation

From April 1941, within the occupied area which the Nazis called Serbia-Banat (*Serbien-Banat*), the western Banat had special economic significance. Mere days after Yugoslavia's defeat, an official from the Southeastern Europe Society (*Südosteuropa Gesellschaft*, a Nazi think-tank for Balkan policy founded in 1940) toured the newly conquered area to assess its economic potential. The resulting report linked the natural fruitfulness of the land to the presence of the hard-working Germans and the German share of ownership in various economic sectors, not to mention the relative ease with which Jews participating in the local economy could be removed from the equation. The report also noted that the invasion had barely disrupted preparations for the sowing season and harvest.[16]

The intention of treating the Banat's agriculture as a convenience of the Reich's war economy – and the Banat German peasants as an economic asset – was evident from the start of the occupation. The Reich specifically needed the Banat's contributions due to both the disproportionately large agricultural output of this small region, which was already evident in the interwar era, and the fact that the Reich planners' hopes of syphoning off food from other occupied territories proved difficult to realize, even before the invasion of Yugoslavia, due precisely to the disruptions the Nazi invasion and occupation caused. A report by the SS-administered Ethnic German Liaison Office (*Volksdeutsche Mittelstelle* – VOMI) in early 1943 pointed out that grain shipments from Southeastern Europe could reach the Reich within days, rather than the weeks it took them to arrive from Ukraine. Starting in summer 1941, widespread resistance activity in many parts of occupied Yugoslavia also made economic extraction from those areas difficult. The Banat, however, mostly remained resistance free, and so the Reich economy prioritized agricultural extraction from it at all costs.[17]

Propaganda in both the Reich and the occupied Banat framed agricultural extraction as both a feature and a prerequisite of belonging to the *Volk*. In March 1944, the *Völkischer Beobachter* (the main Nazi daily newspaper) published a typically grandiose article about the Banat, a region many Reich Germans would have known little about despite its economic importance. The article recycled well-worn tropes about the Banat as a formerly depopulated wasteland, plagued by disease and banditry, which the Germans had settled and civilized two hundred years earlier: the land 'was not given to [the settlers] but was conquered [*erkämpft*] through blood and sweat … German endurance and German diligence, German work and German example [*Vorbild*]'.[18] The article also tied the Banat's economic importance to the rapid Aryanization of Jewish property there. In 1943, the *Donauzeitung*, a German-language newspaper published in (now Hungarian-occupied) Batschka, echoed the message about the 'German' Banat's economic importance to the Reich war effort by stressing that the Banat fed not only the Reich but also the city of Belgrade and the *Wehrmacht* troops in Greece and Italy, and did so of its own free will, a willing participant in a captive market, in contrast to the recalcitrant attitude and the greed of the peasants in Serbia proper as well as the armed resistance there.[19] Lothar Heller, a VOMI economic official who liaised frequently with the Banat German leadership and the Belgrade office of Franz Neuhausen, the General Plenipotentiary for the Economy (*Generalbevollmächtigter für die Wirtschaft* – GBW) in occupied Serbia-Banat, routinely included in his reports a pithy reference to the Banat Germans being one-fifth of the region's population but controlling one-quarter of arable land and producing between one-third and two-fifths of the Banat's agrarian yields.[20] Finally, in his speeches to the community, Josef (Sepp) Janko, the leader of the nazified ethnic German community (*Volksgruppenführer*), linked the sweat of German brows with a specifically and uniquely German bread, which fed the Germans, the other Banat ethnicities (which were dependent on German leadership and kindness) *and* the Reich.[21] Thus the hard work of generations of German peasants guaranteed their place in the Nazi *Volksgemeinschaft*.[22]

These glowing propaganda accounts were, of course, oversimplified, but they also reflected the real value and significance the Banat had for the Reich economy: in spring 1942, the VOMI explicitly framed the Banat economy as a part of the Reich's war economy and stressed the need to 'secure future harvests for the Reich'.[23] Banat German leadership, in turn, used the German peasants' economic importance as a means of crafting a propaganda message to knit the community closer together. It also deployed propaganda to exhort community members to make ever-greater efforts on the Reich's behalf. The Banat Germans understood that the Reich would have little need for the 'German' Banat unless the latter continued to serve as a reliable breadbasket. Agricultural productivity thus promised *Volk* belonging. In practice, relations between the Reich's economic planners and authorities and the Banat German community were complex and often fractious.

After the creation of Serbia-Banat as an occupation zone in April 1941, the daily administration of the Banat became the responsibility of the resident ethnic Germans under the nazified *Volksgruppenführung*. The latter worked under the supervision of the military occupation officials stationed in Belgrade as well as Berlin offices, such as the VOMI, which oversaw ethnic German affairs. To underline the Banat's importance as an economic resource, the Main Office for the National Economy (*Hauptamt für Volkswirtschaft*) was created in May 1941 in order to mediate between the Banat Germans and the GBW as the Reich's chief economic representative in Serbia-Banat. In practice, the *Hauptamt* carried out the GBW's orders; it did not craft or put forth independent economic policy.[24]

While they had to carry out the Reich's wishes, the ethnic Germans were far from mere puppets. The Banat Germans' position in the Nazi hierarchy was ambiguous: they were ethnically German but not quite 'as German as' the Reich Germans. They resided in an occupied area threatened by Hungary's expansionist ambitions.[25] They also had to navigate the tensions between various Nazi institutions (the *Wehrmacht*, the Foreign Ministry, the Ministry of the Four-Year Plan, the VOMI, the SS). While their leaders and many community members collaborated with the Nazis in various ways, their subordinate position in the Nazi racial hierarchy and the requirement that they prove themselves worthy of inclusion in the Nazi *Volksgemeinschaft* meant that the Banat

Germans contended with ever-escalating demands from the Reich. Participation in local administration and in the Holocaust, agricultural deliveries for the Reich's war effort and, eventually, even armed service in the Waffen-SS were all ways in which the Banat Germans tried to secure their foothold in the *Volksgemeinschaft*.

Germans from the Reich accused Banat Germans of putting personal gain ahead of the interests of the *Volk* (in effect, of failure in their racial duty), while Banat Germans claimed the Reich lacked a nuanced understanding of the economic and racial challenges faced by a German community in a multi-ethnic region far from the Reich's borders.[26] These tensions spilled over into Banat-Reich economic relations and were evident also in the further development of the network of economic cooperatives, which numbered 172 chapters (with 40,000 members in total) in the Banat by 1943.[27] The five biggest and most important *Genossenschaften* were *Agraria*, *Agrarprodukt*, *Cereal-Export*, *Donau-Cereal* (testimony to the Banat's importance as a putative breadbasket) and the Belgrade-based *Uljarica* with its Banat subsidiary *Oleum* (which focused on trade in sunflower seeds and oil). Reich experts stressed the cooperatives' key role in securing the delivery of agricultural quotas for export to the Reich as well as in remaking the Banat economy into a part of the Reich economy.[28] Yet tensions were apparent in the cooperatives' work. This was mainly due to the influx of privately owned companies from the Reich, which bought up properties (including Aryanized land and economic enterprises) in the Banat and founded new firms with the collusion of leading Banat Germans (who often sat on the boards of directors of multiple firms), bypassing the *Hauptamt für Volkswirtschaft* as the relevant local authority and defying the GBW's ostensible sole authority in directing economic activities in Serbia-Banat. Banat cooperatives, too, snapped up Aryanized properties as part of a larger process through which property seized from the Banat Jews (who were transported to Belgrade in August 1941 to be interned and eventually killed in autumn 1941 and spring 1942) passed to the German state, but also to individual ethnic Germans and their organizations.[29] Aryanization was also part of the Reich's investment in food-processing, canning and storage capacities in the occupied Banat. Examples included the takeover of mills and silos once owned by Jewish grain merchants, or the case of the sugar factory in Grossbetschkerek, whose Jewish owner was publicly hanged soon after the start of the occupation.[30]

The *Volksgruppenführung*'s attempts to chart its own economic policy as an equal partner to the Reich gained no traction in Berlin. Clashes between the Banat Germans, the GBW and/or various Berlin offices and firms ultimately complicated but did not slow down or diminish the extent of economic extraction. Reich officials were not shy about expressing both their satisfaction with the extraction and their ambitious plans for the Banat. In the last year of the occupation, Lothar Heller of the VOMI described the Banat as 'so small in area, so towering in achievement', and that it could 'of late gladly be called the Reich's front garden [*Vorgarten*] or domain [*Domäne*]'. He also called for *even more* regimentation and utilization of the entire southeast's economic potential,[31] while Franz Neuhausen, the GBW in Serbia-Banat, likened the Banat to a 'German *Heimatgau* [administrative unit in the Third Reich]' in fulfilling its 'duty' to Reich and *Volk*.[32]

Agricultural extraction and wartime trade

How significant was the occupied western Banat's agricultural yield in numerical terms? Official figures vary, yet by any estimate the Banat's output was prodigious. Working with both Reich and Banat German records, the historian Karl-Heinz Schlarp estimates that, after setting aside the produce and fodder necessary to feed the Banat itself and to secure the seed for the next year's sowing, the harvests of the years 1940–43 produced a cumulative surplus of about 900,000 tonnes of grain and produce, including 316,000 tonnes of wheat (enough to supply the entire city of Berlin with bread for eight whole months); 335,000 tonnes of ears of corn; 159,000 tonnes of sunflower seeds; plus barley, oats, potatoes, other vegetables and fruit. In addition, by spring 1943 alone, the Banat exported 16 million eggs and 305,000 live pigs, as well as canned meat and vegetables, marmalade and dried prunes, wine from the vineyards in the southern Banat hills, live heads of cattle, milk and dairy products, pig fat (cheaper than butter and therefore much sought after in both the Banat and in Serbia proper) and almost its entire crop of hemp.[33] A report written in July 1943 claimed that the harvests of 1940–41 and 1941–42 plus the projections for the 1942–43 harvest yielded over 510,000 tonnes of wheat; nearly 740,000 tonnes of corn;[34] nearly 110,000 tonnes of sunflower seeds; nearly 190,000 tonnes of sugar beets; 305,000 live pigs and 2,504 wagonloads of sugar.[35] Felix Benzler, the German Foreign Office's (*Auswärtiges Amt*) representative in occupied Belgrade and one of the Banat Germans' main points of contact with Berlin, prefaced this report with the statement that 'the German Volksgruppe puts in the greatest possible effort on the outer and the inner front'.[36] Also in 1943, Neuhausen estimated that over half of the wheat sent to the Reich from Serbia-Banat would come from the (more fertile, more peaceful, but also far smaller) Banat, as would half of the corn shipment; ethnic Germans claimed the corn harvest undershot Neuhausen's projections, but the expected quota of corn to be shipped to the Reich remained the same.[37] In order to ensure the expected quotas were met, the Reich Germans and the Banat *Volksgruppenführung* turned the Banat into a captive market, prescribed areas of land that had to be sown with various crops every year, and instituted rules for reporting and delivering surpluses beyond the amounts that were officially calculated as necessary for a family to feed itself.[38] Not surprisingly, producers often chafed against both these restrictions and the prices the Reich was willing to pay, leading to peasants and even entire villages receiving repeated official warnings if they delayed the Reich's deliveries, did not meet the prescribed quotas or held back the produce and pigs while the peasants and the Reich haggled over the purchasing price.[39]

The issue of where – and to feed whom exactly – the Banat sent its agrarian surpluses became a perennial source of complaints from the Banat Germans and tensions between the Banat and the Reich. Grain, pork and wine from the Banat fed both Reich civilians and Reich armed personnel in Serbia proper (including those who guarded and supervised forced labourers toiling in the copper mines in the town of Bor in eastern Serbia, which were crucial to the Reich's war economy), Italy, Hungary, Greece, Albania, Bulgaria, Croatia, Norway and even on the Eastern Front. But on many occasions, the civilian population of the Serbian capital Belgrade depended on the Banat for its bread and fat supply, too. In autumn 1941 alone, 1,000 wagons of wheat were sent to Belgrade from the Banat. In early summer 1942, the city's food situation became so dire that Neuhausen had to give permission for the transportation of additional wheat and fresh fish from the Banat to the city. The worse the security situation in Serbia proper became, the less Neuhausen could rely on grain shipments from there to meet his quotas, and the more he turned to extraction from the Banat.[40] Harald Turner, the head of the Reich's civilian administration in Serbia-Banat, pointed out that a major reason for the chronic shortages of foodstuffs in Serbia proper was that all of the Banat's grain was sent to the Reich – to little avail, as both Neuhausen's ability to protect his administrative fiefdom and the economic imperative to extract as much as possible remained paramount, even when this rapaciousness caused problems in Serbia-Banat. At the turn of 1941–42 rumours that the *Wehrmacht* would be forced to provide rations for Belgrade's civilians and would therefore have to lean on the Banat even more prompted an exchange of memoranda in Berlin aimed at soothing the evident displeasure among Banat Germans (who claimed to speak for the entire Banat population) at being treated as Belgrade's reluctant pantry.[41]

Although Serbia-Banat was one occupation zone, its two halves were, in practice, semi-autonomous from each other economically, as well as, to an extent, in terms of trade and administration. This was evident in Neuhausen's overreliance on the Banat to supply the entire occupation zone's grain and protein needs and export quotas, but also in trade across the Danube, primarily between the Banat and the city of Belgrade. In order to prevent the Banat's agrarian surplus from flowing to Serbia proper unchecked, selling food across the Danube was officially forbidden. Smuggling became rampant.[42] Officials repeatedly attempted to ban the transport of food to Serbia proper as well as to prevent private individuals (Belgrade residents but also *Wehrmacht*, SS and Operation Todt personnel) from crossing into the Banat in order to buy food.[43] Banat Germans sometimes bypassed the regulations that limited their choice of buyer and sold some of their goods (e.g. wine) directly to the *Wehrmacht*, which often paid better and required less demanding logistics than sending bottled wine to the Reich, or they slaughtered pigs and sold the meat 'under the table', invoking their right to do so as the *Wehrmacht*'s suppliers if caught.[44] Once, starting in 1942, the Waffen-SS recruited able-bodied adult men into the division *Prinz Eugen* and deployed them to Serbia proper, Bosnia and Croatia, it had to officially ban the division members from bringing supplies of food and fodder when returning from home leave.[45] Inside the Banat itself, the *Volksgruppenführung* attempted to force producers to only sell their surpluses to authorized economic cooperatives, which served as the Reich's middlemen.[46] It also tried to enforce meatless days in order to control the slaughter of pigs, calves and lambs; banned the informal food trade at street stalls and from door to door; and banned unauthorized trade in or slaughter of horses for meat, since the *Wehrmacht* periodically requisitioned draught horses for its own use.[47]

While Banat producers had the incentive to participate in the illicit trade with Serbia proper, where their wheat and pig fat could fetch much higher prices than on the Banat's controlled internal market, this was undercut by the high wartime inflation and the fact that price controls in the Banat (intended to benefit the Reich as the area's main buyer) diminished the willingness of Serbian tradespeople to sell wood and coal across the Danube.[48] Serbia-Banat constituted a single economic unit for import purposes, and since the Third Reich had little incentive to sell its industrial products in Serbia proper, the Banat also suffered from constant shortages of shoe leather, iron, petroleum, pesticides and agricultural machinery. The value of its exports vastly outstripped the value of its imports. This had a direct negative impact on agricultural productivity. As a flatland on the banks of the Danube and its tributaries (the Theiss/Tisa, the Aranka/Zlatica, the Bega/Begej), the Banat was subject to seasonal flooding and had depended on joint flood prevention implemented by Romania and Yugoslavia. In spring and summer 1942, catastrophic flooding submerged one-third of Serbia-Banat's arable land, caused in large part by the failure of the Romanian state to maintain the flood prevention systems on its side of the border, but also by shortages of the coal that should have powered the irrigation pumps on the Serbian side.[49] All of this made meeting the Reich's economic demands more challenging and prompted bitter complaints from the *Volksgruppenführung* – complaints which found a sympathetic ear in Lothar Heller but failed to move Nazi officials more interested in economic extraction than infrastructure investment as an extension of the racial policies (*Volkstumsarbeit*) in occupied Eastern and Southeastern Europe.[50] In as late as spring and summer 1944, reports from the Banat reiterated well-worn complaints about the requisitioning of horses by the *Wehrmacht*, as well as shortages of oil, firewood and pesticides, and dashed hopes that agricultural machinery withdrawn from the East would be sent to the Banat, all of which – along with increased resistance incursions and the labour shortage – delayed and adversely affected the grain and grape harvests.[51] Despite these setbacks, the Banat's agricultural output remained prodigious. Nazi officials pinpointed the region's potential for further extraction, yet proved unwilling to husband and invest in available resources.

Food and *Volksgemeinschaft*

Contemporary German – both Reich and Banat – reports about the western Banat's titanic agricultural output routinely foregrounded the role of the resident German minority as the main driver of economic success and effective agriculture. They often implied that it was the Germans' industriousness (a mark of their racial quality) and share in various economic sectors alone which legitimized the Banat's claim to being a part of Greater Germany by enabling its own economic exploitation. In reality – which Reich economic reports admitted on occasion – without continuing contributions from peasants of other ethnicities, the Banat's output would have been far less. In as late as summer 1943, the Banat Germans grew 28 per cent of the region's wheat, 25 per cent of its corn, 33.7 per cent of its sunflowers and 30.8 per cent of its sugar beets, and raised 47.5 per cent of its pigs.[52] For the rest – amounting to anywhere from just over one-half to three-quarters of various agricultural quotas – the Reich depended on the hard work and compliance of the Banat Serbs, Hungarians, Romanians and other ethnic groups.

At the same time, the Nazis put in place a system of privileges which signalled the Banat Germans' newly elevated position within their home region and enabled the Banat German peasantry to fulfil the Reich's steep economic demands. These privileges were in the Reich's interest and always remained contingent on the Banat Germans' satisfactory performance of their 'worthiness' to belong to the *Volksgemeinschaft*. The Banat Germans profited from the repeal of the interwar land reform and from access to Aryanized land, to agricultural labour and to preferential rations. Given the manifold sacrifices the Banat Germans were expected to make, including not only their agricultural output but also service in the Waffen-SS, on balance these privileges and benefits were of limited value in and of themselves, while helping to brand the whole Banat German community as collaborators.

In June 1941, two months into the occupation of Serbia-Banat, the Serbian collaborationist government, working under the Reich's supervision, partially repealed the interwar land reform. Only land not being actively cultivated by its current owners could be expropriated. An amendment passed in October 1942 specified that Banat Hungarians could benefit from the repeal, while those Serbs who had settled in the Banat in the 1920s and 1930s and were adversely affected by the repeal could still claim a small parcel of land, enough to build a house and a kitchen garden.[53] In practice, however, while the Reich wanted to both promote ethnic Germans by giving them access to more land and ensure significant economic extraction from the Banat, the former happened only in as far as it did not hinder the latter. In total, the interwar land reform had affected some 220,000–230,000 *Joche* (127,000–132,000 hectares or 312,000–327,000 acres), mostly from the partitioned great estates of the Hungarian nobility. Only a fraction thereof actually changed hands between 1941 and 1944, though the lion's share of that (30,000 *Joche*, 17,000 hectares or 43,000 acres) was then sold to Banat Germans by as early as October 1941.[54] Banat Hungarians made access to this land one of the perennial bones of contention between them (and Hungary) and the Germans in Serbia-Banat, relying on the alliance between the Reich and Hungary to lend their demands legitimacy. Even Banat Serbs could, on occasion, profit from this wartime development. At the very least, few of them lost their livelihoods if they worked in agriculture, as Serbs (and Croats, combined) made up just under half of the western Banat's population, were overwhelmingly peasants by profession and social stratum, and the Reich needed their agricultural contributions.[55]

Before 1941, the Banat Jews had been essential in the food-processing industries and the agricultural trade, less so in the growing of crops and raising of cattle. That being said, some 14,500 *Joche* (8,350 hectares or 20,600 acres) of Jewish-owned land were Aryanized, along with Jewish-owned houses and businesses. About half of that land belonged to three large estates near the villages of Zerne/Crnja, Padej/Padej and Tschoka/Čoka, which were taken over by the Reich in summer 1941, named German Landholdings in the Banat (*Deutsche Güter im Banat*) and used to supply the Operation Todt-run copper mines in Bor with food. The Banat Germans bought up part of this land, while the *Volksgruppenführung* held the rest in trust with a view to using it as a reward for the Banat's Waffen-SS veterans after the Reich's victory. While Reich officials, on occasion, described the Banat German attitude to Aryanization as jealous micromanaging, which obsessively dwelled on every 'dwarf' parcel of land, in reality this was not far removed from the Reich's own interest in Aryanized property, and it certainly helped augment Banat German landholdings.[56]

In 1943 and 1944, Reich estimates of the effects of these reversals in land ownership pegged the Banat Germans' ownership at 25.9 per cent of the entire land surface of the Banat and 30 per cent of its arable land.[57] This suggests that either the pre-1941 estimates of Banat Germans' economic might were inflated (probable) or the multiple disruptions caused by the war, even in the relatively peaceful Banat, in addition to the corruption and thievery inherent in the Nazi system of rule, failed to account for all of the Banat Germans' possessions (possible). Either way, at one-fifth of the resident population and with most adult men away from the Banat serving in the Waffen-SS, the Banat Germans played an outsized role throughout the occupation years as both economic and ideological agents of the Third Reich.

As both the *Volksgruppenführung* and the Serbian collaborationist government repeatedly asserted, ownership of land meant an obligation to cultivate that land. Each year, they ordered the peasants to cultivate as much land as the previous year, preferably more, and sometimes offered incentives, such as monetary bonuses for sowing certain crops or the use of teams of draught horses or oxen to pull ploughs.[58] Mass recruitment of men by the Waffen-SS (more than 21,000 by December 1943, out of a Banat German population of around 120,000[59]) compounded these challenges. In March 1942, the *Volksgruppenführung* created a German Labour Service (*Deutscher Arbeitsdienst*) for Banat German youth, followed in June 1942, by mandatory labour service for non-German youth. Finally, starting in March 1943, in line with the Nazi government's proclamation of total war, the *Volksgruppenführung* instituted labour conscription for all unemployed adults, regardless of ethnicity, which blurred the line between mandatory and forced labour. Discipline may have been lax and the effectiveness of the deployed workers variable, but in every instance, ethnic German households had preferential access to the labour pool.[60]

Finally, rationing of foodstuffs became a fact of life in Serbia-Banat, as it was in much of wartime Europe. In the Banat, rationing was tied to both race and another major signifier of belonging to the *Volk*: armed service on behalf of the Third Reich. Thus, while economic planners presupposed that a peasant household needed to grow and retain a certain quantity of potatoes, onions, beans, peas, lentils and peppers to survive,[61] and that bread was both a key symbol and a bodily necessity, the amount and kind of grain with which to bake bread varied significantly. The preferential ration – greater in weight and composed only or predominantly of wheat rather than corn flour (the exact amounts and kinds of flour could vary from village to village[62]) – was usually reserved for German households. Starting in 1942, in the face of complaints of unfairness from the Hungarians, in particular, this was justified by invoking the Banat Germans' service in the Waffen-SS and the Banat police, as local administrators and as role models for other ethnic groups.[63] The same logic applied with regard to access to such wartime luxuries as sugar: Banat Germans received a bigger ration of sugar due to their special position as both pillars and benefactors of the Reich, but also because Banat German women baked cakes and assembled care packages for the Reich's soldiers on active duty as well as the wounded in SS and *Wehrmacht* hospitals.[64] The black market remained active, but given the trade imbalance between the Banat, Serbia proper and the Reich, and controls on the slaughter and consumption of meat, the Banat diet remained meagre, despite the perks the Banat Germans enjoyed. Yet it never descended to starvation levels as in other parts of occupied Eastern and Southeastern Europe.

Conclusion

The Banat Germans' experiences under occupation in the Second World War were shaped by complex historical legacies of migration, multi-ethnic settlement and economic relations, and constantly shifting dynamics between the centre and the periphery. The twin impacts of the Third Reich's trade relations with interwar Yugoslavia and the Nazification of the Banat Germans accelerated under Nazi occupation, deepening the Banat Germans' perceived ideological and real economic dependence on the Reich's good will and priorities. Propaganda about the hard-working Banat German peasant oversimplified and glossed over the realities of occupation, which always prioritized the Reich's needs. In addition to other forms of collaboration, participation in – even spearheading – significant agricultural extraction from their home region, all to feed the Reich's war economy and support its violent domination of Southeastern Europe and other areas, helped brand the entire Banat German community as collaborators, which resulted in their violent mistreatment and forced departure from their home region in the war's aftermath.

Notes

1 'German' denotes the Yugoslav (interwar) or Banat (wartime) Germans, and 'Reich' or 'Reich German' denotes the German state and its citizens in the Nazi period. I use both German and Serbian toponyms.

2 For more details on the various forms of Banat German collaboration, the Banat Germans' precarious position in the Nazi racial hierarchy and Banat-Reich relations, see Mirna Zakić, *Ethnic Germans and National Socialism in Yugoslavia in World War II* (Cambridge: Cambridge University Press, 2017).

3 Sepp Janko, 'Zur Prinz-Eugen-Feier des Kreises Donau', 15 August 1941, in Sepp Janko, *Reden und Aufsätze* (Betschkerek: Buchreihe der Deutschen Volksgruppe im Banat und in Serbien, 1944), 77.

4 Márta Fata, 'German Settlers (*Donauschwaben*) in Southeastern Europe since the Early Modern Period', in *The Encyclopedia of Migration and Minorities in Europe: From the 17th Century to the Present*, ed. Klaus J. Bade et al. (Cambridge: Cambridge University Press, 2011), 445–6; Karl A. Roider and Robert Forrest, 'German Colonization in the Banat and Transylvania in the Eighteenth Century', in *The Germans and the East*, ed. Charles Ingrao and Franz A. J. Szabo (West Lafayette, IN: Purdue University Press, 2008), 89–94.

5 Zoran Janjetović, *Nemci u Vojvodini* (Belgrade: INIS, 2009), 107–11, 129; Karl-Heinz Schlarp, *Wirtschaft und Besatzung in Serbien. Ein Beitrag zur nationalsozialistischen Wirtschaftspolitik in Südosteuropa* (Stuttgart: Franz Steiner, 1986), 339; Akiko Shimizu, *Die deutsche Okkupation des serbischen Banats 1941–1944 unter besonderer Berücksichtigung der deutschen Volksgruppe in Jugoslawien* (Münster: LIT Verlag, 2003), 384; Ekkehard Völkl, *Der Westbanat 1941–1944. Die deutsche, die ungarische und andere Volksgruppen* (Munich: Dr. Rudolf Trofenik, 1991), 87.

6 Janjetović, *Nemci u Vojvodini*, 114–15; Dietmar Müller, *Bodeneigentum und Nation. Rumänien, Jugoslawien und Polen im europäischen Vergleich 1918–1948* (Göttingen: Wallstein, 2020), 8–10, 410–13.

7 Željko Bjeljac, Marija Drobnjaković and Milan Radovanović, 'Migracije stanovništva Vojvodine uoči i početkom Drugog svetskog rata', in *Srbi i rat u Jugoslaviji 1941. godine: Tematski zbornik radova*, ed. Dragan Aleksić (Belgrade: INIS, 2014), 105–8; Jovica Luković, '"Es ist nicht gerecht, für eine Reform aufkommen zu müssen, die gegen einen selbst gerichtet ist." Die Agrarreform und das bäuerliche Selbstverständnis der Deutschen im jugoslawischen Banat 1918–1941 – Ein Problemaufriss', in *Kulturraum Banat. Deutsche Kultur in einer europäischen Vielvölkerregion*, ed. Walter Engel (Essen: Klartext, 2007), 145–50.

8 Janjetović, *Nemci u Vojvodini*, 115–16; Luković, '"Es ist nicht gerecht"', 150–1.

9 'Der fleissige Schwabe', *Banater Beobachter*, 14 August 1942, 5; David Blackbourn, '"The Garden of Our Hearts": Landscape, Nature, and Local Identity in the German East', in *Localism, Landscape, and the Ambiguities of Place: German-Speaking Central Europe, 1860–1930*, ed. David Blackbourn and James Retallack (Toronto/Buffalo: University of Toronto Press, 2007), 150–8; Annemarie Röder, *Deutsche, Schwaben,Donauschwaben. Ethnisierungsprozesse einer deutschen Minderheit in Südosteuropa* (Marburg: N. G. Elwert, 1998), 8–9, 197.

10 Luković, '"Es ist nicht gerecht"', 160.

11 Janjetović, *Nemci u Vojvodini*, 121–2; Luković, '"Es ist nicht gerecht"', 157–8; Schlarp, *Wirtschaft und Besatzung*, 339.

12 Gesine Gerhard, 'Nie wieder Kohlrüben! Nationalsozialistische Ernährungspolitik im Zeichen des Zweiten Weltkrieges', *Zeitgeschichte: Landwirtschaft und Ernährung im Nationalsozialismus* 45, no. 3 (2018): 273–80; Stephen G. Gross, *Export Empire: German Soft Power in Southeastern Europe, 1890–1945* (Cambridge: Cambridge University Press, 2015).

13 'Serbien – Die Bedeutung des Banats', 17 December 1941, National Archives and Records Administration (henceforth: NARA), RG 242, T-81, roll 544, fr. 5316191; Schlarp, *Wirtschaft und Besatzung*, 338–9.

14 Janjetović, *Nemci u Vojvodini*, 123–5; Luković, '"Es ist nicht gerecht"', 158.

15 Even after the overt Nazification of the *Kulturbund* (the Yugoslav Germans' main political and social organization) in 1939, the cooperatives could not have fulfilled their export obligations without the contributions of producers of non-German (including Jewish) origins. Bernd Robionek, 'A New Light on Yugoslav-German Trade Relations and Economic Anti-Semitism: The Ethnic German Poultry Product Cooperative in the Vojvodina during the 1930s', in *German-Balkan Entangled Histories in the Twentieth Century*, ed. Mirna Zakić and Christopher A. Molnar (Pittsburgh: University of Pittsburgh Press, 2020), 49–53, 55–9.

16 Von Rischka, 2 May 1941, Bundesarchiv Berlin-Lichterfelde (henceforth: BArch) R 63, Band 213, 215–17.

17 'Kurzbericht über die Wirtschaftsarbeit der Volksdeutschen im Jahre 1942', February 1943, Politisches Archiv des Auswärtigen Amts (henceforth: PA AA), Inland II D, R 100533, 24; Gross, *Export Empire*, 307, 315, 318.

18 'Das Banat. Eigener Bericht des VB', *Völkischer Beobachter*, 28 March 1944, BArch, R 8034 II, Band 4780, 38.

19 Peter Staadlbaur, 'Banat – Land des Ackerbaues. Wertvoller Beitrag für die Ernährungssicherung des europäischen Raumes', *Donauzeitung*, 18 April 1943, BArch, R 8034 II, Band 4780, 13.

20 Heller, 17 February 1943, BArch, R 63, Band 138, doc. 163; Heller, 22 December 1943, BArch, R 63, Band 87, 218.

21 Janko, 'Zur Prinz-Eugen-Feier des Kreises Temesch', 24 August 1941, in Janko, *Reden*, 83.

22 Janko, 'Zum Erntedank', 5 October 1941, in Janko, *Reden*, 87–8.
23 VOMI, 12 March 1942, BArch, NS 19, file 1728, fiche 1, fr. 35.
24 Schlarp, *Wirtschaft und Besatzung*, 342; Shimizu, *Die deutsche Okkupation*, 405.
25 Hungary occupied the neighbouring Batschka and insisted in vain on its right to the Banat through to the end of 1941 and occasionally in subsequent years. The Reich resisted this demand, despite having promised the Banat to Hungary in order to entice its ally into participating in the invasion of Yugoslavia in spring 1941, not least due to the likelihood that a Hungarian takeover would rile the Banat population and disrupt the flow of the all-important agricultural surpluses to the Reich. Triska, 31 July 1941, NARA, RG 242, T-120, roll 5782, frs. H297935–936; Reichel, 15 April 1943, PA AA, Inland II Geheim, R 100969, fiche 2498, frs. H299839–840.
26 'Meldungen aus dem Reich', 4 August 1941, BArch, R 58, file 163, fiche 1, fr. 11; Geissler, July 1943, BArch, NS 5 VI, file 29277/a, 146–7.
27 Shimizu, *Die deutsche Okkupation*, 399; Völkl, *Der Westbanat*, 114.
28 Heller, 11 February 1942, BArch, NS 19, file 1728, fiche 1, 33–4.
29 Rimann, 15 November 1941, PA AA, Inland II D, R 100615, fiche 6, frs. 166–8; Heller, 15 January 1942, PA AA, Inland II D, R 100615, fiche 5, fr. 152; 'Meldungen aus dem Reich', 12 March 1942, BArch, R 58, file 170, fiche 2, frs. 134–5; Shimizu, *Die deutsche Okkupation*, 285–7, 400–5.
30 Von Rischka, 2 May 1941, BArch, R 63, Band 213, 219; Gurski, 23 March 1945, NARA, RG 242, T-75, roll 53, fr. 591.
31 Heller, 22 December 1943, BArch, R 63, Band 87, 220; Heller, 18 January 1944, PA AA, Inland II D, R 100588, 125–6.
32 Neuhausen, January 1944, NARA, RG 242, T-75, roll 69, fr. 164.
33 Schlarp, *Wirtschaft und Besatzung*, 353–4.
34 The discrepancy between this and Schlarp's estimate may have been due to overly optimistic projections for the 1943 harvest.
35 'Kriegseinsatz der Volksgruppe', July 1943, PA AA, Inland II C, R 100380, 94.
36 Benzler, 22 July 1943, PA AA, Inland II C, R 100380, 92.
37 Shimizu, *Die deutsche Okkupation*, 385–6.
38 'Naredba', *Službene novine*, 17 November 1942, 3–4; Amelung, 'Anordnung', *Amtsblatt für das Banat*, 12/19 November 1942, 2; Josef Lapp, 'Aufruf an sämtliche Landwirte im Banat!', *Amtsblatt für das Banat*, 26 November 1942, 2–3; Lapp, 'Anordnung', *Amtsblatt für das Banat*, 17 September 1943, 1; 'Plan für die planmässige landwirtschaftliche Erzeugung im Banat für das Wirtschaftsjahr 1943/44', *Amtsblatt für das Banat*, 18 December 1943, 1–3.
39 Gemeindeamt Soltur, 8 December 1941, Istorijski arhiv Kikinda, fonds 84, box 1, 424; 'Naredba o isporuci pšenice i mešanju kukuruznog sa pšeničnim brašnom u Banatu', *Službene novine*, 30 January 1942, 2; Nakodorf Bürgermeister und Notar, 6 August 1942, Istorijski arhiv Kikinda, fonds 84, box 3.
40 Turner, 3 July 1942, Bundesarchiv-Militärarchiv Freiburg (henceforth BArch-MA), RW 40, file 195, 10; Gross, *Export Empire*, 318–19; Shimizu, *Die deutsche Okkupation*, 385.
41 Turner, 6 September 1941, BArch-MA, RW 40, file 186, 5; VOMI, 13 November 1941, PA AA, Inland II D, R 100615, fiche 6, fr. 170; VOMI, 16 January 1942, PA AA, Inland II D, R 100615, fiche 5, fr. 150.
42 Geissler, July 1943, BArch, NS 5 VI, file 29277/a, 144; Shimizu, *Die deutsche Okkupation*, 391–2.
43 Landratsamt Grosskikinda, 3 October 1941, Istorijski arhiv Kikinda, fonds 84, box 1; Beer, 3 April 1942, Vojni arhiv Republike Srbije, Nemački arhiv, box 27-A, folder 5,

doc. 51; Janko, 17 July 1942, Vojni arhiv Republike Srbije, Nemački arhiv, box 27-A, folder 5, doc. 70; 'Naredba o putovanju u Banat', *Službene novine*, 25 August 1942, 5–6; Neuhausen, 'Durchführungsverordnung (Bewirtschaftung von Obst, Obsterzeugnissen, Gemüse u. Kartoffeln)', *Amtsblatt für das Banat*, 12–19 November 1942, 1; Rentsch, 25 November 1942, Vojni arhiv Republike Srbije, Nemački arhiv, box 27-C, folder 4, doc. 37.

44 Pragai and Richa, 20 January 1942, Istorijski arhiv Kikinda, fonds 84, box 1; Zimmer, 14 March 1944, BArch, R 63, Band 138, 63.

45 'Warenausfuhr aus dem Banat', 7 July 1943, BArch-MA, RS 3-7, file 1, 43.

46 'Naredba o prometu suncokretovim semenom u Banatu za godinu 1942', *Službene novine*, 20 March 1942, 7–8; Lapp, 'Anordnung betreffend die Weizenablieferung der Ernte 1943', *Amtsblatt für das Banat*, 17 September 1943, 1.

47 Grossbetschkerek Bürgermeisteramt, 12 May 1941, Istorijski arhiv Zrenjanin, fonds 131, miscellanea box, miscellanea folder, doc. 434; Lapp, 'Anordnung', *Amtsblatt für das Banat*, 12 March 1942, 1–2; Lapp, 'Verfügung betreffend Verbot des Strassenhandels mit landwirtschaftlichen Produkten', *Amtsblatt für das Banat*, 2/9 July 1942, 1.

48 With few forests, no natural deposits of oil or coal and no hydroelectric dam on the Lower Danube till the 1970s, the western Banat was energy poor.

49 Egger, 31 March 1942, PA AA, Inland II D, R 100615, fiche 4, frs. 109–10; Shimizu, *Die deutsche Okkupation*, 393–4.

50 Opštinska uprava Padej, 10 December 1941, Istorijski arhiv Kikinda, fonds 84, box 1, 421; Gemeindeamt Heufeld, 7 February 1942, Istorijski arhiv Kikinda, fonds 84, box 1, 464; 'Betrachtungen zur Banater Wirtschaftslage', 27 May 1942, PA AA, Inland II D, R 100615, fiche 3, frs. 85–7; Heller, 17 February 1943, BArch, R 63, Band 138, doc. 163; Shimizu, *Die deutsche Okkupation*, 390–1, 393; Völkl, *Der Westbanat*, 87–8, 90.

51 'Monatsbericht April 1944 über die Lage in den Deutschen Volksgruppen', NARA, RG 242, T-120, roll 1005, fr. 393494; 'Monatsbericht Juli 1944 des Hauptamtes Volksdeutsche Mittelstelle', NARA, RG 242, T-120, roll 1005, frs. 393335, 393341–342; 'Monatsbericht August 1944 des Hauptamtes Volksdeutsche Mittelstelle', NARA, RG 242, T-120, roll 1030, fr. 408957.

52 'Kriegseinsatz der Volksgruppe', July 1943, PA AA, Inland II C, R 100380, 95.

53 'Uredba o delimičnom ukidanju mera izvršenih na osnovu Zakona o agrarnoj reformi', *Službene novine*, 20 June 1941, 1; 'Uredba o davanju naknade licima oštećenim ukidanjem mera izvršenih na osnovu Zakona o agrarnoj reformi', *Službene novine*, 30 October 1942, 1.

54 VOMI, 27 October 1941, PA AA, Inland II D, R 100614, fiche 7, fr. 213; Shimizu, *Die deutsche Okkupation*, 413.

55 'Uredba o ukidanju eksproprijacija izvršenih na osnovu Zakona o agrarnoj reformi u pogledu nekretnina u opštinama Jabuka, Glogonj, Toba, Martinica i Lazarevo', *Službene novine*, 17 February 1942, 12; Beauftragter für den Vierjahresplan, 21 March 1942, PA AA, Inland II D, R 100614, fiche 5, fr. 157; Völkl, *Der Westbanat*, 162–3, 165–8.

56 Janko, 'Anordnung des Volksgruppenführers über die Übertragung von jüdischen Vermögen an Angehörige der Deutschen Volksgruppe', *Verordnungsblatt der Volksgruppenführung der deutschen Volksgruppe im Banat und Serbien*, 1 March 1942, 8–9; Geissler, July 1943, BArch, NS 5 VI, file 29277/a, 144, 146; Gurski, 23 March 1945, NARA, RG 242, T-75, roll 53, frs. 567, 577; Völkl, *Der Westbanat*, 173–4, 176, 178.

57 Benzler, July 1943, PA AA, Inland II C, R 100380, 95; Geissler, July 1943, BArch, NS 5 VI, file 29277/a, 145; 'Neueingängeverzeichnis', August 1944, BArch, R 59, file 65, fiche 2, fr. 81.
58 Lapp, 'Anordnung', *Amtsblatt für das Banat*, 10 October 1941, 1–2; Lapp, 'Aufruf', *Amtsblatt für das Banat*, 26 November 1942, 1; Lapp, 'Anordnung', *Amtsblatt für das Banat*, 17 September 1943, 1.
59 'Volksdeutsche in der Waffen-SS', 12 December 1943, NARA, RG 238, entry 174, box 2, doc. NO-2015, 3.
60 Janko, 'Verordnung über die Errichtung des Deutschen Arbeitsdienstes (DAD)', *Verordnungsblatt der Volksgruppenführung der deutschen Volksgruppe im Banat und Serbien*, 1 March 1942, 6; Lapp, 'Verfügung über die Mobilmachung gewisser Jahrgänge zum Zwecke des Pflichtarbeitsdienstes und der Verwendung der mobilisierten Arbeiter', *Amtsblatt für das Banat*, 18/25 June 1942, 1–3; 'Naredba za Banat o upućivanju na obavezan rad. Alkoholičari i asocijalni tipovi obrazuju zasebnu grupu', *Vreme*, 21 March 1943, BArch, NS 5 VI, file 29277/a, 195.
61 Amelung, 'Anordnung', *Amtsblatt für das Banat*, 12/19 November 1942, 2.
62 See testimonials collected in the Bundesarchiv Lastenausgleichsarchiv Bayreuth, Ost-Dokumentation 17.
63 Benzler, 2 November 1942, PA AA, Inland II D, R 100548, 87–8; Referat D VIII, 23 November 1942, PA AA, Inland II D, R 100548, 86; Benzler, 18 March 1943, PA AA, Inland II D, R 100549, 43; Egger, 30 July 1943, PA AA, Inland II Geheim, R 101094, fiche 2822.
64 Beer, 'Opferleistungen der Deutschen Volksgruppe. Reichsdurchschnitt stellenweise übertroffen', *Banater Beobachter*, 9 May 1943, 2; 'Aufzeichnung zur ungarischen Verbalnote vom 16.6.1943 unter Berücksichtigung der Stellungnahme der Dienststelle in Gross-Betschekerek', 7 July 1943, PA AA, Inland II Geheim, R 100969, fiche 2497, fr. H299804; Benzler, July 1943, PA AA, Inland II C, R 100380, 94; Egger, 30 July 1943, PA AA, Inland II Geheim, R 101094, fiche 2822.

2

Coal and copper for the German war effort: Food and labour in Yugoslav mining industries

Sabine Rutar

To date, there is no comprehensive economic history of the Second World War as it played out in Yugoslavia as a whole. Several scholars have addressed the German economic exploitation and the German idea of an economic 'supplementary area' (*Ergänzungsraum*) in Southeastern Europe. Yet, very little attention has been paid to the question of food supplies, whether for the army or for civilians.[1] Scholars have generally taken a structural bird's eye view of economic exploitation, including the exploitation of the labour force. These studies have, for the most part, focused on Yugoslavia's fragmented parts rather than looking at the country within its prewar borders.[2]

During the interwar period, Yugoslavia's economy was heavily dependent not only on Germany, but also on France and Great Britain. In some sectors of the economy, the share of foreign capital reached almost 100 per cent, and the copper industry was one such sector. In 1940, the copper mine in Bor in eastern Serbia, for instance, exported a record quantity of copper ore (43,646 tonnes). The French company *Mines de Bor* saw its capital increase from an initial 5.5 million francs (1905) to 15 million (1933), and three years later to as much as 60 million. By 1939, the figure amounted to 120 million francs.[3] In 1940, Germany occupied France and quickly took over the French assets in Europe's biggest copper mine.[4] At that time, the German rhetoric emphasized friendship with Yugoslavia: 'In light of the fact that the headquarters of *Mines de Bor* in Paris is now part of the German-administered territories, the German authorities have introduced the appropriate measures to guarantee the continued smooth operation of the mine, in line with the Yugoslav wishes.'[5]

When Germany invaded Yugoslavia in April 1941, it also added to its 'administered territories' mines that had been controlled by British capital and technological know-how, such as the lead and zinc mines in Mežica in northern Slovenia and in Trepça in northern Kosovo (see Maps 1, 3 and 4). The Yugoslav mining industries as well as the Banat's 'breadbasket' were important for the German war economy. Due to the British sea blockade of 1939, the Germans no longer had access to copper and other ores from overseas. Thus Serbian copper became essential, as did the exploitation of the other mines in the German-controlled areas.[6]

Histories of supply, food, shortages and hunger tend to focus on the distribution of agricultural goods and on Nazi agricultural policies, the most horrific of which was the so-called 'hunger plan' that killed millions of prisoners of war and civilians in the Soviet Union.[7] When Lizzie Collingham published *The Taste of War. World War II and the Battle for Food* in 2011, she had little more than Violetta Hionidou's pioneering study on the horrific famine in Greece to draw on for Southeastern Europe. Her book has a global perspective, in which the Balkans beyond Greece remain a blank spot.[8]

In this chapter, I focus on the question of how the mining industries in Yugoslavia functioned during the war in terms of food and provisioning. The copper mine in Bor in eastern Serbia and the coalfields in the Zasavje region of southern Styria in Slovenia serve as case studies. I use the company files to shed light on the question, illustrating how work in the mining regions was impacted by experiences of violence, survival and death in locally contingent ways. While shortage, deprivation and hunger prevailed everywhere, in the context of Yugoslavia as a whole, the copper mine in Bor was different from the mining industry in the north of the country (Slovenia). I first provide a more general impression of the role of physical labourers in Yugoslavia, and of miners in particular, in the nutrition schemes conditioned by the war even before the Axis attack of April 1941. I then give an overview of how Yugoslavia reacted to the outbreak of war with food supply regulations. And finally, I look at how, in the mining regions, the issue of food supplies was intertwined with that of labour supply regimes after Yugoslavia was dismembered and occupied.

Food schemes conditioned by the war

Lizzie Collingham notes how physical activity increased dramatically as a consequence of the war because of the breakdown of infrastructures (such as public transport), which made it necessary to walk much more, and because of all manner of other shortages. She points out that peasants were recruited into the army, leaving their fields unattended, or rather, leaving all the work to their families on the home front. Thus the need for food actually increased for almost everybody.[9] The mining industries required and searched for skilled miners, and throughout the war there was tension between the army's recruitment efforts and those of the mines. Hans-Christoph Seidel provides detailed insights into the complex entanglements between labour in the mines, conscription into the army and food schemes in the Ruhr Valley, Germany's most important coal mining and steel-producing region.[10]

Workers in heavy industry became less productive when they were under-nourished, and this was all the more true for the increasingly unskilled and overworked workforce. For example, because of the war-induced food shortages, Ruhr Valley miners lost up to 6 kilograms of their body weight during the winter of 1941–42. Their productivity decreased by between 15 and 43 per cent. It was observations like this that prompted the Nazi leadership to look towards the occupied territories for food stocks – without regard for the consequences this would have for the local populations.[11]

While governments everywhere broadly accepted that the military should be prioritized when it came to food supply, the issue of how to allocate extra rations to those engaged in heavy physical labour, such as miners, steel workers and arms industry workers, was addressed differently, depending on local conditions. To give just two examples that reflect the extremes: in Britain, equal rations were distributed across the adult population, whereas in the Soviet Union the government struggled to provide its army and its industrial workforce with enough to eat, let alone the rest of the population. That said, although Britain managed to feed its army, the government's 'equal' ration policy demonstrably disadvantaged miners and other physical labourers, who were soon significantly less well-nourished than the middle class. The government did not react to this situation until 1943, when it made it compulsory for all firms employing more than 250 people to set up canteens where men could buy additional meals at low cost.[12]

In Germany, the *Wehrmacht* was the best-supplied institution and workers began to demand the same rations. While the German rationing system acknowledged physical labourers' need for larger quantities of food, in reality the quantities of available provisions were simply too low for the physically demanding war industries. In the German mining industries, miners suffered from severe symptoms of fatigue from 1942 at the latest. In March 1939, a government decree had extended their eight-hour working day by forty-five minutes, and since 1941 they had been obliged to work overtime on Sundays and holidays, sometimes resulting in them working for three weeks straight without a day off. These regulations were extended to the occupied northern Yugoslav (Slovenian) regions after April 1941. On the other hand, from the 1920s, experts in the emerging field of labour physiology had regarded the miners, whose physical fitness remained indispensable despite increasing mechanization, as an apt case study to increase knowledge about the effects of good nutrition on efficiency. In the first two years of the war, the miners, while impacted by the general shortages, especially in animal fat supplies, were still in a very privileged position when it came to rationing. From spring 1942 at the latest, however, the worsening general shortages took their toll precisely because of the heavy nature of the miners' work.[13] What is more, when it came to feeding the foreign workers who had come to populate the German heavy industries, the importance of efficient use of food resources was obscured by a mass of ideological principles. While forced labourers from Western Europe received only marginally less food than the German workers, the rations received by the East Europeans were completely inadequate.[14]

With regard to the Nazi policies and actions which resulted in millions of people dying of hunger in the Soviet Union, a mix of anti-Slavic racist ideology, military strategy and economic exploitation has been identified. Adam Tooze emphasizes that the existing documents concerning the 'hunger plan' reveal a language that is more explicit, colder and refers more directly to mass murder than the documents on the destruction of the Jews.[15] It is only through works such as these that the centrality of food – and of agrarian ideology – as an engine of the Second World War has become apparent (as opposed to racial and ideological motivations). Generally, scholars who have researched the 'hunger plan' have come to a consensus that the National Socialist economic policy in the East was a deliberate tool of mass extermination, directed against Slavic or Soviet peoples, as well as Jews and other 'undesirable' groups.[16] Even though there is no equivalent to the 'hunger plan' for Southeastern Europe, the region's envisaged role as a 'supplementary space' (*Ergänzungsraum*) for German needs had consequences that essentially comprised the same economic, racist and ideological mix.

Yugoslav food schemes

In the late 1930s, many European countries started to conduct preparations for maintaining a viable supply regime. Their experiences from the First World War were still fresh in their minds, and they were concerned about the German political situation and, indeed, a potential German military invasion. When from 1939 onwards, imports and exports were severely reduced and many transport connections interrupted, this resulted in decreased production rates and subsequent price increases. Speculative trading also increased. The situation was further aggravated by many anxious consumers emptying the stores and worried savers knocking on the doors of the banks. These problems did not bypass Yugoslavia, which was economically weak and dependent on other European countries.[17]

Soon after the start of the war in Europe in September 1939 with the German attack on Poland, scarcity and profiteering arrived in Yugoslavia. Protests against price rises and against the support of the Axis powers intensified. Before the war, the subsistence garden had been a key necessity for many, and the world economic crisis had exacerbated the situation considerably. In Yugoslavia, the number of unemployed hovered between 360,000 and 500,000. The huge surplus of workers allowed wages to be kept low. Between 1930 and 1937, the average income of a Yugoslav miner was about 38 per cent of the subsistence level of a family of four. Given that this figure comes from the statistics for the Croatia-Slavonia region, which represented the Yugoslav average, it can be assumed that it was more or less accurate for Slovenia, too. In Serbia, on the other hand, where industrial workers only numbered 110,000–150,000 people with below-average wages, the miners' situation was even more dire.[18] In September 1940, German sources refer to Serbian wages being as low as 25 per cent of the subsistence level.[19] The Yugoslav average corresponded to one-sixth of what a miner earned in the Ruhr Valley, while the latter's productivity was three times higher than that of the average Yugoslav miner.[20] Miners' wages were not only lower than during the crisis years of 1932–33, they were even lower than in 1913–14, prior to the outbreak of the First World War. When it came to the copper mine of Bor, the mine's monopoly had certainly helped it navigate relatively successfully through the economic crisis.[21] But the measures the French mining company took in order to succeed during these years did include lowering the miners' wages to a critical minimum.[22]

In the spring of 1940, everyday life in Yugoslavia was marked by the first war-induced food supply shortages, and in the autumn of the same year a regulated economy was introduced. First, decrees were issued that aimed at controlling prices. Then in May 1940, there was a decree aimed at reducing meat consumption by making Tuesdays and Fridays meatless days. Butchers were not allowed to sell meat on these days, and restaurants were not allowed to serve dishes that contained it. In his *Economic Blockade*, William N. Medlicott, a member of the British Cabinet Office

Historical Section during the war and thus an insider, quotes a collaborator of the British Ministry of Food who expressed the opinion that the Yugoslav government was cutting down its population's meat supplies in response to German pressure, rather than because of a real scarcity of foodstuffs.[23]

As the shortages continued to increase, so too did the regulatory provisions introduced to control the distribution of other goods. Price movements were monitored, as were merchants, in an attempt to prevent the black market from growing. In 1940, the harvest was poor – there were 100,000 rail cars of grain less than in 1939. Yugoslavia was forced to import wheat from Germany and deliver ore and other raw materials as payment. In doing so, the Yugoslav government came into conflict with non-German foreign mining enterprises active in the country. In the lead and zinc mine in Mežica on the border with Austria, for example, the need to provide the Germans with ores meant the Yugoslav state commissioner had to de facto expropriate the mine's British management, who protested fiercely. However, at the end of the winter, in April 1941, the disintegration of Yugoslavia and its occupation by Germany and its allies made such protests futile.[24]

The wheat imports had led to even greater economic dependence on Germany. Still, the movement of wheat and maize was regulated in terms of both price and use in the production of bread, in an attempt to evenly distribute the available agricultural produce. By early 1941, just a few weeks before Yugoslavia was broken up and occupied, the amount of wheat flour in bread dough was first limited to 70 per cent and shortly after that further reduced to 40 per cent. The rest had to be made up of corn flour. This still only left enough wheat to last for two months. The next step was the introduction of bread ration cards in February 1941. These acknowledged, for the first time, the increased nutritional requirements of heavy manual labourers. While adults received 4 kilograms of wheat flour per month and children 2 or 3 kilograms, depending on their age, men performing heavy physical work were entitled to one additional kilo of flour per month.[25] When, a couple of weeks later, Yugoslavia rapidly succumbed to the attack of the German, Italian, Hungarian and Bulgarian troops, the population's suffering began to grow exponentially throughout the country.

Coal miners in German-occupied Slovenia

In annexed Austria, which the German-occupied Yugoslav regions of Southern Styria and Southern Carinthia became a de facto part of in 1941, the Germans had, in 1938, established a framework that was to steer the economy and the exploitation of raw materials. The workforce was screened and most Jewish enterprises were quickly closed or expropriated. A similar screening procedure was carried out in the Yugoslav Drava Banate (i.e. Slovenia) in the spring of 1941; only here the aim was not so much to segregate the Jews – hardly any lived here – but to establish whether a given Slovene was deemed fit to be Germanized or rather qualified for quick deportation. In the first stage, in terms of its economy, Slovenia was added on to Austria in the sense of enlarging Austrian structures to 'return' the former imperial crown lands Styria, Carinthia and Carniola (see Map 4). The occupiers' view was that they were reunifying the century-old imperial lands that had been 'artificially' cut off from each other by the provisions of the 1918 Versailles Treaty and the founding of the state of Yugoslavia.[26] Because of the events of the war, however, the Germans repeatedly postponed the de jure annexation of the northern Yugoslav regions to the German Reich – this was also something the Slovene Partisan movement helped prevent.[27]

Thus, the first policies aimed at appeasement. A couple of weeks after the occupation, the miners' salaries were raised to equal those in the Austrian mines. *Reichsführer-SS* Heinrich Himmler issued a decree that would largely exempt the miners from the mass deportations of Slovenes that began within weeks of Yugoslavia's surrender. The district (*Gau*) administration articulated their plan to treat the mining regions like concentration camps. As the chief administrator of Graz, Otto Müller-Haccius, put it in a briefing on 30 April 1941, the traditionally communist-leaning miners needed 'a certain amount of surveillance'. He mentioned 214 miners' families from the Zasavje coalfields around the central mining towns of Trbovlje and Velenje, altogether 976 individuals, who had been exempted from deportation because their labour was important for the German war economy, or rather, for the annexed Austrian industries.[28]

If there had been a belief, or even hope, among the population that the German takeover meant some sort of return of the times of the Austrian Empire, the occupiers quickly disabused them of this notion. Their *Heim ins Reich* ('Back home to the Reich') policies only included those they saw fit to be Germanized. Within weeks, violence became one of the main features of the occupation. Food supplies had already been stretched to their limits, so at the moment of the attack in April 1941, shops and depots only held enough comestibles to meet about fifteen days of demand. This situation was soon further exacerbated by the poor exchange rate of the Yugoslav dinar against the currencies used by the three occupying forces, i.e. the German mark, Italian lira and Hungarian pengö. The system of rationed food supply established before the occupation essentially remained in place, but was updated several times between the summer of 1941 and the spring of 1945. An increasing number of foodstuffs and other necessities could only be purchased with ration cards, if they were even available at all. Provisions continued to decline in quantity and also in quality. This applied to flour, bread, pasta, meat, potatoes, rice, milk, salt, sugar, oils and lard, as well as fuel, soap, clothes, footwear and tobacco.[29]

The situation of the miners remained ambivalent. They were privileged in terms of food rationing; they were likely to be exempt from deportation even if seen 'unfit' for Germanization; and many of them could rely on home-grown fruits and vegetables as well as forms of small animal husbandry such as poultry, rabbit or bee farming. In these deteriorating circumstances, the mining families thus started off in a better position than many others.[30] Yet, as was the case elsewhere, with the general decline in nutrition, physical labourers lost this advantage exactly because of the type of work they were doing. It wore them down more quickly. In addition, in the Zasavje coal mining region in the course of 1942 the workflow was adapted to the one used in the Reich proper. Gradually, a piecework system (*Gedinge*) was introduced, which meant that work was no longer paid per hour, but per amount of coal extracted.[31] A lot of fine-tuning and discussion were invested in optimizing the extraction rate with the least possible expenditure, as a report by the mining authority of the German occupying forces in the southern Styrian town of Celje illustrates. Interestingly, the report establishes a link between food provisioning and work performance on racist grounds:

> Nowadays, the underground pit miner does not have access to a diet as nourishing as it was before the military campaign, because back then he had access to all sorts of foodstuffs. This has to be seriously considered when looking at work performance. It is necessary to establish a situation in which the pit miner receives sufficient fats, sugar and meat. The Slovenian miner does not possess the strength of mind to compensate for the shortage of food through willpower …, as, for example, the northern German worker would. … A very important aspect is [thus] the provisioning of the underground pit mining workforce with very nourishing food … if an increase in performance is to be achieved.[32]

In April 1942, the minutes of the monthly directors' meeting of the Zasavje coalfields referred to extra rations having been distributed. These consisted of cigarettes, tobacco, spirits and a lot of canned fish: 29,292 cans in June 1942, 13,500 in August and 29,874 in October. In June, the extra rations also included 2,447.5 kilograms of bacon, 4,895 kilograms of flour, 2,447.5 kilograms of lard and 4,895 kilograms of beans. The miners also received monthly rations of extra vitamins.[33] However, the eligibility for these extra rations was tied to work performance: the extra rations were only given to those underground pit miners who had worked all obligatory Sunday shifts and never missed a regular shift either. Anyone with a good reason for not working a shift, e.g. because of illness or leave of absence, only remained eligible for the extra rations if he worked an extra shift on another occasion. Young people under the age of eighteen were not eligible for cigarettes and spirits, and neither were women. Open pit workers were never eligible for any of these extra rations.[34]

In 1943, the distribution of extra foodstuffs continued, but the minutes of the monthly directors' meetings no longer mention any specifics. By mid-1943, a large part of these minutes consisted of reporting on acts of sabotage at the various mining facilities. Although the company sources do not reveal any connection between such Partisan sabotage and food provisioning, it is highly probable that they were linked.[35]

Miners in German-occupied Serbia

In Serbia, too, it was the German occupation regime that ruined a once viable, albeit not exactly prosperous economy in this part of Yugoslavia. The copper mine in Bor, located in eastern Serbia close to the border with Bulgaria and Romania, was the largest of its kind in Europe and the main target of German exploitation in Yugoslavia during the war (see Map 3). The socio-economic situation in Bor had traits of colonial power relations, of an 'informal empire'.[36] Since 1905, the mine had been managed by the French enterprise *Mines de Bor*. In the interwar period, the engineers and skilled workers were an international population from literally all Yugoslav regions, as well as from France, Italy, Romania, Germany and Czechoslovakia. The mine absorbed the surplus labour force in rural eastern Serbia, which means that the dangerous job of copper extraction was performed predominantly by unskilled workers, namely peasants seeking a source of income when there was little or nothing for them to do in the fields.[37]

However, the mine, with its sulphur dioxide emissions and water pollution with sulphur and other metals, also played a major role in destroying the region's agriculture. In as early as 1907, the peasants had protested violently against the ecological destruction the new mining industry had brought in its wake.[38] Almost thirty years later, in 1935, 4,000 peasants revolted against the French mining company. Bernard Michel assumes the strike was 'a peasant protest of a distinctly archaic character against the industrial plant',[39] but it seems that the protest was in fact jointly led by politically aware miners and peasants, important enough to have been immortalized by the artist Đorđe Andrejević Kun, who was present in Bor at the time. Kun created twenty-eight wood carvings that tell the story of the social(ist) revolt, a sort of graphic novel *ante litteram*.[40] The Communist Party and trade unions were forbidden in Yugoslavia at that time. *Mines de Bor* reacted to the protest with violence, killing one worker and injuring a dozen. It paid minimal compensation to the peasants, continued its copper extraction and eventually invested in filters that reduced the sulphur dioxide in the air.[41]

Thus, when the French enterprise initiated copper extraction at the beginning of the twentieth century, they had set up 'a modern company in an agricultural region',[42] which had created a locally contingent mix of agrarian and industrial social consciousness among the population. By 1939, the Bor mine employed 5,836 people and had achieved both an advanced technological level and a secure financial situation.[43] Still, Bor would have to wait until 1947 to be granted the status of a town, having reached 8,000 inhabitants.[44] When the Germans took over Bor in April 1941, they rapidly exploited the features of 'informal empire' that the French had established and transformed the mine into an elaborate system of obligatory and forced labour.[45]

A few months into the occupation, a promotional letter was sent to the director of the mine by the company Berkefeld-Filter, the German inventor of a water-purifying filter system and an international vendor with an office in Belgrade. They offered to help with regard to the 'extraordinarily bad' water conditions in the copper mine.[46] It is unclear whether the contaminated water was a problem caused by the overall polluting effects of copper extraction or whether this situation was created on purpose by the retreating Yugoslav army who did their best to destroy the mine's facilities. In order to safeguard the networks of food deliveries to the mine, the garrison commander (*Standortkommandatur*) in Bor and the director of the mine issued special permits for those who had been delivering foodstuffs to the mine, sometimes for many years, in order to allow free movement where this had been restricted. The engineers and administrative employees had been receiving a monthly average of 60 kilograms of butter, 20 kilograms of cream and 50 kilograms of cheese from the village of Veliki Izvor near Zaječar since 1928.[47] Other foodstuff suppliers focused on the workforce, buying, in various districts in the vicinity, items such as flour, grain, maize, potatoes, pigs and milk, and delivering them to Bor.[48] The chef in the workers' kitchen, Bora Vasić, was tasked with labour recruitment. He was sent to the region between Šabac and Krupanj in western Serbia 'to bring around 150 workers to Bor, possibly previously employed workers who have not returned back [to work in the mine] yet'.[49] Similar special permits were also issued to other employees that were deemed trustworthy, such as the ethnic German (*Volksdeutscher*) Alojs Hostnik, first pit foreman Anton Guran and foreman Radisav Jovanović, who were sent to the coal mining town of Knjaževac 70 kilometres to the south tasked with recruiting '200 underground miners for the copper mine in Bor'.[50]

Labour service was made mandatory in Serbia at the end of 1941. By summer 1942, this labour regime privileged the mines over agriculture – the operation of the mines was prioritized above maximizing the agricultural harvest, as decree no. 10 on the deployment of workers in the occupied territories of 22 August 1942 reveals: 'In the occupied territories they [the available labourers] are to be deployed according to the following priority ranking: a) for necessary tasks of the troops, the offices of the occupiers and the civil administration; b) for German armament tasks; c) for tasks in the food and agricultural economy.'[51] Workers were to be sent to the mines or other war industries as a top priority, both in the Reich and in the occupied territories, including Serbia. In the German Reich, the number of workers and prisoners of war from Serbia between 1941 and October 1942 rose from approximately 75,000 to 150,000. In Serbia, thousands of citizens were deployed in the mines, most of them in Bor, as a consequence of which there was 'a lack of workers for cultivating the fields'.[52]

Nevertheless, unlike the previous year, the harvest of 1941 was abundant. Between August 1941 and July 1942, about 100,000 tonnes of wheat and 70,000 tonnes of maize were exported to Germany. However, the confusion following the occupation as well as inefficient recording and distribution of foodstuffs in Serbia had led to a lack of supplies, so the grain from the Banat ultimately had to provide not only Germany but also the troops in occupied Serbia, as well as the general population. When it came to provisions, priority was given to workers in the war economy, which included the miners.[53]

The winter of 1941–42 was very harsh. The various reports sent by the German copper mine management to the Zemun office of the Plenipotentiary for the Economy in Serbia in February 1942 illustrate this well. Copper extraction was delayed for many weeks due to the heavy winter, which made it necessary to deploy 'several hundred of workers' to free the railway tracks of snow when 'more than one thousand men from the more remote villages could not reach their workplace'. Urgently needed materials and machines, such as turbines, compressors, explosives and wood, had not reached Bor for over a month, being stuck in Belgrade, or even in the Reich, given that materials had also been sent from Cologne. The production plan could not be fulfilled, especially as, one report concluded, 'in the upcoming months, what will be of decisive importance for the level of production will be the question of the size of the workforce as well as supplies of food and shoes'.[54] A report sent a week earlier had gone into more detail:

> Food supplies, which had been more or less secured through grain and pulses until February, are now unfavourable. Especially noticeable is the shortage of lard and meat. In December, the scarce provisions allowed a ration of 500 grams, and

> in January and February 400 grams, which exhausted the stocks with no prospect of new deliveries, despite all our efforts. The quantities of lard that have been given out are quite insufficient to maintain the physical strength and the will to work. … Most definitely insufficient are also the shoes and clothes provided. For a workforce of more than 5,000 men we received 450 pairs of workers' shoes within ten months, which is but a drop in the ocean. For working both in the underground and the open pit as well as for the long distances walked to work, good footwear is indispensable, especially in winter.[55]

The German occupiers provided the copper mine, as well as the *Wehrmacht* units deployed in the region, with seeds for both vegetables and flower beds. In March 1942, a woman from Pančevo near Belgrade was commissioned to buy sixty-five different varieties of seeds, among them as many as twenty-six varieties of flower seeds, and transport them to Bor. The vegetables included dwarf beans, various sorts of cabbage and salad, peas, beetroot, onions, spinach, tomatoes, cucumbers and about a dozen herbs.[56] In July 1942, a total of fifty mother sows were brought to Bor from the municipality of Čoka in the northern Banat, for which the available pigsty had to be considerably enlarged.[57] In November 1942, 'larger amounts of potatoes' were expected to arrive and were ordered to be distributed to the workers who lived near the mine at a price of 14 dinars per kilogram, which was to be deducted from the workers' salaries of the following four months.[58] In order to 'secure the food supply situation for the workforce', workers were encouraged to bring food from their farmsteads or local markets to Bor. This could be a dangerous endeavour, as Chetniks operated in the region. A certificate issued to a worker in the construction department testifies that 4 kilograms of cheese, 5 kilograms of flour, 1.5 kilograms of lard and 28 kilograms of maize were stolen from him just a few kilometres from his home village of Rečka, about 50 kilometres east of Bor, where he had been taking a few days leave. It seems that the considerable amount of maize he transported had been intended for exchange with copper sulphate.[59]

Bor was in a clearly privileged position when it came to the assignment of workers.[60] In the aforementioned competition between the army and the mine, Bor definitely 'won'. In March 1942, the Serbian minister of the interior decreed compulsory labour for all miners, including those who had already been conscripted into the army. Skilled personnel in Bor who sought to join the army were forbidden to do so. A construction technician, for example, was informed that he was absolutely indispensable 'for the execution of the upcoming tasks of reconstruction and enlargement of the mine'.[61] In August 1942, all deportations of Serbian citizens to the Reich were stopped in order to supply Bor with more workers.[62]

The company made huge efforts to provide the workforce with the necessary foodstuffs, successfully increasing the fat rations above the quota prescribed by the special commissioner for foodstuffs and agriculture: 1,000 grams of fat and a flour ration of 20 kilograms per month for underground pit miners and smelting workers, and 800 grams of fat and 15 kilograms of flour for the rest of the workforce, while family members received 400 grams of fat and 5 kilograms of flour.[63] Butchers were only allowed to sell their produce to workers and employees in Bor, and at mandatory prices of 37 dinars per kilogram of beef, 38 dinars for veal and 39 dinars for pork.[64]

In the meantime, the overall food supply situation deteriorated. On the same day in October 1942 that workers were summoned to collect provisions for themselves from a larger delivery of cabbage at the price of 6 dinars per kilogram, all workshops in the mine were informed that the family members of workers engaged in compulsory labour from Belgrade were to be prioritized in the distribution of wood and coal for heating, as well as of potatoes, beans and cabbage.[65] Workers who had pigs to feed were instructed to put their names on a list in order to receive fodder, such as pumpkins, a wagon of which had just arrived.[66] At the same time, the willingness to work extra hours was rewarded with extra rations of bread: those obliged to work on Sundays who had already worked for the six days prior were to receive 860 additional grams of bread for performing this shift and were also prioritized for receiving clothing.[67]

In the winter of 1942–43 then, only a fraction of the planned rations could be distributed. The regular price of 8 dinars for a kilogram of flour became a myth as there were hardly any goods on sale anymore. Only 37 per cent of the required flour was available, as well as only 56 per cent of the meat and 0.05 per cent of the fat. Vendors on the Belgrade black market charged the following prices: 500 dinars for a kilogram of wheat flour and 350 dinars for a kilogram of maize; between 1,800 and 2,500 dinars for a kilogram of lard, butter or *kajmak*; 1,000 dinars for a kilogram of sugar; 100 dinars for potatoes and 12,000 dinars for coffee. They asked for between 8,000 and 12,000 dinars for a tonne of hard coal, between 4,000 and 6,000 dinars for a tonne of lignite and between 18,000 and 20,000 dinars for a pair of shoes.[68] Legally acquired alcohol was cheap in comparison, as 295 dinars bought two litres of schnapps, which the engineer in charge distributed to 'cheer up the workers who were doing nightshifts to install a concrete base for the flotation platform'. He was reimbursed for the purchase by the construction department's directorate.[69]

It is difficult to put these numbers into perspective by comparing them with the wages the workers received, at least those who continued or began working in the mine on compulsory service (rather than as forced labourers). A report from late 1941 on labour deployment in Yugoslavia mentions that the post-occupation confusion and the ensuing lack of workers saw wages rise – a minimum of 100 dinars per day is mentioned, which is five times the prewar average. Qualified personnel received double or triple this average.[70] Towards the end of the occupation, in April 1944, sources mention between 120 and 250 dinars per day for unskilled workers, and between 500 and 600 dinars for skilled workers. Purchasing power had fallen substantially, however. A report from April or May 1944 on labour deployment in the Bor region refers to low wages as one of the main reasons people were leaving the workplace.[71]

The precariousness of the situation is reflected in a decree issued on 27 October 1943, which prioritized food hunting over Partisan hunting: the German army, with the support of the Serbian police, had to give priority to collecting food even if this meant weakening their fight against the Partisans. For example, in the district of Užice at the end of April 1944, all manner of foodstuffs were stolen in order to provide for the German troops. As a consequence of these food raids, the civilian population suffered increasing hunger.[72]

By February 1943, it had become obvious that it was impossible to satisfy the demand for labour merely by recruiting workers in Serbia. To address the fact that workers were increasingly leaving their jobs in order to escape the unbearable working and living conditions, the occupiers took several measures. Alongside the local workforce, the German occupiers had turned Bor into a huge labour camp, where an increasingly wide variety of forced labourers toiled and lived under horrific conditions. One of the measures taken was the deployment of approximately 6,000 Hungarian compulsory labourers, most of them Jews. In accordance with the Hungarian compulsory labour laws, these workers were put at the disposal of the Germans in exchange for copper ore. This system of labour service was organized in a military manner and became the fate of all those who were deemed unreliable or unfit for military service. In the late 1930s, these had included Hungary's ethnic minorities, such as Romanians, Serbs and Slovaks. Later the labour service largely involved the Jewish population.[73]

In addition to this large group from Hungary, only a few of whom would survive, Bor had seen the arrival of Russian and Polish prisoners of war, Serbs and Greeks who had left 'Greater Albania' and, after the Italian capitulation of September 1943, about 3,000 Italian military internees. In July 1944, there was an estimated workforce of as many as 80,000. By this time, the workers were in such poor condition that it required four of them to load a railway car where two had once been enough.[74]

Those Yugoslav citizens who, after the war, testified before the State Commission for Investigating the Crimes of the Occupiers and their Collaborators recalled how their diet had gone from bad to worse. It had often consisted of a breakfast of coffee without sugar and a slice of straw and corn flour bread, with the latter frequently spoiled; a lunch and a dinner of cabbage or bean soup, sometimes potatoes, often rotten. The bread ration consisted of 500–700 grams made of millet and wheat flour mixed with straw, often two weeks old or mouldy. Those who did not have money of their own to buy food on the black market faced hunger. The war had turned Bor into a place with a food and labour regime that treated workers differently depending on the 'status' they occupied according to Nazi ideology. For their lunch, those at the bottom of Nazi food hierarchies had to walk twenty minutes to the place where they received an insubstantial meal and were exposed to abuse, even beatings, from the guards. For them, their paltry meal was accompanied by harassment and violence. The brutal way in which racist and political ideology spilled over into food provisioning schemes often deliberately worked against the goal of serving the war economy.[75]

Conclusion

As elsewhere in Europe, miners in Yugoslavia were socially conscious and often communist-leaning workers, which prompted the German occupiers to install specific systems of surveillance while seeking to extract ores and coal. The food and labour supply regimes in the Yugoslav mining industries reveal how the dismembered country was subjected – in both systemic and arbitrary ways – to contingencies dictated by the German occupiers, their war economy activities and their racial ideological world views, and often enough simply by situational practices. Food and labour supply regimes coincided, but were also heavily influenced by racist dispositions and the accompanying violence.

In the course of the war, the precariousness that had begun to be felt before the occupation and had already seen the first food regulations implemented by the Yugoslav state became the main feature of the occupied populations in both Slovenia and Serbia. In Serbia, with its pervasive compulsory and forced labour regime, the way the groups who ranked lowest in the Nazi worldview were provisioned was a deliberate strategy to exacerbate their plight. Food deprivation was used as punishment for any sort of 'misbehaviour', or simply as a matter of ideological 'principle'.

At the same time, the cross-cutting issues of, first, how to supply the mines with labourers, second, how to feed them and keep them in a condition that enabled them to still work, and third, how to counter sabotage, haunted the occupiers throughout the war. The contradiction is obvious: on the one hand, the occupiers pursued policies to provide the war economy with a larger labour force in a futile battle against the ever-increasing scarcity of labour and food; on the other hand, they cynically continued to abuse, mistreat and ultimately kill certain groups of labourers. The latter completely undermined the goal of a functioning war economy.

Notes

1 See Sanela Schmid and Milovan Pisarri, eds, *Forced Labour in Serbia. Producers, Consumers and Consequences of Forced Labour 1941–1944* (Belgrade: CHRE, 2018), which provides a good overview of the state of the art of research. This chapter is a refocused and updated version of my own contribution to this volume, 'Physical Labour and Survival. Supplying Miners in Yugoslavia', 62–81, and I am grateful to Sanela Schmid, to the editors, to Nikola Radić Lucati, and to the Center for Holocaust Research and Education, Belgrade, for allowing me to reuse parts of that chapter.

2 For the most recent overview, see Paolo Fonzi, 'Besatzungswirtschaft in Süd- und Südosteuropa: Jugoslawien, Griechenland und Italien', in *Handbuch Wirtschaft im Nationalsozialismus*, ed. Marcel Boldorf and Jonas Scherner (Berlin, Boston: De Gruyter, 2023), 821–43. See also Carl Freytag, *Deutschlands 'Drang nach Südosten.' Der Mitteleuropäische Wirtschaftstag und der 'Ergänzungsraum Südosteuropa' 1931–1945* (Göttingen: V&R, 2012); Milan Ristović, *Nemački 'novi poredak' i jugoistočna Evropa 1940/41–1945. Planovi o budućnosti i praksa*, 2nd edn (Belgrade: Službeni Glasnik, 2005); and Zoran Janjetović, *'U skladu sa nastalom potrebom ...' Prinudni rad u okupiranoj Srbiji 1941–1944* (Belgrade: INIS, 2012).

3 See Sergije Dimitrijević, *Das ausländische Kapital in Jugoslawien vor dem Zweiten Weltkrieg* (Berlin: Rütten & Loening, 1963), 52–4, 180, 198; Dragan Aleksić, 'Medjunarodni privredni položaj Jugoslavije pred drugi svetski rat', in *Srbija u modernizacijskim procesima XX. veka*, ed. Latinka Perović et al. (Belgrade: Institut za noviju istoriju Srbije, 1994), 123–32, 126–7, 131. From a French perspective, see Bernard Michel, 'La Compagnie française des mines de Bor. Une entreprise étrangère en Serbie (1905–1940)', in *Les entreprises et leurs réseaux. Hommes, capitaux, techniques et pouvoirs XIXe – Xxe siècles*, ed. Michèle Merger and Dominique Barjot (Paris: Presses de l'Université de Paris-Sorbonne, 1998), 487–99, esp. 488, 493.

4 Tomislav Pajić, *Prinudni rad i otpor u logorima Borskog rudnika 1941–1944* (Belgrade: Institut za savremenu istoriju, 1989), 21–6; Michel, 'La Compagnie française des mines de Bor', 497.

5 'Widerstand gegen die Politik der französischen und britischen Bergwerksgesellschaften in Jugoslawien', *Montanistische Rundschau* 32, no. 16 (1940): 274.

6 See the elaborate account of the British blockade by William N. Medlicott, *The Economic Blockade*, vol. 1 (London: Longmans, Green and Co., 1952), including a detailed description of the role of the Balkans in the British economic and food schemes at the outbreak of war. On the Banat, see Mirna Zakić's chapter in this volume.

7 Christoph Dieckmann, 'Das Scheitern des Hungerplans und die Praxis der selektiven Hungerpolitik im deutschen Krieg gegen die Sowjetunion', in *Kriegführung und Hunger 1939–1945. Zum Verhältnis von militärischen, wirtschaftlichen und politischen Interessen*, ed. Christoph Dieckmann and Babette Quinkert (Göttingen: Wallstein, 2015), 88–122; Christian Gerlach, *Krieg, Ernährung, Völkermord. Forschungen zur deutschen Vernichtungspolitik im Zweiten Weltkrieg* (Hamburg: Hamburger Edition, 1998); Gustavo Corni and Horst Gies, *Brot – Butter – Kanonen. Die Ernährungswirtschaft in Deutschland unter der Diktatur Hitlers* (Berlin: Akademie Verlag, 1997).

8 Lizzie Collingham, *The Taste of War. World War Two and the Battle for Food* (London et al.: Allen Lane, 2011); Violetta Hionidou, *Famine and Death in Occupied Greece, 1941–1944* (Cambridge: Cambridge University Press, 2006).

9 Collingham, *The Taste of War*, 8–9.

10 Hans-Christoph Seidel, *Der Ruhrbergbau im Zweiten Weltkrieg. Zechen – Bergarbeiter – Zwangsarbeiter* (Essen: Klartext, 2010). On the British variant of conscripting coal miners into the mines, see the website 'The Wartime Memories Project – Bevin Boys', http://www.wartimememories.co.uk/bevinboys.html (accessed 27 July 2023).

11 Collingham, *Taste of War*, 9.

12 Collingham, *Taste of War*, 320–39, 363–7.

13 Hans-Christoph Seidel, 'Gesundheitspolitik und "Arbeitseinsatz" im Ruhrbergbau während des Zweiten Weltkrieges', *Mitteilungsblatt des Instituts für soziale Bewegungen* 28 (2003): 203–27, 215–23.

14 Dietrich Eichholtz, *Geschichte der deutschen Kriegswirtschaft 1939–1945*, vol. 1: 1939–41 (Munich: Saur, 2003), 216–17.

15 Adam Tooze, *The Wages of Destruction. The Making and Breaking of the Nazi Economy* (London: Penguin, 2006), 476–7.

16 In addition to Tooze, *The Wages of Destruction*, see Gerlach, *Krieg, Ernährung, Völkermord*; Jörg Ganzenmüller, *Das belagerte Leningrad 1941–1944. Die Stadt in den Strategien von Angreifern und Verteidigern*, 2nd edn (Paderborn: Schöningh, 2007), 41–53; and Dieter Pohl, *Die Herrschaft der Wehrmacht. Deutsche Militärbesatzung und einheimische Bevölkerung in der Sowjetunion 1941–1944* (Munich: Oldenbourg, 2008), 65–6.

17 Karl Olshausen, *Zwischenspiel auf dem Balkan. Die deutsche Politik gegenüber Jugoslawien und Griechenland von März bis Juli 1941* (Stuttgart: Deutsche Verlagsanstalt, 1973), was among the first to study the interdependencies of the economy and politics with regard to Yugoslavia and Greece.

18 Sergije Dimitrijević, *Karakteristike industrije i rudarstva bivše Jugoslavije* (Belgrade: Biblioteka Društva Ekonomista Srbije, 1949), 43.
19 See Milan Ristović, 'General M. Nedić. Diktatur, Kollaboration und die patriarchalische Gesellschaft Serbiens 1941–1944', in *Autoritäre Regime in Ostmittel- und Südosteuropa 1919–44*, ed. Erwin Oberländer (Paderborn: Schöningh, 2001), 633–87, 662.
20 Ferdinand Friedensburg, 'Kohle, Eisen und Bauxit in Jugoslawien', *Glückauf. Berg- und Hüttenmännische Zeitschrift* 75, no. 46 (18 November 1939): 897–903, 913–19, 897.
21 Roland Schönfeld, 'Deutsche Rohstoffsicherungspolitik in Jugoslawien 1934–1944', *Vierteljahreshefte für Zeitgeschichte* 24, no. 3 (1976): 215–58, 252.
22 Pajić, *Prinudni rad*, 18–19.
23 Medlicott, *The Economic Blockade*, 247.
24 Ibid., 261–5, 595–6.
25 Mojca Šorn, 'Life in Occupied Slovenia during World War II', in *Between the House of Habsburg and Tito. A Look at the Slovenian Past 1861–1980*, ed. Jurij Perovšek and Bojan Godeša (Ljubljana: Inštitut za novejšo zgodovino, 2016), http://www.sistory.si/cdn/publikacije/36001-37000/36293/ch09.html. See also Šorn's chapter in this volume.
26 See Sabine Rutar, 'Zwischen Volkstumspolitik und Volksbefreiungskampf. Braunkohlenabbau im deutsch besetzten Slowenien', in *Zwangsarbeit im Bergwerk. Der Arbeitseinsatz im Kohlenbergbau des Deutschen Reiches und der besetzten Gebiete im Ersten und Zweiten Weltkrieg*, ed. Klaus Tenfelde and Hans-Christoph Seidel (Essen: Klartext, 2005), 537–69.
27 'Schreiben der Reichskanzlei über die Zurückstellung der Eingliederung der besetzten slowenischen Gebiete ins Deutsche Reich', 22 January 1942, in Tone Ferenc, *Quellen zur nationalsozialistischen Entnationalisierungspolitik in Slowenien 1941–1945 / Viri o nacistični raznarodnovalni politiki v Sloveniji 1941–1945* (Maribor: Obzorja, 1980), document no. 194.
28 'Richtlinien und Anweisungen des Reichskommissars für die Festigung deutschen Volkstums zur Aussiedlung von Slowenen und Ansiedlung von Deutschen in der Untersteiermark', 18 April 1941, in Ferenc, *Quellen*, document no. 23; see Tone Ferenc, *Nacistična raznarodnovalna politika v Sloveniji v letih 1941–1945* (Maribor: Obzorja, 1968), 257–89, 322–7.
29 On the situation in Slovenia's two largest cities, Ljubljana and Maribor, see Marjan Žnidarič, *Do pekla in nazaj. Nacistična okupacija in narodnoosvobodilni boj v Mariboru 1941–1945* (Maribor: Muzej narodne osvoboditve, 1997), 146; Šorn, 'Life in Occupied Slovenia'; as well as Šorn's chapter in this volume.
30 See the description of the miners' social situation in 'Beschreibung des Kohlenwerkes Trifail', 20 April 1941, Arhiv Republike Slovenije (ARS), Energieversorgung Südsteiermark (EV Süd), folder 4; and Friedensburg, 'Kohle', 897.
31 'An die E. V. Süd A. G., Technische Direktion der Bergbaue in Cilli, Betr.: Besuch des Gedingeprüfers Pg. Preissler', 9 August 1942, ARS, EV Süd, folder 95.
32 'Lagebericht über Gedinge und Verdienstangelegenheiten der Kohlenwerke E.V. Süd', 4 February 1942, ARS, EV Süd, folder 95, 3.
33 'Niederschrift über die Monatsbesprechung am 13. Mai 1942 in Cilli, Hotel Europa', n.d.; 'Niederschrift über die Monatsbesprechung am 2. Juli 1942 in Cilli, Hotel Europa', n.d.; 'Niederschrift über die Monatsbesprechung am 18. September 1942 in Cilli, Hotel Europa', n.d.; 'Niederschrift über die

Monatsbesprechung am 17. Dezember 1942 in Cilli, Hotel Europa', n.d., all in ARS, EV Süd, folder 67, 6, 9, 11, 13.

34 'Bezirksgruppe Ostmark der Wirtschaftsgruppe Bergbau, Sonderzuteilungen. Unser Rundschreiben Nr. 320 vom 15.12.1941', 13 August 1942, ARS, EV Süd, folder 31a.

35 'Niederschrift über die Monatsbesprechung am 26. März 1943 in Cilli, Hotel Europa', 8 April 1943, ARS, EV Süd, folder 67, 10.

36 Vladimir Lj. Cvetković, 'La présence économique de la France en Yougoslavie 1918–1940. Intérêts, enjeux, portées', in *La Serbie et la France. Une alliance atypique*, ed. Dušan T. Bataković (Belgrade: Institut des Études balkaniques, SANU, 2010), 557–74, who does not use the term 'informal empire'. David Todd, *A Velvet Empire. French Informal Imperialism in the 19th Century* (Princeton: Princeton University Press, 2021), does use it but makes no mention of France's economic interests in Southeastern Europe.

37 Michel, 'La Compagnie française des mines de Bor', 489.

38 Ibid., 490–1.

39 Ibid., 497.

40 Đorđe Andrejević Kun, *Krvavo zlato. 28 originalnih drevoreza* (Belgrade: Štamparija Jovana Luksa, St. Bečej, 1937). See Ana Stevanović and Saša Ilić, 'Strike at the Bor Mine in the 1930s: Europe's First Environmental Protest?', *Europeana Blog*, 5 December 2019, https://www.europeana.eu/de/blog/power-and-pollution-at-the-bor-mine-serbias-first-environmental-protest (accessed 27 July 2023). The authors do not mention any historical sources beyond the artist's wood carvings to underpin their narrative.

41 Pajić, *Prinudni rad*, 16–17.

42 Michel, 'La Compagnie française des mines de Bor', 487.

43 Ibid., 497.

44 See the website of the Bor municipality, Istorijski razvoj, https://bor.rs/istorijski-razvoj/?0=lat (accessed 27 July 2023).

45 See Stephen G. Gross, *Export Empire. German Soft Power in Southeastern Europe* (Cambridge: Cambridge University Press, 2015); Paul N. Hehn, *A Low Dishonest Decade. The Great Powers, Eastern Europe, and the Economic Origins of World War II, 1930–1941* (New York: Continuum, 2002), 99–117.

46 'Berkefeld-Filter Gesellschaft m.b.H. / Celle, Herrn Direktor Pialat, Mines de Bor, Serbien', 12 August 1941, Istorijski arhiv Negotin, Odeljenje u Boru (IAN Bor), Rudnik Bakra Bor (RBB), folder I 18, 4.

47 'Sonderausweis', 22 December 1941, IAN Bor, RBB, folder I 18, 7. A similar *Sonderausweis* (special permit) was issued for another foodstuffs deliverer to the company elite on 8 October 1941.

48 'Sonderausweise' of 17 June, 12 August, 8 October 1941, IAN Bor, RBB, folder I 18, 7.

49 'Sonderausweis', 24 July 1941, IAN Bor, RBB, folder I 18, 7.

50 'Sonderausweis', 18 November 1941; and two 'Sonderausweise' of 15 November 1941, IAN Bor, RBB, folder I 18, 7.

51 Friedrich Didier, ed., *Handbuch für die Dienststellen des Generalbevollmächtigten für den Arbeitseinsatz und die interessierten Reichsstellen im Großdeutschen Reich und in den besetzten Gebieten* (Berlin: Der Generalbevollmächtigte für den Arbeitseinsatz, 1944), 97–8, 97.

52 'Aus einer Aufzeichnung von Felix Benzler vom 19. Oktober 1942 über eine Besprechung mit Milan Nedić, Ministerpräsident der Kollaborationsregierung, zur Ausbeutung und zum Terror in Serbien', in *Die Okkupationspolitik des deutschen Faschismus in Jugoslawien, Griechenland, Albanien, Italien und Ungarn (1941–45)*,

ed. Bundesarchiv Koblenz (Berlin: Hüthig, 1992), document no. 104. See Ristović, 'General M. Nedić', 663.

53 Olshausen, *Zwischenspiel*, 291.

54 'Generalbevollmächtigter für die Wirtschaft in Serbien, Referat Wi 8, Semlin', 14 February 1942, IAN Bor, RBB, folder I 17, 3.

55 'Dem Präsidenten der Compagnie Française des Mines de Bor, Herrn N.S.F.K. Gruppenführer Neuhausen, Semlin', 5 February 1942, IAN Bor, RBB, folder I 17, 3, 9.

56 'Bescheinigung: Frau Helene Gutwein ...', 22 March 1942, IAN Bor, RBB, folder I 16, 8.

57 'Notiz (Bauabteilung)', 23 July 1942, IAN Bor, RBB, folder I 16, 8.

58 'Rundschreiben an alle Abteilungen', 12 November 1942, IAN Bor, RBB, folder I 19, 1.

59 'Bescheinigung (Bauabteilung)', 14 June 1942, IAN Bor, RBB, folder I 16, 8.

60 See the extensive material collected by the State Commission for Investigating the Crimes of the Occupiers and their Collaborators, 'Izveštaj anketne komisije o prinudnim radu u Borskom rudniku od 6 aprila 1941. g. do 3 oktobra 1944. god', Arhiv Jugoslavije (AJ), Državna komisija za utvrdjivanje zločina okupatora i njihovih pomagača (DK), box 598, folder 648. Details in Sabine Rutar, 'Arbeit und Überleben in Serbien. Das Kupfererzbergwerk Bor im Zweiten Weltkrieg', *Geschichte und Gesellschaft* 31, no. 1 (2005): 101–34.

61 'Herrn Andreas Georg, dipl. Bautechniker', 7 March 1942, IAN Bor, RBB, folder I 16, 8.

62 'Die Arbeitskräfte für den Bergbau Serbiens', *Montanistische Rundschau* 34, no. 8 (1942): 129. See Jozo Tomasevich, *War and Revolution in Yugoslavia, 1941–1945. Occupation and Collaboration* (Stanford, CA: Stanford University Press, 2001), 655.

63 'Bekanntmachung: Betrifft: Abt. Hütte, Grube, Lebensmittelverteilung', 15 July 1942; and 'Bekanntmachung Lebensmittelverteilung', 16 July 1942, IAN Bor, RBB, folder I 19, 1.

64 'Bekanntmachung: In dieser Fleischbank ...', 20 April 1942, IAN Bor, RBB, folder I 19, 1.

65 'Bekanntmachung an alle Betriebe und Abteilungen', 26 October 1942; and 'Bekanntmachung an alle Betriebe und Abteilungen, Betrifft: Versorgung der Familienangehörigen der aus Belgrad dienstverpflichteten Arbeiter', 26 October 1942, IAN Bor, RBB, folder I 19, 1.

66 'Bekanntmachung: Alle Arbeiter und Angestellten die Schlachtschweine füttern ...', 15 October 1942, IAN Bor, RBB, folder I 19, 1.

67 'Bekanntmachung für die Grube', 8 October 1942, IAN Bor, RBB, folder I 19, 1.

68 'Le travail', n.d., but before December 1941, Arhiv Jugoslavije (AJ), Fond 103: Emigrantska vlada Kraljevine Jugoslavije (EV), box 5, folder 54.

69 'Rechnung über 295 Dinar (Bauabteilung)', 15 April 1942, IAN Bor, RBB, folder I 16, 8.

70 'Le travail', n.d., AJ, EV, box 5, folder 54; 'Der Arbeitslohn im ehemaligen Jugoslawien', in *Jahrbuch 1940/41*, vol. 2, ed. Arbeitswissenschaftliches Institut der Deutschen Arbeitsfront (Berlin: Arbeitswiss. Verlag, 1941), 850–9, confirms this in its analysis of the growing gap between nominal and real wages in relation to the rising cost of living.

71 'Arbeitseinsatz im Kreise Zaječar', n.d. (but probably end of April or beginning of May 1944), AJ, DK, box 598, folder 648.

72 'Izveštaj okružnog komiteta KPJ Zaječar (bez datuma, verovatno je od kraja januara 1943.) pokrajinskom komitetu KPJ za Srbiju o stanju i situaciji u Borskom rudniku', in *Istočna Srbija u ratu i revoluciji. Zbornik nemačkih dokumenata (Ekonomska*

eksploatacija), ed. Živko Avramovski (Zaječar: Istorijski arhiv 'Timočka krajina', 1989), 193–6, 195; see Žarko Jovanović, 'Poljoprivreda Srbije u ratu 1941–1945', in *Srbija u modernizacijskim procesima XX veka*, ed. Perović et al., 143–50, 148.

73 'Note by Fränk of the Organisation Todt Regarding the Need for Hungarian Jews to Work in the Copper Mines of Bor', and 'Letter from Jagow to the Foreign Office Transmitting the Text of the Agreement Signed by Neyer and Ruszkiczay-Rüdiger Concerning the Transfer of Hungarian Jews to Bor', 6 July 1943, in Randolph L. Braham, *The Destruction of Hungarian Jewry. A Documentary Account* (New York: Pro Arte for the World Federation of Hungarian Jews, 1963), document no. 58 and 62. See also Randolph L. Braham, *The Hungarian Labor Service System 1939–45* (Boulder, CO: Columbia University Press, 1977), and Randolph L. Braham, ed., *The Wartime System of Labor Service in Hungary. Varieties of Experiences* (Boulder, CO: Columbia University Press, 1995). Hungarian scholars in particular have shed light on the history of these labourers; see Tamás Csapody, *Bortól szombathelyig. Tanulmányok a bori munkaszolgálatról és a bori munkaszolgálatosok részleges névlistája* (Budapest: Zrínyi, 2014).

74 'Anforderung einer Wehrmachtseinheit für die Arbeiterrekrutierung im Kreis Zaječar', 29 April 1944; and 'Arbeitseinsatz im Kreise Zaječar', n.d., AJ, DK, box 598, folder 648. See 'Aus dem Lagebericht von Generalmajor Erwin Braumüller, Chef des Wehrwirtschaftsstabs Südost, für Juli 1944 über die wirtschaftliche Ausbeutung Serbiens', in *Okkupationspolitik*, ed. Bundesarchiv Koblenz, document no. 294.

75 Testimonies of Rastislav Ognjanović, Milan Bučan, Milan Tatalović and Milan Šarenac, 6 June 1945, AJ, DK, box 599, fasc. 649.

Part Two

Italy: Instrumentalizing food

3

Between chaos and economic weakness: Italian food policies in Albania (1939–43)

Alberto Basciani

In the early hours of 7 April 1939, Operation Overseas Tirana (*Operazione Oltre Mare Tirana*) began. An Italian expeditionary force of about 22,000 men invaded Albania and, within a few hours, the first vanguard of motorcycle-mounted *Bersaglieri* entered Tirana. Despite some logistical difficulties, the operation was in fact a military promenade and the fascist regime was more concerned with legitimizing the new military conquest, both at home and abroad, than with actual military operations. At the same time as the invasion, a vast propaganda campaign was launched from Rome to mask the occupation of the neighbouring country. The campaign portrayed the invasion as a sort of international police operation aimed at re-establishing law and order, which the despotic, corrupt and tribal government of King Zog had disrupted. The fascist leadership presented itself as a harbinger of progress in the new Albania. According to the propaganda, including Albania in the fascist imperial community put the country on the path towards modernity and prosperity. At the same time, Italy claimed to be respectful of the ethnic identities and religious pluralism of the Albanian population.[1]

Of the territories of Southeastern Europe occupied by Italy immediately before and during the Second World War, Albania is a peculiar case both in terms of the institutional architecture which tied this country to Italy and in terms of the economic objectives Rome set itself when it planned Albania's inclusion in Italy's fascist empire. Rome's intention was for the Albanian economy to be strongly integrated with Italy's. Fascist policymakers had high hopes that by virtue of these ties the driving force of fascism – including the planned immigration projects which would see settlers populate the coastal areas once they had been reclaimed – would initiate extensive modernization of Albania, which, in turn, would make a significant contribution to the Italian economy (especially through the exploitation of mineral resources). Italy's goals were ambitious, aiming to use institutional reforms and investments to stimulate rapid development in Albania's agriculture, manufacturing industry – especially the agro-food sector – and trade, thus making the country self-sufficient in terms of food consumption. Yet, the Italian policy was premised on shaky foundations. Thus, instead of following a rational plan, Italy's economic policy in Albania between 1939 and 1943 came to resemble more of a set of ad hoc measures introduced in an attempt to overcome widespread crisis phenomena, such as the general food shortage and the spread of the black market, than a modernization drive. It can therefore be said that up until September 1943, Italy's food policy, designed to garner support for the occupiers among the local populations by improving living standards and to develop an economy that complemented Italy's, ended in utter failure. In this chapter, I will investigate why Italy's food policy in Albania was so unsuccessful, paying particular attention to the distortions that, in the space of a few months, hindered the realization of its plans, causing the Albanian system of food production and distribution to fall into a deep crisis.

The political and economic union between Italy and Albania

In the weeks following the invasion of Albania, the country's integration into the Italian empire was determined by the authorities in Rome according to Italy's interests in the region. While a team of legal experts from various universities on the Italian peninsula elaborated a new Albanian constitution, essentially based on Italian constitutional law, Rome carried out a de facto annexation in the form of a personal union between the crown of Albania and Italy. This saw Vittorio Emanuele III acquire another title in addition to that of King of Italy and Emperor of Ethiopia. Meanwhile, in Tirana, after a brief transitional executive, a new Albanian government was installed, entrusted to Shefqet Vërlaci, an influential bey and one of the country's largest landowners. Despite the existence of a formally independent government, two Italian institutions were to be in charge of actual decision-making on the political, economic, social, scholastic and cultural life of Albania. These were the Lieutenancy of the Kingdom in Tirana, entrusted to Francesco Jacomoni di San Savino (until then minister plenipotentiary of Italy in Albania), and the Undersecretariat for Albanian Affairs (*Sottosegretariato agli Affari Albanesi* – SSAA) established at the Ministry of Foreign Affairs and entrusted to an associate of Galeazzo Ciano, Zenone Benini. Italy set up a legislative assembly, the Corporative Fascist Supreme Council (*Consiglio Superiore Fascista Corporativo*), whose members – fourteen of whom were Italians – were appointed by the king. In this context, one unusual development in the history of fascist expansionism in Europe and the colonies was the creation of the Albanian Fascist Party (*Partia Fashiste e Shqipërisë* – PFSh). The first minister secretary of the party – which Rome intended to act as a powerful transmission belt between the regime and Albanian society – was an Albanian notable, Tefik Mborja. Finally, Italy appointed permanent advisors to each of the Albanian ministries who were to closely monitor the work of the executive. These were sort of director generals of the ministry appointed by the lieutenant, who always selected Italian nationals for the posts. The permanent advisors were the highest-ranking officials in the entire hierarchical structure of the Albanian state bureaucracy and, therefore, the real decision-makers in the various ministries. In short, a rather complex institutional architecture was created that also generated a certain amount of bureaucratic chaos, since the duties of the various institutions were not always clearly defined and, therefore, conflicts and misunderstandings – especially between the Lieutenancy and the SSAA – were a recurring feature.[2]

The Italians put great effort into defining the economic integration of Albania with Italy, a task eased by the fact that Italian-Albanian ties had been particularly close, even before the occupation.[3] One of the objectives was to ensure that Albania's natural resources be intensively exploited to the advantage of the Italian economy.[4] On 20 April 1939, Lieutenant Jacomoni and the Albanian minister of finance Fejzi Alizotti concluded an agreement that strengthened economic, customs and financial collaboration between the two countries and saw the merging of Italy and Albania into a single economic territory. On the Albanian side, the existing trade agreements were terminated, while on the Italian side, all trade relations that had existed prior to April 1939 were extended to Albania. Although Albanian goods could freely circulate in Italy, they were subject to considerable restrictions when exported to other provinces of the empire, for example, the Dodecanese Islands.[5] Finally, the Albanian franga or franc was decoupled from the Latin parity and tied to the Italian lira at a fixed rate of 6.25 lire with a link to gold similar to that in force for the lira.[6] In practice, this created a 'mini currency area' of the lira. With this exchange rate, the lira was undervalued in order to increase Italian exports to Albania. Albanian foreign trade was almost entirely with Italy. It is undoubtedly true that from this moment on, Italy monopolized the entire Albanian import and export sector, but it would be mistaken to consider this economic policy as being akin to that which was implemented by Germany in the Balkans. Indeed, in the Italian case, no consistent scheme of economic and financial exploitation is really detectable. While Italy admittedly had plans to modernize the country, its trade relations with Albania were rather the result of unforeseen factors that brought all its existing plans into disarray, a situation very similar to that seen in the Italian colonies.[7]

An unsustainable normality: Production and supply crisis

In 1939, Italy took over a country characterized by an under-developed economy that was based on backward agriculture dominated by large landed estates, marked by low productivity and an infrastructure network that was little more than primitive. For reasons of political expediency, the Italians decided to shelve any plans for agrarian reform[8] but, at the same time, they launched a large-scale plan for the exploitation of natural resources, the ambitious expansion of the infrastructure network and urban development. The sudden increase in population with the arrival of thousands of soldiers, clerks, civil servants and workers from Italy altered the delicate balance of Albanian society with negative repercussions on the distribution and price of goods. As early as the beginning of 1940, a report by the Lieutenancy alarmingly denounced that peasants and shepherds were increasingly tending to leave their occupations, attracted by the possibility of earning higher salaries on the many building sites springing up across the country and in the new mining plants.[9] In other cases, local authorities prevented the peasants from tending the soil by forcibly employing them in construction works of strategic and military relevance. For instance, in April 1940, the Vlorë provincial office of the Lieutenancy forwarded to Jacomoni a complaint from the villagers of Çukë, who the sub-prefect of Sarandë had forced to work at a road construction site on the Çukë-

Butrint carriageway, thus causing them to neglect their fields at a particularly important time of the agricultural season.[10] According to Jacomoni's memoirs, published in 1966, cereal production, which up to 1939 had always been sufficient to meet Albania's needs (though other sources refute this claim), significantly declined from the 1940 harvest onwards due to the abandonment of the countryside. Against the backdrop of this reduced production, there was a bigger population to feed, swelled by the arrival of a considerable number of Italian civilians and soldiers. To meet the needs of this larger population, a million quintals of cereal and flour had to be imported from Italy.[11] Moreover, even in the middle of winter, when, in previous years, stocks had been entirely sufficient to meet the needs of the population, several urban centres in Albania experienced serious supply difficulties. On 27 January 1940, the economic office of the Lieutenancy at the Fascist Federation of Durrës sent an alarmed note to Piero Parini, secretary general of the Lieutenancy of Tirana, reporting the concerns of the Fascist Federation of the city. The note communicated the following:

> The mills in Durrës have only 1,000 quintals of wheat in stock, whereas, as is known, Durrës and Tirana need about 500 quintals per day. The stocks of maize are also low (amounting to just 2,500 quintals). The Shkodër Federation has also reported that the mills are short of grain and that the prefecture, in order to somehow ensure local needs are met, has had to organize searches in the neighbouring municipalities … the population is not impressed.[12]

Similar communications arrived a few weeks later from the Fascist Federations of Vlorë and Peshkopi.[13] However, the stocks of grain and cereals brought from Italy somehow managed to stabilize the situation while waiting for the new harvest. In the summer of 1940, the grain emergency was no longer pressing but the lack of salt made itself felt. On 8 July, Piero Parini wrote to the Public Limited Company for Trade and Industry (*Società Anonima Commerciale e Industriale* – SITA), which was responsible for salt extraction, informing him that several Fascist Federations, especially the one in Peshkopi, had criticized the serious lack of salt.[14] A reply came from SITA a few days later, signalling that both the production and distribution of salt were higher than the actual Albanian needs. However, supply problems were caused by the 'very strong market demand for hoarding … in many regions, especially in the periphery; sales have doubled, tripled and sometimes even quadrupled. It is our firm view that this must be attributed to purchases beyond the real and immediate needs'.[15]

The solution devised by the Lieutenancy was the creation of an ad hoc Commissariat for the procurement of foodstuffs, headed by Vincenzo Rocco, an official who had been living in Albania for years and who had Jacomoni's full confidence. The Lieutenancy hoped, in particular, that the Commissariat,

> in exercising control over the purchase and sale prices of basic necessities, could fix wholesale prices, while the fixing of retail prices remained the responsibility of the Party … It was, however, … necessary to ensure coordination between the action of the Party and that of the Commissariat and it was therefore established … that, when fixing retail prices, the Party act in concert with the Commissariat.[16]

On 1 August 1940, a new price list came into force, which would regulate the prices of some of the most important commodities, including flour, sugar, olive oil, pasta, rice, butter, etc. The Italians hoped that, in addition to the regulations, the local fascist authorities would, with the help of the *Carabinieri*, carry out strict controls to ensure that the population complied with the regulations.[17] Indeed, at the beginning of January 1941, the Central Police Directorate set up special rationing squads in Tirana, Vlorë, Durrës and a few other major towns. These squads consisted of a non-commissioned officer and a few police officers assisted by one or two members of the *Guardia di Finanza* and the urban police.[18] Despite their efforts – evidenced by the large number of fines, seizures of goods and a few arrests – these small police units could not stem the harmful effects generated by the imposition of regulated prices. In several provinces, foodstuffs disappeared from the markets and could only be purchased on the black market at significantly increased prices. Ordinances, intensified controls and threats were not enough to repress the phenomenon. Thus the Lieutenancy and the PFSh Inspectorate had no choice but to blame the lack of control of the markets on the local fascist organizations, as in the case of Shkodër, which was openly reproached for failing to ensure the application of the rules and the proper behaviour of traders and wholesalers.[19] In the years that followed, the newly created Commissioner's Office failed to establish itself as an efficient administrative body and to implement a proper food policy. Both Albanian and Italian citizens often accused this office of corruption and patronage, which they saw as the real cause of its inefficiency.[20]

Internal industrial and handicraft production did not fare much better than the agricultural sector. A small manufacturing sector had developed before the war in the Shkodër and Korçë regions, based mainly on mills, pasta factories, breweries and small mechanical workshops. A few weeks after the Italian invasion, with the progressive integration of the Albanian economy into the Italian one, the Italian authorities noted the mounting problems of the small Albanian industrial and handicraft enterprises, often family-run, increasingly undermined by competition from Italian imports, but also by the growing difficulties of 'procuring the necessary raw materials'.[21] The case of the *Dragusha* pasta factory in Shkodër is telling in this regard. Though equipped with modern machinery, 'this pasta factory, which was noted for the quality of its product, operated for three months and then had to close due to a lack of raw materials (it imported semolina from Tunisia) and competition from the Italian industry, which poured its products into Albania'.[22] The ever-increasing incidence of these phenomena contributed to the spiral of unchecked price increases in the country, already visible in the first weeks after the union. In a report classified as 'highly confidential', an inspector from the Bank of Italy on a mission across the Adriatic in April 1940 noted that shops and markets in Tirana generally appeared well stocked but observed with dismay that the prices of many goods were twice as high as those in Italy.[23] In the inspector's view, the problem was not easy to solve because it was caused, among other things, by the large influx of Italians 'with the not inconsiderable allowances that they receive'. Because 'of the public works policy that has accustomed our labour force, unfortunately also including the indigenous workers, to very high wages', the report continued, 'there has been an abundance of money circulating and therefore an increase in prices – which, however, is partly due to the higher cost and greater difficulty of transporting goods from Italy – and the feeling has spread, especially among the ignorant and distrustful indigenous element, that inflation on paper is perhaps more than in reality'.[24] The only feasible solution, according to the report, was to accelerate the economic and financial integration of Albania with Italy, through robust injections of money from Rome – calculated at 40–50 billion lire over ten years – to stabilize the Albanian state budget but also through a massive influx of Italians, preferably not unskilled labourers but workers with the necessary technical and practical knowledge to rapidly start exploiting the local natural resources.[25] For Albania, this seemed the only viable way to ensure 'food autonomy, develop the mining industry … or, what is important from a political point of view, become real Italian territory as a consequence of the prevalence that the Italian population would gain'.[26]

The solution proposed by the Bank of Italy official, however, proved unfeasible after June 1940, when, with Italy's entry into the war on the side of Germany, investments destined for Albania were immediately redirected towards other war aims. The war brought considerable difficulties due to the increase in extraordinary expenses for the Italian and Albanian state budgets. In Albania these additional expenses were covered through increases in indirect taxation (which was particularly hard on the peasants) and emergency transfers from the Italian state, amounting to 5.5 million Albanian francs.[27] Negative effects on the price stability and the circulation of goods were not long in coming. A document dated July 1940 denounced 'the tendency among the public to build up stocks of various kinds, and among merchants of all ranks to apply high prices to goods that were absolutely unjustified'.[28] The situation became even more complicated from the end of October of the same year, when Italy attacked Greece, a move that would, within just a few days, prove a military debacle for Italy and have dire repercussions on the stability of Italian rule in Albania.

Indeed, by the summer of 1941, that is, in the aftermath of Germany's direct military intervention in the Balkans, resulting in the destruction of Yugoslavia and the defeat of Greece, the wholesale food price index had risen by 46 per cent. The average wholesale price index from 31 August 1941 to 15 December of the same year had risen from 345.7 to 504.8, that of other consumer goods had risen from 427 to 528.1 and, more generally, the overall price index had increased from 378.2 to 513.3. The average retail price index had jumped from 347.3 to 445.2. However, a memo dated December 1941 remarked that

> the actual increases are more pronounced than those reported, since many of the foodstuffs being monitored (including the most important ones) are subject to the black market everywhere. It would really be superfluous to present facts and figures, when daily observations give us the clear impression that the cost of living is much higher than can be deduced from, shall we say, the official figures.[299]

Rising labour costs, rising production prices and increased money circulation could only partly justify such price hikes, which could actually be explained 'by a deliberate rarefaction of products, which diminishes supply in relation to demand', a phenomenon itself generated by the desire of small producers to

> hoard goods, because they are sure that prices will rise … [and], in view of the mechanisms triggered, tended to keep as many non-perishable products as possible … in order to be able to use them as bargaining chips in exchange for other goods and … out of mistrust of paper money, so you try to buy as much as you can and sell as little as possible.[30]

As early as the autumn of 1939, the Italian *Guardia di Finanza* denounced the unjustified increases of oil to 0.50 and 0.60 gold francs per kilogram despite the fact that wholesale prices had fallen by 25–30 per cent. The intensified controls had also made it possible to identify traders who were removing goods such as coffee, sugar, pasta and flour from the shelves in order to sell them to customers under the counter at prices far higher than those set by the official price authorities. Smuggling to Greece, Bulgaria and Yugoslavia, where goods would be sold at even higher prices, was already rampant.[31] The black market had already begun to spread in as early as 1939, but with the onset of the war on Greece it took on a different scale. At the end of November 1940, a few weeks after the start of hostilities against Greece, the prefect of Durrës denounced how in his town 'wholesalers and traders fearing destruction of the foodstuffs stockpiled there are asking for permission to transport them out of Durrës … to avoid speculative stockpiling and regular supply', demanding the intervention of the *Carabinieri* and the local chamber of commerce.[32] A few weeks later, the Fascist Federation of Gjirokastër complained about the scarcity of both Albanian and Italian cigarettes, while in several localities of the kingdom, even textiles were beginning to disappear from the official market.[33] It was not only the civilian population that suffered from supply problems but also the thousands of Italian workers who had arrived in Albania in the meantime. In June 1940, an anonymous report informed the Lieutenancy Office in Shkodër that only 50 of the 200 quintals of flour had been distributed to cover the bread consumption of 6,000 Italian workers hired for public works in the region. 'The officer in charge of the warehouse', the report noted, 'told us that he does not know when he will be able to meet our needs.'[34] In the province of Peshkopi, the difficulties in supplying grain were so severe that 'hundreds of breadless people were wandering around the town waiting for the arrival of grain'.[35] In Korçë, on the other hand, the inhabitants complained about the shortage of beef, eggs, vegetables and poultry. According to the inspector sent by the Italian Fascist Party, the prefecture's territory, but also, and more importantly, to the fact that 'many traders were hoarding almost all the goods … in order to export them to other provinces'.[36] Finally, there were also instances of bitter conflict between the local authorities and the leaders of the various *Fasci* or Fascist Federations established by the Italians in most Albanian cities, who evidently thought they could gain visibility and consensus by fighting against real or supposed speculation. Towards the end of 1940, the leaders of the *Fascio* of Kukës wrote to their superiors in Tirana that, in view of the sharp rise in flour prices, they had decided to get rid of the middlemen by assuming the task of 'taking flour from the mills in Shkodër and transporting it to Kukës to distribute it to the bakers under strict control'. According to the report, '[i]n the preceding months, Adem Luli, the commissioner of supplies in the prefectures of Kukës and Shkodër engaged in black market trading himself, earning between 4 and 7.50 Albanian francs per quintal, causing the wholesale price of flour to rise from 55 to 60 francs per quintal'.[37] The fascists of Kukës had no doubt that speculative operations of this kind were only possible with the direct complicity of the local Albanian authorities, both the prefecture and the municipalities.[38]

Apart from the scarcity due to the redirecting of resources, the war against Greece burdened the small country's economy with the large influx of troops and organizational chaos. The situation was exacerbated by the limited capacity of the small Albanian ports, which were totally ill-equipped to unload and sort supplies quickly and in an orderly manner. In addition, part of the supplies arriving from Italy, especially foodstuffs, ended up on the black market. Special packages of biscuits, chocolate, milk, coffee, clothing, pasta and tinned meat destined for the soldiers at the front appeared in the 'back shops' and were often even sold openly. The officers and troops were greatly disappointed when, driven by necessity, they were forced to buy products in private shops that their corps should have theoretically received directly and free of charge. And such incidents were certainly not uncommon. According to the Army General Staff, there was little doubt as to who was responsible for this unfortunate situation:

> The task of distributing collective parcels and comfort goods … had been devolved to the Albanian Fascist Party … as a result of this all the parcels were collected on their arrival in the ports of Vlorë and Durrës by PFSh representatives and then … distributed to the troops. The Albanian Supreme Headquarters … limited itself to informing the Party of the units' main needs … In the specific case reported … the head of the squadron [*capo manipolo*] Biagioli Edmondo … personally came to announce … that the sale of condensed milk '*Nutrice*' was carried out by the uniformed personnel of the Albanian Fascist Party … and the goods were loaded onto private lorries.[39]

As the war progressed, it became increasingly difficult to rely on aid from Italy. Indeed, the peninsula's civilian population – in particular the urban population – was beginning to feel the effects of the war effort and the shift from a peace economy back to a war economy, which began to affect the production and distribution of foodstuffs. Though the situation still appeared tolerable in 1940, it was destined to worsen rapidly, and already in 1942–43, between 7 and 13 million Italian city dwellers lived off a diet considered by specialists to be 'below the physiological minimum' from both a calorific and qualitative point of view.[40] In February 1941, the SSAA sent a note directly to Mussolini indicating the need, because of the growing shortage in Italy, to slow the delivery of oils and fats across the Adriatic by setting 'a monthly minimum … of 200 quintals of edible oil, … 125 quintals of lard or similar products and 75 quintals of butter' for future deliveries. The needs of the Italian troops and workers would have been met directly by the Military Subsistence Section.[41]

The war against Greece had revealed the fragility of the Albanian productive base and distribution network, but the creation of Greater Albania in the spring of 1941 – achieved through the annexation of Kosovo (except the province of Mitrovica), the

province of Dibër (except Ohrid) and some territories of Montenegro – far from improving the economic situation, in fact considerably worsened it. With the creation of Greater Albania, an additional 14,924 square kilometres with 754,000 inhabitants became part of the old kingdom (see Map 5).[42]

In 1941 the economic situation was dire, as the war had forced Italy to close many public works and the large number of soldiers quartered on Albanian territory had exacerbated the shortage of food, fuel and salt supplies. Many southern prefectures still suffered from the consequences of the war operations, especially the destruction of private houses, schools and infrastructure. With these issues not yet solved, the fragile Italo-Albanian political and administrative structure now had to integrate the new provinces – themselves already economically depressed and generally poorly administered. It did not take long for the consequences to be felt. In his history of Albania during the Second World War, Bernd Fischer wrote that Kosovo, characterized by a relatively abundant production of wheat and cereals and less populated than the old Albania, became a sort of granary of the kingdom, which, with this territorial expansion, solved its chronic supply problems, especially when it came to wheat and cereals.[43] In fact, Italian records paint a different picture. While the Italians deemed Kosovo and the Dibër area capable of solving the supply problems, the inefficient administrative structure established in the region and the disruption of public order caused by the internal ethnic conflicts dashed any hopes of this happening. During the summer of 1942, according to a report of the Bank of Albania, the city of Tetovë had seen a great flourishing of trade and 'the influx of abundant cereal and legume commodities at the weekly markets attracted from the capital, Durrës and other smaller towns ... [There are] many merchant buyers ... everyone is busy trading in these products ..., everyone is busy buying, either to resell, at their own pace with large profits or to supply their families during the winter months'.[44] As this report shows, therefore, the new provinces, far from being surplus regions, soon became deficit areas themselves, supplied with foodstuffs from the rest of Albania. The now chronic problems affecting the old Albanian territory, starting with the difficulties of commercial transport, exacerbated by the scarcity of vehicles, the shortage of spare parts and the bad roads, did not spare the new provinces either, with the consequence that many localities in Kosovo began to suffer from the lack of salt. In several localities, the local populations also complained about the scarcity of tobacco, vegetable oils, pasta and rice. In autumn 1941 in Kosovo and the Dibër area, it was only possible to buy salt if one was prepared to pay double the official tariffs, while the price of other foodstuffs had risen by around 40 per cent.[45]

The war highlighted the major problems afflicting Albanian agriculture, which, as mentioned above, the Italians had, for political reasons, preferred not to tackle with a radical agrarian reform. Instead, the Italian authorities had limited their interventions to improving minor aspects, such as the construction of a certain number of modern stables, animal health control and the increased use of fertilizers and modern machinery. However, they only took these measures in a small number of cases, almost always in farms managed by Italian colonists or companies with Italian capital. In the absence of decisive intervention on the part of the central authorities, peasants increasingly abandoned their land in favour of employment in construction or mining. The war also accentuated another phenomenon, namely the predisposition to produce only certain goods, i.e. those that could easily be sold at high prices to the Italian armed forces. Towards the spring of 1942, it became clear that in the countryside of the prefectures of Berat and Vlorë, many farms had neglected to sow cereals in the previous autumn in order to obtain hay from the land to sell to the Italian army. This phenomenon, too, had greatly contributed to the sharp rise in prices. Wheat, for example, had increased from 90 Albanian francs per quintal in 1940 to 160 in 1942.[46] Since the results of the harvest were disappointing throughout the country, in regions unaffected by the war operations, the poor results were mostly attributed to unfavourable weather: 'too much rain in the first sprouting and ripening period, and too much drought in the period of growth'.[47] Nevertheless, some provinces, especially in the south, recorded a not inconsiderable increase in cultivated area, which, on the other hand, decreased significantly in all the new territories of Greater Albania. In Kosovo, for example, 15,000 fewer hectares were cultivated.

Tirana, more than other population centres, immediately felt the impact of market distortions. According to Jacomoni, the general shortage of consumer goods, fuel and building materials of all kinds had forced many construction sites to close or slow down their operations, resulting in the dismissal of their workers.[48] Food supplies and price hikes remained the most serious problems throughout 1942. A report drawn up by the Bank of Albania emphasized that the deterioration of the economic situation in Tirana had reached dangerous levels,

> inasmuch as the hoarding of all kinds of goods is continually intensifying, resulting in ever higher prices. In view of the difficulties in obtaining supplies abroad, the merchant class is oriented towards hoarding domestic products, wool, hides, oil, etc., products that are constantly increasing in price due to the great demand.[49]

While merchants with large sums of money were increasingly oriented towards speculation (and this category swelled steadily due to the easy profits promised), for the rest of the population 'the cost of living rose continuously' and in the squares and streets of the neighbourhoods people began to engage in barter of foodstuffs: rice and sugar in exchange for flour, potatoes and beans for pasta. Assaults on lorries carrying grain, flour and salt were not uncommon.[50] It is worth adding that throughout 1942, there was a marked increase in smuggling activity from Albania to neighbouring countries, especially Greece and Montenegro, but also Serbia under German administration. This practice was not only prevalent among the local population but, according to a report by the Ministry of Foreign Affairs, also among Italian officers and the Italian financial police.[51]

Administrative attempts to tackle price increases

In May 1941, the Italian authorities decided to dissolve the Commissariat for the Procurement of Foodstuffs and the Ministry of National Economy took over its responsibilities, but only for a short time. In fact, in July 1942, after securing Jacomoni's assent, Prime Minister Mustafa Merlika Kruja, who succeeded the Vërlaci government on 4 December 1941, set up a new body at the Ministry of the Economy. This new department was the Central Commissariat for Supplies and Consumption, also headed by Vincenzo Rocco and staffed by members of the Ministry of the Economy, which would be supported by provincial and district committees to be established in the local sections of the PFSh. The life of this new body was rather troubled, especially because of various conflicts between the Commissariat and the so-called external members, i.e. officers from the army, the *Carabinieri* and the *Guardia di Finanza*, Just a few weeks later, accusing the ministry of denying them the data they needed to work with, including up-to-date statistics, these external members resigned from their posts.[52]

In 1942, the Italian authorities created the Albanian Society for Agricultural Trade (*Società Albanese Commerciale Agricola/Shoqi Anonime Shqiptare Tregtare Bujqësore* – SASTEB). This was a sort of cartel of different companies, formed essentially with Albanian capital, whose activities were focused on marketing agro-food products. According to Giancarlo Caselli and Grid Thoma, far from tackling inflation, the SASTEB caused further price increases, as its monopolistic position – as well as the powerful political backing it enjoyed in Tirana – allowed it to buy from producers at very low prices and sell on the markets at high prices.[53] In the same year, the authorities also tried to set up a comprehensive aid system that would enable the white-collar class to better withstand the continuous price increases. This step needed to be taken as a matter of urgency because, as the monthly reports of the *Carabinieri* pointed out, corruption and bribery in a group whose number had swelled with the creation of thirty prefectures and sub-prefectures, had reached such dimensions that they jeopardized the effective functioning of the bureaucratic administrative apparatus of the country. In 1940, the PFSh had promoted the creation of a procurement company: the Procurement Agency for State Employees (*Ente Approvvigionamento per gli Impiegati dello Stato* – EAIS) entrusted to a committee consisting of a representative of the PFSh, one from the Ministry of Finance and one from the Ministry of Industry and Trade. The objectives of the organization were essentially threefold: (1) to provide employees with foodstuffs and other consumer goods at significantly reduced prices, (2) to regulate the sale of goods through orderly and strict forms of membership and (3) to extend the sale of products to other centres in Albania.[54] The results obtained by the organization were not, however, particularly noteworthy due to the scarcity of financial means, leaving the situation of the clerical class substantially unchanged and, as a consequence, not improving the efficiency of the Albanian state administration.

In the last weeks of 1942, the index of wholesale prices increased by 5 per cent, and that of retail prices by 5.6 per cent, but this was only the national average. On a local scale inflation could be more marked. In Vlorë, increases of 10 per cent were recorded for retail prices, reaching as much as 16.5 per cent in Gjirokastër. The Bank of Albania noted that while in 1941 the gap between the wholesale prices of foodstuffs and the corresponding index of other products had been 15.9 per cent, in 1942 it had reached 63.2 per cent. During the year, the index for foodstuffs increased by 118 per cent compared to 55 per cent for other goods.[55] In several provinces, including Shkodër, some products had disappeared from the market altogether. 'In the Dukagjini and Mirditë', wrote the Shkodër Fascist Federation, 'people are suffering from a total lack of grain and salt. Many are forced to walk for days to reach Shkodër in order to buy a few kilograms of grain, paying very high prices, ranging from 15 to 20 lek per kilogram. This, however, shows that there are speculators in possession of stocks of grain and salt'.[56]

In the eyes of the experts sent to Albania to examine the local situation and try to come up with solutions, the diagnosis was straightforward: first the union with Italy and then the war had broken the precarious equilibrium of a poor country whose economy, unable to 'meet the needs of consumption, must import everything it requires, thus making commerce the only vital aspect'. Until 1939, in certain areas, local agriculture and pastoralism had somehow managed to meet the low consumption demands of the population. The union and the war had altered that balance due to the sudden and constant increase in inhabitants and their growing needs, which resulted in commercial activities becoming the main sector of the Albanian economy.[57] Once peace was restored, stated the report, the Albanian market would need to be radically restructured to enable it to operate under normal conditions. It would, therefore, be necessary 'to take precautionary measures to ensure at least a stabilization of prices and the consumption of stored goods …, measures that could include the prohibition of the import of any product and classification of commercial activity … prohibitions and discipline that would give immediate results'.[58] It would also be necessary to completely reorganize the commercial transport system, as transportation costs had shot up because operations were performed by a large number of firms.[59]

Efforts were indeed made by the provincial economic offices to try to control the markets, the movement of goods and the behaviour of sellers, but these were little more than feeble attempts hampered by the lack of cooperation from other institutions or by the lack of any real data on which to base real action. While the aforementioned report pointed to the distortions of the transport system, a July 1942 report by the Fascist Federation of Korçë drew attention to the endemic backwardness of the entire sector. The lack of an agrarian reform was only part of the problem. Added to but also as a consequence of this was 'the lack of agricultural science and the limitation of cultivated land'.[60] In Korçë, for example, only 454 square kilometres of the available 3,312 square kilometres were cultivated, the land was often flooded due to the lack of canalization works and embankments, not to mention the complete lack of modern machinery, fertilizers, irrigation systems, etc. In the region, 'farmers work the land with local ploughs made of wood … which plough the land insufficiently'.[61] Of course, even in the territory of Korçë, like much of the rest of the country, market trends faced major imbalances as well as a particularly acute phenomenon at that time – the large-scale smuggling of a significant number of goods to Bulgaria and Greece.[62] However, even in this case, to tackle this problem, the police only made a few isolated arrests or imposed fines, because they lacked the intelligence needed to identify the culprits. 'Unfortunately, as in all the other provinces, no technical service exists in Korçë to control and register the inter-provincial export movement'.[63] In the province of Korçë, as elsewhere, not all goods were regulated and controlled. On the contrary,

> the prices of those in greatest demand, such as wheat, grain and barley, are left to fluctuate freely. Depending on the demand, they are subject to very significant

> increases; last week, wheat, maize and barley reached the following prices: 340, 260 and 180 Albanian francs per quintal, respectively. However, because they cannot be controlled, the prices of manufactured goods and fabrics are continually rising, sometimes reaching exorbitant prices.[64]

The year 1942 witnessed a general worsening of the situation in Kosovo, despite the apparent abundance of agro-industrial products. Admittedly, the local fascists complained, the region was suffering from the poor administration of the former Yugoslav regime and the colonization process that had favoured the Serbian veterans over the Albanian population, but the deplorable state of the new province was also due to

> speculative traders and wholesalers, either local or from the various provinces of Albania, who, wishing to exploit producers and consumers to the hilt, have created a kind of anarchy that is taking on larger proportions day by day … the greatest responsibility for this anarchy … lies with the governmental bodies, which have so far not been able to solve the problem of basic foodstuffs, including the simple transport of salt, nor have they put a limit, or carried out an accurate control on transport … is the responsibility of the government bodies, which have so far been unable to solve the problem of basic foodstuffs, including the simple problem of transporting salt, or to set a limit, or to carry out a thorough control of transport … leaving the way open for smuggling, which has raised the price of salt to 20/25 lek, and oil to 50 lek.[65]

The peasants were the first to be affected by such extreme price hikes and in response increased 'the price of meat from 8 to 20 lek, wheat from 2 to 10 lek, maize from 1 to 7 lek and butter from 20 to 70 lek'.[66] The following year brought little change, let alone any noticeable improvement. On the contrary, it can be said that the overall deterioration of public order, the spread of the Partisan movement and the increasing difficulties the Italian occupier had in keeping Albania under its firm control led to a further worsening of the supply, price and production situation in the agricultural sector.

Conclusion

Until the end of the Italian rule in September 1943, Italy proved unable to implement a coherent economic policy in Albania, not to mention a food policy capable of ensuring a steady supply of agro-food products to the major hubs of the Albanian state. A burgeoning black market sidelined the official economy, thwarting any attempts by the Italians and the Albanian institutions to control the production and distribution of food products, a situation that was to the advantage of the Partisan movement, which managed to acquire a substantial share of the produce instead. This largely undermined the ability of the Italians to gain approval for fascist Italy among the local population.

This failure derived from the contradictions of the Italian policy. Although poor planning was certainly a major cause, local conditions also played a key role in undermining the Italian attempt to modernize the country. Since the Italians decided to rule the country by establishing an alliance with the great landowners, they refrained from conducting an agrarian reform that would solely have increased agricultural output. Moreover, as a consequence of the influx of a large number of Italians burdening the already-struggling economy, and the injection of capital for modernization projects disrupting the Albanian economic balance, the food situation deteriorated further. Finally, the administrative system established by the Italians in Albania was largely inefficient, marred by corruption and competition between different power centres as well as limited ability to operate efficiently on the local level. In 1939, Rome decided not to take over the administration of the country, but instead created a complicated system in which Albanian institutions were formally granted considerable autonomy, while in reality they were devoid of real power, which largely remained in the hands of their Italian supervisors. This doubling up of tasks and responsibilities had significant negative effects on the motivation of state officials to perform their duties and on the ability of the institutions to operate effectively.

Among the efforts undertaken to tackle this situation one stands out, namely the attempt made by the authorities to safeguard the purchasing power of public employees through the establishment of the Procurement Agency for State Employees (EAIS). Since clerks were a category of employee which received low wages, both state and municipal workers were among the hardest hit by the wave of sharp price increases that occurred a few weeks after the union with Italy. The creation of the EAIS was meant to be a clear sign of the institutions' interest in the clerical class in an attempt to sustain their loyalty and limit the increasingly widespread phenomena of corruption. Although the intentions behind this move may have been right, it was made too late and did not prove sufficient to bind the clerks to the state.

Notes

1 Ministry of Popular Culture to Mussolini, n.d., Archivio Centrale dello Stato (henceforth: ACS), Ministero della Cultura Popolare (henceforth: MinCulPop), DGP, Nu.P.I.I.E, box 3.

2 For an overview of the integration of Albania into the Italian domains, see Alberto Basciani, *L'impero nei Balcani. L'occupazione italiana dell'Albania (1939–1943)* (Rome: Viella, 2022), 37–64. See also Giovanni Villari, 'Il sistema di occupazione fascista in Albania', in *Gli ebrei in Albania sotto il fascismo. Una storia da ricostruire*, ed. Laura Brazzo and Michele Sarfatti (Florence: Giuntina, 2010), 93–124.

3 Alessandro Roselli, *Italia e Albania: relazioni finanziarie nel Ventennio fascista* (Bologna: Il Mulino, 1986).

4 In the months following the military occupation, fascist propaganda focused on extolling the wealth of the Albanian subsoil and the potential of agriculture; Basciani, *L'impero nei Balcani*, 40–3.

5 See ibid., 63; also, Roselli, *Italia e Albania: relazioni finanziarie*, 166–70. 'The conspicuous investments planned for Albania had to specify the contribution of the means necessary

to revive economic activity (provisions, equipment, stocks, etc.) without giving rise to an exodus of foreign currency', Amedeo Gambino, 'Le relazioni economiche tra l'Italia e l'Albania', *Rivista internazionale di Scienze Sociali* 11, no. 3 (1940): 408–423, 423.

6 In the interwar period and during the war, Albania had a dual currency system. The franc was the currency used in banking and financial transactions, whereas the lek was the currency of circulation.

7 Giancarlo Caselli and Grid Thoma, *L'economia Albanese durante il secondo conflitto mondiale e il primo tentativo di pianificazione* (Modena/Reggio Emilia: University of Modena and Reggio Emilia Department of Political Economy, 2001), 3–6.

8 Basciani, *L'Impero nei Balcani*, 124.

9 Document signed by Jacomoni, 26 February 1940, Arkivi Qëndor i Shtetit Shqipëtar (henceforth: AQSh), Fond Ministeria Brendesheme (henceforth: MB), box 20/1940.

10 The Provincial Office of the Lieutenancy to the Lieutenancy in Tirana, 9 April 1940, AQSh-MB, box 64/1940.

11 See Francesco Jacomoni, *La politica italiana in Albania nelle testimonianze del Luogotenente del Re Francesco Jacomoni di San Savino* (Bologna: Cappelli Editore, 1966), 293. A quintal is a traditional unit of weight in France, Italy, Portugal and Spain equal to 100 kilograms.

12 Economic office of the Lieutenancy Tirana, 27 January 1940, AQSh, Fond Partia Fashiste e Shqipërisë (henceforth: PFSh), box 40/1940.

13 Memorandum for Piero Parini, classified as 'urgent', 1 February 1940, AQSh, PFSh, box 40/1940.

14 Piero Parini to the SITA Company, 5 July 1940, AQSh, PFSh, box 40/1940.

15 Sita's general manager (signature not legible) to Piero Parini, 11 July 1940, AQSh, PFSh, box 40/1940.

16 Piero Parini to the Fascist Federations, 5 July 1940, AQSh, PFSh, box 40/1940.

17 Ibid.

18 Circular to the prefectures of the General Directorate of the PFSh, 17 January 1941, AQSh, PFSh, box 58/1941.

19 Piero Parini to the Commissariat for the Procurement of Foodstuffs, 4 September 1940, AQSh, PFSh, box 58/1941. From October 1940, the fixing of wholesale prices was entrusted to specific provincial commissions, the Commissariat for the Procurement of Foodstuffs to the Chambers of Commerce and the Directorate of the PFSh, 1 October 1940, AQSh, PFSh, box 237/1940.

20 Unsigned note dated 26 March 1943, Archivio di Stato Venezia (henceforth: ASV) – Fondo Pariani (henceforth: FP), b. 11; 'Rocco, a former *Carabinieri* brigadier ... monopolized all domestic and foreign trade and military supplies and stole a few hundred million', Sefedin Gurakugi, 'Il Luogotenente Jacomoni "Padre del popolo albanese"', *L'Italia Libera*, 17 May 1945.

21 'Visita alle industrie albanesi 3-17 maggio 1940', Archivio Storico-Diplomatico Ministero Affari Esteri (henceforth: ASDAMAE), Sottosegretariato per gli Affari Albanesi (henceforth: SSAA), box 155/1.

22 Ibid.

23 'Relazione del Consiglio per l'Assemblea del 16 aprile 1940-XVIII', Archivio Storico Banca d'Italia (henceforth: ASBI), Fondo Direttorato Introna – Pratiche (henceforth: FDI-P), file 3.

24 Ibid.

25 Ibid.

26 Ibid.

27 Caselli and Thoma, *L'economia Albanese durante il secondo conflitto mondiale*, 15.

28 Document without heading, signature or addressee, 7 July 1940, AQSh, PFSh, box 40/1940.

29 'Promemoria del dicembre del 1941', n.d., AQSh, MB, box 642/1941.

30 Ibid.

31 Minutes of the Tirana PTI Unit of 13 October and 14 December 1939, respectively, Archivio Museo Storico della Guardia di Finanza (henceforth: AMSGdF), Atti Particolari (henceforth: AP), file 12, sheet 662.

32 Prefect Kodheli to the Commissariat for the Procurement of Foodstuffs, 23 February 1940, AQSh, PFSh, box 40/1940.

33 Gjirokastër Federation of the PFSh to the General Inspector of the *Partito Nazionale Fascista* (National Fascist Party – PNF), 29 July 1940; Dürres Federation of the PFSh to the Prefect of Durrës and the Central Directorate of the PFSh, 25 October 1940, AQSh, PFSh, box 40/1940. According to the Gjirokastër Federation of the PFSh, there was often a shortage of goods because of a lack of transport and for a long time goods, including perishable ones, were stored in Durrës, Gjirokastër Federation of the PFSh to the PFSh Central Directorate, 12 November 1940, AQSh, PFSh, box 40/1940.

34 Dispatch without signature or heading, 6 June 1940, AQSh, PFSh, box 40/1940. While complaints about hoarding by Shkodër merchants poured in, one of the most active hoarders allegedly being the owner of the most important mill in the city, the Italian workers' canteens reportedly offered products of very poor quality: '[D]uring a visit to our building sites we found that the oil taken from the Military Subsistence Section yesterday, although made from olive oil, had a really unpleasant smell which certainly sparked workers' protests, in some cases justified', PFSh Central Directorate to the Shkodër Federation of the PFSh, n.d., 19 June 1940, AQSh, PFSh, box 40/1940.

35 Federal Secretary Ziani to the PFSh central directorate, 9 September 1940, AQSh, PFSh, box 40/1940.

36 Korçë Fascist Federation of the PFSh to the PFSh Central Directorate, 1 October 1940, ASQh, PFSh, box 40/1940.

37 Kukës Fascist Federation of the PFSh to the PFSh, 3 December 1940, AQSh, PFSh, box 40/1940.

38 Ibid.

39 Army General Staff – Propaganda Office, to the PNF inspector, Alessandro Frontoni, 19 June 1941, AQSh, PFSh, box 53/1941. The same individual sent a letter on 23 July to the central directorate of the PNF requesting that an enquiry be conducted into this occurrence. New reports with further requests to put an end to the situation were sent from Rome on 10 September 1941 to the PNF inspector in Albania, Pasquale Lugini.

40 Alberto De Bernardi, 'Alimentazione di guerra', in *1943. Guerra e Società*, ed. Luca Alessandrini and Matteo Pasetti (Rome: Viella, 2015), 131.

41 SSAA to Mussolini, 11 February 1941, ASDMAE, Gabinetto Albania (henceforth: GA), box 107.

42 On the definition of the new borders and the difficulties encountered by Italy in the negotiations with Germany and Bulgaria, see Luca Micheletta, *La resa dei conti. Il Kosovo, l'Italia e la dissoluzione della Jugoslavia (1939–1941)* (Rome: Nuova Cultura, 2008), 114–30.

43 See Bernd J. Fischer, *Albania at War 1939–1945* (West Lafayette, IN: Purdue University Press, 1999), 87.

44 Tetovo Agency of the National Bank of Albania, 28.08.1942, ASDMAE, SSAA, box 233/18.
45 Basciani, *L'impero nei Balcani*, 180.
46 'Informazioni economiche e commerciali – Campagna grano 1941 – grano e cerali minori', 22 March 1942, AQSh, PFSh, box 115/1942.
47 'Esito campagna 1942', October 1942, AQSh, PFSh, box 115/1942.
48 Jacomoni, *La politica dell'Italia in Albania*, 301.
49 Report of the Tirana branch of the National Bank of Albania on the general economic situation in December 1942, 3 February 1943, ASDMAE, SSAA, box 238/18.
50 Ibid.
51 MFA to the General Command of the Guardia di Finanza, 28 September 1942, AMSGF, AP, scheda 662, fasc. 6/1942.
52 Basciani, *L'impero nei Balcani*, 220–1.
53 Caselli and Thoma, *L'economia Albanese durante il secondo conflitto mondiale*, 11. In 1942 and 1943, SASTEB, later acquired by a consortium of Italian banks, made profits of 2,500,000 Albanian francs.
54 'Appunto per l'eccellenza il Luogotenente del Re – Azienda Approvvigionamento del PNFA e Conto FAPI', n.d., ASV- FP, box 11.
55 'Relazione della Banca d'Albania sui prezzi in Albania', 19 February 1943, ASDMAE, SSAA, box 238/18.
56 Shkodër Fascist Federation of the PFSh, 'Rapporto sulla situazione nel Maggio 1942', 16 June 1942, AQSh, PFSh, box 115/1942.
57 Zeno Ricci to Vittorio Agnioli, 27 June 1942, AQSh, PFSh, box 115/1942.
58 Ibid.
59 Ibid.
60 PFSh Federal Secretary Lluka Bibi and PFSh Federal Inspector Edoardo Bardazza to the National Directorate of the PFSh, 1 July 1942, AQSh, PFSh, box 115/1942.
61 In the entire province of Pristina, Kosovo, there were still no tractors operating in 1942, Federal Secretary of the PFSh, Mahmut Çela to the National Directorate of the PFSh, 12 March 1942, AQSh, PFSh, box 115/1942.
62 Zeno Ricci, head of the federal labour office, to Vittorio Agnioli, head of the PFSh national labour services, 27 July 1942, AQSh, PFSh, box 115/1942.
63 Ibid.
64 Ibid.
65 PFSh Federal Secretary Tahir Zaimi to the Central Directorate, 13 November 1942, AQSh, PFSh, box 115/1942.
66 Ibid.

4

Imperial humanitarianism: Italy and the Greek famine during the Second World War (1941–43)

Paolo Fonzi

After the sweeping German invasion in April 1941 that forced the Greek army to seek an armistice, the Axis forces occupied Greece. Italy was assigned slightly more than a half of the country, with its territory comprising the Peloponnese, Thessaly, Epirus, Western Macedonia and so-called Central Greece,[1] the majority of the Aegean and the Ionian Islands – a total of approximately 74,000 square kilometres with a population of 3,264,245 inhabitants.[2] German troops occupied Central Macedonia, including Salonika, three-quarters of Crete, a number of Aegean islands and a strip of territory on the border with Turkey. Bulgaria seized Thrace and eastern Macedonia, turning them into a new Bulgarian province it named Belomorje (see Map 6). Just a few weeks into occupation, a food crisis made itself felt both in the German- and Italian-occupied areas. Though developing at different times and pace in different regions, the famine was to plague the country until liberation in 1944. While it is difficult to establish the exact number of victims, several historical accounts give 300,000 as a reliable figure for population loss as a result of hunger and malnutrition.[3] To relieve the effects of the famine in the first year of occupation the Italian authorities delivered foodstuffs to Greece, at a time when Italy itself was suffering from food scarcity.

In the postwar period, Italian propaganda extolled the food aid the country had sent to Greece during the war as an act of humanity, marking a clear difference between Italy's occupation practice and Germany's harsh conduct. Yet, although there are a small number of histories of occupation and famine dealing with Italy's food policy,[4] we are yet to see a systematic analysis. This chapter conducts such an analysis but is not concerned with the long-debated issue of Italy's relatively benevolent conduct in the occupied territories. Rather, it will address this topic as an example of how food assistance can be seen as a constituent part of imperialist policies. As shown by recent research on the history of humanitarianism, humanitarian interventions are inextricably tied to imperial relations.[5] I will show how, against the backdrop of a widespread food crisis and associated weak statehood, the Italian authorities used food supply as an instrument of short-term governance and long-term imperial policies. To this end, I consider Italy's food policy as part of its occupation policies more generally, in particular of its strategy to penetrate the Greek economy.

The causes of the Greek food crisis

During occupation, the Greek authorities estimated that, on average, agricultural output dropped by 40–50 per cent.[6] Therefore, the collapse of agricultural production has traditionally been considered one of the key causes of the famine. However, recent scholarship has concluded that official statistics systematically underestimated production, meaning that actual output decline may not have been as dramatic as reported.[7] Since none of these studies has come up with a reliable estimate of total food production, it is very difficult to assess the actual role played by output decline in the outbreak of the famine. Further factors contributed to the decrease in the availability of foodstuffs. After annexing Thrace and eastern Macedonia, which accounted for 25–30 per cent of the Greek agricultural production, the Bulgarian authorities decided to curb exchange between these areas and other regions of Greece. Similarly, the Italians prevented some of the areas under their rule, namely the Ionian Islands, the Cyclades and eastern Crete, from delivering crops to the rest of the country.[8] A further factor leading to a decline in food availability was the sudden interruption of food imports. Before the war, between 20 and 40 per cent of Greece's internal consumption had been covered by imports.[9] The naval blockade imposed by the Allies resulted in a dramatic drop in these imports.[10] As a result of all these factors combined, food availability per person decreased, on average, from an annual amount of 170 kilograms per person in 1939 to 100 kilograms in 1941.[11]

As suggested by modern theories of famine, a drop in food availability cannot fully explain food crises, however. Changes in the existing patterns of entitlement, namely the conditions of people's access to food, also need to be considered.[12] As in most instances of famine, in wartime Greece, too, market fragmentation played a key role in preventing access to food. One of the immediate causes of this was the national transport crisis exacerbated by a lack of vehicles and fuel. Besides transport problems, exchanges through official channels were also made less profitable by the hyperinflation caused by the reduced availability of goods and, most importantly, by the increase in money supply.[13] The requests for occupation costs made by the occupying powers, especially the Germans, largely exceeded the country's capacity, amounting during the first year of occupation to 113.7 per cent of its GDP.[14] To meet such demanding requests the Greek government had no other choice but to resort to the money press. As a consequence of inflation, the drachma no longer served as an exchange tool and the official economy was increasingly sidelined by the black market. Owing to the spread of corruption, the unreliability of the gendarmerie and the weak legitimacy of public institutions, the Greek state apparatus lost its grip on society and public crop collection was an utter failure in the first occupation winter.[15]

Although there are no statistics allowing us to gauge the relevance of this factor, the consumption of local produce by the occupying troops surely placed a heavy burden on the local economy, too. When the Greek army capitulated in April 1941, the whole country was first occupied by German troops, who then handed over to Italy the regions the latter had been assigned. During this interregnum, the German authorities purchased or requisitioned substantial strategic material from the Greek economy, including foodstuffs such as olive oil, currants and sultanas.[16] Initially, the Italians acted no differently in this respect. However, in September 1941, a German-Italian agreement stipulated that troops were to be supplied not only from the local economy but also through food imports,[17] placing much less of a strain on local resources. In August 1942, for example, half of the Italian troops' food requirements were covered through purchases on the Greek market, while the other half was brought in by the Army General Staff.[18] Yet, direct consumption was not the only way the occupying armies impacted food availability for the population. Demand for forage crops meant there was less arable land for food production, and extensive use of the railway system for military purposes hampered the circulation of food within the country. Finally, apart from organized consumption of local resources, Italian and German soldiers purchased or requisitioned products from the local economy on an individual basis. Not unlike the German soldiers, the Italian soldiers sent large amounts of food from Greece to their families. Indeed, they had been instructed to do so by the Italian authorities who were concerned by the fact that the soldiers were transferring a large part of their earnings back home, thus increasing money circulation in Italy.[19] With the growth of armed resistance in 1942–43, isolated garrisons and troops engaged in mopping-up operations increasingly fed themselves off the land.

In addition, the occupiers exported foodstuffs from the country. Both Germans and Italians ordered so-called 'blockades' (*blocco*) of certain products, which meant these items were reserved for occupiers to purchase themselves. These were usually commercial crops that the country had exported prior to the war and were therefore relatively abundant.[20] Thus, these exports did not cause shortages on a local scale, but preventing them from being exported to other regions of Greece impacted the national economy as a whole.[21] Therefore, although the occupiers' policy was not the sole reason for market fragmentation, it significantly contributed to it by exacerbating the disruption of prewar supply chains. On Crete for example, in order to overcome the peasants' resistance to selling their olive oil, the occupiers paid in grain instead of money. This resulted in the paradoxical consequence of the island having relatively better conditions than other regions,[22] but, since the oil was exported to Italy and Germany, it also led to a dire lack of olive oil in other parts of the country.

Besides exporting foodstuffs, one of the main ways in which the occupiers exacerbated the food crisis was by hindering internal exchanges of goods.[23] To seal off their area of occupation from the others, but also within their own area, both Germans and Italians imposed a substantial layer of bureaucracy on Greek society, which significantly slowed down interregional trade and led to the spread of corruption.

Feeding the Greeks: Italy, Germany and the food crisis

In the summer of 1941, Italian and German representatives in Athens reported to Rome and Berlin that food reserves were becoming scarce and there was a risk of famine. As the Greek economy was cut off from international markets owing to the British blockade and the general crisis of trade, the Allied countries considered it the occupiers' duty to procure alternative sources of supply.[24] The spread of the famine threatened to undermine the maintenance of public order, leading to a considerable increase in criminality and the outbreak of strikes in the cities.[25] Italians were particularly concerned about the possibility that, as a consequence of the famine, the urban middle class could drift 'towards the obscure ranks of the proletariat',[26] unleashing a communist uprising.

The first attempts to set a common agenda on how to provide food to the country resulted in Italian and German representatives agreeing, in Rome at the beginning of September 1941, on a long-term plan to supply Greece up to June 1942 with a total amount of 150,000 tonnes of cereals and 30,000 tonnes of sugar (half from each occupying power), to be delivered in monthly transfers.[27] As the Italians admitted in a secret memorandum, this quantity of cereals was only half of the country's actual requirements.[28] The food plan based on this scheme foresaw the distribution of a daily ration of 128 grams of bread, 320 grams of oil and sugar and 1.2 grams of pulses.[29] Both Axis powers initially considered their food export 'advances' to be compensated for with a corresponding amount of foodstuffs from Bulgaria, Turkey and Romania.[30]

It was not long before the Italians realized that the Germans were delayed with their deliveries and that any possibility of compensating for these foodstuffs through imports from Bulgaria was precluded by the latter's unwillingness to release any cereals from Thrace.[31] Also, in a telegram to its Axis ally, the German government clarified that the food issue in Greece was to be solely Italy's responsibility, as the latter had been granted 'political preponderance' in the country.[32] The German authorities were clearly unwilling to supply a country with limited economic and military importance for the Reich. In the same period, the Italians became more concerned about the food crisis. In October, the Italian plenipotentiary in Greece, Pellegrino Ghigi, went to Rome and told Italian foreign minister Galeazzo Ciano as well as Benito Mussolini that he expected 'ferocious revolts by those who know they have nothing to lose'.[33] Therefore, the Italian Foreign Ministry proposed that, if Germany did not honour its obligations, Italy would take over part of the German share, supplying Greece with 100,000 tonnes of cereals until 30 June 1942. Mussolini accepted the proposal and gave the order to 'start with 500,000 quintals'.[34]

The different attitudes displayed by the Italians and the Germans with regard to the food issue can be explained by various factors. Almost all Reich institutions firmly opposed the prospect of reducing the consumption of the German population in favour of the Greeks, as the Nazi leadership, influenced by the experience of the First World War, when the Germans had suffered food scarcity due to the embargo by the Entente,[35] feared that any reduction in food rations might result in the collapse of the internal front. Moreover, the awareness that the Italians occupied most of the country played a key role here as it meant that suppressing social unrest resulting from famine conditions would be almost exclusively the duty of the Italian military.

By December 1941, Germany had only sent Greece 10,000 tonnes of cereals from the Banat and 1,000 tonnes of sugar from unknown sources,[36] while Italy had delivered 42,000 tonnes of cereals from its own reserves by January 1942.[37] In the next round of talks, which took place in January/February 1942, Italy insisted on Germany delivering its share but the Reich representatives stuck to the line of refusing to 'commit to a supply plan for Greece'.[38] Only after lengthy negotiation did the two sides agree, on 14 March, on a new plan aimed at 'soldiering on until the next harvest'. Germany undertook to deliver 56,000 tonnes of cereals – 38,000 tonnes of which was to be provided from the Serb Banat – only a fraction of its commitments according to the September agreement. By the same token, the Axis partners decided to discontinue all exports of foodstuffs from the country except for olive oil and wine, much of which had already been contracted from the previous harvest.[39] The Third Reich only fulfilled the terms of the new agreement under strong Italian pressure.[40]

Part of the foodstuffs Italy exported to Greece was sold to the Greek Ministry of Supply, which paid four times the original price, as their selling price on the Greek market was much higher than in Italy. The sums earned in this way were deposited by the Italian authorities in a special account from which the Public Limited Company for Italo-Greek Trade (*Società Anonima per il Commercio Italo-Greco* – SACIG, an Italian firm founded in September 1941 as a monopolist to handle trade between the two countries) drew funds to purchase goods in Greece and sell them at lower prices on the Italian market.[41] Another share of the food exports went directly to the so-called 'reserved areas'.[42] These were areas earmarked by Italy for direct annexation (for example, the Ionian Islands) or for annexation to Albania (e.g. Chameria/Thesprotia, Epirus), where the Italian civil authorities were appointed.[43] The geography of the Italian food deliveries clearly shows that political considerations prevailed over humanitarianism. Of the 42,000 tonnes that Italy had delivered to Greece by January 1942, 20,000 tonnes had been sent to the 'reserved areas'.[44] If we consider that the population of these areas amounted to one-quarter of the rest of Greece and that Athens was by then the epicentre of the famine, it is clear that these imports were not dispatched to the places where they were most needed but were disseminated according to political priorities, specifically building consent to Italian rule. Moreover, most of the Greek raw materials imported by Italy originated from these areas and, consequently, Italy had a particular interest in keeping the local economy running.[45] The relatively privileged status of these regions is reflected in the monthly reports of the 26th Army Corps Command supervising Chameria, Epirus and Aetolia-Acarnania. While the two former regions enjoyed deliveries of food from Albania, the latter region's food situation was regularly described as dire.[46]

Supply from non-Axis sources

Apart from the deliveries from the Axis powers, until the start of the international relief operation in August 1942 – on which more later – Greece was mainly supplied via Turkey, which was within the blockaded area. This first relief scheme ran from October 1941 to August 1942 and was financed by American philhellenic associations under the aegis of Great Britain. As a result, a total amount of 17,000 tonnes of foodstuffs – not including wheat – were shipped to Greece. Although this was no real solution to the country's food crisis, it was nevertheless a vital contribution.[47] In the same period, Turkey proposed the inclusion of the Cyclades, a group of islands ravaged by hunger, in the operation, as they could easily be supplied by steamers from Turkish ports. The proposal was dropped due to strong Italian opposition, however.[48] The Cyclades received food aid in the summer of 1942 and then only sporadically until the summer of 1943.

A commission of the Greek Red Cross[49] under the direction of a Central Administrative Committee (*Comité de haute direction*) created in November 1941 undertook the distribution of the Turkish shipments and other minor envoys from different sources. Among its members was Guglielmo Arnò, the representative of the Italian Red Cross in Athens, along with representatives of the German, Greek and International Red Cross. The Italian Foreign Ministry allowed the Committee to be created on condition that it would only be responsible for the distribution of non-Italian food aid.[50] The ministry argued that entrusting the distribution of Italian aid to an international board would have deprived it of its 'characteristic Italian provenance', thus eliminating its propaganda impact.[51]

In January 1942, the Axis authorities were informed that the Allies were willing to partially lift the blockade on imports to Greece and Sweden was prepared to transport those imports to Greece.[52] Mussolini expressed his willingness to accept the offer, even asking for the operation to include food imports from other countries. A month later, the American and British governments requested that the Swedish government start negotiations with the Axis powers on allowing shipments of food from North America. By mid-March, the Swedish Embassy had informed the Italian and German governments of the Allied proposal to allow more foodstuffs from Canada (15,000 tonnes of grain a month) to be shipped to Greece. The Italians immediately expressed their readiness to start negotiations so as to reach an agreement but they also set a series of conditions that delayed the start of the operation by several months.[53]

One of the most contentious issues in the negotiations stemmed from the obvious mistrust between countries at war with each other. The Allies requested guarantees that the dispatched food would solely benefit the Greek population and that the Axis powers would not exploit it for their own ends. Despite immediate verbal assurances, the problem remained as to who was to ensure that the actual distribution of food complied with this rule. The Italians insisted on entrusting this task to the Central Administrative Committee, since the composition of the board gave them a certain preponderance when it came to managing the distribution. The American and British governments, however, immediately made their consent conditional on the creation of a new committee, staffed with Swedish and Swiss representatives, to oversee the distribution. When in mid-March, the Swedish government's official note reached Italian representative Luca Pietromarchi, the latter explained to the Swedish legate that an oversight board already existed and that it was 'out of the question to substitute it with a Swedish commission'.[54] A second source of conflict was the fact that the Allies requested assurances that the food produced in Greece be consumed exclusively by the Greek population. This meant, in practice, that the occupying powers should replenish the entire quantity of foodstuffs they consumed by importing food with an equivalent number of calories.[55] This request clearly derived from the concern that the occupiers could have 'indirectly' exploited the external food relief, leaving the wheat provided by the relief scheme to the local population and feeding the troops off the local produce. Another consequence of this ruling was that the occupiers would submit to 'external' control, as the Allies mistrusted not only the occupiers but also the Greek collaborationist government and the Greek Red Cross.[56]

To avoid submitting completely to the control of neutral observers, Italy tried to limit the distribution of relief to mainland Greece and the Peloponnese, excluding most of the 'reserved areas'. Pietromarchi informed his German counterpart of this proposal, stressing that its aim was 'to reserve for Italy and Germany the Greek agricultural surplus agreed upon in the last negotiations conducted in Rome'. He continued:

> This way the [Red Cross] supplies would only be destined for Continental Greece and the Peloponnese, where they could meet the conditions set by the American and English governments, i.e. that food produced in Greece should be reserved exclusively for the local population. The Italian and German governments would continue supplying the occupied Greek islands with foodstuffs and of course they would claim the locally produced food they consider useful to the economies of the two countries.[57]

The Italian authorities were extremely worried about the prospect of having neutral observers on the Ionian Islands, the Cyclades and Sporades. This was primarily motivated by concerns over military security but also by the fact that these areas were to be annexed by Italy after the war. Here the Italian authorities were especially committed to implementing their policy of food distribution as a means to acquire political consent.[58] This applies to the Ionian Islands, in particular, where at the very start of the occupation, the Italian Civilian Commissioner Piero Parini and his wife instituted a charity organization. Food imports regularly arrived from Italy in the first year of occupation, keeping mortality relatively low compared to the mainland. The situation changed rapidly in the winter of 1942–43, however, when it became increasingly difficult to ship cereals from Italy, resulting in rising death rates. In the same period, the arrival of Red Cross relief improved the situation in Athens and other regions of mainland Greece. Thus, while in 1941–42, the population of the Ionian Islands had been spared the dramatic conditions prevailing in many Greek regions, over the following year the situation reversed. In a report to Rome in February 1943, Parini expressed his concern that this might undermine his efforts to convince the inhabitants of the benefits of submitting to Italian rule.[59] When in the summer of 1943, the population requested that Canadian grain be allowed to reach the island, Parini pointed out: 'If only one kilogram of flour [of Canadian origin] were to be transported to the Ionian Islands, this would immediately destroy the Italian Civil Administration's policy.'[60]

Not surprisingly, the German attitude towards the relief operation was positive from its very inception. Since the Reich did not have any political interest in Greece, it raised only minor objections to the terms of agreement and accepted that all areas under its rule be included in the operation.[61]

The agreement, finally reached at the end of June 1942, foresaw the creation of a new board, the Commission of Administration (*Commission de gestion*), comprising representatives of the Swedish and Swiss Red Cross.[62] The Italians accepted many of the conditions imposed by the Allies because in March/April 1942, the food situation in Italy itself had become particularly worrying and the authorities in Rome had signalled that they were not in a position to continue supplying Greece.[63] Also, as Ghigi wrote from Athens, Allied propaganda began spreading accusations among the Greeks that the Axis powers were hindering the conclusion of the agreement.[64] The agreement, which was formulated ambiguously, stated that the Commission of Administration was to act in cooperation with the already-existing Central Administrative Committee. This made it acceptable for the Italians who believed that this would enable them to keep control of the relief distribution.[65] Yet, contrary to their expectations, over the following months, the Commission of Administration gained more and more power and the Central Administrative Committee rapidly lost its authority, holding just a few meetings until the Italian capitulation on 8 September 1943, after which it was finally dissolved.[66]

On 7 August 1942, the first shipment was transported from Montreal to Greece with a load of 15,000 tonnes of cereals of Canadian provenance. Shipped on a monthly basis until the very end of the occupation in October 1944, these cereals represented the main source of nourishment for the country up to liberation. From the end of 1942, the relief reached more and more peripheral areas. As stressed by Violetta Hionidou, the Commission of Administration was, formally speaking, not an institution of the International Red Cross. Swedish representatives, for instance, had a strong influence over the board from the very beginning. It was presided over by a representative of the Swedish government and the *chargé d'affaire* of the Swedish government in Sofia had extensive powers to intervene in its operations. Committee members were selected and paid by the Swedish government and did not always comply with their role as neutral observers. There is evidence that they extensively reported to the Allies on the internal situation of Greece, providing information on military matters.[67] Besides this, the relief organization became increasingly powerful owing to the sheer size of the relief scheme, which became a kind of 'state within the state'. Apart from the Red Cross delegates – dispatched throughout the country to oversee food distribution – there was a network of local committees known as Central Committees for the Distribution of the Red Cross (*Kentrikes Epitropes Dianomon Erythrou Stavrou* – KEDES). These committees numbered around 30 at the end of 1942, increasing to as many as 100 by 1944.[68]

Rome's acceptance of the conditions set by the Allies might be seen as surrender, which is partially true, because its inability to stem the famine forced it to allow foreign aid into Greece with limited scope for controlling it. Yet, the existing evidence suggests that the Italians saw the relief operation as just a stopgap measure until the collection of the next harvest.[69] In spring 1942, hopes were high among the Italian authorities that the new harvest would stabilize the country's economy, reducing the need for foreign aid. As mandatory crop collection failed almost entirely in 1941, the Greek government decided to adopt a different strategy, forcing the peasants to yield their produce by means of harsh repressive methods, including the death penalty for those who hid produce. The government's plan to 'attack the countryside' largely depended on Italian support. In May 1942, the Italian command in Athens and the Greek government concluded an agreement which saw the Italian army commit itself to overseeing the harvest and crop collection. In several regions of Greece, especially in Thessaly, one of the most productive plains of Greece, the Italian military was deployed in the fields to guard the harvest against banditry. Special units composed of Italian soldiers, gendarmes and rural guards were tasked with surveillance duties and were ordered to 'shoot on the spot' anyone they caught red-handed. The Italian army was also entrusted with civilian duties such as calculating the extension of cultivated land and compiling lists of farmers and their respective land parcels in order to assess collection quotas.[70] Finally, every battalion was ordered to cultivate about 100 hectares of land to supply the occupying troops.[71] This 'militarization of agriculture', however, produced only limited results and failed to overcome the peasants' resistance. The 1942 crop collection campaign resulted in just 8–15 per cent of the harvest being obtained.[72] This eventually dashed any hopes of reducing the size of the international relief operation, leaving the Italian authorities with no other choice but to accept the managing board's extension of its powers.

Having lost the struggle to control food imports, the Italian authorities tried to at least take charge of the 'last mile' of food distribution.[73] The final report of the Commission of Administration, published in 1949, stressed repeatedly that, while relations with the Germans ran smoothly, the Italians hampered the work of the delegates.[74] The Italians suspected the Swedish representatives of feeding the resistance movement and, as Arnò proposed in April 1943, even considered taking over supplying the capital to show that Italy was able to manage the situation on its own.[75] When the Partisan movement gained control of extensive areas between autumn 1942 and spring 1943, the Italians applied a strategy of food denial, banning relief from regions that fell under Partisan control. Moreover, from January 1943, Italian counter-insurgency increasingly used material destruction to starve out the Partisans, which resulted in a considerable number of homeless civilians having to rely on Red Cross food aid. Finally, in many instances the Italian military authorities prevented the use of ports under their jurisdiction,[76] which resulted in some regions, such as Epirus, receiving only scant relief owing to transport difficulties. This move resulted from military security considerations but, as evidence suggests, in many instances also from the fact that the Italians regarded the relief operation as a threat to their authority in a country that was to become part of the Italian Empire.

According to the relief operation agreement, the Italian and German authorities had to refrain from exporting and consuming food produced inside Greece. The Commission of Administration kept track of the Italian and German consumption of Greek food and the import of the requisite amounts to fulfil the obligations of the agreement. According to its report, from September 1942 to the end of the Italian occupation in September 1943, Italian troops had requisitioned 45 billion calories of foodstuffs, importing 55 billion calories as compensation.[77] Yet, as the report acknowledged, there was a large grey area of unchecked consumption by the occupation army, e.g. for mopping-up operations and exports to Italy. While in most cases it is impossible to describe these developments in full, the existing evidence suggests that Italy continued to export consistent quantities of foodstuffs, not only from the areas exempted from the relief operation but also from those under the supervision of the neutral delegates. In December 1942, for example, the Greek government and the Commission of Administration organized an operation where oil could be exchanged for wheat.[78] Yet, according to the final report of the Economic Section of the Office of the German Plenipotentiary in Athens, Italy consigned only one-sixth of the oil that it had committed to collect.[79]

Food exports and Italian economic policy in Greece

If contextualized within Italy's overall economic policy towards wartime Greece, its food policy acquires the contours of a rational strategy of exploitation. In most countries occupied by the Axis powers, payments deriving from cross-border trade were handled in a clearing system, according to which they are not settled in currency but registered on a bilateral account. In a clearing system, if not settled otherwise, imbalances amount to a credit concession from the surplus to the deficit country. With the exception of Greece, where unusual conditions prevented this from happening, the Reich used clearing as an instrument of exploitation to extract forced credits from occupied countries and satellites.[80] For most of the occupation period, the clearing account between Italy and Greece showed a Greek deficit, resulting mainly from Italian food exports. From September 1942, when the international relief operation was underway, Italy's exports to Greece decreased. Yet, this never completely offset the Greek deficit.[81]

However, the clearing balance sheet does not provide a complete picture of Italy's economic exchange with Greece. Trade with the 'reserved areas' was excluded from the general Italo-Greek clearing account from the beginning of occupation until June 1943.[82] This was particularly true for the Ionian Islands, from which Italy imported large amounts of olive oil throughout the occupation.[83] In addition, many of the imports from the remaining areas of Greece to Italy, especially raw materials, were not paid through the clearing system. Based on Italian records, the Greek historian Vasileios Manousakis has estimated that from one-third to one-half of Italian imports from Greece were not reported on the clearing balance sheet, but were purchased by the military authorities using different methods, making it difficult to fully account for these imports.[84]

It is thus hardly surprising that, far from seeing trade with Greece as a burden, the Italians considered it a rather profitable affair. In his first economic report to Rome, in September 1941, the Italian representative in Athens Pellegrino Ghigi wrote that up to then, the country had 'contributed to alleviating rather than exacerbating our economy and our finances',[85] a situation that had apparently not changed a year later, when a report by the Commercial Section of the Italian representation in Athens remarked:

> If one takes into consideration all the goods that have streamed into Italy in other ways, especially through the military command, and that have been paid for with drachmas from the funds available to the Treasury without going through the clearing system, what this representation indicated in its report on the first year of occupation, namely that Greece has given to Italy many more goods than it has received, is clearly confirmed.[86]

According to the same report, the goods exported outside the clearing system included 'the oil that civilians and the military have brought home for their own use and that has certainly reached considerable quantities'.[87] It can be concluded, therefore, that although Italy had to relinquish to Greece a certain amount of its food reserves, which were an extremely scarce commodity in wartime, it was able to make virtue out of necessity by importing goods in similarly short supply onto its home market.

Moreover, food deliveries were tied to capital penetration. Italy used the drachmas obtained from selling foodstuffs to the Greek government to acquire substantial shareholdings in Greek enterprises. Initially, the idea of investing the proceeds of food exports was intended to preserve the value of that income in the face of the rapid devaluation of the drachma. However, it soon became a consistent strategy for the 'penetration of the Greek industry with the dual goal of securing raw materials for Italy to consume and exchange and of exerting control over specific branches with the potential of developing a certain degree of competition vis-à-vis our national industry'.[88] In October 1941, the Italian government created the Italian Company for the Mediterranean Orient (*Compagnia Italiana per l'Oriente Mediterraneo* – CIOM), a firm whose role was to 'promote Italian trade and industrial expansion in the territories of the Eastern Mediterranean', using the drachmas the Italian Treasury had obtained from trade imbalances.[89] After March 1942, when the Germans granted Italy part of the capital shares it had purchased in the first months of occupation, the CIOM acquired important shareholdings in key sectors of Greek raw material production, such as brown coal. The acquisition scheme was so ambitious that in July 1942 the company had already run out of funds and had to request more from the Italian Treasury.[90] Trade imbalances can thus be regarded as a means used by an imperialist power with limited resources to penetrate the economy of a subject country without triggering inflation.[91] This finding is supported by a memo drafted in preparation for a German-Italian meeting held in Berlin in June 1941. One section of the text reported that the Italian military authorities had already distributed food on the spot and that it would probably be necessary to distribute larger quantities in the future. 'The relative value', the memo read, 'should be seen as an export from us to Greece and added to the clearing balance. In exchange for surpluses, we should obtain investments or concessions (customs, ports, industries)'.[92]

Apart from the direct economic advantages, Italy's willingness to deliver food to Greece was motivated by its attempt to develop complementarities between the markets of the two countries with a view to establishing an Italian foothold in the occupied regions. In other words, exporting to Greece was considered a means of drawing this country into Rome's sphere of influence. Italy's economic imperialism was at a disadvantage vis-à-vis Germany's because Italian industrial exports were not competitive on foreign markets. As internal memos repeatedly stressed, the occupation of the Balkans was seen as a chance to turn these countries into a future outlet for Italy's industrial products.[93] With this goal in mind, exports of agricultural products were regarded as a means of fighting off German competition while waiting for 'Italian products' to be allowed to 'establish themselves on this market'.[94]

Similarly, the Italian authorities saw food deliveries as leverage to be used in German-Italian negotiations. This strategy paid off, for example, in October 1941, when in return for their food exports, Italy's share of Greek exports was consistently increased.[95] Moreover, while the food crisis in Greece was the subject of negotiations with the Axis powers, the Italians managed to convince Germany to assign them food deliveries from surplus areas such as the Banat and the Bačka.[96]

Conclusion

How Italy dealt with food issues in occupied Greece was shaped by different factors. While a general preoccupation with the idea that public order might slip out of control as a result of the food crisis played an important role, a strategy centred on the use of food to establish political control was also a key factor. These two aspects were closely intertwined and, interestingly, to a great extent developed in parallel. This is revealed by a report filed by the Italian Minister for Communications, Giovanni Host-Venturi, to Mussolini in August 1941, upon his return from a trip to Greece undertaken to inspect the state of internal communications and gain a first-hand impression of the recently occupied country. The food supply situation, Host-Venturi observed, had become such a concern to the Greeks that 'it can be said that anyone able to ensure the necessary supply [to Greece] will have the country in their hands'.[97]

The use of food aid for political purposes was by no means a strategy that was unique to the Italians. As suggested by Violetta Hionidou, during the Greek famine, most political actors – the Greek government, the resistance movement and the Allies – used food as a source of legitimacy,[98] a finding that is largely consistent with recent theories of famine.[99] Interestingly, in regions inhabited by sizable ethnic minorities, such as Macedonia and Epirus, external powers tried to gain a foothold by granting members of their kin groups privileged access to food. The Bulgarian authorities, for example, used food distribution as a form of propaganda among the Slav-speaking population in the Italian- and German-occupied areas of Macedonia. Similarly, the Romanian government delivered food to the Vlach minority of Pindus and Thessaly in an attempt to establish its political hegemony among what they considered to be ethnic Romanians.[100]

Italy's policy was not devoid of a distinctive notion of humanitarianism, albeit one that would certainly not be in keeping with the contemporary meaning of this word. Yet, contrasting the use of food for political purposes with 'pure' humanitarianism would amount to an historical anachronism. Indeed, the Italian actors did not see any contradiction between what they perceived as humanitarian aid and their overall occupation policy. From a scholarly point of view, regarding Italy's food policy as part of its imperial praxis allows us to understand the apparently contradictory rationales behind Rome exporting food to Greece and at the same time depriving that same country of foodstuffs to feed the Italian population. It also explains how the Italians could prevent relief from reaching the Ionian Islands and distribute food according to political priorities. Finally, it sheds light on how Italy regarded its food deliveries as part and parcel of a long-term strategy of economic penetration pursued against the backdrop of intense competition with Germany.

Notes

1 This comprised Attica, Boeotia, Evritania, Euboea, Pthiothis and Aetolia-Acarnania.

2 These figures are taken from the official statistics of 1940, Yannis Skalidakis, *I Elefhteri Ellada. I exousia tou EAM sta hronia tis katohis (1943–1944)* (Athens: Asini, 2015), 26.

3 This figure, commonly found in many Greek accounts, is questioned by Hagen Fleischer, *Im Kreuzschatten der Mächte. Griechenland 1941–1944 (Okkupation – Resistance – Kollaboration)* (Frankfurt am Main/Bern/New York: Peter Lang, 1986), 117–18, who proposes a more conservative estimate of 100,000.

4 Mark Mazower, *Inside Hitler's Greece. The Experience of Occupation 1941–44* (New Haven: Yale University Press, 1993), 30–2; Gabriella Etmektsoglou-Koehn, *Axis Exploitation in Wartime Greece 1941–1943* (PhD Diss., Department of History, Emory University, 1995), 404–66; Violetta Hionidou, *Famine and Death in Occupied Greece, 1941–1944* (Cambridge: Cambridge University Press, 2006), passim, mainly focused on Syros.

5 For an overview of the literature on the topic, see Rob Skinner and Alan Lester, 'Humanitarianism and Empire: New Research Agendas', *The Journal of Imperial and Commonwealth History* 40, no. 5 (2012): 729–47.

6 'Die Versorgung Griechenlands während der deutschen Besatzung. Zeit 1941–1944. Beitrag zum Tätigkeitsbericht der Wirtschaftsabteilung der Dienststelle des Sonderbevollmächtigten des Auswärtigen Amtes für den Südosten Athen', 12 April 1945, Politisches Archiv – Auswärtiges Amt Berlin (henceforth: PA AA), R27320 folio 227–36.

7 Hionidou, *Famine and Death*, 68–81. Hionidou provides no estimates of actual production but states that 'the production was probably as high as that of a "normal" year', 81. A thorough discussion of available figures can be found in Skalidakis, *I Elefhteri Ellada*, 35–47.

8 For the Cyclades, see Hionidou, *Famine and Death*, 53–5 and Sheila Lecoeur, *Mussolini's Greek Island: Fascism and the Italian Occupation of Syros in World War II* (London: Tauris Academic Studies, 2009); on Crete, see Paolo Fonzi, 'The Italian Occupation of Crete during the Second World War', in *Italy and the Second World War*, ed. Emanuele Sica and Richard Carrier (Leiden: Brill, 2018), 51–75.

9 Hionidou, *Famine and Death*, 11.

10 The role of the Allied blockade and the responsibility borne by the British government for its refusal to lift the blockade are emphasized in Fleischer, *Im Kreuzschatten der Mächte*, 116–27.

11 Bengt Helger, *Ravitaillement de la Grèce pendant l'occupation 1941–1944 et pendant le premiers cinq mois après la libération. Rapport final de la Commission de gestion pour le secours en Grèce sous les auspices du Comité international de la Croix-Rouge* (Athens: Société hellénique d'édition, 1949), 28.

12 See the classic work Amartya Sen, *Poverty and Famines: An Essay on Entitlement and Deprivation* (Oxford: Oxford University Press, 1982).

13 Dimitrios Delivanis and William C. Cleveland, *Greek Monetary Developments 1939–1948* (Bloomington, IN: Indiana University Press, 1949), 80–2.

14 In the same period, Norway paid 69 per cent of its GDP in occupation costs, Belgium 24 per cent, the Netherlands 18 per cent, Gabriella Etmektoglou, 'Gli alleati dissonanti: L'Asse e i costi dell'occupazione della Grecia', *Italia contemporanea*, no. 209–210 (1997): 109–42, 115.

15 Giorgos Margaritis, *Proaggelia thyellodon anemon. O polemos stin Alvania kai i proti periodos tis Katohis* (Athens: Bibliorama, 2009), 250–68; Mazower, *Inside Hitler's Greece*, 53–64; Hionidou, *Famine and Death*, 82–108.

16 Etmektsoglou-Koehn, *Axis Exploitation*, 277–85.

17 Helger, *Ravitaillement*, 98.

18 Intendenza Comando Superiore FF. AA. Grecia, 'Sguardo schematico a attività servizi di intendenza, agosto-settembre 1942', 30 September 1942, Ufficio Storico – Stato maggiore dell'Esercito (henceforth: USSME) N-11, box 1054. In the following month, the ratio between imported and consumed foodstuffs changed. For wine, imports remained half of consumption, for olive oil they amounted to two-thirds and for hay three-quarters.
19 Ministero delle Finanze to Amministrazione Centrale della Banca d'Italia (Ufficio Rapporti Finanziari con l'Estero), 20 September 1941, Archivio centrale dello Stato (henceforth: ACS), INCE, box 130.
20 An Italian report drafted in 1941 calculated that half of the 120,000 tons of oil produced annually in Greece covered internal consumption. Since exports were hindered by war and the economic blockade there were large reserves that could be exported, Comando XI Armata-Ufficio I, 'Informazioni fino alle 20 del giorno 24 giugno 1941', 24 June 1941, USSME L13, box 85.
21 Hionidou, *Famine and Death*, 64.
22 Helger, *Ravitaillement*, 389.
23 Mazower, *Inside Hitler's Greece*, 27, acknowledges this in relation to the first weeks of occupation.
24 This was based on an extensive interpretation of art. 43 of the 1907 Hague Convention, Hristos Sterpis, *Diethnis voitheia kai episitismos stin katohiki Ellada (1941–1944)* (MA Diss., Department for Political Sciences and History, Panteion University, 2016), 14.
25 See Gabriella Etmektsoglou, 'Changes in the Civilian Economy as a Factor in the Radicalization of Popular Opposition in Greece, 1941–1944', in *Die 'Neuordnung' Europas: NS-Wirtschaftspolitik in den besetzten Gebieten*, ed. Richard J. Overy, Gerhard Otto and Johannes Houwink ten Cate (Berlin: Metropol, 1997), 193–240.
26 Regia Rappresentanza Italiana in Grecia, 'Rapporto su comunicazioni', 13 August 1941, USSME L15, box 22.
27 Clodius-Mackensen to Auswärtiges Amt, 2 September 1941, Bundesarchiv (henceforth: BArch), R901, box 110326.
28 Regia Rappresentanza Italiana in Grecia (Ufficio coordinamento approvvigionamenti), 'Appunto per l'eccellenza il Plenipotenziario', annex 6, 18 September 1941. The *Ufficio coordinamento* suggested revising the agreement and increasing the amount due from 150,000 to 276,000 tons; see Archivio Storico del Ministero degli Affari Esteri (henceforth: ASMAE), DGAC Grecia, box 1941–1942.
29 'Die Versorgung Griechenlands während der deutschen Besatzungszeit 1941–1944. Beitrag zum Tätigkeitsbericht der Wirtschaftsabteilung der Dienststelle des Sonderbevollmächtigten des Auswärtigen Amtes für den Südosten Athen', 12 April 1945, PA AA, R27320 folio 227–36.
30 Mackensen to Auswärtiges Amt, 10 October 1941, PA AA, R105921, containing the text of a memorandum by Luca Pietromarchi.
31 'Aufzeichnung betreffend Lebensmittelversorgung Griechenlands (Emil Wiehl)', 15 September 1941, PA AA, R29880.
32 Mackensen to Auswärtiges Amt, 10 October 1941, PA AA, R105921.
33 Renzo De Felice, *Galeazzo Ciano. Diario 1937–1943* (Milano: Rizzoli, 1980), 451. See also Forte to Azzolini, 30 September 1941, Archivio Storico della Banca d'Italia (henceforth: ASBI), Direttorio Azzolini, Pratiche, n. 21.0, file 11.

34 Galeazzo Ciano to Ministero agricoltura e foreste, 'Rifornimenti di cereali alla Grecia', 2 November 1941, ASMAE, DGAC 1941. The Italian decision was communicated to the Germans on 11 October, von Bismarck to Auswärtiges Amt, 11 October 1941, PA AA R105921. A quintal is a traditional unit of weight in France, Italy, Portugal and Spain equal to 100 kilograms.
35 Gustavo Corni and Horst Gies, *Brot – Butter – Kanonen. Die Ernährungswirtschaft in Deutschland unter der Diktatur Hitlers* (Berlin: Akademie Verlag, 1997), 399–410.
36 Ghigi to Ministero degli Affari Esteri, 8 December 1941, ASMAE DGAC, Grecia, box 1941–1942.
37 Ufficio Speciale di Coordinamento, 'Riunione preparatoria dei rappresentanti italiani del 19 gennaio 1942', 19 January 1942, ASBI USC, Pratiche, n. 300, file 52.
38 Clodius to Altenburg, 18 November 1941, BArch R901, box 110326, folio 503.
39 Ministero degli Affari Esteri, Gabinetto A. P. Grecia, 'Appunto', 24 March 1942, ASMAE, Gab. Min. e Segr. Gen. 1923–43, box 1487.
40 Altenburg to Auswärtiges Amt, 23 October 1942, BArch R901, box 110327, f. 721.
41 Ministero delle Finanze to Ministero degli Affari Esteri, 'Anticipazione SACIG', 12 December 1941, ACS, INCE, box 130.
42 Ufficio coordinamento approvvigionamenti, 'Annex 6. Appunto per l'eccellenza il plenipotenziario', 18 September 1941, ASMAE, DGAC, Grecia, box 1941–1942 (3.1/4.1-5).
43 Civilian Commissars were, however, never appointed in Chameria, as Italy feared an uprising of the local Greek inhabitants against this decision.
44 Ufficio Speciale di Coordinamento, 'Riunione preparatoria dei rappresentanti italiani del 19 gennaio 1942', 19 January 1942, ASBI USC, Pratiche, n. 300, file 52. The figures quoted from October 1941 show a similar pattern of distribution; see Mazower, *Inside Hitler's Greece*, 31.
45 For example, in 1942, Italy imported 53,200 kilograms of leather and 46,000 kilograms of wool from Chameria, which equalled half the amount of imports of the same raw materials from the whole of Albania in the same period; Ente Albanese Gestione Ammassi, 'Relazione del Consiglio di Amministrazione all'Assemblea dei soci sul bilancio al 31 dicembre 1942 XI', 31 December 1942, ACS, SVEA, box 241.
46 See, e.g. Comando XXVI CdA (Ufficio affari civili), 'Relazione quindicinale', 20 October 1941, USSME N-1-11, box 376, where the situation in Aetolia-Acarnania is reported to be more difficult than in Epirus because of the lack of food deliveries from the Greek government.
47 The initial plan foresaw the delivery of 50,000 tons; see Giorgos Kazamias, *Allied Policy towards Occupied Greece: the 1941–1944 Famine* (PhD diss., Department of European Studies. Bradford, University of Bradford. 1990), 91–9.
48 German Embassy Ankara to Auswärtiges Amt, 13 January 1942, PA AA, R43055, fr. 724.
49 This was named the 'Committee for the Administration of Food Deliveries of the Red Cross International Committee' (Commission de gestion des envois de vivres du C.I.C.R.), was directed by the Swiss Albert Gredinger and included a number of Greek personalities; Sterpis, *Diethnis voitheia*, 34.
50 Ministero degli Affari Esteri to Ghigi, 12 December 1941, ASMAE, AP 1931–45, Grecia, box 21.
51 Croce Rossa Italiana (Comitato centrale) to Ministero degli Affari Esteri, 28 November 1941, ASMAE, AP 1931–45, Grecia, box 21.

52 Ciano to Croce Rossa Italiana, 28 January 1942, ASMAE, AP 1931–45, Grecia, box 20; German Consulate in Bern to Auswärtiges Amt, 10 February 1942; 'Einsatz des schwedischen Motorschiffs Hallaren durch das schwedische Rote Kreuz für Lebensmittelsendungen von der Türkei nach Griechenland', 2 February 1942, PA AA, box R43055. This operation concerned only 8,000 tons of cereals from Egypt; see 'Extracts from "A survey of Greek Relief April 1941 to December 1943" by Foreign Economic Administration – Liberated Areas Division in collaboration with the State Department', n.d., Archives du Comité international de la Croix-Rouge (henceforth: ACICR) B SEC CGSG B9.

53 Ministero degli Affari Esteri (Gabap-Grecia) to Swedish Legation Rome, 17 March 1942, ASMAE, Gab. Min. e Segr. Gen. 1923–43, box 1487.

54 German Embassy in Rome to Auswärtiges Amt, 25 March 1942, PA AA, R43055.

55 Swedish Legation in Berlin to Auswärtiges Amt, 20 March 1942, PA AA, R43055.

56 'Extracts from "A survey of Greek Relief April 1941 to December 1943" by Foreign Economic Administration – Liberated Areas Division in collaboration with the State Department', n.d., ACICR B SEC CGSG B9.

57 German Embassy in Rome to Auswärtiges Amt, 28 March 1942, PA AA, box R43056.

58 Arnò to Pietromarchi, 12 January 1943, ASMAE, Gab. Min. e Segr. Gen. 1923–43, box 1487.

59 Parini to Ministero degli Affari Esteri, 6 February 1943, ASMAE, Gab. Min. e Segr. Gen. 1923–43, box 1489.

60 Parini to Ministero degli Affari Esteri, 28 July 1943, ASMAE, Gab. Min. e Segr. Gen. 1923–43, box 1489. In 1969, a trial *in absentia* took place at the Greek Special Court for War Crimes against Piero Parini and other Italians who had served in the Ionian Islands during the war. One of the charges brought against Parini was of having impeded the Red Cross from supplying the islands. The accused were all acquitted, all charges being statute barred; see Spyros Gasparinatos, *Oi ellenikes katohikes kyberniseis. Dikes katohikon dosilogon kai egklimation polemou* (Athens: Vivliopoleion tis Estias, 2015), 429.

61 Regia Rappresentanza Italiana in Grecia to Ministero degli Affari Esteri (Gabap), 9 April 1942, ASMAE, AP 1931–45, Grecia, box 21.

62 See 'Extracts from "A survey of Greek Relief April 1941 to December 1943" by Foreign Economic Administration – Liberated Areas Division in collaboration with the State Department', n.d., ACICR B SEC CGSG B9; Helger, *Ravitaillement*, passim. The name 'Joint Relief Committee', erroneously reported by Violetta Hionidou, 'Relief and Politics in Occupied Greece, 1941–4', *Journal of Contemporary History* 48, no. 4 (2013): 761–83, 764–5, most probably gives the translation of the name of a different commission, namely the 'Commission mixte de secours de la Croix-Rouge internationale'.

63 Ministero degli Affari Esteri (Gabap) to Italian Consulate in Geneva, 7 March 1942, ASMAE, AP 1931–45 Grecia, box 21; see also Swiss Representative in Rome to Huber, President of the ICRC, 7 April 1942, Bundesarchiv Bern, E2001 D 1000/1552 bd 181, B.55.11.5.

64 Regia Rappresentanza Italiana in Grecia to Ministero degli Affari Esteri (Gabap-Grecia), 15 May 1942, ASMAE, AP 1931–45, Grecia, box 21.

65 The Italians had initially proposed the formulation 'under control of the Central Administrative Committee', Arnò to Ministero degli Affari Esteri (Gabap), 20 June 1942, ASMAE, AP 1931–45, Grecia, box 21.

66 Helger, *Ravitaillement*, 80–1.

67 Hionidou, *Relief and Politics*.
68 Helger, *Ravitaillement*, 113.
69 Ministero degli Affari Esteri (D'Ajeta) to Ghigi, 8 May 1942, ASMAE, AP 1931–45, Grecia, box 21.
70 Comando III CdA (Ufficio Affari Civili), 'Provvedimenti vari per la tutela della proprietà fondiaria e rustiche e dei raccolti agricoli', 10 May 1942, USSME N1-11, box 713.
71 'Relazione sull'opera svolta dal Comando Superiore FF.AA. Grecia nel campo politico economico durante il primo anno di occupazione, maggio 1941-maggio 1942', n.d., USSME L15, box 22.
72 Helger, *Ravitaillement*, 126.
73 'Control of the "last mile" in the aid chain is decisive when it comes to whose stomachs will be filled, and it allows for a strong claim of paternalistic credit vis-à-vis the final recipients'; Norbert Götz, Georgina Brewis and Steffen Werther, *Humanitarianism in the Modern World: The Moral Economy of Famine Relief* (Cambridge: Cambridge University Press, 2020), 12.
74 Helger, *Ravitaillement*, passim; see also Sterpis, *Diethnis voitheia*, 66–71.
75 Arnò to Ministero degli Affari Esteri, 'Applicazione dei Protocolli di Roma per la distribuzione del grano canadese alla Grecia', 29 April 1943, ASMAE, Gab. Min. e Segr. Gen. 1923–43, box 1487.
76 In December 1942, for example, Italy denied sending food shipments away at Patras and Kalamata, which made supplying Crete and the Peloponnese extremely difficult; 'Séance du Comité exécutif de la Commission de gestion qui a eu lieu le mercredi, 2 décembre, à 9 ½ h', Bundesarchiv Bern, E 2200.28 - 02 1000/440 Band 14, RR42/7.
77 Helger, *Ravitaillement*, 102. In the same period, the amount consumed and imported by the Germans was 75,520 million and 142,500 million calories.
78 Altenburg to Auswärtiges Amt, 5 April 1943, BArch R901, box 68610, folio 6–8.
79 'Die Versorgung Griechenlands während der deutschen Besatzung, Zeit 1941–1944. Beitrag zum Tätigkeitsbericht der Wirtschaftsabteilung der Dienststelle des Sonderbevollmächtigten des Auswärtigen Amtes für den Südosten Athen', 12 April 1945, PA AA, R27320 folio 227–36, 233.
80 While Germany accumulated a conspicuous amount of clearing debt in 1942, in 1943 and 1944 this was offset by a Greek deficit; see Etmektsoglou-Koehn, *Axis Exploitation*, 362–78; according to Jürgen Kilian, *Krieg auf Kosten anderer: das Reichsministerium der Finanzen und die wirtschaftliche Mobilisierung Europas für Hitlers Krieg* (Berlin: De Gruyter Oldenbourg, 2017), 294–318, the clearing played a relatively minor role in the exploitation of Greece.
81 Regia Rappresentanza Italiana in Grecia (Ufficio Commerciale) Ministero per gli Scambi e le Valute, 'Situazione clearing italo-greco', 28 September 1942, ASMAE, DGAC, Grecia, box 1942–1943.
82 Istituto Nazionale per i Cambi con l'Estero to Regia Rappresentanza Italiana in Grecia, Regia Luogotenenza Tirana, Capo Affari Civili Corfù, Regio Governo Rodi, Ministero delle Finanze, Ministero degli Scambi e Valute, 7 October 1941, ACS, INCE, box 130.
83 Existing records do not allow us to assess the amount of olive oil actually imported. However, the fact that in the summer of 1942, a total of 67 per cent of the entire produce of the island of Cephalonia was exported to Italy does give us an idea, Consulente dell'isola di Cefalonia to Parini, 13 July 1942, ASMAE, Ufficio Isole Ionie, box 49.

84 Vasileios Manousakis, *Oikonomia kai Politiki stin Ellada tou B'Pagkosmiou Polemou (1940–1944)* (PhD Diss., Department of Law, Economic and Political Sciences, Aristotle University Salonika 2014), 79–80.
85 Ghigi to Ciano, 'Relazione sulla Grecia', 29 September 1941, ASMAE, DGAC, box 1941–1942.
86 Regia Rappresentanza Italiana in Grecia (Ufficio Commerciale) to Ministero per gli Scambi e le Valute, 'Situazione clearing italo-greco', 28 September 1942, ASMAE, DGAC, Grecia, box 1942–1943.
87 Ibid.
88 CIOM to Ministero delle Finanze, n. 44, [December 1942], ACS, SVEA, box 213.
89 Promemoria per il Ministro delle Finanze, 'Compagnia per l'Oriente Mediterraneo in liq.', 31 August 1944, ACS, IRI serie nera, STO/539.
90 CIOM to Ministero delle Finanze, 11 July 1942, ACS, SVEA, box 213.
91 Ufficio Speciale di Coordinamento, 'Riunione preparatoria dei rappresentanti italiani del 19 gennaio 1942', 19 January 1942, ASBI USC, Pratiche, n. 300, file 52.
92 'Appunto per Berlino', n.d., ACS, INCE, box 130.
93 See, e.g. a memo from the Italian company Gruppo Volpi (soc.Galileo - Atene), 'L'industria elettrica in Grecia, Atene', 2 June 1941, ACS, INCE, box 130.
94 Regia Rappresentanza Italiana in Grecia to Ministero degli Affari Esteri, 'Situazione clearing italo-greco', 31 May 1942, ACS, INCE, box 130.
95 Clodius to Altenburg, 18 November 1941, BArch R901, box 110326.
96 For instance, by August 1942, Italy had received 20 per cent of the 1941 Banat harvest and 40 per cent of the Bačka maize production, 'Vermerk über eine Besprechung bei Herrn Ministerialdirektor Dr. Moritz am 6. Juli 1942 um 16.30 Uhr', 7 July 1942, BArch R3601, box 3124d.
97 Ministro delle Comunicazioni, 'Promemoria per IL DUCE', 8 August 1941, ACS, PCM, Guerra europea 1940, G-7/1, 228/3.
98 Hionidou, *Relief and Politics*, 774.
99 In partial correction of Amartya Sen's analysis, new approaches stress the role of 'personal' forces in the outbreak and development of famines, see Stephen Devereux, ed., *The New Famines. Why Famines Persist in an Era of Globalization* (London: Routledge, 2007).
100 Ministero degli Affari Esteri (Gabap) to Comando Supremo and Regia Rappresentanza Italiana in Grecia, 29 April 1942, ASMAE, AP 1931–45, Grecia, box 21.

Part Three

Cities: Searching for food

5

The rationing system and self-sufficiency efforts in Ljubljana during the Second World War

Mojca Šorn

Introduction

When it comes to the Second World War, Slovenian historiography boasts a relatively large number of scholarly works. However, most of these studies focus mainly on political and military issues. This is also true for the city of Ljubljana and its inhabitants. On reading a newspaper article published in early 1945, I came across the following quote: 'In spite of the momentous events that are taking place in the world ... the citizens of Ljubljana remain focused on acquiring the essential foodstuffs.'[1] This quote prompted me to research the causes and consequences of the lack of basic necessities during the years of occupation, focusing on the food policy and rationing system in the Slovenian capital. After Germany, Italy and Hungary attacked and divided the Slovene-inhabited territories of Yugoslavia (the Drava Banate) in April 1941, the border between the German and Italian occupation zones cut Ljubljana off from its vital hinterland in the north (see Map 4). Surrounded by a barbed wire fence in February 1942, the city was also severed from the rest of its hinterlands and thus virtually entirely isolated from the outside world. In this chapter, I discuss the strategies and methods Ljubljana's political and administrative institutions used in an attempt to address the city's food shortages from 1939 until the liberation in 1945.

On the one hand, my study reflects the complexity of the supply issue and the intricacies of food policy, while on the other, it reflects the experience of food shortages of Ljubljana's inhabitants. Neither adapted diets nor attempts at self-sufficiency could alleviate the emergency. When the war and its consequences led to the collapse of the supply system in the second half of 1944, food shortages not only manifested themselves in declining health, rampant disease, increasing mortality and a dwindling birth rate; they also meant people's daily rhythm had to adapt, which undoubtedly had a severe impact on the mental and psychological health of the inhabitants of the capital city of the Province of Ljubljana as well.

The works of Tone Ferenc, especially his book *Okupacijski sistemi med drugo svetovno vojno* ('Occupation Systems during the Second World War'), helped me place the Slovenian lands, the Province of Ljubljana and the city of Ljubljana in the proper temporal and spatial context. My study is mainly based on the materials kept in the Archives of the Republic of Slovenia and the Historical Archives Ljubljana, especially those contained in the folders of the head of the provincial administration in Ljubljana, the Provincial Food Institute, *Prevod*, 1941–44, and the City Supply Office of Ljubljana (*Mestni preskrbovalni urad Ljubljana*). I also had access to private collections, which include valuable personal diaries and correspondence. On the whole, archival materials, especially for the period of the German occupation, are relatively scarce. Much documentation was destroyed during and after the war, and the German occupiers also took some of it with them when they retreated. The memoirs written by the inhabitants of wartime Ljubljana and, up to a point, also the wartime press served as good indicators of the situation in the city. However, the newspaper reports were neither precise nor very revealing, as from the very onset of the war they were censored. Later the newspapers also suffered from paper shortages, which led to their content being reduced further.

Before the Axis attack on Yugoslavia

Much like the other European countries, neutral Yugoslavia started to prepare for war in the second half of the 1930s, concerned about the political situation in Germany, fearing a potential military attack, and based on its experience regarding the supply situation during the First World War.[2] It paid particular attention to supplying the population with food. In July 1939, the Yugoslav government issued the Food Reserve Decree. The minister of agriculture was empowered to procure and store the supplies required for the civilian population, while the minister of finance was tasked with establishing and administering the National Food Reserve Fund. Municipalities were obliged to provide a share of the resources themselves. In many places, however, it proved impossible to implement this decree fully.[3]

With the German attack on Poland in September 1939 marking the onset of war, imports were disrupted, driving up the prices of basic necessities. The Yugoslav government at the end of September 1939 issued a decree intended to keep price increases in check. It regulated prices for food, clothing, footwear, fuel and power, and prohibited stockpiling of other goods.[4] In October 1939, a committee tasked with controlling prices was established in Ljubljana. This was to ensure that all necessities available to merchants were sold and at the same time prices were monitored.[5] Despite the regulation, prices soared. Therefore, a Price Control Decree was issued in February 1940.[6] The basic foodstuffs covered by this decree included bread, flour, pasta, rice, coffee, tea, cooking oil, lard and meat. Importers, wholesalers and producers had to report any price increases related to these foods to the Price Control Office, which either approved or rejected the increase, while often capping prices.[7] Nevertheless, in the months leading up to the Axis attack on Yugoslavia on 6 April 1941, the prices of food and fodder had increased by between 20 and 50 per cent.[8]

In 1940, the Drava Banate – the Yugoslav administrative unit that included most of the Slovene-inhabited lands – faced its first supply restrictions. Due to increased consumption of meat, which could be attributed to reservists on military manoeuvres,[9] a regulation on meat saving was adopted in May, specifying that two days a week must be meat-free days. However, butcher's shops and taverns still offered mutton, goat and poultry every day. As the economic situation continued to deteriorate, Marko Natlačen, the Ban of the Drava Banate, decided to introduce a so-called command economy. In autumn 1940, the Ljubljana-based Banate Food Institute (*Banovinski prehranjevalni zavod*, also known as *Prevod*) was founded on his initiative. The Institute was tasked with organizing and executing the entire supply process; the principle of freedom of economic activity was abandoned.[10]

On the first day of 1941, Natlačen issued another major regulation, prescribing a 'single type of bread' or 'folk bread' be baked, made of 40 per cent wheat and 60 per cent maize flour.[11] As of 1939, the import of wheat from abroad and from Vojvodina, the so-called 'breadbasket of Yugoslavia', had become increasingly unreliable,[12] and the Drava Banate had only 1,100 wagons of wheat in stock (with a monthly consumption of at least 600 wagons).[13] Thus, on 20 January 1941, the Ban's administration issued a decree on ration cards for flour and bread. On 1 February 1941, the Drava Banate was in fact the first of the Yugoslav provinces (*banovine*) to introduce ration cards for bread and flour, pasta and other products made from wheat and rye flour. These were available to people who did not own land as well as to anyone who owned a small enough parcel of land to be exempt from the national land tax. The monthly bread allowance amounted to just over 13 kilograms for adults, a little over 6.5 kilograms for children up to the age of six, and up to 10 kilograms for children between the ages of six and fourteen. Heavy manual labourers, however, received just over 16.5 kilograms

Figure 5.1 The sign reads: 'Bread is sold out'. Source: Muzej novejše in sodobne zgodovine Slovenije, Collection Tekoče gradivo, inv. no. 1245/50.

of bread each month.[14] Shortly before the military attack on Yugoslavia, the *Prevod* Food Institute provided assurances that Slovenia had extensive stocks of foodstuffs set aside in case of war.[15] However, such assessments and promises soon proved to be completely false.

The attack on Yugoslavia and the occupation of Slovenia

As a consequence of the Axis attack on the Kingdom of Yugoslavia on 6 April 1941, the Drava Banate was occupied and the Slovene-inhabited territory divided, driven both by the German desire to reach the northern Adriatic coast and the Italian aspiration to control access to the Danube basin. The largest part of Slovenia – Lower Styria, the northern part of Lower Carniola and Upper Carniola, with a total of 800,000 inhabitants – was seized by Germany. Italy occupied the province of Inner Carniola and most of Lower Carniola, with almost 340,000 inhabitants, while Hungary occupied the Prekmurje region, which had approximately 100,000 inhabitants (see Map 4). On 3 May 1941, after introducing their civil administration, the Italians annexed the parts of Slovenia they had occupied. The Hungarians did the same on 16 December 1941. The Germans postponed the planned annexation several times and ultimately never formally implemented it. Nevertheless, they gradually integrated the occupied areas of Slovenia into their social order in flagrant violation of provisions set out in international law on war and occupation.[16]

However, the occupiers did not treat the Slovenian provinces as territories to be exploited and plundered, as was the case in other occupied countries throughout Europe, but rather as areas that were to be economically incorporated into their state system. In the years before the war, 60 per cent of Slovenia's population (700,000 people) was engaged in agriculture. Nevertheless, despite the fact that some areas were exceedingly fertile and well developed agriculturally and viticulturally, the Slovenian lands were not self-sufficient in terms of supply. Much as they did in the Reich, the German occupiers waged a 'battle for production' (*Erzeugungsschlacht*) in occupied Slovenia, especially in Styria. By providing materials such as artificial fertilizers, machinery and breeding stock, they in fact succeeded in increasing agricultural yields.[17] This led to an improved economic situation in rural areas and increased the farmers' standards of living, but had little to no effect on the urban populations.[18]

The provinces taken over by the Italian occupiers did not benefit to the same extent. In July 1941, the Province of Ljubljana, as the Italians named the territory, had 340,000 inhabitants and measured 4,544.94 square kilometres. It had the worst economic situation of all the Slovenian regions, as it had no noteworthy industry or well-developed farmland. Less than 58 per cent of the land was suitable for arable farming, of which only 30 per cent was actually farmland, with most of it consisting of forests, meadows and pastures. Livestock production was not a particular strength of the Province of Ljubljana either; in 1939, records show 220,000 head of livestock: 17,482 horses, 117,361 cattle, 74,727 pigs, 7,199 sheep and 2,654 goats.[19]

The city of Ljubljana was the centre of the newly established Province of Ljubljana. Before the Second World War, with its 80,000 inhabitants, it had been the political, administrative, economic, cultural and – with the only university in Slovenia – scientific centre of the Drava Banate. On the other hand, the Italian-occupied province also had a rural character, with meadows and fields accounting for more than half of its area.[20] Agriculturally, it was not well developed: the 1939 statistics show that farming represented the only source of income for just 590 people. The majority of Ljubljana's workforce – 10,152 people – were employed in crafts and industry; 7,216 worked in trade and transport; 8,335 in public services, the liberal professions and the army; while 8,855 had no occupation or were classified as 'other'.[21]

Under Italian occupation

After the annexation of the Province of Ljubljana to Italy, the Ministry of Agriculture and Forests in Rome (*Ministero dell'Agricoltura e delle Foreste*), or rather the main food directorate under its auspices, was in charge of food supply. In Ljubljana, just as before the war, the *Prevod* Food Institute, which operated across the entire province, was responsible for supplying the population. Its tasks remained the same: to study the population's needs and organize an appropriate supply of food, fuel and power. The only changes that the Institute was subject to under Italian occupation were related to its personnel: the managerial positions were filled by Italian officers,[22] who were now in charge of all the critical supply issues, in agreement with the High Commissioner, Emilio Grazioli. The City Supply Office of Ljubljana, which employed more than 150 people, continued to operate under the auspices of the *Prevod* Food Institute.[23] Until May 1945, this office, a part of the Ljubljana City Administration, was responsible for managing the food supply to the city's inhabitants.[24]

After the occupation, the people of Ljubljana found themselves in an unenviable food supply situation. When the Italian occupiers took over the city on 11 April 1941, the amount of food in the stores and warehouses was only sufficient for another fifteen days. As the new state border cut off the city from its economic hinterlands in the north, which were occupied by the Germans, the Italians were forced to import 110 tonnes of flour from Italy and other regions by mid-May. In June, they imported 2,200 tonnes of flour, 400 tonnes of pasta and 400 tonnes of maize. During the first three months of the occupation, Ljubljana received eighteen wagons of fat, half from the province of Rijeka and half from other parts of the newly established Independent State of Croatia (*Nezavisna Država Hrvatska* – NDH). Rice, sugar, oil, bacon, butter, cheese, condensed milk and even potatoes were imported from Italy as well.[25]

At the same time, however, Ljubljana was already flooded with refugees from the area occupied by the Germans. This was due to the more lenient policy that the Italian occupiers adopted. Aiming to win the favour of the local population, they took the Slovenian cultural and educational institutions, press, judiciary and to some extent the administration into account.[26] More than 20,000 people sought refuge in the Province of Ljubljana, and in October 1941 more than 11,000 of these were registered in Ljubljana. They had left their homes because of the Nazi policy to destroy the Slovenian nation, which largely consisted of three points: the mass expulsion of Slovenians, especially 'persons hostile to Germans'; the mass settlement of Germans;

and the Germanization of those Slovenians remaining in their homes. Between 220,000 and 260,000 people were to be deported from the German-occupied areas by October 1941. Due to numerous obstacles, including transport and accommodation problems as well as Partisan actions, the Germans were unable to fully implement their plan, but they did deport 63,500 people (most of them to Germany, many to the Independent State of Croatia and several also to Serbia and other parts of Yugoslavia).[27] In Ljubljana, the refugees accounted for as much as one-eighth of the city's population and, as (new) residents, were entitled to ration cards throughout the war.[28]

Many accounts reported that in Ljubljana at the beginning of April 1941, people were stocking up on the various goods that were still available in the stores and looting the abandoned Yugoslav military food warehouses. Italian soldiers joined the locals in their purchases. It turned out that they, like the German soldiers, were sending thousands of parcels home.[29] Francesco Semi, an art and literary historian born in 1910 in Capodistria/Koper and a member of the Italian army in Ljubljana at the beginning of the occupation, wrote in his war diary: 'Officers are rushing to the stores to buy precious silver foxes and other furs, cloth, leather .... The groceries and drugstores are also full of military personnel purchasing coffee for their superior officers. They will send it to Italy, where it will fetch three times the price.'[30]

Emilio Grazioli, the High Commissioner for the Province of Ljubljana, reported on the first food-related activities at the end of April 1941. His inspection of food stocks revealed that these were negligible and particularly short of wheat, maize flour and fat. This difficult situation was also obvious from the notices put up in individual taverns advising guests to 'bring their own bread'.[31] The authorities mistakenly assumed that the diversion of the trade routes would ensure a more regular supply, enough to resolve the situation.[32] However, the warehouses remained empty and the rationing of bread and flour followed in June 1941. The system was identical to the one used before the war. It was based on a policy of bread and flour vouchers, but the amounts specified were different: each individual could only purchase 7.5 kilograms of bread per month (in the German occupation zone everyone over the age of ten received 9 kilograms). According to the same decree, everyone was also entitled to 1 kilogram of rice and 1 kilogram of pasta.[33] Later, following the example of the supply system in Italy, High Commissioner Grazioli also introduced the rationing of other foodstuffs. Fat was rationed in July 1941: an individual could purchase 220 grams of lard, 100 grams of bacon and 100 grams of cooking oil per month. At the same time, only 700 grams of sugar was available per person per month. In the summer of 1941, meat consumption was also restricted. Residents of Ljubljana had to purchase their meat from specific butchers, who in turn had to provide their customers with booklets in which to record the quantities of meat bought and when. Meat could not be purchased without these booklets.[34] Food was rationed for the entire population, although people who owned land and/or livestock were not entitled to flour and/or meat and fat. A report written by Grazioli for Italian Prime Minister Benito Mussolini on 18 September 1941 reveals that all the regulations bringing the supply system in line with that of the Kingdom of Italy were implemented in just over four months.[35]

In addition to food rationing, the High Commissioner adopted several other measures concerning supply. From the autumn of 1941, a provision on the compulsory

Figure 5.2 Waiting for meat. Source: Muzej novejše in sodobne zgodovine Slovenije, Collection Tekoče gradivo, inv. no. P100.

delivery of all produce and livestock came into force. At the same time, some of the measures adopted by the former Yugoslav authorities were maintained, including the meat-free days. Beef could be sold on Saturdays, Sundays and Mondays; pork, mutton and horsemeat on Tuesdays; cured ham, sausages, etc., on Tuesdays, Wednesdays and Thursdays; while offal, game and rabbit could in fact be sold every day of the week. This schedule changed in March 1942, as butchers began to simply sell meat whenever they could get it.[36]

Ljubljana was also deprived of the milk it had received from the hinterlands before April 1941. By April 1942, milk, too, was subject to rationing. The *Prevod* Food Institute decreed that milk had to be distributed by district. Dairies received 'milk purchase books' subject to prior registration. On this basis, infants up to a year old were entitled to one litre per day (the decree did not expressly state that nursing mothers could not consume this milk), children aged one to seven were allowed half a litre, children aged eight to ten a quarter of a litre, while persons over the age of sixty, the sick and pregnant women were entitled to half a litre a day.[37] However, the office in charge of milk distribution was unable to ensure these quantities. Only children under the age of three and health institutions received enough milk on a daily basis, while all other beneficiaries only received their milk ration every second or third day.

Scarcity went hand in hand with price increases. By the end of 1941, prices for all necessities, including rationed food (except rice, which was relatively abundant in Italy as a rice-producing country), had risen sharply. The average increase in food prices was 43 per cent. Day after day, the High Commissioner would give assurances that the Italian administration would prevent prices from increasing or would ensure better wages and pensions. Yet it failed to do much more than occasionally officially specify – or set an upper limit for – the prices of rationed foodstuffs.

By the beginning of 1942, the liberation movement in the Province of Ljubljana had expanded considerably. Thus, Mussolini issued orders for the army to take over the defence of the province and ensure public order. The commander of the 11th Army Corps, General Mario Robotti, welcomed the orders as he perceived the province as a combat area. The Granatieri di Sardegna Division was tasked with addressing the issue of Ljubljana, which was considered the centre of the resistance movement in the Italian occupation zone. In an attempt to prevent any contact between the city and the countryside, Italian soldiers started laying barbed wire around Ljubljana on 19 February 1942, and by 23 February, the city was surrounded by it. Fortifications called 'blocks' were constructed at the eleven entrances to the city, manned by twenty-four-hour guards to ensure that only those with the appropriate documents were allowed to pass.[38] The High Commissioner's decree on the introduction of a travel pass for the municipality of Ljubljana had already been published in the Official Journal on 7 February, stipulating that from 20 February 1942, all those over the age of fourteen had to show a 'regular travel pass' (*lasciapassare*) to enter and leave the city.[39] The complete fencing off of the city was thus based on previous measures aimed at controlling the movement of citizens.

There is no information to indicate that the citizens of Ljubljana resisted or attempted to sabotage this Italian action. However, the differences in people's perceptions are illustrated by the following notes, written by two young individuals at the time, one of whom made the following diary entry: 'I forgot to mention that Ljubljana has been locked down for almost a week now.'[40] The other relived these difficult moments decades later in a published account: 'When … the Italians surrounded Ljubljana with bunkers and barbed wire barriers, we started to feel like concentration camp internees.'[41]

This severed Ljubljana's last connections with its immediate surroundings and caused the complete collapse of food supply. No source indicates that the High Commissioner may have opposed the implementation of the fortification system. Grazioli does not seem to have presented any suitable plan to facilitate the provision of supplies to the city from February 1942 onwards. After the city was enclosed by barbed wire, extensive raids and arrests followed, particularly targeting individuals suspected of opposing the Italian regime. By Christmas 1942, a total of 44,000 people had been investigated, 5,400 of whom were then interned. This removal of political opponents may have influenced the decision of the Italian occupiers to include everyone remaining in their homes in the ration coupon distribution. The Italian occupiers did not use the supply system for political purposes – this is also confirmed by the fact that, in the whole Province of Ljubljana, 342,615 sugar vouchers were distributed in February 1942 and 97,000 food vouchers in Ljubljana in December 1941.[42]

Due to censorship, newspapers offer little information about life under occupation, and especially about the food supply situation in Ljubljana after the city was surrounded by barbed wire. Some modest insights are available from journal entries and memoirs, as evidenced throughout this chapter. The diary of *družina K.* (family K.), for example, indicates that the people from the areas surrounding the city who had supplied the food market until that point could only get as far as the 'blocks', where a provisional market developed. Later, however, the vendors received passes to enter the city after all.[43]

For the people of Ljubljana, the consequences of their city being enclosed in barbed wire, and of the war as such, worsened each year. By the end of 1942, their cost of living had risen by 140–160 per cent compared to 1939, and food prices had increased even more.[44] A growing number of basic necessities could only be purchased with ration cards, while the quantities permitted decreased from month to month. At the beginning of 1943, every individual received 4.5 kilograms of bread, 1 kilograms of rice, 1 kilogram of pasta, 500 grams of sugar, 100 grams of bacon, 200 grams of butter and 100 millilitres of oil per month. From the first day of 1943, salt was rationed and the monthly allowance was 600 grams per person. The monthly salt quota was relatively generous, as salt was used for both cooking and food preservation – a vital household activity at a time when refrigerators did not yet exist. The decree that introduced bread and flour ration cards in 1941 divided children into two age groups: those under the age of six and those between six and fourteen. Later, children were divided into three groups: up to three, from three to nine and from nine to eighteen. Based on the recipients' needs, the largest amount of food went to the third group, while the first group received the least. From April 1942, ration cards for pregnant women and the sick were also in circulation, in addition to the regular food vouchers and those intended for manual workers.[45]

Under German occupation

After the capitulation of Italy on 8 September 1943, the Province of Ljubljana was merged with parts of the Italian territory – the Slovenian Littoral, Istria and Friuli – which was then occupied by the German Army. The German operational zone, called the Adriatic Littoral (*Adriatisches Küstenland*), was administered from its capital city of Trieste by High Commissioner Friedrich Rainer. He issued a decree appointing Leon Rupnik, a general of the Army of the Kingdom of Yugoslavia, as president of the administration of the Province of Ljubljana. No major organizational changes in either the provincial or the municipal administration took place, though of course the (high-ranking) Italian officials were replaced by German ones. Initially, the new authorities supplied most of the food from the Italian stocks they had appropriated in the border regions after the capitulation of Italy. Later, foodstuffs were imported mostly from Italy, Germany and from the areas that had already been under German occupation since April 1941. Rupnik ordered all rationed economy measures to remain in force. The *Prevod* Food Institute remained in charge of supply and distribution for the entire occupation zone of the Adriatic Littoral, even after the establishment of the Central Food and Agriculture Office in Trieste in the autumn of 1944.[46]

Basic necessities continued to be rationed and only available to people with ration cards.[47] In October 1943, the occupation authorities distributed just 137,714 vouchers in the Province of Ljubljana. Of these, 93,714 were given out in the city of Ljubljana (the census of 31 July 1941 indicated that approximately 92,000 people – including 12,000 refugees – lived in the city) and 44,000 in the countryside (in June 1944, the quota for coupons in the countryside was increased again and 93,172 vouchers were distributed).[48] The authorities wanted to force the rural population to produce more staple foods, while also hoping to increase the quantities of rationed foods for the urban population. Ration cards could only be issued to permanent residents of Ljubljana, while those who had moved to the city from elsewhere had to present an official certificate stating that they had de-registered at their former place of residence and that they were no longer in receipt of ration cards there. The urban guerrilla movement in Ljubljana was strong and mainly consisted of Ljubljana inhabitants – only a few dozen of its members were not permanent residents. They were provided with forged documents and other illegally printed materials, including food vouchers, through the technical services of the Communist Party.[49]

The German authorities soon discovered that the rationed food supply was more abundant in the areas under German occupation since the beginning of the war than in the territory previously under Italian occupation. In Lower Styria, which was de facto treated as a part of Germany, the amounts of rationed food were only slightly lower than in the Reich.[50] Here, at the end of September 1939, an adult had received 2.4 kilograms of bread, 500 grams of meat, 270 grams of fats, 62.5 grams of cheese, 100 grams of marmalade and 250 grams of sugar per week.[51] In the first years of the war, people received 2,400 calories per day. Towards the end of the war, this amount had decreased to 1,670 calories.[52] In 1943, the food situation in the province of Upper Carniola was still twice as good as in the city of Ljubljana. The German authorities aimed at improving the supply situation, but the inventory of crucial necessities convinced them that this would be very difficult to achieve. Indeed, they failed to make the situation any better despite the compulsory submission of agricultural produce and livestock being strictly monitored – except for a short period in 1944, detailed below. In Ljubljana, at the end of 1943, the amount of rationed food obtainable with ration cards was no bigger than at the start of the year. Each individual was entitled to 4.5 kilograms of bread, 2 kilograms of soup ingredients (rice, pasta), 400 grams of fat, 500 grams of sugar and 500 grams of salt each month.[53] The sick could use an additional ration card to receive 100 grams of bread and 100 grams of meat per day. Only infants would regularly receive a litre of milk, which would be entered into a special booklet, while older children and other beneficiaries (the sick and those over the age of sixty-five) would only occasionally receive the 'guaranteed' amounts. In November 1943, potato ration cards were introduced in response to a growing potato shortage.[54]

From January 1944, people no longer needed different ration cards to purchase foodstuffs: everything could now be bought with a new 'basic' ration card. Supplementary ration cards for workers, pregnant women, young people and the sick remained in use. Family ration cards were also in circulation. These were used to obtain firewood, kerosene and matches, as well as a few one-off allocations of foodstuffs in 1944 and 1945. On holidays and other special occasions, inhabitants were given extra rations of food – a practice the Italian occupiers did not indulge in. For example, in 1944, on Hitler's birthday (20 April), beneficiaries received an additional 500 grams of jam, 100 grams of fruit syrup, 200 grams of tomato paste, 400 millilitres of liquor and 200 grams of hard cheese. In fact, in the first half of 1944, the *Prevod* Food Institute managed to temporarily increase daily food quantities, probably at the expense of the

Figure 5.3 Waiting for bread. Source: Muzej novejše in sodobne zgodovine Slovenije, Collection Tekoče gradivo, inv. no. 1245/66.

rural population, which received far fewer vouchers between October 1943 and June 1944 than in the months before and afterwards. Each individual was thus entitled to 225 grams of bread, 16.6 grams of rice, 50 grams of pasta, 7.2 grams of fat and 16.6 grams of sugar per day.[55]

However, the authorities did not manage to control prices, which continued to increase. Towards the end of 1943, a linear wage increase (of approximately one-third) was implemented in the Province of Ljubljana, but this had little noticeable effect, as wages could not keep up with inflation. In March 1944, High Commissioner Rainer issued a new decree to ensure that basic goods were supplied at affordable prices, stipulating that the prices for essential goods could only be set by the price commissioners appointed by him personally. Initially, the district and county courts were responsible for dealing with violations of price control measures.[56] However, a Public Security Court was established in Ljubljana in 1944, based on the High Commissioner's decree on the exercise of justice in the Adriatic Littoral of 19 October 1943. It consisted of a three-member panel and a judge and could impose sentences of up to five years in prison and unlimited fines on black marketeers and other violators of the price control regulations.[57] In the first month after the implementation of this new decree, 129 misdemeanors led to fines in the amount of 178,600 lire for its violation. In four cases, establishments were closed down, one person was sentenced to sixty days in prison and a large amount of goods were confiscated.[58] As Tables 5.1 and 5.2 show, in the last year of the war, the food shortage in Ljubljana became increasingly acute.

Due to coal shortages and the constant Allied bombing of (rail) transport connections, transport was practically paralysed, making purchases in Italy exceedingly difficult. The lack of artificial fertilizers and consequent poor agricultural yields, the shortage of human labour and draught animals, as well as a ban on walking in the woods and the occupiers' intentional burning of forests where the resistance forces had found shelter, further exacerbated the situation.[59] Ljubljana, dubbed 'poor city'

Table 5.1 Daily quantities of rationed foodstuffs between 1941 and 1945

Daily quantity of rationed foods	1941 (g)	The first half of 1943 (g)	Beginning of 1944 (g)	1945 (g)
Bread	250	150	225	150
Rice	33.3	33.3	16.6	33.3
Pasta	33.3	33.3	50	
Fats	13.9	13.3	7.2	5.33
Sugar	23.3	16.6	16.6	8.3
Vegetables (peas or beans)				33.3
Total	**353.8**	**246.5**	**315.5**	**230.2**

Source: Mojca Šorn, *Življenje Ljubljančanov med drugo svetovno vojno* (Ljubljana: Inštitut za novejšo zgodovino, 2007), 124–93. In 1945, instead of pasta, people received 1 kilogram of vegetables and 1 kilogram of rice every month (SI AS 202, fond 76, II-442/25).

Table 5.2 Daily quantities of rationed foodstuffs and conversions into calories between 1941 and 1945

Year	Daily quantity of rationed foods (g)	Calories
1941	353.9	**1,030.13**
The first half of 1943	246.5	**771.66**
End of 1943	246.2	**766.81**
Beginning of 1944	315.4	**888.73**
1945	230.2	**674.85**

Source: Šorn, *Življenje Ljubljančanov med drugo svetovno vojno*, 175, 184, 191, 192. The conversion of the daily quantity of rationed food into calories was conducted by David Kumer, Executive Chef at Gostinstvo David Kumer s.p. in Kamnik, Slovenia (www.mangotree.si).

(*Revnograd*) by its citizens, depended almost entirely on the food it managed to produce itself or obtain throughout the province.[60] However, after the capitulation of Italy, a part of the province was liberated and then controlled by the Partisan forces. Because the Partisan Army had to supply itself as well as take care of the needs of the civilian population, which had become cut off from the supply centres, it depended on requisitions in addition to donations and purchases. A circular of the Economic Section of the Partisan Army Headquarters of 26 December 1943 indicated that each individual Partisan was entitled to a daily breakfast consisting of 250 grams of maize flour, 150 grams of unrefined flour and 10 grams of fat, together with a daily lunch or dinner consisting of 300 grams of beef or 200 grams of pork (one day a week was meat-free) or 50 grams of dried mushrooms, 400 grams of flour, 500 grams of beans or potatoes and 1,000 grams of kohlrabi, turnips or cabbage.[61] The question of whether this decree could actually be enforced remains open.

The general shortage was also reflected in the selection of foodstuffs brought to the main market to be sold freely by farmers:

> Apparently, there are no fats to be had, and only home-grown vegetables arrive at the market, none of it is imported. As far as fruits are concerned, you are extremely lucky if you can get blueberries ... You cannot even buy beans unless a greengrocer does you a favour. Only cabbage and kale abound for now ... Our stomachs are like gardens, with only greenery floating inside, mixed with pasta in every possible form.[62]

Only the turnip and cabbage stalls were well stocked, and occasionally home-grown apples were available. Women and children who picked and sold forest fruit would bring strawberries, raspberries, mushrooms and chestnuts to the market. Just before the end of the war, buyers could enjoy dandelions and fresh nettles.[63]

During the last months of the war, citizens' pleas to Ljubljana Town Hall for help went unheeded. Not even the decree on compulsory submission of livestock, which had been in force since April 1941, or rewards offered to successful livestock farmers could do anything to improve the situation. The reward for 1 kilogram of bacon was 600 grams of salt, 300 grams of sugar, 25 cigarettes, 2 boxes of matches, 50 grams of yeast and 100 grams of soap but it was rare for anyone to be eligible for this reward. At the *Prevod* Food Institute, farmers preferred to submit animals that would not be missed, such as old animals. The situation in agriculture was no better. During the war, field produce, which had already been modest in peacetime, was further reduced. The efforts of the *Prevod* Food Institute and the Chamber of Agriculture in Trieste, which offered prizes (artificial fertilizers in the form of lime saltpetre and ammonium sulphate) to anyone bringing 10 kilograms of spinach, carrots, kohlrabi and peas to the Ljubljana market, were more or less in vain.[64]

Coal remained scarce throughout the war, as it was mainly used by the railways and military transport. In 1944, even the city slaughterhouse, hospital and power station were occasionally without, but households suffered the most. When the German economic advisor to the provincial administration put a stop to the sale of coal for heating homes and cooking on 11 October 1944, the inhabitants turned to firewood.[65] At the beginning of 1944, the City Supply Office decided that firewood should no longer be sold in amounts large enough to stockpile (50 kilograms) but only enough for the current month and in accordance with supply.[66] Hoping to find at least a few suitable trees to cut down to enable people to keep warm and cook until spring, the commissioner in charge of supplying Ljubljana had the trees in the city's forests and parks inspected, upon which the expert commission approved a considerable amount of felling, especially in the Tivoli city park. Nevertheless, in April and May 1944, the beneficiaries did not receive any firewood. They would burn old crates and cut down fences and benches, which people appropriated even on Castle Hill and along the Ljubljanica River. Fuel was also sought through newspaper advertisements: some offered a financial reward for firewood, while others offered wool and fur coats in exchange for fuel.[67] For the period between April and November 1944, the Economic Council allocated 200 kilograms of firewood per household, which amounted to less than 1 kilogram of firewood per day. In March 1945, Ljubljana received only 775 tonnes of firewood.[68] Besides private dwellings, public institutions were also unheated. The preparation of hot meals was a serious problem. Many people were forced to eat in canteens or public kitchens.

Initially, it was unlikely that the agricultural and semi-agricultural population in the province or the wealthier inhabitants of Ljubljana would experience any health problems due to inadequate nutrition. However, the latter only accounted for around 15 per cent of the city's total population. In addition to markets and stores, they were also able to shop at the so-called free market: 'Whatever we could get for food stamps was far from enough. Gradually, I had no choice but to start selling kitchenware, jewellery, crystal and cloth. I sold the coir carpets from the hallway to Hotel Union. I had to sell precious silverware … and so on and so forth.'[69] In 1944 and 1945, black market prices were almost ten times higher than the official prices. For comparison, a bank employee received a monthly salary of 1,120 to 1,556 lire,[70] while a kilogram of beef cost 100 lire, a kilogram of butter 350 lire, a kilogram of lard 450 lire, a kilogram of sugar 150 lire, a kilogram of flour 70 lire and an egg 10 lire.[71] The black market, used by men and women, young and old, flourished until 1945, when even this potential source of livelihood declined due to the general shortage.[72]

Inadequate nutrition and its consequences became apparent as early as 1943. In addition to a decline in birth rate, an alarming rise in tuberculosis cases and increased mortality rates among infants under one and the elderly were recorded. In 1943, a total of 10,367 people were claiming sickness benefits, although more than 31,000 citizens had submitted the required medical certificates to the City Health Office.[73] The city doctor reported malnutrition in children, and adults also suffered from the typical consequences of nutrient deficiencies: weight loss, anaemia, nervous exhaustion, weakened heart, skin diseases and irregular or absent menstruation in women.[74] Many people decided to try their hand at self-sufficiency in one form or another to improve their nutrition and thus take care of their health. From the very onset of the war, their efforts were supported by the municipality of Ljubljana with no opposition from the Italian, nor later the German occupation authorities.

The municipality was actively involved in social welfare efforts. During the first year of the war, it was still able to allocate some extra funds from the municipal budget to help the city's inhabitants. In 1942, the city administration managed to increase the social policy budget by 34.4 per cent compared to the previous year, while later social welfare became increasingly dependent on charity. As had been the case during the Italian occupation, only charity from fascist institutions was allowed, the socially deprived were mainly helped by the province-level Provincial Support Institution and its city-level committee. Under their auspices, a programme known as Winter Aid (*Zimska pomoč*) and its successor Social Aid (*Socialna pomoč*) operated in Ljubljana, collecting cash and material donations. The only exception to the rule was the Red Cross, which was allowed to operate within the official social system. However, its activities were severely limited, as it was placed under the control of the High Commissariat.[75] When the German occupiers took over, they did not interfere in social affairs, which meant that the Red Cross could now consolidate its humanitarian activities. At the end of September 1943, it renamed itself the Slovenian Red Cross in Ljubljana (*Slovenski Rdeči križ v Ljubljani*).[76] Throughout the war, church organizations and shelters for children and adults engaged in charitable work, while outside the official social system, the charitable institutions of the People's Liberation Movement, the Partisans, established their own social network. The most active institution was what was known as Slovenian People's Aid (*Slovenska narodna pomoč*), which took care of prisoners and internees, and especially their families and the families of those who had joined the Partisan Army. It also provided food for the children of members of the urban guerrilla movement and Partisans.[77]

Attempts at self-sufficiency

Newspapers such as the *Slovenec*, the leading voice of Slovene Catholicism and magazines mainly aimed at women, such as *Gospodinja* (The Housekeeper), played an important role in the supply of food during the war. On the one hand, they urged people to save food, while on the other they encouraged the pursuit of a healthy diet. They wrote that ascribing too much importance to vitamins was just a fad, and they classified meat and eggs as unhealthy foods.[78] Newspapers would publish recipes and even weekly menus to ensure a 'balanced' diet adapted to the reduced availability. By the end of 1941, meat was almost eliminated, while pasta in various forms and rice were still recommended. Potato soup with rice was suggested for lunch and polenta with tomato sauce for supper on Mondays. For Wednesdays, the newspapers suggested Italian-style rice and celery salad for lunch and kale steaks and lettuce for supper.[79] Much attention was devoted to 'substitutes' for staple foods, especially bread. Recipes for bread made from potatoes, as well as kohlrabi, beetroot and carrots, were shared. Editors gave a reward of 10 lire for tasty and practical recipes. In 1945, one could purchase 1 kilogram of beetroot, carrots or cauliflower for that amount.[80] A few cookbooks were also published, focusing on recipes that were appropriate for the times.[81]

Some people could count on help from relatives and friends who lived in the surrounding areas.[82] In the spirit of self-sufficiency, Ljubljana municipality started encouraging all garden owners to cultivate their land. Those who did not have their own land could put their gardening skills to good use on rented plots. The municipality leased gardens and fields to the poorer and larger families for free or for a small fee, thus supporting its citizenry. It organized vegetable-growing courses, strove to purchase and distribute seeds and artificial fertilizers, and in cooperation with the city plant nursery, grew tomatoes, cabbage, kale and other seedlings in greenhouses. Apart from personal gardens, wartime gardens were developed in the city, for which the Town Hall was indirectly responsible. These were tended by the city plant nursery, mainly to supply the kitchens of social institutions with vegetables and potatoes. All city parks and even the green areas next to the Opera House and the National Museum were cultivated. To illustrate, in 1939, the arable land dedicated to maize amounted to 60 hectares, while in 1942 this type of land accounted for an area amounting to 130 hectares. On the other hand, there was 146 hectares of wheat fields in 1939 and 10 hectares less in 1942. Areas dedicated to cabbage and various other vegetables increased, but potatoes saw the biggest increase: from 80 hectares in 1939 to 500 hectares in 1942.[83]

In interwar Ljubljana, breeding small animals had been relatively widespread.[84] The local authorities were aware that keeping small animals could enable people to take care of their diet, at least partially, without having to turn to the black market. Therefore, they supported this activity and tried to help breeders. The focus was on keeping domestic rabbits, which was a worthwhile activity because of their meat, wool, fur and skins.[85] Breeding and caring for these animals seemed simple and cheap. Rabbits could be kept by anyone able to provide them with a little greenery each day and with enough space to set up a few cages. There were two organizations focused on assisting small animal breeders that operated in Ljubljana. These were involved in the purchase of fodder, disseminated expert literature to educate their members and organized lectures and courses. They also encouraged poultry, pigeon, sheep and goat farming, endeavoured to expand guinea pig breeding and were keen on developing bee-keeping.[86]

During the war, the people of Ljubljana unsuspectingly also ate meat from local pets. This fact was discovered in 1944, when detectives stumbled upon a secret slaughter house. At first glance, the place was nothing unusual for the war, but it turned out to be dedicated to slaughtering dogs. For a long time, rumours that pure-bred dogs were being stolen had circulated in the city, but the authorities had been convinced that a gang had been trafficking these animals in exchange for money or food. After the slaughterhouse was exposed, it came to light that fraudsters were selling dog meat on the black market – as veal.[87]

Conclusion

Ljubljana was liberated on 9 May 1945. Radio Free Ljubljana (*Svobodna Ljubljana*) announced the good news early in the morning. Partisan troops marched into the city, and the following day the National Government of Slovenia arrived, having been appointed in the town of Ajdovščina a few days earlier, on 5 May.[88] On 25 May, a day before Marshal Josip Broz Tito visited Ljubljana, its citizens bid farewell to the barbed wire fence: 'On Saturday, just as our Marshal Tito was to arrive, the news that all the checkpoints were open and that it was possible to cross the "Ljubljana borders" without permits or passes spread throughout the city.'[89] After the liberation, the administration was assigned to the Command of the City of Ljubljana, which, in cooperation with the Slovenian government, restored railways and bridges (in June 1946 to Trieste and in August to Zagreb) so that food and other goods could be transported to the city again. However, the time of shortages was far from over. Rationing, which involved a system of allocating goods subject to ration coupons, would remain in place until the early 1950s.[90]

The food policies of the occupiers in the city of Ljubljana were, in many ways, characterized by administrative organizational continuities associated with prewar Yugoslavia. Personnel changes occurred only at senior levels, as both the Italian and then the German occupiers sought to take control of the various institutions. Despite price thresholds, supply restrictions, compulsory submission of crops and livestock, and a rationing system, neither occupying force managed to solve either the chronic shortages of basic foodstuffs and other necessities, nor the price increases. A comparison of the theoretically guaranteed daily food rations in the period from 1941 to 1945 reveals the different phases of shortages at the local level. The situation in Ljubljana, on the brink of a severe famine during the last months of the war, reflected the global food crisis that was characteristic of the Second World War.

Notes

1 'Ljubljana pred pomladjo', *Slovenski narod*, 26 February 1945, 4.
2 Werner Abelshauser, 'Germany: Guns, Butter, and Economic Miracles', in *The Economics of World War II. Six Great Powers in International Comparison*, ed. Mark Harrison (Cambridge: Cambridge University Press, 1998), 122–76.
3 'Občinske finance in uredba o rezervi hrane', *Slovenec*, no. 181, 10 August 1939, 4.
4 'Pol leta nove gospodarske politike v Jugoslaviji', *Sodobnost. Neodvisna slovenska revija*, 1940, 181–7.
5 'Izvrševanje uredbe o pobijanju draginje', 6 November 1939, Zgodovinski arhiv Ljubljana (henceforth: SI ZA LJU), fond 501, container 8, no. 58, 300–1021.
6 'Komisija za preskrbo prebivalstva', 15 March 1940, SI ZA LJU, Fond 501, container 9, no. VIII 1971/24.
7 'Pol leta nove gospodarske politike v Jugoslaviji', *Sodobnost. Neodvisna slovenska revija*,1940, 181–7.
8 'Poslovno poročilo za 12. redno zasedanje banskega sveta', n.d., Arhiv Republike Slovenije (henceforth: SI AS), fond 77, folder 14, 87.
9 'Uredba o delu javnih klavnic', *Službeni list kraljevske banske uprave Dravske banovine*, no. 83, 18 October 1939, 773.
10 Andrej Gosar, *Gospodarstvo po načrtu, njegove naloge in problemi* (Ljubljana: s. n.).
11 'Zasedanja', 17 February 1941, 32–4, SI AS, fond 77, folder 15, 1. seja XIII.
12 'Preskrba Slovenije z živili', *Trgovski list*, no. 9, 22 January 1941, 1.
13 'Zasedanja', 17 February 1941, 32–4, SI AS, fond 77, folder 15 1. seja XIII.
14 'Banova odredba o prodaji moke', *Trgovski list*, no. 1, 1 January 1941, 8.
15 'Za preskrbo Ljubljane s hrano in kurivom', *Slovenec*, no. 60, 13 March 1941, 7.
16 Tone Ferenc, *Izbrana dela. Okupacijski sistemi med drugo svetovno vojno, 3. Nasilje in izkoriščanje gmotnih sil za potrebe okupatorskih držav*, ed. Mitja Ferenc (Ljubljana: Oddelek za zgodovino FF, 2009), 10.
17 Ferenc, *Izbrana dela*, 58.
18 Ibid., 383, 384.
19 Ibid., 388.
20 Anton Melik, *Slovenija. Geografski opis* (Ljubljana: Slovenska matica, 1963).
21 'Statistični letopis mesta Ljubljana za leto 1939', Ljubljana 1940, 6, SI ZA LJU, fond 708, container 3, item 16.
22 Tone Ferenc, *Fašisti brez krinke. Dokumenti 1941–1942* (Maribor: Obzorja, 1987), 33.
23 'Obsežno delo ljubljanskega mestnega preskrbovalnega urada', *Jutro*, no. 11, 15 January 1943, 2.
24 'Zapisnik 1. seje uprave Preskrbovalnega odbora mestne občine ljubljanske', 7 January 1943, SI ZA LJU, fond 490, Mesto Ljubljana, Predsedstvena registratura, Reg. II, folder 52, file 1.
25 Tone Kikelj et al., eds, *Slovenska narodna pomoč v okupirani Ljubljani 1941–1945* (Ljubljana: Mestni odbor medvojnega aktiva OF, 1995), 60.

26 Tone Ferenc, 'Okupacija slovenskega ozemlja', in *Slovenska novejša zgodovina. Od programa Zedinjena Slovenija do mednarodnega priznanja Republike Slovenije*, ed. Jasna Fischer et al. (Ljubljana: Mladinska knjiga and Inštitut za novejšo zgodovino, 2005), 589.
27 Ferenc, 'Raznarodovanje in fašizacija', in ibid., 586–90.
28 *Prebivalstvo Slovenije 1931 in 1941. Demografska statistika, I* (Ljubljana: Statistični urad Slovenije, 1945), 8.
29 Götz Aly, *Hitler's Beneficiaries. Plunder, Racial War, and the Nazi Welfare State* (London/New York: Verso, 2016), 97.
30 The war diary was published in the illustrated journal *Tovariš* in 1996; see Francesco Semi, 'Bojna komedija ali "osvojitev Ljubljane"', *Tovariš*, no. 19, 12 May 1966, 59.
31 Miran Pavlin, *Ljubljana 1941. Pričevanja fotoreporterja* (Ljubljana: Modrijan, 2004), 136.
32 Ferenc, *Fašisti brez krinke*, 113.
33 *Najvažnejši predpisi o prehrani v Ljubljanski pokrajini* (Ljubljana: Ente provinciale dell'alimentazione, 1942), 41.
34 'Mestnemu poglavarstvu – Ljubljana, vsem občinskim uradom in okrajnim načelstvom v vednost in radi kontrole', 5 July 1941, SI AS, fond 213, folder 3, file Okrožnice 1941.
35 Ferenc, *Fašisti brez krinke*, 153–8.
36 'Uvedba enotnega obeda v gostinskih obratih in ureditev prodaje in potrošnje mesa', *Bollettino Ufficiale per la provincia di Lubiana / Službeni list za Ljubljansko pokrajino*, no. 19, 7 March 1942, 126–7.
37 'Uvedba področij za razdeljevanje mleka v Ljubljani', *Slovenec*, no. 75a, 1 April 1942, 2.
38 Niko Lukež and Janez Kos, *Ljubljana 1170 dni v žični zapori 1942–1945* (Ljubljana: Čas, 2002), 15.
39 'Uvedba potne dovolilnice za občino Ljubljana', *Bollettino Ufficiale / Službeni list*, no. 11, 7 February 1942, 70.
40 'Dnevnik Z. B.', 27 February 1942, SI ZA LJU, fond 439, container 2, file 11, IV.
41 Tomaž Weber, *150 zgodb Ljubljančana* (Ljubljana: self-published, 2004), 108.
42 'Ali ima Ljubljana 1000.000 prebivalcev', *Jutro*, no. 34, 12 February 1942, 3.
43 'Dnevnik družine K.', i.e. the diary of family K., the author's personal archive.
44 Ferenc, *Izbrana dela*, 388.
45 'Lanski dodatki racioniranih živil za bolnike', *Slovenski narod*, no. 87, 16 April 1942, 2.
46 'Naredba o ustanovitvi Osrednjega prehranjevalnega in kmetijskega urada', *Službeni list šefa pokrajinske uprave v Ljubljani*, 9 August 1944, 187.
47 'Uredba polkovnika in poveljnika Örtla, Ljubljana', 13 September 1943, SI AS, fond 1886, folder 44, II.
48 Ferenc, *Izbrana dela*, 392.
49 Marica Čepe, 'Centralna tehnika je zrasla iz predvojne partijske tehnike', in *Ljubljana v ilegali, vol. I: V odločilnih dneh*, ed. Vladimir Krivic et al. (Ljubljana: Državna založba Slovenije, 1959), 235.
50 Bojan Himmelreich, *Namesto žemlje črni kruh. Organizacija preskrbe z živili v Celju v času obeh vojn* (Celje: Zgodovinski arhiv Celje, 2001), 187–212.
51 Ibid., 186.
52 Gustavo Corni and Horst Gies, *Brot, Butter,Kanonen. Die Ernährungswirtschaft in Deutschland unter der Diktatur Hitlers* (Berlin: Akademie Verlag, 1997), 581.

53 'Jahresbericht über die gesundheitlichen Verhältnisse in Laibach 1943', 77, SI AS, fond 1886, folder 66.
54 'Dostavljanje živilskih nakaznic za mesec november', 19 October 1943, SI AS, fond 1886, folder 43, XII, no. 2/7256.
55 Mojca Šorn, *Življenje Ljubljančanov med drugo svetovno vojno* (Ljubljana: Inštitut za novejšo zgodovino, 2007), 184.
56 'Naredba proti navijanju cen', *Jutro*, no. 74, 31 March 1944, 2.
57 'Izvršilne določbe k naredbi Visokega komisarja', *Službeni list šefa pokrajinske uprave v Ljubljani*, 17 June 1944, 149.
58 SI AS, fond 202, folder 39, no. 613/4.
59 'Okrožnice iz leta 1943', 29 October 1943, SI ZA LJU, fond 501, container 29, Okrožnice, no. 5.259.
60 'Dnevnik družine K.', i.e. the diary of family K., the author's personal archive.
61 Metod Mikuž, *Slovensko partizansko gospodarstvo v luči partizanskih dokumentov* (Ljubljana: Borec, 1969), 59.
62 'Pismo M. P.', i.e. the letter of. M.P., 20 July 1944, Mestni muzej Ljubljana, no. S31325.
63 'Vsakdanja Ljubljana', *Slovenec*, no. 88, 19 April 1945, 2.
64 'Z zelenjavo na trg!', *Slovenec*, no. 91, 22 April 1945, 4.
65 See also 'Okrožnice iz leta 1944', 4 April 1944, SI ZA LJU, fond 501, container 29, Okrožnice, no. 14487/44.
66 'Oddaja drv za domačinstva', *Trgovski list*, no. 59, 21 July 1944, 1.
67 'Mali oglasi', *Jutro*, no. 2, 4 January 1945, 5.
68 'Gospodarski svet Mestnemu poglavarstvu v Ljubljani', 5 April 1945, SI AS, fond 202, folder 28, Kurivo, no. 1112.
69 Mirjam Tozon, *Rože in trnje* (Celje: Društvo Mohorjeva družba and Celjska Mohorjeva družba, 2005), 183.
70 'Gibanje cen, mezd in zaposlitve v Ljubljanski pokrajini leta 1943', *Slovenski narod*, no. 19, 8 May 1944, 3.
71 'Pisma nam in vam (Pisma bralcev)', *Slovenski dom*, no. 26, 1 July 1944, 4.
72 'Vsakdanja Ljubljana po kronistovih zapiskih. Vlomi v Mostah', *Slovenec*, no. 152, 6 July 1944, 4.
73 'Jahresbericht über die gesundheitliche Verhältnisse in Laibach 1943', January 1944, SI AS, fond 1886, folder 66, Mavricij Rus, Poročilo o zdravstvenih razmerah v Ljubljani.
74 Ivo Pirc, *Zdravje v Sloveniji II* (Ljubljana: Higijenski zavod, 1938), 595.
75 'Postavitev društva rdeči križ pod nadzorstvo', *Bollettino Ufficiale / Službeni list*, no. 86, 25 October 1941, 614.
76 'Slovenski Rdeči križ v Ljubljani,' ibid., no. 78, 29 September 1943, 397.
77 Kikelj et al., eds, *Slovenska narodna pomoč*, 65–90.
78 'Pretirano besedičenje o vitaminih', *Slovenec*, no. 93, 23 April 1944, 3.
79 'Naša prehrana. Jedilniki', *Gospodinja*, December 1941, 66.
80 'Kotiček za praktične gospodinje', *Družinski teden*, 13 November 1941, 6.
81 'Naša prehrana. Nekaj nasvetov naši gospodinji', *Gospodinja*, May 1941, 36–7.
82 'Pismo A. C.', i.e. the letter of A.C., 19 January 1945, SI ZA LJU, fond 439, Zbirka Ulčar, container 3, file 30.
83 'V Ljubljani pridelujemo vse poljske pridelke', *Slovenski narod*, no. 246, 8 November 1943, 3.
84 'Poslovno poročilo Kmetijskega oddelka kraljevske banske uprave za XII. redno zasedanje', 14, 12 February 1940, SI AS, fond 77, folder 14.

85 'Kako je in kako bi moralo biti?', *Mali gospodar*, no. 1, 15 January 1941, 11–12.
86 'Poslovno poročilo Kmetijskega oddelka kraljevske banske uprave za XII. redno zasedanje', 14, 12 February 1940, SI AS, fond 77, folder 14.
87 'Pasja klavnica v mestu odkrita', *Slovenec*, no. 122, 28 May 1944, 4.
88 Aleš Gabrič, 'Osvoboditev in vzpostavitev nove oblasti', in *Slovenska novejša zgodovina*, 831–3.
89 'Blokov ni več', *Ljudska pravica*, no. 29, 29 May 1945.
90 Jože Prinčič, 'Obnova', in, *Slovenska novejša zgodovina*, 869; Zdenko Čepič, 'Preskrba prebivalstva in obvezni odkupi', in *Slovenska novejša zgodovina*, 893–7.

6

Trying the impossible: The Zagreb Jewish Community and the provisioning of female camp inmates (1941–42)

Marija Vulesica

Introduction

On 11 April 1941, on Erev Pesach – the day before Passover or Pesach – Aleksa (Aleksandar) Klein and his fellow members of the Zagreb Jewish Community were working hard in preparation for the upcoming Jewish holiday. The day before, the German military and police forces had entered Zagreb, bringing the fascist Ustashas to power. Just a few hours earlier, the Independent State of Croatia (*Nezavisna Država Hrvatska* – NDH) had been proclaimed (see Map 2). The atmosphere among the members of the Jewish Community, which had probably already been uneasy, took an abrupt and dramatic turn for the worse on this Friday in April, when the tragedy of the Croatian Jews began. At 11 am, the Gestapo entered the premises of the Jewish Community in Palmotićeva Street. All the staff present were arrested, all the funds and archives confiscated, and the building was occupied. Aleksa Klein, along with his colleagues, was arrested and interrogated.[1] He was allowed to return home the next day, but he – and all the other leading figures of the Community – was placed at the Gestapo's disposal. On Sunday, 12 April, the Zagreb Jewish Community was dissolved. For the first time since 1806, the approximately 12,000 Zagreb Jews had no official representative body.

Jews in the Independent State of Croatia and the Ustashas' food policy

Immediately after coming to power, the Ustashas launched an extensive and brutal campaign of terror against the Jewish and Serbian population. They also persecuted political opponents and the Roma. The multiple aspects of the politics of destruction occurred simultaneously and were often intertwined.[2] Within weeks of the proclamation of the Independent State of Croatia, Jews were arrested, disfranchised and publicly humiliated. Their property was looted, and they were deported to camps and murdered.[3] The overall events and developments of the Holocaust in the NDH are well known and have frequently been depicted in scholarly publications. The details, however, the microhistory of certain events, of the different types of camp, of Jewish families and individuals as well as (Jewish) institutions, have been neglected. With the aim of helping to close one of the many gaps when it comes to the historiography of the Holocaust in this region, I focus in this chapter on the Zagreb Jewish Community as an institution and on its clerks as central actors in the first eighteen months of the NDH. Specifically, I seek to address the pivotal question of subsistence and food provision. My aim is to shed light on these actors' efforts to supply food to the female camp inmates, in particular. Where did they get the food provisions from? How did they cope with the constant danger and legal constraints? Did they really feed the Jews who were deported to the camps? And if so, how?

I understand the concept of food policy as a whole conglomerate of practices and strategies of using food for political aims. First, the prevailing circumstances in 1941 and 1942 when the food policy was developed and executed by the governing Ustashas therefore need to be taken into consideration. However, there is still a lack of comprehensive scholarly accounts of the Ustashas' food policy. According to the studies conducted by Holm Sundhaussen, Alexander Korb and Sanela Schmid/Christian Schölzel, the NDH already faced massive economic problems in the first few months of its existence. Inflation, lack of purchasing power, shortages of food, unemployment, looting and corruption characterized large parts of the economy.[4] The occupying forces confiscated many tons of grain. The Ustashas tried to counteract the difficult supply situation by passing a law against hoarding food and against price increases in April 1941.[5] A month later, the regime established a Commission for Nutrition, which was later transformed into a state directorate that was to be the organizational basis for the collection and distribution of food. At the end of 1941, this state directorate was dissolved and replaced by the Section for National Alimentation, tied to the Ministry of Trade, Industry and Commerce. Other laws followed, including one that required peasants to sell their food surplus to the state at prices determined by the state. Yet, it was almost impossible to actually implement and monitor compliance with these laws and measures. Corrupt inspectors enriched themselves; peasants sold their produce at free market prices on the black market or simply abandoned their farms. Payment in kind was established between the city and the countryside, as the national currency steadily lost value. In as early as the summer of 1941, famine broke out in some parts of the NDH. In early 1942, only 30 per cent of the country's arable land had been tilled.[6] According to recent research, the Ustasha government never really gained control over the economy, *a fortiori* not over the food economy.[7] Thus, local actors, individual administrative units or the peasants themselves may have had a food policy, but the government never really did, with perhaps one exception: the practice of making it legally difficult for Jews to access food. For instance, Jews were not allowed to do their grocery shopping before 10 am, by which time the shelves were empty. By arresting and deporting the Jews, by leaving them to starve to death in prisons and camps, by denying them food, the Ustashas did indeed pursue a political goal, namely the total elimination of the Jews. In this case, the Ustashas' food policy was therefore more of a no-food policy, in its determination to rid the country of the Jewish population. The other 'by-product' of deportation to camps was that thousands of consumers were removed from the very limited food market.

In this hopeless situation, the Jewish Community attempted to supply Jewish camp inmates with food. They tried the impossible. Their efforts and their agency are at the centre of this chapter, but also the camp inmates who were supposed to receive the foodstuffs organized by the Community. The key actors here were Aleksa Klein (1898–1974) and Drago Rosenberg (1898–1946). In 1933, Klein, an ardent Zionist, became secretary of the Zagreb Jewish Community. Over the course of the 1930s, he played a central role in the administrative work of the Zagreb Community and was involved in all their decisions, plans and activities. After Klein's flight from Zagreb, first to Italy then to Switzerland in May 1942, Drago Rosenberg became the key figure in the Jewish Community administration. Rosenberg was a lawyer and he, too, was a committed Zionist. In September 1942, however, he too left the NDH for Italy and in December 1943 crossed the border to Switzerland.[8] Both men continued their work on behalf of the Yugoslav refugees in exile but also on behalf of those who were left behind. They established close ties with local and international relief organizations, campaigning for them to help Yugoslav Jews.[9] Rosenberg died unexpectedly in June 1946. Klein emigrated to Palestine in 1947, where he continued his work for Yugoslav immigrants. In 1961, he served as a witness at the Eichmann trial in Jerusalem, testifying about his efforts to make life easier for the (remaining) Jews after 1941.

Klein and Rosenberg were courageous enough to act and to take risks. Both were committed and ambitious. To a great extent, they shaped our (putative) historical knowledge about the events after 1941. Their reports, mostly written in German between 1943 and 1944, provided highly important insights into the situation of the Croatian Jews and their Communities.[10] Living in exile in Switzerland, feeling that they had escaped brutal and life-threatening persecution, they were traumatized, bitterly disappointed and at the same time anxious to help those who were still in danger. With this in mind, their reports should be read empathically but no less critically. For this chapter, I have used several sources created by the Community's officials in the 1940s, during and shortly after the war. These reports are of tremendous importance, since they provide us with essential facts, being at once testimonials of personal and institutional justifications, expressions of the pressure and fear experienced as well as of individual affirmation. However, all these reports and sources remain patchy.

Another source I used is survivors' interviews conducted in the 1990s. To understand the impact of hunger, on the one hand, and food provisions on the other, I introduce four women who experienced the camps and received food provisions from the Jewish Community. These four women survived the Holocaust, and they bore witness for the Visual History Archive of the Shoah Foundation: Jola Gelb (1909–2000), Ružica Breyer (1916–96), Zlata Romano (1920–?) and Vlatka Vajs (1922–2005).[11] I consider these interviews to be valuable sources documenting people's experiences during the Holocaust. But I also acknowledge their complexity, bearing in mind that they document the survivors' way of remembering and coping with past experiences.[12] By listening carefully to their recollections of life in the camps and of the role the

Community played, a more complete picture of this time and space arises. The four women were deported – along with many others – to the Kruščica and Loborgrad camps. These were the first camps in the NDH to be established exclusively for women. Importantly, Loborgrad was created due to the efforts of the Zagreb Community in an attempt to save or at least to help the detained women in Kruščica. The existence of these camps vividly illustrates the situation in which the Community found itself and exemplifies the scope of action the Community believed it had.

The re-establishment of the Jewish Community in May 1941

The dissolution of the Jewish organizations created a kind of vacuum which proved to be fatal for the Jews, but also for the Ustasha government. Desperate families, particularly those who had lost their income and whose male heads had been arrested, needed contact people to help them organize their lives under these new conditions. At the same time, the Ustashas – and the Gestapo – realized that they needed contacts, too, if they wanted the Jews to adapt to and follow the new laws and regulations. Simultaneously, according to Drago Rosenberg, Aleksa Klein was courageous enough to negotiate with the Ustashas to convince them to reopen the Community. Rosenberg claimed that it was Klein who suggested to the Ustashas and to the Gestapo that Community members be reinstated in office due to their extensive experience and expertise.[13] Klein himself confirmed this information in his report *Nach dem Umbruch*, explaining that he was first allowed to act as a temporary representative of the Community and a few days later was given permission to suggest some staff appointments.[14]

With the permission of the Jewish Section of the Ustasha police and that of the Gestapo, a Jewish Council was created in Zagreb on 14 May, consisting of twelve members. Aleksa Klein assumed the position of an *Amtsleiter* in the administration (equivalent to a secretary).[15] Two days later, the Jewish Council met for the first time at Tomislav Square 4, near the main railway station.[16] The Jewish Council or rather the newly re-established Jewish Religious Community – the latter was its official title even after May 1941 – was subordinate to the Jewish Section (*Židovski odsjek/Judenabteilung*).[17] This Jewish Section, which the Ustasha regime created in May 1941 and restructured at least twice, was in charge of the Ustashas' whole anti-Jewish policy.[18] To the Jewish Section, the Jewish Council or rather the Jewish Community served as a means to an end, a means to practise discrimination and persecution. Despite their totally different motives and political positions, these two institutions collaborated.

To this day, there is no research or academic debate on the collaboration between the Jewish Community and the Ustashas, nor on the role of the Zagreb Jewish Council in the NDH. Zdenko Levental – a Holocaust survivor and former member of the Community – already referred to this issue in his memoirs, published in the 1990s.[19] In my view, the question of collaboration[20] – a controversial term and at the same time an important subject of research – is crucial, touching on a sensitive issue and challenging long-standing narratives. However, this is neither the time nor the place to describe this debate in more detail. The Jews' experience in the NDH was, however, similar, albeit distinctive, to the complex role of the Jewish Councils (*Judenräte*) set up by the Nazis in numerous occupied European cities, which has been a subject of controversial debates for many decades.[21] In the NDH, the Jewish Community was an institution whose leading actors succeeded – at least for a very short period – in providing Croatian Jews with a valuable infrastructure and food. It is, however, *not* about the *raison d'être* of the Jewish Council and does not comprise a retrospective evaluation of its moral role.

Jewish agency in a time of terror

After the Council was installed, Aleksa Klein could build up an administrative team comprising twelve clerks and assistants.[22] By the end of July 1941, the Jewish Community consisted of fourteen different sections and employed about seventy staff members.[23] Giving Zagreb Jews work, making them part of the Community's staff, also meant protecting them from arrest and deportation, at least temporarily. Although he enjoyed certain rights and status, Aleksa Klein himself was still arrested and imprisoned from August to November 1941. He was brutally interrogated, beaten and tortured.[24]

No Jewish woman or man was ever safe from arrest and deportation. Only those who intermarried or had useful contacts had a slight of chance of being spared or being freed from a camp after they had been deported. The reason Klein was freed was most probably due to his – or the Community's – connection with Vilko Kühnel (1912–45), who became the head of the Jewish Section in September 1941. Kühnel would become a key actor in the implementation of anti-Jewish policy, yet, ironically, at the same time also assisted the Jewish Community and its members in supplying camp inmates with food and even explicitly helped individual Jews escape death. Kühnel was certainly a complex personality who played a leading – but until today completely unresearched – role in the history of the Holocaust in the NDH.

A consequence of the frequent arrests and deportations for the Zagreb Community was that, over time, its staff disappeared. After May 1943, there were almost no Jews left in Zagreb or the NDH – except those in hiding and those who were spared due to intermarriage. In the period between May 1941 and the spring of 1943, the remaining Community members did everything within their power to make life easier for Jews – including, not infrequently, alleviating their pain and suffering. Within months, local Jewish Communities were closed, their members and staff deported. Only the Communities in Osijek, Brod and Sarajevo were allowed to continue their work, although the Sarajevo Communities (Ashkenazi and Sephardim) were assigned non-Jewish commissioners[25] – two judges by the names of Srećko Bujas and Branko Milaković. According to Drago Rosenberg, both men worked 'altruistically' and were 'devoted' to the cause of the Sarajevo Jews.[26]

In June 1941, the Jewish Section allowed a soup kitchen to be opened for the Zagreb Jews.[27] How this decision came about is unclear. Most likely, however, the Community demanded a soup kitchen because the remaining Jews in Zagreb had barely any access to regular food. A major challenge for the Community was indeed how to feed the

Jewish population in the city, in the Zagreb transit camp (*Zbor*) and in all the other camps which rapidly proliferated throughout the country. To address this challenge, the Community needed significant financial means. Even though the state had set the prices for food, it was the black market or the individual farmer who ultimately determined how much food would cost. In response to the constant pleas of the Community's staff, in late June 1941, the Ministry of National Economy unfroze several (Jewish) accounts.[28] In the course of 1941 and 1942, the Jewish Community sent several requests to the various ministries and directorates to unfreeze accounts, also asking for 'commissioners' of Jewish businesses to pay community taxes. The Zagreb Community also urged the Communities in Osijek and Sarajevo to send as much money as they could.[29] In December 1941, Drago Rosenberg and Aleksa Klein succeeded – with support of Vilko Kühnel – in landing an in-person meeting with the Minister of Finance Vladimir Košak (1908–47) to inform him about the challenges and financial problems the Community was facing. Košak consented to transfer some of the confiscated 'Jewish' money to the Community, but only if international Jewish aid organizations agreed to cover at least part of the Community's expenses.[30] In fact, the Community, and particularly Aleksa Klein, had been in touch with the American Jewish Joint Distribution Committee, also known as JOINT or JDC,[31] for years. In July 1941, Klein was even allowed to travel to Budapest to negotiate with the JDC office directly to ask them for support. The JDC agreed to help financially, but they also imposed the condition that the Croatian state help cover the Community's expenses as well. Between December 1941 and July 1942, the Community received regular payments to partially cover the costs of the Loborgrad and Đakovo camps and to send food and medicine to Jasenovac and Stara Gradiška.[32] But these donations were far from sufficient and Klein and Rosenberg therefore had to take two more trips to Budapest – in February and in April 1942. Once again, they urged the JDC, as well as the Jewish institutions in Hungary, to help them. They all made 'big promises' but 'the results failed to materialize', Drago Rosenberg wrote in his report.[33] Despite the concessions Minister Košak made, it became very difficult for the Community to cooperate with the Ustasha administration because the latter's clerks delayed issues and created obstacles whenever they could.[34]

Thus, the first step in terms of organizing food supplies was to secure the financial means. A huge amount of money was required to buy the hundreds of kilograms of food needed or to rent vans and coaches for the transport of the supplies, or even to bribe officials. In addition to financial support, the Jewish Community also received food rations from government agencies. The Municipal Food Supply (*Gradska aprovizacija*), for instance, was instructed by the Jewish Section in August 1942 to continue supplying the Jewish soup kitchen with produce because they needed to cook two meals a day for approximately 350 people.[35] Similarly, in August 1942, the Jewish Section asked the Ministry of Trade, Industry and Commerce, and in particular its Section for National Alimentation, to continue to provide the Jewish Community with food, since it had to take care of those who were being transported 'in the context of the resettlement of the Jews' and of the elderly and the sick. The Section was advised to make 3,000 kilograms of wheat and 200 kilograms of sugar available.[36] It is unclear whether the Community actually received these supplies and if it did, whether it was able to prepare meals for the several thousands of people who were deported via Zagreb to Jasenovac and – especially in August 1942 – to Auschwitz. In his already widely quoted report, Rosenberg stated that in August 1942, the Community had found out 'at the very last moment' that they were to provide those being transported with flour, beans, bread and jam to last the three-day journey.[37] He did not indicate whether the Jewish prisoners received these rations. Chances are, they did not.

It is noteworthy, however, that government agencies took the Jewish Community into account when providing food. The question arises therefore as to why the regime subsidized the Jewish Community at all. Why should it support Jews being transported to or detained in concentration camps when the Ustashas' aim was to eradicate all traces of Jewish life? It was not the government's policy or desire to help the Jews. The key factor here was rather the determination and persistence of leading Jewish actors – such as Aleksa Klein and Drago Rosenberg – to help the persecuted and deported Jews. No doubt, they are unlikely to have achieved anything without the support – often through bribes – of Vilko Kühnel and others who were in service of the Ustashas. Considering the government's lack of economic power, the role and networks of individual actors when it comes to the provision of food become even clearer.

Supporting the camps, or rather the inmates, with food, clothes and medicine became the biggest challenge faced by the Zagreb Jewish Community in 1941 and 1942. The first groups to be detained were Jewish men, but soon after this in May 1941, Jewish women and children were arrested and deported as well. Survivors' testimonies give the impression that the Ustashas wanted to get rid of the Jews immediately, but they did not exactly know how or where to send them. The first camps to be set up were provisional sites, with unfinished huts or stables housing detainees. Some even had no buildings at all. In these cases, the inmates had to build the premises themselves and, in the meantime, had to sleep on floors, with no shelter. Within weeks, thousands of Jewish men and women were being transported across the country, from one site to another, languishing under terrible conditions, hungry, sick and frightened. The first camps included the 'collection point' or transit camp *Zbor* in Zagreb; *Danica* close to Koprivnica; the *Gospić-Komplex* consisting of camps on the island of Pag and the *Jadovno* camp in the Velebit mountains; *Kruščica*, located between the cities of Travnik and Zenica in Bosnia; *Kerestinec*, a castle near Zagreb; *Loborgrad*, a castle close to the Croatian city of Zlatar; and *Đakovo*, not far from Osijek.[38]

Immediately after the first arrests and deportations, the Care for the Camps Section came into existence. Its initial members – among them family members of the deported – began to intervene on behalf of the detainees. Aleksa Klein and Drago Rosenberg were both heavily involved in the work of this Section from the very start. In his memoirs, Zdenko Levental referred to the nerve-racking campaigns and actions – many of which were kept secret – that Aleksa Klein undertook with other members of the Community to help the Jewish detainees. He insinuated that they even succeeded in sabotaging transport routes and, above all, in bribing and favourably turning higher Ustasha officials.[39] Neither Rosenberg nor Klein considered their own emotions or mental state during such negotiations or after visiting the camps. However, Aleksa Klein's son, Baruch Arnon (1931–), bore witness for the Shoah Foundation and recalled a situation when his father once came home after a visit to a camp. He was heartbroken because he had met an acquaintance there who had begged him for bread.[40] No doubt, such situations caused unimaginable stress and psychological strain for the members of the Jewish Community trying to help.

The Care for the Camps Section was in another location than the Community, namely in Trenkova 9. The premises also housed a Jewish school. These children not infrequently helped to assemble and pack the aid packages.[41] When the Care for Camps Section started its work, their members asked the Jewish Section of the Ustasha police to permit them to send parcels with food, clothes and medicine, and to allow representatives of the Community to visit the detainees in Gospić and Pag. These first attempts were unsuccessful,[42] but at the end of July 1941, the Community was allowed to send food parcels, albeit only via the Croatian Red Cross (*Hrvatski crveni križ* – HCK). The first packages were dispatched on 6 August 1941, but these were never received by the inmates.[43] The role of the Croatian Red Cross at that time remains virtually unexplored, however. Why was it determined to function as a mediator, and why did it fail? These questions require further investigation. What does seem clear, however, is that the HCK was of no help to the Jewish Community in this situation.

According to Rosenberg, the only way of alleviating the horrors of the detainees' situation was to establish direct and personal contact to senior Ustasha staff, and this meant to either the Chief of Police Eugen Dido Kvaternik (1910–62)[44] or Vjekoslav 'Maks' Luburić (1914–69), the head of the department responsible for camps. Kvaternik refused to meet with anyone of Jewish origins, and it was not until September 1941 that Rosenberg – Klein was in prison at that time – managed to meet Luburić in person.[45] The latter, in turn, made 'the most beautiful promises' – such as supplying the Community with lists of Jewish detainees and of those who had already perished – but in the end, Luburić kept almost none of his promises. It was only thanks to constant pleas that, from September 1941, the Community was allowed to send bigger food parcels to Jasenovac and Stara Gradiška. In the months that followed, the Zagreb Community sent hundreds of kilograms of food to the camps, including potatoes, beans, vegetables, cheese and jam. Despite these efforts to supply the Jewish inmates, the Community continued to receive messages that almost nothing or only a very small part of the food being sent was actually reaching the prisoners. The Ustasha guards collected and rifled through the deliveries, keeping the supplies for themselves or selling the food elsewhere.[46]

This became common practice over the next months, and it is fair to say that the remaining Jewish Communities fed and supplied the Ustashas more than the inmates. It is quite likely that the authorities anticipated the deliveries and deliberately exploited the Community's hope and efforts to help the Jewish detainees. By allowing the Community to send foodstuffs to Jasenovac and Stara Gradiška they financially exhausted the remaining Community members and at the same time made sure that the guards and Ustasha forces on the ground were supplied with enough food, which was, after all, a rare commodity across the NDH.

The Kruščica camp was erected in summer 1941. The inmates were ordered to write to the Sarajevo Jewish Community to send them food. Then, when the parcels arrived, the guards plundered them, leaving almost nothing for the women. To make matters worse, they blackmailed the starving women and children by showing them a piece of bread or cheese, telling them they could have it if they handed over their remaining gold or jewellery in exchange. And to top it all, the guards frequently burned the food they did not want to eat.[47] The members of the Jewish Community in Zagreb and in Sarajevo knew about the plunder and misuse of the parcels. However, as Rosenberg put it, if there was at least a glimmer of hope that the inmates would receive some of the food sent, the Community was still willing to arrange these larger deliveries to the camps.[48] By the end of 1941, however, this action had been shut down since it became obvious that the inmates were no longer receiving any of the food. The Community then tried to help in a different way. Rather than dispatching larger deliveries, they started to send individual packages. Remaining family members and friends, but also non-Jews who wanted to help, could make up individual parcels and bring them to the Community. The Care for the Camps Section had to check each parcel since this was a responsibility the Utashas had assigned it.[49]

In autumn 1941, individuals could also send food and other supplies to the Serbian inmates of the camps, but only via the Zagreb Jewish Community.[50] This is how Diana Budisavljević, a humanitarian and wife of the well-known Zagreb physician Julije Budisavljević,[51] found her way to the Jewish Community and to the idea of creating an aid network. According to her 'Diary'[52] she was informed by the Jewish clerks that Serbian women were being held in the Loborgrad camp. She also found out that the Jewish Community had been ordered to take care of these Serbian women.[53] The Community thus recommended creating a Serbian committee which would have responsibility for the detained Serbs.[54] This was the beginning of a major humanitarian action to help Serbs and particularly Serbian children in the Independent State of Croatia. However, the *Aktion DB*, as the enterprise was called, was never granted official permission to operate independently. At least until autumn 1943,[55] all parcels with food, clothes and medicine put together for Serbian women were transported and distributed by the Care for the Camps Section. Budisavljević and her co-workers collected aid supplies, brought them to the Care for the Camps Section (in Trenkova 9) and paid for the transport to the camps.[56] Without the logistical and non-material support of the Jewish Community, the *Aktion DB* could never have been initiated and implemented. That said, judging from her 'Diary', Budisavljević developed strong distrust towards her Jewish partners.[57] It is difficult to say whether this was justified or whether unrealistic expectations or even antisemitism played a role in her adopting this suspicious attitude. Drago Rosenberg, on the other hand, described their cooperation as 'friendly'.[58]

The inmates of Kruščica and Loborgrad: The Jewish Community feeds the condemned

Among the many thousands of women who were arrested and subjected to humiliation, violence, fear and extreme hunger were Jola Gelb, Ružica Breyer, Zlata Romano and Vlatka Vajs. I have listened to their life stories to learn more about the beneficiaries of the Jewish Community's efforts to feed the camp inmates. What did they actually receive, and what did they know about the Community's efforts to provide them with provisions? What are their memories of hunger and the significance of food?

Jola Gelb was arrested in May 1941. She – like many others – was first transported to the prison at Savska cesta in Zagreb, from there to Gospić, Pag, Kruščica, Jastrebarsko, Slavonski Brod and in October 1941, to Loborgrad. She – like so many others – spent days on trains, in trucks or at train stations. While being transported, she often had no idea where she was and there was certainly nothing to eat or drink. According to Gelb's recollection, she spent approximately four weeks in the camp on the island of Pag, where there was almost no food, only a watery broth. Gelb reported that after four weeks, roughly fifty to sixty women were taken from Pag to Jastrebarsko. Here someone came and distributed a piece of bread and some milk to the women, she recalled. From Jastrebarsko, the women were then taken to the main station in Slavonski Brod where they received water, coffee and milk.[59] The Osijek Jewish Community had organized this meagre ration. It is hard to say who exactly helped the women in Jastrebarsko. Some survivors have also reported local peasants approaching the trains and giving them something to eat or drink.

After a short stop at Slavonski Brod, the women were transported to Kruščica. Gelb had very few memories of this camp and the conditions there. She remembered that the Sarajevo Jewish Community sent food parcels which were destroyed by the guards. And she remembered that the women constantly talked about recipes.[60] Many Holocaust survivors remembered that the inmates spoke about food, about what they were going to cook and eat once they were free. They exchanged recipes and sometimes even wrote them down.[61]

Vlatka Vajs was probably on the same transport as Jola Gelb. Arrested in Daruvar at the beginning of August 1941, she was first deported to Gospić where she was held for almost a month. From there, she and a group of other women were transported via Jastrebarsko to Slavonski Brod and then to Kruščica.[62] Vajs recalled that meals were cooked for the Ustashas in large pots, while the women inmates received only a cup of broth with two or three beans in it. One image, a uniquely harrowing experience, is anchored in her memory: a four-year-old girl, Verica, holding an empty cup, repeating over and over, 'Mum, I'm hungry'.[63] Vlatka Vajs could never forget this heart-breaking scene. It is almost impossible to imagine what hell it must be for a mother who has absolutely no way of feeding her hungry child. In these desperate situations, the Ustashas – according to Vajs's recollection – offered the wretched women bread and cheese, demanding jewellery and money in return.[64] Vajs also remembered a new group of women arriving from Sarajevo.

Zlata Romano was on one of the two inmate transports that arrived at Kruščica from Sarajevo at the beginning of September 1941, bringing approximately 1,000 Jewish women (and an estimated 300 Serb), as well as a few men to the camp. Romano was pregnant with her first child. The night she was arrested, she recalled, she had prepared loaves of bread to bake. She was sorry to leave the unfinished bread behind, so she rang the bell of a non-Jewish neighbour and asked him to take care of it. The neighbour showed compassion and concern and stuffed her jacket pockets full of sugar cubes.[65] Obviously these sugar cubes helped her get through these first days and nights en route to the camp. When the interviewer asked Romano about food in the camp, she made a puzzled face, as if she did not understand how anyone could ask about food in the camp. There was no food; the inmates ate leaves, she reported. She recalled a farmer who sold apples next to the camp, but the guards killed anyone who tried to reach out to him. She also remembered the Ustashas ordering the inmates to write home or to the Sarajevo Jewish Community to ask them to send food.[66] As described above, these parcels arrived, only to be plundered and destroyed by the Ustashas.

The Kruščica camp existed for approximately two months. Roughly 1,500 women and children were held there. There was almost no food, no light, no water, and the inmates slept in very basic, sparsely furnished barracks. The women experienced hunger, terror and quite often sexual violence. The conditions in this camp must have been so terrible that both the Jewish and non-Jewish population began to react. In fact, information spread across the country about Kruščica.[67] What could the Zagreb Jewish Community do? Here, Drago Rosenberg's report once again provides insight. Apparently, he conducted intensive negotiations with Vilko Kühnel about this camp. He succeeded in persuading Kühnel to approach Eugen Kvaternik and convince him to transfer the camp to Croatia, closer to Zagreb. Furthermore, Kühnel agreed to try to bring the camp under his control and entrust the Jewish Community with its food supply and 'autonomous administration' of the camp, led by the Jewish Community. Rosenberg further stated in his report: 'In this sense, we also had other influential people who intervened at various points and prepared the terrain, so to speak.'[68] Seemingly, the actors from the Jewish Community mobilized all their connections and contacts to improve the situation in Kruščica. It remains unclear, however, who these 'influential people' were, what exactly they did and how. It is even more remarkable that in a time of terror and systematic destruction of Jewish life, the members of the Jewish Community still had some room for manoeuvre. It is also noteworthy how persistent, well-connected and willing to take risks some of the Jewish actors were. Apparently, within the Ustashas, there was a network of helpers, confidants and corrupt officials. The Ustasha regime was permeable, at least on certain points and at the beginning of its rule. It was thanks to this circumstance that the Jewish actors managed to bring food into the camps at all.

Initially, it seemed as though the Jewish Community had succeeded in realizing the transfer of 'Kruščica', or 'the project' as Rosenberg referred to it. Drago Rosenberg and Kühnel's staff member had found a suitable building in Loborgrad Castle. It was large enough for several hundred people and was located in the vicinity of Zagreb. According to Rosenberg, it was agreed that the camp would be placed under the control of the Jewish Community. The Community was to be responsible for its administration and supply. Furthermore, there was to be only 'local police security' and no Ustasha guards. However, these agreements were only partially implemented. Instead of under the Ustashas, the camp was placed under the command of ethnic Germans (*Volksdeutsche*), who, with Karl Heger (1906–96) at its head, took over the camp management and surveillance.[69] The Jewish Community continued to be responsible for the care of the women prisoners, but had virtually no control over the distribution of relief supplies. Diana Budisavljević herself noted that Heger hoarded food in his office until it spoiled or was chewed up by dogs.[70] More than 1,500 women, as well as numerous children, arrived from Kruščica. However, Rosenberg and his staff had assumed there would be about 700–800 women,[71] which meant that Loborgrad was too small from the very start.

The trains from Kruščica ran via Zagreb. They were accompanied by Ustasha guards who, on arrival, handed over the command to the *Volksdeutsche*. Among the points agreed with the Ustashas was that the women in Slavonski Brod and Zagreb would be provided with food and would, in Zagreb, be allowed to shower and change clothes. Jola Gelb recollects that the train stopped at the final station. Here they were permitted to use the lavatories belonging to the railway employees. After a short stop, the women were loaded onto passenger trains and deported to Loborgrad. Zlata Romano went into labour in Zagreb, where she was hospitalized. She fled from the hospital but was rearrested and taken to Loborgrad. She does not remember receiving real food, only watery soups.[72]

Despite the agreement with the Ustashas and the efforts of the Jewish Community to provide the women with food, clothing and medicine, most of them were desperately hungry. Vlatka Vajs recalled boiling up potato peels in the camp. She also remembered food deliveries from the Community, but the women received very little or only leftovers, such as hard bread. She reported having broken two teeth after biting into a stale loaf of bread. Her mother, who was also arrested with her and transported from camp to camp, found employment in the camp kitchen, and here, at least, she had a little more to eat. Jola Gelb also remembered the deliveries as well as the camp kitchen. She volunteered for kitchen duty and took over the cooking for the camp commander Karl Heger and his brother Waldemar (1919–2007). The Zagreb Jewish Community not only supplied the women with food, but also Heger and his crew. This meant that they delivered 20 litres of milk daily and occasionally better-quality foods, such as luxurious mushrooms. Jola Gelb remembered an occasion when Heger came to her late one evening asking her to cook ‘a first-class dinner’ (*ein erstklassiges Nachtmahl*). She described how she managed to rustle up such a first-class dinner – including an appetizer and a dessert – with just a few ingredients. She sauteed the stems of the yellow boletus mushroom with onion. From eggs and flour, she then made pancakes (*palaćinke*), which she filled with the mushrooms and had them served as an appetizer. For the main course, she breaded the mushroom heads and boiled potatoes, seasoned with parsley. For dessert she was left with flour, eggs and milk. Again, she prepared pancakes, this time frying them only on one side and sprinkling the other with sugar, finally topping them with whipped egg white, so that the pancakes looked like a cake. Heger and his crew were delighted.[73] That evening, she acquired something of a special status along with some protection. Her work in the kitchen also gave her, admittedly clandestine, access to food, which, according to her testimony, she gave to others as well.[74]

Jola Gelb enjoyed another form of protection after her husband – Maksimilian Gelb – was transferred from the Stara Gradiška camp to Loborgrad at the beginning of 1942. Only a few Jewish men were detained at Loborgrad, mostly physicians who were needed to combat the typhus outbreaks at the end of 1941 or the beginning of 1942. One of these physicians was Karlo Breyer (1905–85). A gynaecologist from Zagreb, Breyer was also a member of the re-established Jewish Community and supported Aleksa Klein and Drago Rosenberg in their efforts to help detained women by organizing medicine and sending it to the camps. Breyer was arrested in July 1941.

At first, he was held in Zagreb and, in December 1941, deported to Jasenovac, then on to Stara Gradiška. According to Ružica Breyer's testimony, she and her husband had a good relationship with Vilko Kühnel. Consequently, it was Kühnel who managed to get Breyer out of Stara Gradiška, sending him – as a physician – to Loborgrad to help combat typhus.[75] Then, when Karlo Breyer met Jola Gelb in Loborgrad, he promised to help get her husband, once a well-known dentist in Zagreb, out of Gradiška.[76] Ružica Breyer, however, managed to remain hidden in Zagreb until June 1942. Her 'friends' – she never mentions any names – and neighbours in Zagreb hid her and brought her food. These same 'friends' provided her with supplies and she was even able to bring some food to her husband while he was imprisoned in Zagreb. Ružica Breyer was arrested in May 1942. She spent three months in Loborgrad. Shortly before the camp was dismantled, she and her husband were 'released', i.e. Karlo Breyer was sent – once again with the help of Vilko Kühnel – to Bosnia to fight the typhus epidemic raging there.[77]

In her account, Ružica Breyer does not go into much detail about the camp itself, nor the living conditions of the detained women. In fact, in June 1942, she claimed that the women 'looked good', which implies that they did not look as if they were starving. Breyer also mentions a garden, set up by the inmates, where they had planted vegetables and other crops.[78] Indeed, the commander of Loborgrad sent a report to the Jewish Section in July 1942 informing them that all the land which belonged to the camp had been cultivated by 196 female inmates. He also listed how many plants had been cultivated and how many kilograms of seeds had been used. For instance, he indicated that there were 4,500 tomato plants, 500 cabbage plants, 300 kilograms of potatoes and 5 kilograms of beans and other items.[79] Obviously, Heger had given the order to cultivate the land and most likely exploited the detained women, using them as forced labour. It is also quite certain that the detained women did not profit from this work or their seedlings, especially since they were deported in August that same year. From July 1942 at the latest, Croatian and German authorities worked together in pursuit of the 'Final Solution'. Approximately 1,200 Jewish women from Loborgrad were deported to Auschwitz. Five transports brought 4,927 Croatian and Bosnian Jews to Auschwitz in August 1942.[80] Jola Gelb and her husband, the dentist, were left in Loborgrad as camp staff. A few weeks later they were allowed to travel to Zagreb. Once in Zagreb, they went into hiding.[81] Ružica Breyer and her husband went to Bosnia and joined the Partisans, Zlata Romano escaped Loborgrad and, like Vlatka Vajs, joined the Partisans in autumn 1943. In the course of 1942, Aleksa Klein and Drago Rosenberg fled the NDH. Others had to take care of the remaining Jews in Zagreb and those in the concentration camps.

Conclusion

The Pag, Kruščica and Loborgrad camps were 'just' the beginning of the Holocaust in the NDH. Various other camps were established over the years. In the first year of the Ustasha rule, it looked as if key actors in the Jewish Community were still capable of having an impact. They worked hard, used their contacts, mobilized helpers and sympathizers, and used funds to bribe officials. However, both Aleksa Klein and

Drago Rosenberg soon sensed that their own ability to act was an illusion. Leading Ustasha officials were not really open to negotiation – and if they were, it was only with the aim of continuing to rob and bleed the community dry in every way. During this time of terror and constant danger, the Jewish Community and its leading representatives developed something akin to a relief agency: they organized food, clothing and medicine and made their transport secure, always hoping to help the interned women. However, those women who survived the camps and the Holocaust described in their memoirs that there were supplies, but that they hardly received any of them. Hunger shaped their existence in the camps. Italian Auschwitz survivor Primo Levi emphasized the omnipresence of hunger, writing in 1947: 'The Lager *is* hunger: we ourselves are hunger, living hunger.'[82] This applied to the women in the Ustasha camps, too. Hunger was omnipresent. The women certainly did not receive what they needed, at most only a fraction. But the fact that they received anything at all was thanks to a few Jewish actors. In a country where the economy was in tatters and food was in short supply, the camp guards and commanders kept supplies for themselves. In fact, the Ustashas completely exploited the Jewish Communities and their efforts.

The question therefore arises: Did the Community feed the beast that ultimately wanted to eat them? Did the Community sustain the perpetrators, thus indirectly supporting their policy of extermination? Based on historical evidence, it would seem that they did. However, the Community's motives to engage in this form of collaboration were shaped by the hope of being able to care for the women and men in the camps. They wanted to keep them alive and to help them. It was never their goal to preserve the system in the process or even to profit from it. The relationship between the Jewish Community and the Ustasha apparatus was one characterized by fear, terror and threat. The efforts of the Jewish Community in 1941 and 1942 to attempt to provide Jews with the necessities of life – such as food – reveal the sheer magnitude of the Ustasha terror. At the same time, the work of the Jewish Community also reflects the survival strategies of the persecuted Jews. The perspective taken in this chapter provides insight into a once strong Community, supported by committed personalities, who at least initially believed that they could extract concessions and relief for Croatian and Bosnian Jews from the Ustasha regime. Very soon, however, it became apparent that their options for action were extremely limited and their room for manoeuvre almost non-existent. In view of their ineffectiveness and the real danger to their own lives, the two leading actors of 1941 and 1942 finally had no choice but to flee. The Jewish Community continued its work until the end of the war. After the last large-scale deportations to Auschwitz in May 1943, only a small number of actors – protected due to their intermarriages – were left and it fell to them to try to take care of the elderly Jews who remained in the city and of the few survivors in the Croatian camps.

Notes

1 Aleksa Klein, *Nach dem Umbruch (10.4.1941)*, Central Archive for the History of the Jewish People (henceforth CAHJP), Eventov-Archive, B-49; report written in September 1945 in Lausanne.

2 Alexander Korb, *Im Schatten des Weltkrieges. Massengewalt der Ustaša gegen Serben, Juden und Roma in Kroatien 1941–1945* (Hamburg: Hamburger Edition, 2013).

3 Ivo Goldstein, *Holokaust u Zagrebu* (Zagreb: Novi Liber, 2002).

4 Sanela Hodzic and Christian Schölzel, *Zwangsarbeit und der 'Unabhängige Staat Kroatien' 1941–1945* (Berlin: LIT-Verlag, 2013), 23.

5 Holm Sundhaussen, *Wirtschaftsgeschichte Kroatiens im nationalsozialistischen Großraum 1941–1945. Das Scheitern einer Ausbeutungsstrategie* (Stuttgart: DVA, 1983), 265.

6 Ibid., 266–71.

7 Korb, *Im Schatten des Weltkrieges*, 239–45.

8 CAHJP, Eventov-Archive, A-08, file Dragutin Rosenberg.

9 CAHJP, Eventov-Archive, A-08 file Rosenberg; A-172 file Aleksa Klein (Arnon).

10 Aleksa Klein, *Zehn Jahre jüdischen Flüchtlingshilfswerks in Jugoslavien 1933–1942*, in CAHJP, Eventov-Archive, G-873; Drago Rosenberg, 'Die Lage und das Schicksal der Juden im "Unabhängigen Staate Kroatien" /"N.D.H"/ seit dem 10.IV.1941', in Central Zionist Archives (henceforth: CZA), L-17\327. The report was printed in Zdenko Levental, *Auf glühendem Boden. Ein jüdisches Überlebensschicksal in Jugoslawien 1941–1947. Mit einer Dokumentation* (Konstanz: Hartung-Gorre Verlag, 1994), 215–53. In the following, I quote from the printed version.

11 The USC Shoah Foundation collected more than 54,000 interviews with Holocaust survivors worldwide in the period between 1994 and 2001. The project was initiated by Steven Spielberg in collaboration with Croatian Holocaust survivor and Hollywood producer Branko Lustig (1932–2019).

12 On oral history as a method, see Julia Obertreis, ed., *Oral History* (Stuttgart: Franz Steiner Verlag, 2012); Linde Apel and Karin Orth, 'Oral History in der akademischen Lehre', *BIOS. Zeitschrift für Biographieforschung, Oral History und Lebensverlaufanalysen* 31, no. 1 (2018): 3–8.

13 Rosenberg, 'Bericht', in Levental, *Auf glühendem Boden*, 225.

14 Klein, *Nach dem Umbruch*, 3, CAHJP, Eventov-Archive, B-49.

15 'Ravnateljstvo ustaškog redarstva – Židovski odsjek', Hrvatski državni arhiv (henceforth: HR-HDA), HR-HDA-252, box 2, doc. 506/1941, inv. br. 27327; Mihail Sobolevski, 'Zagrebačka židovska općina od 1941. do 1945. godine', in *Dva stoljeća povijesti i kulture Židova u Zagrebu i Hrvatskoj*, ed. Ognjen Kraus (Zagreb: Židovska općina, 1998), 28–46, 31.

16 Goldstein, *Holokaust u Zagrebu*, 234.

17 Klein, *Nach dem Umbruch*, 3, CAHJP, Eventov-Archive, B-49.

18 Ivan Beuc, *Povijest institucija državne vlasti u Hrvatskoj* (Zagreb: Arhiv Hrvatske, 1969); Fikreta Jelić-Butić, *Ustaše i NDH* (Zagreb: Liber/Školska knjiga, 1978).

19 Levental, *Auf glühendem Boden*, 47.

20 Grzegorz Rossolinski-Liebe, 'Kollaboration im Zweiten Weltkrieg und im Holocaust – Ein analytisches Konzept', Version: 2.0 (2020), *Docupedia-Zeitgeschichte*, http://docupedia.de/zg/RossolinskiLiebe_kollaboration_v2_de_2020 (accessed 4 April 2022).

21 See Dan Diner, 'Die Perspektive des "Judenrats". Zur universellen Bedeutung einer partikularen Erfahrung', in *'Wer zum Leben, wer zum Tod …'. Strategien jüdischen Überlebens im Getto*, ed. Doron Kiesel (Frankfurt am Main: Campus Verlag, 1992), 11–36; Dan Michman, 'Kontroversen über die Judenräte in der jüdischen Welt 1945–2005. Das Ineinandergreifen von öffentlichem Gedächtnis und Geschichtsschreibung', in *Der Judenrat von Bialystok*, ed. Freia Anders, Katrin Stoll and Karsten Wilke (Paderborn et al.: Ferdinand Schöningh, 2010), 311–17.

22 Sobolevski, 'Zagrebačka židovska općina', 31f.
23 Ibid., 33.
24 Aleksa Arnon (Klein), 'Moje tamnovanje na Savskoj cesti', *Jevrejski Almanah* 1, no. 1 (1954): 230–6; Baruch Arnon, Interview 12668. Segments 36–42, Visual History Archive, USC Shoah Foundation, 1996 (accessed 8 September 2021).
25 Jewish businesses and some Jewish organizations – such as the Jewish Communities in Sarajevo – were given provisional administrators, so-called commissioners, in the course of 1941.
26 Rosenberg, 'Bericht', in Levental, *Auf glühendem Boden*, 228; 'Letter from Srećko Bujas to the Jewish Community of Zagreb', Sarajevo, 23 November 1941, United States Holocaust Memorial Museum (henceforth: USHMM), https://perspectives.ushmm.org/item/letter-from-srecko-bujas-to-the-jewish-community-of-zagreb (accessed 27 July 2023).
27 HR-HDA-252, box 2, doc. 815/1941, inv. br. 27453.
28 HR-HDA-252, box 2, doc. 633/1941, inv. br. 27317; Sobolevski, 'Zagrebačka židovska općina', 34.
29 'Bujas Asks for Zagreb to Confirm It Has Received the Money', USHMM, https://perspectives.ushmm.org/item/letter-from-srecko-bujas-to-the-jewish-community-of-zagreb (accessed 27 July 2023).
30 Rosenberg, 'Bericht', in Levental, *Auf glühendem Boden*, 246f.
31 The American Jewish Joint Distribution Committee (abbreviated as JOINT or JDC) was founded in 1914 to aid Jews in Europe and in the Middle East. Yehuda Bauer, *My Brother's Keeper* (Philadelphia: The Jewish Publication Society of America, 1974).
32 Rosenberg, 'Bericht', in Levental, *Auf glühendem Boden*, 248; Sobolevski, 'Zagrebačka židovska općina', 36–8.
33 Rosenberg, 'Bericht', in Levental, *Auf glühendem Boden*, 249.
34 Ibid., 249.
35 HR-HDA-252, box 15, doc. 5230/1942, inv. br. 29869.
36 HR-HDA-252, box 15, doc. 5141/1942, inv. br. 29824.
37 Rosenberg, 'Bericht', in Levental, *Auf glühendem Boden*, 241.
38 For a more detailed account about the camps, see Zdravko Dizdar, 'Logori na području sjeverozapadne Hrvatske u toku drugoga svjetskog rata 1941–1945. godine', *Časopis za suvremenu povijest* 22, no. 1–2 (1990): 83–110; Marija Vulesica, 'Kroatien', in *Der Ort des Terrors. Geschichte der nationalsozialistischen Konzentrationslager*, volume 9, ed. Wolfgang Benz and Barbara Distel (Munich: Beck, 2009), 313–16.
39 Levental, *Auf glühendem Boden*, 49; see also the recollection of Sabitaj Buki Finci, *Sećanja* (Belgrade: Jevrejski kulturni i humanitarni fond 'Sabitaj Buki Finci', 1995), 16.
40 Baruch Arnon, Interview 12668. Segments 54, Visual History Archive, USC Shoah Foundation, 1996 (accessed 8 September 2021).
41 Joško Indig, 'Kuća u Trenkovoj ulici 9', *Bilten Hitahdut Olej Jugoslavija* 27, no. 6–8 (1979): 8–9.
42 Rosenberg, 'Bericht', in Levental, *Auf glühendem Boden*, 230, 232; Sobolevski, 'Zagrebačka židovska općina', 38f.
43 Sobolevski, 'Zagrebačka židovska općina', 39f.
44 Kvaternik oversaw the Gestapo-like Directorate for Public Order and Security (*Ravnateljstvo za javni red i sigurnost* – RAVSIGUR). He created an independent Ustasha police force, called the Supervisory Service (*Ustaška nadzorna služba* – UNS). Its Department III, the Defence Service, was assigned responsibility for the

establishment, control and organization of the camps in the NDH. Kvaternik was dismissed in September 1942.

45 Rosenberg, 'Bericht', in Levental, *Auf glühendem Boden*, 233.

46 Ibid., 234.

47 Zlata Romano, Interview 23916. Segments 46, Visual History Archive, USC Shoah Foundation, 1996 (accessed 8 September 2021).

48 Rosenberg, 'Bericht', in Levental, *Auf glühendem Boden*, 234.

49 Ibid.

50 Ibid.

51 Diana Budisavljević (1891–1978) was married to Julije Budisavljević, a Serb. Due to the latter's importance, he was not arrested. In 2003, Diana Budisavljević's granddaughter Silvija Szabo published her grandmother's diary. Since then, several works have been published about her. In 2019, a documentary drama, directed by Dana Budisavljević, attracted considerable attention in Croatia. In 2020, Croatian historian Nataša Mataušić published a study on Diana's humanitarian work during the Second World War. Nataša Mataušić, *Prešućena heroina Drugog Svjetskog rata* (Zagreb: Ljevak, 2020).

52 Budisavljević's diary is more of a report, written almost entirely after 1945. In none of the publications on her 'Diary' has there been any critical reflection on this circumstance, nor on the fact that the original was written in German and is not accessible to researchers or the public.

53 In the documentary drama released in 2019, there is a scene where the leading figure – Diana – says that the Jewish Community is taking care of the Jews, and nobody was taking care of the Serbs. This scene does not correspond either to the 'Diary' or to existing sources.

54 *Dnevnik Diane Budisavljević* (Zagreb: Hrvatski Državni Arhiv, 2003), 13–14.

55 From then on Diana Budisavljević cooperated with the Croatian Red Cross.

56 *Dnevnik Diane Budisavljević*, 30.

57 Ibid., 49.

58 Rosenberg, 'Bericht', in Levental, *Auf glühendem Boden*, 238.

59 Jola Gelb, Interview 5093. Segments 68, Visual History Archive, USC Shoah Foundation, 1995 (accessed 8 September 2021).

60 Jola Gelb, Interview 5093. Segments 72, 76.

61 Thirteen years ago, I visited the Documentation Center Jasenovac. A little notebook, written by inmates and displayed as part of the permanent exhibition, caught my attention. It was a collection of recipes. The exhibition guides considered these collections to be proof of the supply of food. They did not question the provenance of or motivation for these recipe collections.

62 The first transport of women arrived at Kruščica on 28 August 1941. See Eli Tauber, *Holokaust u Bosni i Hercegovini* (Sarajevo: Institut za istraživanje zločina protiv čovječnosti i međunarodnog prava, 2014), 174.

63 Vlatka Vajs, Interview 49111. Segment 73, Visual History Archive, USC Shoah Foundation, 1998 (accessed 8 September 2021).

64 Vlatka Vajs, Interview 49111. Segment 73.

65 Zlata Romano, Interview 23916. Segment 36, Visual History Archive, USC Shoah Foundation, 1996 (accessed 8 September 2021).

66 Zlata Romano, Interview 23916. Segment 46.

67 Sara Berger, Erwin Levin, Sanela Schmid and Maria Vassilikou, 'Besetztes Südosteuropa und Italien', in *Die Verfolgung und Ermordung der europäischen Juden*

durch das nationalsozialistische Deutschland 1933–1945, volume 14, ed. Susanne Heim (Berlin/Boston: De Gruyter, 2017), 418–19.

68 Rosenberg, 'Bericht', in Levental, *Auf glühendem Boden*, 236.

69 Carl Bethke, 'Das Frauen-und Kinderkonzentrationslager Loborgrad in Kroatien (1941–1942)', in *Logori, zatvori i prisilni rad u Hrvatskoj/Jugoslaviji 1941–1945, 1945–1951*, ed. Vladimir Geiger, Martina Grahek Ravančić and Marica Karakaš Obradov (Zagreb: Hrvatski institut za povijest, 2010), 57–73.

70 *Dnevnik Diane Budisavljević*, 49.

71 Rosenberg, 'Bericht', in Levental, *Auf glühendem Boden*, 237.

72 Zlata Romano, Interview 23916. Segments 62.

73 Jola Gelb, Interview 5093. Segments 99–101.

74 Jola Gelb, Interview 5093. Segments 103.

75 Ružica Breyer, Interview 4952. Segments 82, Visual History Archive, USC Shoah Foundation, 1995 (accessed 8 September 2021).

76 Jola Gelb, Interview 5093. Segments 105–8.

77 Ružica Breyer, Interview 4952. Segments 95–6.

78 Ružica Breyer, Interview 4952. Segments 92.

79 HR-HDA-252, box 14, doc. 902/1942, inv. br. 29677.

80 Korb, *Im Schatten des Weltkrieges*, 413–19.

81 Jola Gelb, Interview 5093. Segments 116–18.

82 Primo Levi, *If This Is a Man* (New York: The Orion Press, 1959, It. original *Se questo è un uomo*, 1958), 83.

Part Four

Contested territories: Fighting for food

7

Food and food policies in central Dalmatia from April 1941 to the Italian capitulation in September 1943

Nikica Barić

Introduction

This chapter is focused on food supply and food policies in central Dalmatia in the period from the Axis invasion of the Kingdom of Yugoslavia in April 1941 until the capitulation of the Kingdom of Italy in September 1943. More precisely, the chapter will deal with the Great County of Cetina (*Velika župa Cetina*), an administrative unit of the Independent State of Croatia (*Nezavisna Država Hrvatska* - NDH). From 1941 to 1943, this county was located on the border between the parts of central Dalmatia annexed by Italy and those controlled by the NDH. It was also where the Partisan movement began to take shape. As a result, the Great County of Cetina was a place where, in a context of general food shortages, the competition for the control of the local population and the use of food to this end was particularly visible. In order to study the aforementioned food policies, we will draw on documents found in the Croatian State Archives, as well as those reproduced in the collection *The People's Liberation Struggle in Dalmatia* published in the 1980s,[1] originating from the NDH authorities and the Partisan movement, and, to a lesser extent, from the Italian army. The period from September 1943 to October 1944, during which the NDH regained control of the entirety of Dalmatia and German troops replaced the Italian ones, is not covered by this chapter.[2]

Central Dalmatia between the NDH and Italy

The establishment of the NDH was proclaimed in April 1941, during the Axis invasion of Yugoslavia, and the state was placed under the control of the Ustasha movement headed by Ante Pavelić, who had lived in Italian exile until then. In May 1941, the NDH and the Kingdom of Italy signed the Treaties of Rome. On this basis, Italy annexed, among other territories, parts of the littoral of northern and central Dalmatia, including the city of Split (see Map 2). The treaties also stipulated the creation, on

NDH territory, of a so-called 'demilitarized zone', which was around 50–70 kilometres wide and stretched along the Adriatic Sea. The NDH committed not to maintain a navy or erect fortifications in that area. Although Italy and the NDH were, in principle, allies, the Italian annexation of part of the Croatian littoral soured relations between Rome and Zagreb until the Italian capitulation in September 1943.

Soon after its creation, the NDH initiated a policy of state terror against the ethnic Serbs, who made up a large part of the population of the NDH. This led to their uprising against the Ustasha regime. In September 1941, the Italian army used this situation as a pretext to occupy the demilitarized zone. The Italian Second Army ordered the Croatian Home Guard, the regular army of the NDH, to withdraw the majority of its forces from the demilitarized zone. The Italian military command took control of the remaining Croatian units, and the NDH gendarmerie had to cooperate with the Italian *Carabinieri*. The Italian army took responsibility for all public safety issues, while the NDH administration was in charge of civilian affairs, including supplying the local population with food. The NDH established a General Administrative Commission (*Opće upravno povjereništvo*) to coordinate its activities with the Italian Second Army. With the occupation of the demilitarized zone, the Italians further reduced the influence of the NDH along the Adriatic Sea. The Italian army retained control of this zone until the capitulation of Italy in September 1943.

In the meantime, the insurgents in the NDH gradually split into two opposing camps. One remained loyal to the Kingdom of Yugoslavia and formed Chetnik units, composed mostly of ethnic Serbs, while the Communist Party of Yugoslavia (*Komunistička partija Jugoslavije* – KPJ) formed the People's Liberation Movement (*Narodnooslobodilački pokret* – NOP) with its Partisan army. In other parts of the NDH, ethnic Serbs initially dominated the Partisan ranks, but in central Dalmatia, a region almost entirely inhabited by Croats, the Partisan movement could count on many Croats joining.

After the Treaties of Rome had been signed, the part of central Dalmatia remaining within the NDH became the Great County of Cetina, with its seat in the coastal town of Omiš. The county consisted of six districts: two were islands (Brač and Hvar), two were on the Adriatic coast (Omiš and Makarska) and two were in the hinterland (Imotski and Sinj) (see Map 7). The Great County of Cetina had around 250,000 inhabitants.

The terrain in this area consists of a narrow coastal belt along the Adriatic Sea, with a range of mountains separating it from the hinterland, which is mostly a karst region with a few larger arable plains. In the interwar period, central Dalmatia was largely under-developed and rural. There were olive groves and vineyards on the coast, as well as fishing and seafaring. In the hinterland, in addition to agriculture, the peasants were also engaged in cattle breeding (sheep). From the end of the nineteenth century until the world economic crisis in 1929, a significant number of people migrated to North and South America, sending remittances to support those who stayed.[3]

Because of these characteristics, central Dalmatia was considered a 'passive area', which depended on food imports from 'active' agricultural areas north of the Sava River (see Map 2).[4] Between 1939 and 1941, already before the Axis invasion, there were problems with the supply of foodstuffs. But this was just a foretaste of the dire situation that was to be unleashed by the competition between the NDH, the Italian army and the Partisans.

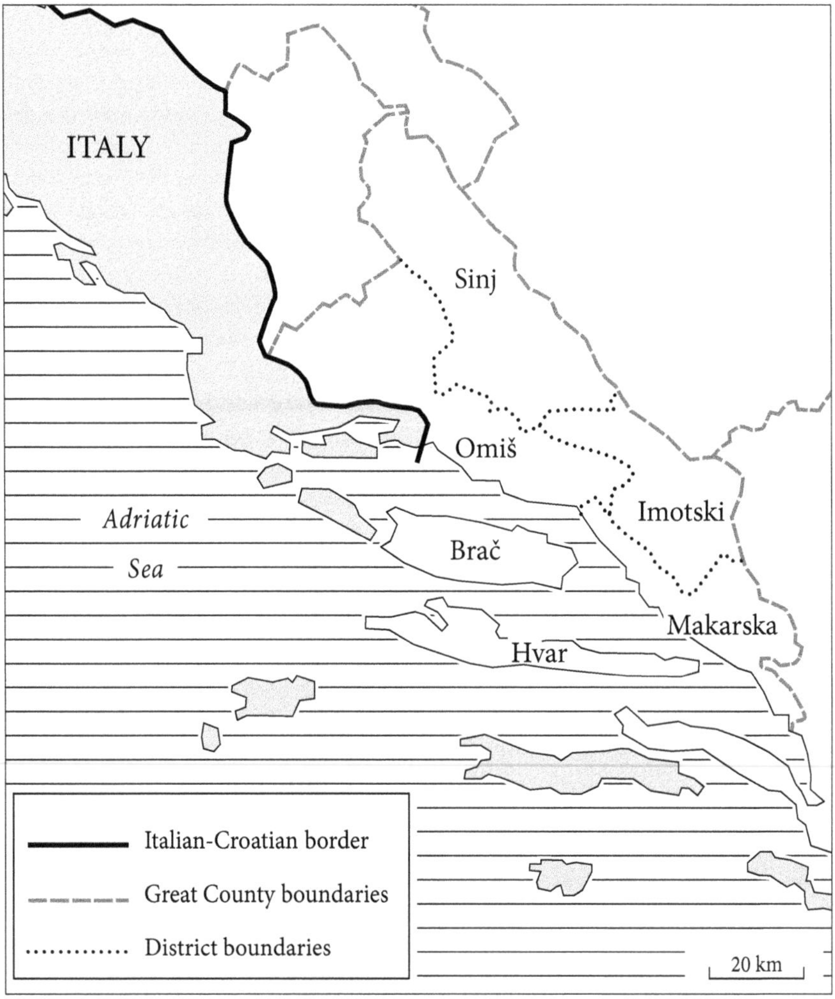

Map 7 The Great County of Cetina in 1941.

The food supply system in the NDH and central Dalmatia

While the NDH lost certain parts of Dalmatia, it did encompass Slavonia and Syrmia, two rich agricultural regions located north of the Sava River (see Map 2). Despite this, supplying the population was a growing problem for the NDH authorities.[5] A major obstacle to the transportation of food to the passive areas south of the Sava River, including Dalmatia, were the overburdened railway lines, which soon became the target of repeated Partisan attacks.

The Bosnian railway line from Brod na Savi in Slavonia, through Sarajevo and Mostar in Bosnia-Herzegovina, to Metković and Dubrovnik on the Adriatic coast was crucial for the supply of central Dalmatia.[6] Trains were mostly destined for the port of Metković, where food was loaded onto ships and transported to the islands of Brač and Hvar and the ports of Makarska and Omiš, and then by road from Omiš to Sinj. In addition, from the summer of 1942, some of the food for northern and central Dalmatia was sent to the Italian port of Fiume/Rijeka, on the northern Adriatic coast and from there shipped to Dalmatia. After the food arrived in the Great County of Cetina, a network of district, municipal and village committees established by the NDH authorities was responsible for the fair allocation of food rations and distributing them to the population.

The first signs of the food crisis that was about to unfold were reported in late 1941. Local authorities in the Great County of Cetina drew attention to the difficulties with food supplies. In December 1941, the gendarmerie in Omiš reported that the population had received insufficient quantities of cereals and had not received any other type of food either (lard, pasta, oil, etc.).[7] In the same month, the Supetar district (Brač) noted that during the summer, fish and home-grown vegetables were added to the population's diet, but by the end of the year, with no food being sent to the island, the situation had become very difficult. There had even been cases of villagers slaughtering their mules or donkeys to feed their children.[8]

In January 1942, the head of the Makarska municipality informed Zagreb that the shortage of food contributed to the spread of 'communist propaganda'.[9] The gendarmerie in Sinj also reported that a significant part of the population was dissatisfied with the current regime, or even hostile to it, a situation which was likely to escalate due to the inadequate food supplies.[10] In response to this and similar reports, the Ministry of Crafts, Trade and Industry stated in late January 1942 that it had done everything within its powers to feed Bosnia, Herzegovina and Dalmatia. In the past month, the NDH authorities had sent a total of 250 wagons of food to the Great County of Cetina. This should have been enough to provide each inhabitant with 150 grams of food (cereals) per day. The ministry acknowledged that this was barely sufficient to 'sustain life', but until the new harvest, larger quantities could not be expected.[11] In addition, the 150 grams the ministry referred to were only intended for those who had no home-grown resources or did not receive food supplies from another source (as those serving in the Croatian Home Guard did, for example).[12]

In late February 1942, the Great County of Cetina complained to the Ministry of Crafts, Trade and Industry that the problem was not only the shortage of cereals, but a general lack of all types of food. Of a total population of around 250,000, only 20,000 had sufficient grain until the next harvest, 100,000 had enough grain for the next few months, while the rest of the population had no food at all. Such a poorly fed population could not be expected to toil in the fields during the following months. In light of this, the Great County of Cetina demanded an increase in the daily supply of cereals per capita to 400 grams for adults and 200 grams for children.[13]

But from September 1941 to April 1942, the NDH authorities were unable to meet this demand and could not even secure the modest 150 grams of cereals per person per day. Food did not arrive regularly and was not distributed evenly. In April 1942, representatives from the authorities in Zagreb visited central Dalmatia to inspect the situation. They concluded that even before the war, Dalmatia had not been able to sustain itself with its own meagre resources. In the past, fishing, seafaring, tourism and remittances from citizens living abroad had brought some money into the region, but, with the war, all these sources of income had disappeared. Consequently, in 1941–42, the Dalmatians had a 'very difficult winter' and the 'expression of hunger' could be seen in their faces.[14]

In mid-1942, the military developments in the hinterland brought new problems. In its advance westward through Bosnia, the core of the Partisan brigades, led by Josip Broz Tito, had destroyed part of the Sarajevo-Mostar railway line, which meant no trains ran for several weeks. In early August 1942, the Great County of Cetina reported that it had not received any food in the last three months.[15] From August to October 1942, some food did arrive, but again far less than the minimum requirements. According to some estimates, the NDH authorities delivered only 2.4 kilograms of cereals and 6.4 kilograms of potatoes per capita during this period, while the minimum requirements were 6 kilograms of cereals and 9 kilograms of potatoes.[16]

As the next winter was approaching, the gendarmerie in Omiš reported in late 1942 that 'general starvation' was imminent.[17] In March 1943, military operations in Bosnia aggravated the situation once more. As the Partisans were withdrawing before the Axis forces, they blew up the bridge on the Sarajevo-Mostar railway line, interrupting supplies to Dalmatia for several weeks again.[18]

During April and May 1943, a certain amount of maize and potatoes was delivered, but again, this was insufficient.[19] With the arrival of spring, farmers could count on their own vegetable production, and there were also hopes that the coming harvest would provide grain for at least part of the population. However, the NDH authorities feared that the Partisans might gather the harvest themselves.[20] The command of the Croatian Home Guard in Sinj asked the Italian army to provide security for the harvesters, and the Italians expressed willingness to help.[21] However, in August 1943, an NDH intelligence report stated that the region of Sinj, which had produced an abundant crop, was under the control of the Partisans.[22]

The NDH was therefore often unable to provide central Dalmatia with even the minimum amount of food, and this weakened its legitimacy. In July 1943, the gendarmerie in Omiš concluded that poor supply of food was one of the main reasons for the population's negative attitude towards the NDH regime.[23] Two months later, the Croatian minister of economy stated that the NDH had 'the smallest ration of bread' in Europe.[24]

Confronted with an inadequate supply of food from Zagreb, the Great County of Cetina took measures to promote fishing in order to secure fish for its population. But from the summer of 1942, the Italian army began restricting the movement of fishing boats in the Adriatic Sea to prevent the Partisans from using them.[25] The Italian authorities gathered these boats in the ports under their control, and limited their freedom of movement to the vicinity of Italian garrisons.[26] These measures greatly restricted fishing. The gendarmerie in Omiš reported in November 1942 that the Italians had deprived the local inhabitants of the opportunity to procure fish, which could have been used as food during the coming winter.[27] When the summer fishing season began in April 1943, fish was available at the markets, but it was expensive, and many citizens could not afford to buy it.[28] As this example shows, the competition between the Italian and NDH authorities in central Dalmatia made an already-difficult situation even more complex.

Local consequences of inadequate food provision

The difficulties in transporting food, compounded by rivalries between Italy and the NDH and acts of sabotage by the Partisans, were not the only cause of the dire situation on the ground. Another factor was the uneven distribution of food at the local level. For example, in early 1942, representatives of the central authorities in Zagreb noticed that the district of Imotski was much better supplied than other parts of the Great County of Cetina. The food arrived in Imotski through various channels and the responsible authorities were completely oblivious to this. The quantity of maize transported to Imotski was so high that the local population was able to sell it in the neighbouring districts or exchange it for olive oil and wine.[29] It seems that the reason Imotski managed to secure such a favourable position was because a significant number of local Ustashas had been in Italian exile with Ante Pavelić and had subsequently obtained senior positions, which enabled them to bypass the regular supply system and secure more food for their native district.[30]

In early 1942, the Great County of Cetina issued various guidelines to ensure the fair and equal distribution of the available food. Members of the committees in charge at the local level had to be 'honest people' who enjoyed the trust of their community. The aim of these measures was to placate the aggrieved population.[31] A report sent to Zagreb in April 1942 stated that the fact that no one was held responsible for abusing the system disappointed the people. As the author added, the population did not expect 'abundance', but it did expect 'justice'.[32]

Despite the measures implemented by the NDH authorities, the distribution of food remained uneven. In early 1943, residents of Omiš and its immediate surroundings received a ration of 150 grams of food a day, and industrial workers received twice as much. But this rationing system did not function in other localities where food was simply unavailable.[33] Under these conditions, the price of food on the free market steadily rose. The price of a kilogram of meat stood at 90 kunas in January 1942, but by August 1943, it was as high as 500 kunas, while the cost of a litre of oil rose from 200 kunas to 1,300–1,500 kunas in the same period.[34] In August 1943, an NDH intelligence report about the Great County of Cetina stated that the population had no access to food rations at a controlled price, while food prices on the free market were so high that most people could not afford to pay them.[35] Additionally, wheat, maize and some other products were often unavailable, even on the free market.

In these circumstances, barter replaced purchase. In late 1941 and early 1942, peasants exchanged 1 litre of olive oil for a few kilograms of maize or beans.[36] This ratio appears to have been to the detriment of the oil producers, as the usual value of olive oil was much higher. In February 1942, the Great County of Cetina asked the authorities in Zagreb to provide ten wagons of maize to be used to exchange for olive oil.[37] It seems that this was seen as the most efficient way to obtain the quantity of oil required by the state.

As mentioned above, the NDH was transporting food by rail from Slavonia and Syrmia to the passive southern areas of the state. At the same time, many people from these areas travelled north to purchase food or to work in agriculture. These agricultural workers were often paid in grain, which they then took back home. Very soon, the trains travelling southward became a hotbed for food smuggling, which disrupted the state supply system. The NDH authorities introduced a series of measures to curb these illegal activities and to stop individuals travelling north in order to obtain food. That said, they knew that they were unable to provide enough food to the passive areas and, therefore, for political reasons, never attempted to completely prevent people from acquiring certain quantities of food from the areas north of the Sava River.[38] At the same time, inadequate supply of food also led to theft. In late 1941, theft of cattle and vegetables became widespread on the island of Brač. The NDH gendarmerie and the Italian army organized patrols to protect the property that was being targeted.[39]

Another sign of the population's despair were public demonstrations against food shortages. In late 1941 and early 1942, large groups of people, mostly women, organized demonstrations in Makarska and Omiš, as well as in Selce (Brač). In Makarska, the NDH authorities arrested several women and sentenced them to ten days in prison. Nonetheless, the same authorities relented, distributing food, or declaring that they would devote more attention to the issue.[40] In June 1942, a total of 200 women gathered in Makarska. The group tried to storm food warehouses but the gendarmes dispersed them. Ultimately the women managed to break into a warehouse, taking 400 kilograms of maize. The authorities arrested the eight 'ringleaders'.[41] Not long after this, women and children held protests in Supetar (Brač).[42] These events are all the more significant, since in the NDH, it was illegal to protest publicly against the regime. Whether these demonstrations were spontaneous or organized by the Communists remains an open question. In a report from March 1942, for example, a representative of the Central Committee of the KPJ refers to 300 women gathering in Stari Grad (Hvar) to demand food. But the report criticized the local Communists for remaining passive, thus missing the opportunity to give the demonstration 'political character'.[43]

In mid-1942, the General Administrative Commission of the NDH asked the Great County of Cetina whether the Partisan movement in central Dalmatia could be suppressed by denying food rations to families whose members had joined the Partisans. The Great County of Cetina rejected the proposal, stating that, due to the NDH's military weakness in the region, such a measure would be counterproductive.[44]

Ultimately, in some cases, the lack of food even led to starvation. In late 1941, the district of Supetar (Brač) reported eight cases of people dying of starvation. These were mostly children, but there were regular cases of the elderly dying of 'general weakness'.[45] In spring 1942, on the same island, there were several cases of people with swollen limbs due to malnutrition, which is a symptom of pellagra or vitamin B3 deficiency.[46] In late 1942, the district of Supetar reported further cases of children and elderly members of the population who were 'swollen and weak'. In fact, several children died of starvation, while dozens of others across the island became 'skeletal' due to lack of food.[47] In May 1943, the NDH authorities also reported the deaths of twenty-three people in the villages of Grabovac and Zagvozd (Imotski).[48]

According to Vladimir Sabolić, from April 1941 to November 1944, almost 5,000 people died of starvation on a territory roughly corresponding to the area of the Great County of Cetina.[49] However, this figure includes the people who died between the capitulation of Italy in September 1943 and the final takeover of Dalmatia by the Partisans in late 1944, a period not covered by this chapter. It can be assumed that the lion's share of the deaths caused by starvation in central Dalmatia occurred after September 1943, when the population found itself in an even more difficult position as regards food provision.

The food policy of the Royal Italian Army

By taking control of the demilitarized zone in September 1941, the Italians also put the NDH authorities in an unfavourable economic position. In October 1941, the NDH agreed to provide food for the Italian troops stationed on its territory, as well as the civilian population living in the parts of Dalmatia annexed by Italy. Both received some supplies from the Italian mainland, but the Italian authorities obviously wanted to supplement these deliveries with food from NDH sources, thus placing an additional burden on Zagreb. Moreover, besides this official arrangement, it did not take very long for people to begin smuggling foodstuffs from the NDH to the annexed areas of Dalmatia, with the complicity of Italian army units stationed in the NDH.[50] In the spring of 1942, for example, the NDH authorities discovered that a significant part of the food allocated to the Great County of Cetina ended up in the city of Split, which the Italians had annexed.[51]

The NDH authorities sought to destroy the Partisans and, with this in mind, supported the counter-insurgency operations conducted by the Italian army in 1942 and 1943. However, these operations also involved harsh measures against the civilian population, including the destruction of houses, cattle and stocks of food. In June 1942, the Italian army conducted one such operation in the Makarska district. The NDH authorities concluded that it had been unable to suppress the Partisans, but that it had inflicted significant suffering on the local population, whose property had been plundered by Italian soldiers. Local NDH authorities reported to their superiors that people should urgently be supplied with food, and that the Italians should avoid conducting further operations, since they would only force the people to find refuge in the woods, and possibly join the Partisans.[52]

In August 1942, the Great County of Cetina claimed that the population was distrustful of the Italian army, whose soldiers were destroying or looting orchards, vineyards and vegetable gardens.[53] In an attempt to prevent unnecessary Italian reprisals against people deemed loyal to the NDH, its representatives tried to appoint liaison officers within the Italian units, who would advise the Italians to refrain from blind repression.[54]

However, in the summer of 1943, shortly before its capitulation, the Italian army conducted a new large-scale operation against the Partisans in the area of Mount

Biokovo (Makarska). The Italian command boasted that it had inflicted significant losses on the enemy, but also reported the complete destruction of infrastructure, as well as the seizure of significant quantities of food that 'certainly belonged to the Partisans'.[55] From the perspective of the NDH authorities, however, this was primarily unnecessary harassment of the Croatian population. In a report on the situation, Croatian Home Guard Colonel Franjo Šimić concluded that the aim of the Italian operation had been only to plunder and destroy.[56]

In other cases, the Italian army took control of the distribution of food, denying provisions to those families with members who belonged to the Partisans. For instance, the Italian army implemented such a measure on the island of Hvar in late 1942. The local NDH authorities were of the view that the Italians did not have accurate information about the Partisans and their families.[57] However, the Communists on Hvar later reported that, by denying food to 'many villages', the Italians had put peasants under pressure and that some of them had agreed to become informants in exchange for food.[58]

The destruction of food stocks and withholding of food rations from Partisan families were only one aspect of the Italian army's policy. Paradoxically, at the same time, the Italian Second Army urged the NDH authorities to improve food supply to the population, warning that any delay could worsen the situation and incite people to join the Partisans.[59]

The NDH authorities also feared that the Italians could use their stronger position to annex some parts of the demilitarized zone and persuade the Croatian people to accept this annexation by proving that Italy, unlike the NDH, was able to provide them with enough food. In April 1942, representatives of the central NDH authorities concluded that the provision of food was much better in Italian-annexed Dalmatia than in the Great County of Cetina, and that this could have a negative impact on the population on the Croatian side of the border.[60]

The competition between Italy and the NDH had very tangible implications for their food policies. In early 1942, for example, the Ustasha Youth (*Ustaška mladež*) in the Great County of Cetina established ninety soup kitchens for children. Ustasha officials considered this an important initiative which aimed to strengthen the legitimacy of the NDH among the population, but they also saw it as a way of preventing the Italian army from doing the same.[61] In reality, the kitchens of the Ustasha Youth in the Great County of Cetina provided food for 11,000 children, but by April 1942, some of them were already closed due to lack of supplies.[62]

A year later, a significant number of children in the town of Hvar had left the Croatian primary school and enrolled in the local Italian one. This was due to the fact that, unlike the Croatian school, the Italian one offered meals to its students. The head of the Hvar district reported to his superiors that it was a pity that Croatian children were being 'denationalized' like this and demanded that meals also be provided for the pupils of the Croatian primary school.[63] It appears therefore that the NDH and Italy were competing not only for the political allegiance of the local population but also, in some cases, for its very national identity.

Moreover, in early 1943, as the Partisans interrupted the Bosnian railway line yet again, even the NDH gendarmerie in Omiš began receiving food rations from the Italian army. Rumours circulated that the Italians were about to take over the entire supply system and, eventually, annex other parts of Dalmatia belonging to the NDH. The gendarmerie also noticed that the Italians were attempting to influence the population of Brač and Hvar, claiming that the food sent to the islands by the NDH authorities via Sušak, a port annexed by Italy, were in fact provided by the Italian authorities.[64]

In early 1943, the General Administrative Commission responsible for coordination between the NDH authorities and the Italian army in the demilitarized zone reached the pessimistic conclusion that in the parts of Dalmatia annexed by the Italians and in Italian-controlled Montenegro, the food supply system 'functioned normally and in an orderly fashion', unlike in the part of the coastal belt controlled by the NDH, where it was largely deficient.[65] It appears therefore that the Italian food policy was multi-layered and to some extent also paradoxical, denying any food supply and destroying food stocks in the areas deemed supportive of the Partisans, but using the provision of food in other areas to gain the political allegiance of the local population and to weaken the influence of the NDH.

The People's Liberation Movement: From hunger as a propaganda tool to the requisition of food

The Partisan movement in Dalmatia could rely on the prewar networks of the Communist Party of Croatia (*Komunistička partija Hrvatske* – KPH), a subdivision of the KPJ created in 1937, as well as on the Croatian (and Yugoslav) patriotic sentiment which opposed Italian imperialism. In late 1941, there were around 800 Partisans in Dalmatia, around 230 of which were in central Dalmatia.[66] Just a year later, this number had risen to 2,100 Partisans in Dalmatia, while around 4,000 Dalmatians had joined the Partisan brigades operating in Bosnia. In September 1943, on the eve of Italian capitulation, the Partisan units in Dalmatia were around 4,500 strong.[67] Large parts of the countryside, where there were no Italian or NDH garrisons, were under the control of the Partisans.[68]

From the beginning, the subject of hunger was an important element of the communist propaganda. It proved an effective approach because the NDH had indeed failed to organize systematic provision of food to the population of central Dalmatia. But spreading propaganda against the Ustasha regime was an easy task. Supplying the Partisan units was more difficult.

In early 1942, Josip Broz Tito, the supreme commander of the Partisan army, stated that the army should primarily be supplied through 'voluntary contributions' from the population, and that Partisan units could also purchase what they needed. When necessary, the Partisans would 'requisition' supplies from the 'wealthier citizens'. In this case, a receipt for the requisitioned goods should be issued to the owner, payable at the end of the war. In addition, 'confiscation' was a measure that the Partisans used against the 'enemies of the people', whose property could be taken for the benefit of the Partisan movement.[69]

In mid-1942, the KPH and the Partisan leadership in Dalmatia concluded that their units had grown in number, but still lacked fighting spirit and discipline. Many of those who had joined the Partisans simply wanted to escape being recruited by the Croatian Home Guard. Such recruits were not motivated to fight. Food supply to the Partisan units was also highlighted as a significant problem. The population itself was largely destitute. This meant that Partisans had to resort to requisitions and confiscations, resulting in some Croatian peasants accepting weapons from the NDH authorities in order to protect their property from the Partisans.[70]

In mid-1942, a report by the NDH authorities describing the situation in the districts of Makarska and Omiš stated that the Partisans were attacking and looting 'our people'.[71] Local NDH authorities in central Dalmatia regularly reported that the Partisans were taking food from the population, as well as cattle grazing in the fields or being transported to towns to be sold.[72] On 26 November 1942, for example, the Partisans intercepted two merchants on their way to the cattle fair in Zadvarje (Imotski) and took 260 sheep, worth 350,000 kunas.[73]

It remains unclear what the Partisans' criteria for requisitioning or confiscating food and cattle were and whether these criteria were evenly and fairly adhered to. In some cases, the Partisans only targeted people who were loyal to the NDH. For example, in late May 1942, a group of Partisans entered the village of Postire (Brač) during the night. They took food and other goods from just three of the people living there and the NDH authorities later reported that this had been done because the victims were 'loyal citizens' and members of the Ustasha movement.[74]

As mentioned above, Tito stipulated that the Partisans had to provide the owner of requisitioned goods with a receipt. It is not known, however, to what extent the Partisans actually issued such receipts. However, the NDH authorities reported that, in August 1942, the Partisans had taken 360 kilograms of grain from a miller in the village of Čaporice (Sinj). They gave the miller a receipt for the confiscated food and instructed him to ask for reimbursement at the headquarters of their Partisan battalion.[75]

In late 1942 and early 1943, the Partisans organized several attacks on villages in the Makarska, Omiš and Sinj districts. These operations took place at night, and the peasants defended themselves with arms provided by the NDH authorities. Through such operations, the Partisans managed to take possession of hundreds, sometimes even thousands of heads of cattle.[76] In other cases, they seized foodstuffs, which they then distributed to the population. In the summer of 1942, for example, the Partisans took large quantities of canned fish and oil from several sardine factories on the islands of Brač and Hvar, which it, for the most part, gave to the local population.[77] For the Partisans, food was not only essential for the maintenance of their military units, but they also used it to consolidate their legitimacy among the civilian population.

The role of the People's Liberation Committees

Along with the Partisan army, the KPJ also set up People's Liberation Committees (*Narodnooslobodilački odbori* – NOO). In October 1941, the communist leadership explained that these committees, which were 'directly and freely' elected by the people, were to become the true organs of the people's power. Their first task was to supply the

Partisan units with all necessities. In addition, they had to feed the population, paying particular attention to the families of the Partisan soldiers. The NOOs required certain resources to be provided by those prepared to sacrifice everything for the struggle and to give up 'peacetime habits and comforts'.[78] Some people gave material support to the NOOs voluntarily, but obviously others did so in order to avoid Partisan retaliation. The Partisans established their network of NOOs in central Dalmatia largely during the second half of 1942. In the towns and villages controlled by the enemy, their activity was clandestine.[79] In early 1943, the Provincial NOO of Dalmatia was established as a body superior to all district, municipal, city and village NOOs.[80]

The island of Brač provides an example of how the NOOs operated. It seems that their aim was to achieve some form of 'redistribution'. Thus, their representatives sometimes pressured the richer peasants to give part of their wine and olive oil to the poor, and exerted similar pressure on fishermen to employ poor people.[81] People's Liberation Committees on Brač also confiscated the property of 'speculators'.[82] In late 1942, the NOO for Sutivan (Brač) organized a public trial of a group of people who had stolen food. The thieves received a suspended death sentence. Their freedom of movement was restricted, and they had to compensate the people they had stolen from. After the trial, the president of the NOO for Sutivan addressed the people who had gathered there, telling them that they should not be worried about their property, because it was protected by the local NOO. After the speech, people cheered the Red Army, Stalin, Tito and the Partisans, and the report by the local committee of the Communist Party in Sutivan concludes that the trial had greatly improved the reputation of the NOO.[83]

In as early as summer 1942, the Partisans organized the harvest as well. For example, Partisan units came to collect the grain belonging to the peasants of the village of Glavaš, located at the foothills of Mount Dinara. But these peasants were loyal to and armed by the NDH, so while conducting the harvest, the Partisans had to repel their attacks.[84] A year later, as a new harvest was approaching, the NDH authorities hoped to collect significant amounts of food but were also worried that the Partisans would take the crops for themselves. Indeed, the NOO for central Dalmatia organized special commissions whose duty was to harvest all fields under Partisan control as well as those belonging to the 'enemies of the people', while other peasants were expected to give 'voluntary contributions'.[85]

Despite the growing strength of the Partisan movement in Dalmatia, it too faced the problem of the lack of resources in that region. In the summer of 1943, the communist leadership for Dalmatia concluded that the NOOs had been reduced to mere 'auxiliary supply bodies', neglecting their political role as organs of the people's power.[86] But such a transformation of the role of the NOOs was hardly surprising given the fact that the Partisans' units could not count on the kind of supply system regular armies enjoyed. In light of these circumstances, the NOO for Dalmatia criticized the district NOO for Hvar for not doing enough to supply the Partisans, emphasizing that the 'consciousness of the people' could only be raised through 'persistent struggle, constant efforts and sacrifices'. The people should learn to make sacrifices in order to gain freedom. It was therefore in the 'interest' of the people to 'give everything for the army'. The people of Hvar should be made aware that, unlike in other regions, such as Bosnia, they did not have to feed thousands of Partisans in even more difficult circumstances.[87]

The Partisan movement achieved significant success in central Dalmatia in the period from 1941 to 1943. Many people joined the Partisan army or supported it. The NDH authorities, in comparison, were weak and largely unpopular, while Italian counter-insurgency operations were often counterproductive, wreaking havoc upon the civilian population and sending it into the arms of the Partisan movement. But, by 1943, the lack of food was also a cause for concern for the Partisans themselves. In May 1943, the Provincial Committee of the KPH for Dalmatia reported:

> Clearly, on our part, we cannot provide any economic assistance to the population in the liberated part of the territory, since we are ourselves dependent on it. … This economic situation has greatly influenced and is still influencing the momentum of the masses for the struggle. Our daily contact and conversations with the people give us the reason: We supported you, we participated in the struggle, we sent our sons to the [Partisan] army, but today we are hungry, we can't support ourselves, and we especially cannot support you, so it would be best if you left us alone.[88]

In April 1943, the gendarmerie in Omiš also reported that, due to war and limited provision of food, the population was exhausted to the point that they no longer trusted the 'communist ideology', despite the fact that they had previously supported it '100 per cent'.[89] However, just five months later, the capitulation of the Kingdom of Italy and the collapse of Italian power on the eastern Adriatic coast gave the Partisan movement the opportunity to strengthen its military and political hold on Dalmatia. Like the other political and military actors of central Dalmatia, however, the Partisans had to develop their own food policy in order to achieve final victory.

Conclusion

During the period from April 1941 to September 1943, central Dalmatia experienced a general food shortage. This region had, in fact, already depended on the import of grain and other food staples before the war. After 1941, the partition of Dalmatia between the NDH and Italy, on the one hand, and the acts of sabotage by the Partisans, on the other, made food supply even more difficult.

The NDH authorities, already weakened by the loss of part of the Adriatic coast, failed to organize food imports from the 'active' regions north of the Sava River to the 'passive' region of central Dalmatia. This failure was due not only to frequent interruptions to railway traffic, but also to the general disorganization of the NDH and, in some cases, to the incompetence or corruption of local authorities. The increasing food shortage in the areas controlled by the NDH further undermined its legitimacy in the eyes of the population.

In the part of central Dalmatia annexed by Italy, food supply was more regular, and the Italian army considered it an important instrument for the maintenance of public order. It also used the supply of food to compete with the NDH authorities in the demilitarized zone created in September 1941, as illustrated by the case of the Great County of Cetina. Officials from the NDH even feared that the Italians would be able to get local support for the annexation of other parts of Dalmatia by supplying the food that the NDH authorities themselves were unable to provide. At the same time, the Italian army was fighting the Partisan movement by systematically destroying agricultural resources in the areas under its control and by denying food aid to the villages supporting the Partisans.

For their part, the Partisans sought to exacerbate the food shortages in the areas controlled by the NDH in order to stir up the discontent of the population. However, as they gained control of larger parts of central Dalmatia, they also had to set up their own food supply system, based on 'voluntary contributions' from the local population, but also on forced requisitions and confiscation of the property of the 'enemies of the people'. In so doing, the Partisans ran the risk of arousing anger about their own food policy and damaging their own legitimacy.

The case of central Dalmatia, and more specifically of the Great County of Cetina, provides a better understanding of the food policies pursued by some of the major protagonists of the Second World War in Southeastern Europe. Providing or denying food was a way of strengthening one's hold on the population. Since the amount of food available during the whole period from April 1941 to September 1943 was insufficient, food thus became an effective weapon.

Notes

1 *Narodnooslobodilačka borba u Dalmaciji 1941–1945. Zbornik dokumenata*, 10 vols., ed. Vinko Branica et al. (Split: Institut za historiju radničkog pokreta Dalmacije, 1981–1986) (henceforth: *NOB u Dalmaciji*).

2 For more on this period, see Nikica Barić, *Ustaše na Jadranu. Uprava Nezavisne Države Hrvatske u jadranskoj Hrvatskoj nakon kapitulacije Kraljevine Italije* (Zagreb: Hrvatski institut za povijest, 2012).

3 For a more detailed account of Dalmatia in the interwar period, see Aleksandar Jakir, *Dalmatien zwischen den Weltkriegen* (Munich: R. Oldenbourg, 1999).

4 See Marica Karakaš Obradov, 'On Nutrition, Harvest and Purchase of Food in the Second World War: Examples from Slavonia and Srijema', *Review of Croatian History* 17, no. 1 (2021): 331–54.

5 For an account of the situation regarding agriculture in the NDH, see Holm Sundhaussen, *Wirtschaftsgeschichte Kroatiens im nationalsocialistischen Großraum 1941–1945* (Stuttgart: DVA, 1983), 263–76; Nikica Barić, 'ZEMPRO/DEPOS: prisilni otkup poljodjelskih proizvoda u NDH', *Scrinia slavonica* 23, no. 1 (2023), 285–315.

6 Nikica Barić, 'Željezničke prometnice u obalnom pojasu Nezavisne Države Hrvatske do kapitulacije Kraljevine Italije', *Časopis za suvremenu povijest* 51, no. 3 (2019): 879–910.

7 Zapovjedništvo oružničkog krila Omiš, 13 December 1941, in *NOB u Dalmaciji*, vol. 1, 1981, doc. 427.

8 Kotarska oblast Supetar, 31 December 1941, Hrvatski državni arhiv (henceforth: HR-HDA), HR-HDA-223, Ministarstvo unutarnjih poslova Nezavisne Države Hrvatske, box 38, doc. 120/1942, I. A.

9 Povjerenik općine Makarska, 15 January 1942, HR-HDA-223, box 39, doc. 676/1942, I. A.

10 Zapovjedništvo oružničkog voda Sinj, 11 January 1942, HR-HDA-491, Opće upravno povjereništvo Nezavisne Države Hrvatske kod II. armate talijanske vojske/ Višeg zapovjedništva talijanskih oružanih snaga 'Slovenija-Dalmacija', box 11, doc. 1063/1942.

11 Glavno tajništvo Predsjedništva vlade NDH, 5 February 1942, HR-HDA-223, box 41, doc. 1376/1942., I. A.

12 'Izvještaj o podjeli hrane i drugih namirnica u Velikoj župi Cetina', 28 April 1942, HR-HDA-211, Hrvatski državni sabor Nezavisne Države Hrvatske, box 9, doc. 1705/1942.

13 Ibid.

14 Ibid.

15 Velika župa Cetina, 9 August 1942, in *NOB u Dalmaciji*, vol. 3, 1982, doc. 264.

16 Povjereništvo za opskrbu obalnog pojasa u Zagrebu, 2 November 1942, HR-HDA-491, box 28, doc. 12.625/1942.

17 Zapovjedništvo oružničkog krila Omiš, 18 November 1942, in *NOB u Dalmaciji*, vol. 4, 1983, doc. 376.

18 Zapovjedništvo oružničkog krila Omiš, 18 March 1943, in *NOB u Dalmaciji*, vol. 5, 1983, doc. 319; Barić, 'Željezničke prometnice', 902–3.

19 Zapovjedništvo oružničkog krila Omiš, 4 May 1943, in *NOB u Dalmaciji*, vol. 6, 1984, doc. 286; Velika župa Cetina, 4 June 1943, ibid., doc. 296.

20 Velika župa Cetina, 30 June 1943, HR-HDA-491, box 43, doc. 5880/1943; Zapovjedništvo oružničkog krila Omiš, 3 July 1943, in *NOB u Dalmaciji*, vol. 7, 1984, doc. 287.

21 Opće upravno povjereništvo NDH, 7 June 1943, HR-HDA-491, box 40, doc. 4913/1943; Opće upravno povjereništvo NDH, 16 June 1943, HR-HDA-491, box 41, doc. 5136/1943.

22 Glavno ravnateljstvo za javni red i sigurnost, agent "Broj 500", 17 August 1943, HR-HDA-1549, Zbirka zapisa upravnih i vojnih vlasti Nezavisne Države Hrvatske i Narodnooslobodilačkog pokreta, I-53/891-897.

23 Zapovjedništvo oružničkog krila Omiš, 17 July 1943, in *NOB u Dalmaciji*, vol. 7, 1984, doc. 297.

24 Ministar narodnog gospodarstva, 30 September 1943, HR-HDA-211, box 5, Predsjednički spisi, doc. 847/1943.

25 Zapovjedništvo Mornarice NDH, 19 September 1942, HR-HDA-491, box 26, doc. 10.501/1942; Ministarstvo vanjskih poslova NDH, 22 September 1942, HR-HDA-491, box 26, doc. 10.512/1942.

26 'Upute talijanskog Vojno-pomorskog zapovjedništva Dalmacije za borbu protiv partizana na moru', 10 April 1943, in *NOB u Dalmaciji*, vol. 6, doc. 126.

27 Zapovjedništvo oružničkog krila Omiš, 18 November 1942, in *NOB u Dalmaciji*, vol. 4, doc. 376.

28 Zapovjedništvo oružničkog krila Omiš, 4 May 1943, in *NOB u Dalmaciji*, vol. 6, doc. 286.

29 'Izvještaj o podjeli hrane i drugih namirnica u Velikoj župi Cetina', 28 April 1942, HR-HDA-211, box 9, doc. 1705/1942.

30 Župska promidžba Velike župe Cetina, 29 April 1942, HR-HDA-237, Glavno ravnateljstvo za promičbu pri Predsjedništvu vlade NDH, box 2, secret doc. 496/1942.

31 'Izvještaj o podjeli hrane i drugih namirnica u Velikoj župi Cetina', 28 April 1942, HR-HDA-211, box 9, doc. 1705/1942.

32 Don Frane Komić, 19 April 1942, in *NOB u Dalmaciji*, vol. 2, doc. 486.
33 Opće upravno povjereništvo NDH, 9 January 1943, HR-HDA-491, box 32, doc. 973/1943.
34 Prices from January 1942 in fact refer to Sinj; see Zapovjedništvo oružničkog voda Sinj, 11 January 1942, HR-HDA-491, box 11, doc. 1063/1942. For data on prices from August 1943, see Zapovjedništvo oružničkog krila Omiš, 3 September 1943, in *NOB u Dalmaciji*, vol. 8, 1985, doc. 458 and Glavno ravnateljstvo za javni red i sigurnost, agent "Broj 550", 25 August 1943, HR-HDA-1549, I-53/964-5.
35 Glavno ravnateljstvo za javni red i sigurnost, agent "Broj 550", 25 August 1943, HR-HDA-1549, I-53/964-965.
36 Kotarska oblast Supetar, 31 December 1941, HR-HDA-223, box 38, doc. 120/1942, I. A; Zapovjedništvo oružničkog krila Omiš, 17 January 1942, in *NOB u Dalmaciji*, vol. 2, doc. 435.
37 'Izvještaj o podjeli hrane i drugih namirnica u Velikoj župi Cetina', 28 April 1942, HR-HDA-211, box 9, doc. 1705/1942.
38 Nikica Barić, 'Brod na Savi i krijumčarenje hrane na željeznicama za vrijeme Nezavisne Države Hrvatske', *Prilozi za povijest Broda i okolice* 2 (2015): 163–93.
39 Kotarska oblast Supetar, 30 November 1941, HR-HDA-223, box 37, doc. 5034/1941, I. A.
40 'Naš izvještaj', 30.12.1941, in *NOB u Dalmaciji*, vol. 1, doc. 137; 'Naš izvještaj', 23 January 1942, *NOB u Dalmaciji*, vol. 2, doc. 13; 'Naš izvještaj', 14 February 1942, ibid., doc. 22; Velika župa Cetina, 28 January 1942, ibid., doc. 439.
41 Velika župa Cetina, 9 June 1942, in *NOB u Dalmaciji*, vol. 2, doc. 507.
42 Velika župa Cetina, 21 June 1942, HR-HDA-491, box 34, doc. 1826/1943.
43 Delegat CK KPJ i VŠ NOP i DVJ, 17 March 1942, in *NOB u Dalmaciji*, vol. 2, doc. 34.
44 Velika župa Cetina, 19 May 1942, HR-HDA-491, box 20, doc. 6856/1942.
45 Kotarska oblast Supetar, 30 November 1941, HR-HDA-223, box 37, doc. 5034/1941, I. A.
46 'Izvještaj o podjeli hrane i drugih namirnica u Velikoj župi Cetina', 28 April 1942, HR-HDA-211, box 9, doc. 1705/1942.
47 Opće upravno povjereništvo NDH, 2 December 1942, HR-HDA-491, box 28, doc. 13.220/1942.
48 Velika župa Cetina, 24 May 1943, HR-HDA-491, box 40, doc. 4985/1943; Velika župa Cetina, 4 June 1943, in *NOB u Dalmaciji*, vol. 6, doc. 296.
49 Vladimir Sabolić, 'Osnovna pitanja djelovanja KPH na području južne Dalmacije 1944–1945. godine', in *Dubrovnik u Narodnooslobodilačkoj borbi i socijalističkoj revoluciji 1941–1945*, ed. Miroslav Ćurin (Split: Institut za historiju radničkog pokreta Dalmacije, 1985), 343.
50 'Report by the NDH authorities submitted to German representatives on economic relations between the NDH and Italy', n.d., National Archives and Records Administration, Washington DC, T-120, roll 744, frames 362083-92; Oddone Talpo, *Dalmazia, Una cronaca per la storia (1941)* (Rome: Stato maggiore dell'esercito, Ufficio storico, 1995), 840–1; Sanela Schmid, *Deutsche und italienische Besatzung im Unabhängigen Staat Kroatien, 1941 bis 1943/45* (Berlin/Boston: De Gruyter, 2020), 130–1.
51 'Izvještaj o podjeli hrane i drugih namirnica u Velikoj župi Cetina', 28 April 1942, HR-HDA-211, box 9, doc. 1705/1942.
52 Velika župa Cetina, 29 January 1943, HR-HDA-491, box 34, doc. 7388/1942.

53 Velika župa Cetina, 9 August 1942, in *NOB u Dalmaciji*, vol. 3, doc. 264.
54 Opće upravno povjereništvo NDH, 28 January 1943, HR-HDA-491, box 34, doc. 1988/1943.
55 Zapovjedništvo talijanskog 6. armijskog zbora, 22 July 1943, in *NOB u Dalmaciji*, vol. 7, doc. 196.
56 Zapovjedništvo 6. pješačke divizije, 22 July 1943, ibid., doc. 300.
57 Kotarska oblast Hvar, 29 December 1942, HR-HDA-491, box 34, doc. 1976/1943.
58 Općinski NOO Stari Grad, n.d. [February 1943], in *NOB u Dalmaciji*, vol. 5, doc. 50.
59 Comando della 2nda armata, Ufficio affari civili, 12 March 1942, HR-HDA-491, box 13, doc. 2498/1942; Opće upravno povjereništvo NDH, 9 January 1943, HR-HDA-491, box 32, doc. 973/1943.
60 'Izvještaj o podjeli hrane i drugih namirnica u Velikoj župi Cetina', 28 April 1942, HR-HDA-211, box 9, doc. 1705/1942; Opće upravno povjereništvo NDH, 7 April 1942, HR-HDA-491, box 15, doc. 3314/1942.
61 Župska promidžba Velike župe Cetina, 29 April 1942, HR-HDA-237, box 2, secret doc. 496/1942.
62 'Izvještaj o podjeli hrane i drugih namirnica u Velikoj župi Cetina', 28 April 1942, HR-HDA-211, box 9, doc. 1705/1942.
63 Velika župa Cetina, 27 April 1943, HR-HDA-491, box 39, doc. 4264/1943.
64 Zapovjedništvo oružničkog krila Omiš, 4 April 1943, in *NOB u Dalmaciji*, vol. 6, doc. 278; Zapovjedništvo oružničkog krila Omiš, 4 May 1943, ibid., doc. 286.
65 Opće upravno povjereništvo NDH, 12 March 1943, HR-HDA-491, box 37, doc. 3179/1943.
66 Drago Gizdić, *Dalmacija 1941, Prilozi historiji Narodnooslobodilačke borbe* (Zagreb: Izdavačko poduzeće '27. srpanj', 1959), 472–6.
67 Barić, *Ustaše na Jadranu*, 61–2.
68 Drago Gizdić, *Dalmacija 1942, Prilozi historiji Narodnooslobodilačke borbe* (Zagreb: Glavni odbor Saveza boraca Hrvatske, 1959), 768–9.
69 Vrhovni komandant NOP i DVJ, January 1942, in *Zbornik dokumenata i podataka o Narodnooslobodilačkom ratu jugoslovenskih naroda*, series II, vol. 2 (Belgrade: Vojnoizdavački zavod 'Vojno delo', 1954), doc. 115.
70 Pokrajinski komitet KPH za Dalmaciju, April 1942, in *NOB u Dalmaciji*, vol. 2, doc. 50; Pokrajinski komitet KPH za Dalmaciju, May 1942, ibid., doc. 75; Štab 4. operativne zone, 7 June 1942, ibid., doc. 108.
71 Ministarstvo vanjskih poslova NDH, 19 June 1942, HR-HDA-491, box 20, doc. 6674/1942.
72 Velika župa Cetina, 25 November 1942, HR-HDA-491, box 29, doc. 13.656/1942.
73 Velika župa Cetina, 30 September 1942, in *NOB u Dalmaciji*, vol. 4, doc. 382.
74 Velika župa Cetina, 2 June 1942, HR-HDA-491, box 19, doc. 6188/1942.
75 Velika župa Cetina, 3 October 1942, in *NOB u Dalmaciji*, vol. 4, doc. 351.
76 Velika župa Cetina, 19 April 1943, HR-HDA-491, box 38, doc. 4119/1943; Velika župa Cetina, 24 May 1943, HR-HDA-491, box 40, doc. 4985/1943; Velika župa Cetina, 7 June 1943, HR-HDA-491, box 41, doc. 5375/1943; Velika župa Cetina, 12 December 1942, in *NOB u Dalmaciji*, vol. 4, doc. 388; Velika župa Cetina, 29 December 1942, ibid., doc. 402.
77 Velika župa Cetina, 3 August 1942, HR-HDA-491, box 24, doc. 8852/1942; Četa bračkih partizana, July 1942, NOB u Dalmaciji, vol. 2, doc. 176; Velika župa Cetina, 12 July 1942, ibid., doc. 536.

78 'Narodnooslobodilački odbori moraju postati istinski privremeni nosioci narodne vlasti', *Borba*, 19 October 1941, in *Istorijski arhiv Komunističke partije Jugoslavije*, series 1, vol. 1 (Belgrade: Istorijski odelenje CK KPJ, 1949), 18–20.
79 Sekretarijat Pokrajinskog NOO-a Dalmacije, 25 July 1943, in *NOB u Dalmaciji*, vol. 7, doc. 37.
80 'Zapisnik s prve sjednice Pokrajinskog NOO-a Dalmacije', 28–29 January 1943, in *NOB u Dalmaciji*, vol. 5, doc. 40; 'NOO Dalmacije', 7 February 1943, ibid., doc. 57.
81 Velika župa Cetina, 19 June 1942, HR-HDA-491, box 20, doc. 6811/1942.
82 Mjesni komitet KPH Bol, 26 August 1942, in *NOB u Dalmaciji*, vol. 3, doc. 69; Mjesni komitet KPH Bol, 5 October 1942, HR-HDA-1847, Okružni komitet KPH za srednje dalmatinsko otočje, box 1, doc. KP-325/5542.
83 Mjesni komitet KPH Sutivan, 31 January 1943, HR-HDA-1847, box 1, doc. KP-325/5550.
84 Štab srednjodalmatinskog NOP odreda, 1 July 1942, in *NOB u Dalmaciji*, vol. 2, doc. 150; Štab srednjodalmatinskog NOP odreda, 9 September 1942, ibid., doc. 162; Štab srednjodalmatinskog NOP odreda, 9 July 1942, ibid., doc. 164.
85 Okružni komitet KPH za srednju Dalmaciju, 12 August 1943, in *NOB u Dalmaciji*, vol. 7, doc. 18.
86 Pokrajinski komitet KPH za Dalmaciju, 5 August 1943, ibid., doc. 68.
87 Sekretarijat Predsjedništva NOO Dalmacije, 22 March 1943, in *NOB u Dalmaciji*, vol. 5, doc. 111.
88 Pokrajinski komitet KPH za Dalmaciju, 17 May 1943, in *NOB u Dalmaciji*, vol. 6, doc. 39.
89 Zapovjedništvo oružničkog krila Omiš, 19 April 1943, ibid., doc. 283.

8

'To live by the gun': Food insecurity, ethnic violence and political mobilization in occupied Greece (1941–44)

Spyros Tsoutsoumpis

What is the impact of economic and material shortages on inter- and intra-communal relations? How does food scarcity and material insecurity affect ethnic conflict and political mobilization? Or, conversely, how and to what extent does ethnic violence contribute to food insecurity? This chapter addresses these questions by focusing on the ethnic conflict between the Greek and Albanian communities in the region of Thesprotia from 1941 to 1944. Wartime Greece experienced a protracted nutrition crisis which resulted in a devastating famine. While scholars have recognized the role of food insecurity, and the concomitant social transformations caused by famine and scarcity, as a key factor in the rise of the resistance, they remain agnostic on its impact on ethnic conflict within and beyond this part of the world.[1] As a result, the political economies of ethnic violence, in general, and the intersection between violence and food insecurity, in particular, both remain under-researched and under-theorized.[2] The absence of relevant studies is no less pronounced outside the confines of occupied Greece. Recent studies have provided important insights on the use of food as part of the Axis and Allied wartime strategies, yet they have rarely considered the role of food insecurity in the onset and escalation of ethnic conflict.[3]

Thesprotia provides a unique vantage point to explore these issues. Between 1941 and 1944, the area experienced both high levels of ethnic violence and a major nutrition crisis. In mid-1942 the Red Cross described the region as being in the 'grip of famine-like conditions'. The situation was particularly serious in upland areas, where hunger caused numerous deaths.[4] While these processes developed synchronously, they have rarely been studied together. As a result, the interrelationship between food insecurity and violence is neglected in most studies, which treat the conflict in Thesprotia as a by-product of deep-seated ethnic cleavages.[5]

This chapter builds on this scholarship by placing food at the centre of the enquiry and reassessing its role as a driver and motivator of violence. Food insecurity has primarily been analysed through the lens of the state. The body of literature that emerged was thus interested in determining why scarcity occurred and the role of the state in adopting and dealing with its exigencies. This chapter, in contrast, focuses on the social dynamics of scarcity, exploring how food insecurity produced the social conditions which facilitated ethnic violence. In doing so, it develops an understanding of food insecurity as a process of social transformation which connected and shaped the distinct social, economic and political dynamics contributing to ethnic conflict. The chapter pays particular attention to meso-level transformations and the role and experiences of local actors, including elites, militia chieftains and guerrilla leaders. This approach brings the national and local levels and their respective dynamics together, thereby providing a more nuanced picture of the causes and patterns of violence in the area.[6] The analysis draws from a large array of published and unpublished sources, including local histories, memories and oral testimonies, as well as archival material generated by the Greek state, the Red Cross and the resistance organizations that operated in the area. The material allows a more concise reconstruction of these dynamics from both civilian and military perspectives.

Food, violence and politics in the interwar period

Thesprotia is located on the northwestern edge of Epirus (see Map 5). The area was part of the Ottoman Empire before it was incorporated into the Greek state after the Balkan Wars of 1912–13. Over 80 per cent of the area is mountainous, with narrow valleys and a small coastal plain providing the only fertile land.[7] This location has contributed to the area's cultural and economic isolation. In the prewar period, a significant segment of the population made a living out of seasonal or permanent migration to southern Greece, the United States and Egypt. A smaller percentage of the population were farmers, foresters and shepherds. The main cash crops were maize and olive oil.[8] Extreme poverty was common, especially in the mountains.[9] The situation was marginally better in some of the lowland villages, particularly the Albanian communities located along the Ionian coast and the Kalamas valley.[10]

The Greek state tried to alleviate this situation through a combination of land distribution and public works in 1923–24. Land distribution in the area was part of a state-wide scheme to resettle refugees from Asia Minor by breaking up landed estates and church-owned land. This move had two aims. The first was to accelerate the pace of Hellenization and homogenize the border areas which had significant minority populations; the second was to modernize patterns of cultivation and alleviate rural poverty.[11] In Thesprotia, much of the best land was held by Albanian peasants. The distribution thus affected them disproportionately, reducing many of them to poverty without attenuating the situation among upland peasants, who were only able to obtain inferior quality land.[12] The Albanian population complained that the distribution went too far, while many Greek citizens claimed that the state had not been bold enough. Land scarcity exacerbated social tensions.[13] Land-hungry peasants attempted to enclose their properties and open up new lands in the hills, which sparked a hostile reaction from the pastoralists who traditionally used the land for their flocks.[14] Rivalry between villagers escalated into violent skirmishes, although most of the violence was directed towards co-ethnics rather than members of other ethnic groups.[15]

From 1928 to 1932, the government of liberal premier Eleftherios Venizelos took various measures in an attempt to tackle these problems. It tried, for example, to normalize relations with the country's neighbours and managed to resolve some of the issues surrounding the appropriation of estates and the plight of local minorities. The government reimbursed landowners and returned urban properties that were illegally appropriated by the state.[16] These changes met with a positive response from the Albanian population. However, the lack of infrastructure meant that the problems affecting agriculture persisted. Malnutrition was common and diseases such as malaria, scurvy and tuberculosis wreaked havoc among the local peasants. They continued to flee the rural areas to seek employment abroad, while poverty-fuelled crime remained endemic in the area. The economic crisis of 1929 and the concomitant restrictions on immigration from Europe to America further exacerbated the situation. By the 1930s the area had slipped into extreme poverty.[17] The establishment of General Ioannes Metaxas' dictatorship did little to alleviate the situation, while some of its policies, such as the replacement of Albanian mayors and councilmen with Greeks, further alienated the minority.[18]

That said, none of these developments led to the political radicalization of either the Greek or the Albanian community. The Albanian state was too poor and too chaotic for most local Albanian peasants whose loyalties remained with their home communities, faith and clan. The local Albanian community was divided into different factions or *tarafs* with distinct lineages, interests and political orientations. Violence between the competing clans was commonplace and politics were fragmented and shaped by local rather than nationalist or group interests.[19] Such divisions were no less prominent in nationalist and separatist circles, which were split between the Dino clan of Paramythia with its pro-Italian sympathies and the Demi clan of Filiates with its liberal and social-democratic tendencies.[20] Consequently, neither the local peasantry nor the separatist elements were able to mount an effective challenge to the Greek state.

The Italian occupation of Albania in 1939 did little to change this. The nationalizing propaganda of the Greek state had failed to garner support among the local Greek population, who continued to view the state with suspicion if not with downright hostility. Lastly, the communist left was unable to make any headway since its efforts were constantly hindered by the deeply conservative nature of the peasantry, the reactions of local elites and the repressive measures of the Metaxas regime.[21] On the eve of the war, little had changed in the area, which remained blighted by poverty, beset by conflict and isolated from the political mainstream. The isolation was not to last long, however. The arrival of new political and military actors and the beginning of the 'New Order' imposed by the Axis powers were about to plunge this marginal area into an unforeseen political maelstrom.

Occupation and the rise of the resistance

The Second World War arrived in the area on 28 October 1940, when Italian troops invaded Greece and crossed into Thesprotia. The first days of the war were marked by panic and confusion caused by the indiscriminate bombing of border towns such as

Filiates and the fear that the Albanian minority would rise up and join the advancing troops. Such fears did not materialize, however, at least not to the extent anticipated by the Greek population. Some Albanian communities welcomed the Italians, particularly in the area around the town of Margariti. Yet most fell short of taking a stand, and many even took advantage of the situation to loot their neighbours.[22]

There was, however, no return to normality, even after the Italian army was repelled north of the border. The Greek state displaced thousands of adult Albanian males, forcing them to migrate to southern Greece, as the authorities saw them as a possible fifth column for the invaders. Mass displacement had a whole range of side effects. Local Greeks used the opportunity to harass and rob the remaining population, which mostly comprised women, children and the elderly.[23] Military mobilization, mass displacement and the commandeering of food supplies, material and pack animals by the army also had a profound effect on the local economy. Food production fell sharply as thousands of acres remained fallow due to the lack of working hands and animals, while prices rose sharply because of the increased demand for food and raw material for the war effort. A local contemporary estimated that prices rose over 50 per cent during the war.[24]

The Greek army and state capitulated in April 1941. Greece was subsequently divided into different zones of occupation controlled by the Bulgarian, Italian and German militaries. The area, along with the rest of Epirus, passed into Italian hands. While the Italian army adopted a pro-Albanian line, they fell short of supporting local Albanian separatists as they were wary of alienating the Greek government and inciting resistance among the Greek population. The Italians tried to control reactions and build some support among the local population by provisioning goods and social services. Villagers were provided with free food and seed, and rural communities were, on occasion, visited by veterinarians and doctors.[25]

But the impact of such policies was limited. Basic goods such as petrol, matches, cloth and agricultural implements had all but disappeared from the local market. Accordingly, food prices had skyrocketed. Over 80 per cent of the calories consumed by local peasants before the war came from grains and cereals, the majority of which were imported from Romania, Canada and the United States, for instance. Large quantities of these grains were bought by the state and resold at low prices to peasant communities.[26] The war, the division of Greece into separate zones of authority and the Allied blockade meant that imports were greatly reduced. The Italian administration tried to address this by distributing small quantities of pasta and rice, but these were far from sufficient. This situation created famine-like conditions, particularly in the mountainous regions where peasants were almost entirely dependent on cheap imported grain. The situation was further aggravated by the loss of remittances from abroad and from southern Greece. In the Mourgana area, remittances had provided over half the income of hundreds of families who were now reduced to a state of penury. Deaths from hunger and malnutrition became common, particularly in upland villages.[27]

Peasants responded to the situation in a variety of ways. Some resorted to intense cultivation of once fallow areas and the introduction of new crops. Forested areas were cleared and planted with high-yield crops such as tobacco, which were then resold or exchanged for maize and oil. Barter slowly replaced all other types of economic exchange as the economy was demonetized.[28] Masons built houses in exchange for a few sacks of maize and corn, tailors sold or mended trousers and skirts for a pint of olive oil, while teachers provided tuition in exchange for food, firewood and a place to live. These forms of barter involved entire networks of families and villages and entailed long journeys from the mountains to the plains and vice versa.[29] Those who lacked the means and networks to engage in such activities were reduced to begging or working in exchange for food. Peasants from the mountain villages of Lia, Tsamantas and Babouri travelled north to the Albanian area of Vourkos where they worked as fruit and olive pickers. Women and children, particularly widows and orphans who lacked the kinship networks and support to find work or access goods, became itinerant beggars.[30]

The journeys these impoverished people were forced to take were perilous because the countryside was awash with bandits and highwaymen. The Greek army had abandoned huge quantities of weapons which fell into the hands of the local peasantry. The proliferation of weapons, combined with the gradual collapse of the instruments of justice, such as the courts and the gendarmerie, led to a staggering rise in criminality.[31] Some of the gangs came from the Albanian villages of Gardiki, Margariti and Karvounari, and others from the Greek-speaking uplands of Skala and Souli. Banditry and violence were initially not politically or ethnically motivated. Instead, Albanians often robbed and killed other Albanians and Greeks turned against Greeks. The violence which plagued the Greek villages of Grika, Petrovitsa and Gola was mostly waged between fellow villagers who seized the opportunity to settle personal and communal scores.[32]

This situation gradually deteriorated as escalating poverty and a disastrous harvest drove more and more peasants to use violence as a means of survival and profit. Low rainfall and the exceptionally harsh winter of 1941–42 'had a disastrous effect on the harvest and the lack of rain destroyed stockbreeding ... the situation is altogether tragic, over 60 per cent of the population survives by eating corn stems and grass'.[33] Deaths from hunger increased rapidly, reaching epidemic-like proportions in upland areas such as Souli.[34] This situation, combined with growing nationalist agitation by Albanian separatists, politicized local cleavages, gradually rendering the economy the main field of nationalist conflict. These tensions were exemplified by the riots which broke out in the town of Filiates, where Albanian peasants attacked and looted Greek shops, beat up civil servants and destroyed properties.[35] Emboldened by the inactivity of the Italian forces, many went a step further and began occupying properties which had been distributed to Greek peasants during the interwar land distribution. Those who resisted were manhandled and, in many cases, murdered, with their properties being returned to their former owners and the local ruffians and bandits who were helping them. Others tried to reach a compromise by paying the former landowners a monthly tax amounting to one-third of the produce yielded by these properties.[36]

The rise in criminality had a detrimental effect on barter, trade and agriculture. Gangs targeted travelling merchants who they 'robbed and murdered with impunity'.[37] In many cases peasants stopped tilling their fields out of fear that they would be robbed or held for ransom. This led local communities to mobilize and create home guard units, which patrolled their neighbourhood, fending off robbers and thieves.[38] Initially, these groups had no particular political orientation. A local civil servant described the local militias as a type of 'old-time *haiduks*', or 'honour bandits' whose foremost concern was the defence of kin and reputation.[39] The men who led them came from different backgrounds. Some were 'professional' bandits, like Gakis Bolosis, a rural guard from the upland village of Koristiani in the Souli area.[40] In the village of Tsouknida, located south of Koristiani, the first self-defence group was organized by Spiros Ioannou, a small farmer who sought revenge after an Albanian gang abducted one of his relatives. Ioannou was joined by several kinsmen and peasants from his home community. In the upland village of Seliani, such units were formed and led by Spiros Tsamis, an itinerant peddler whose brother was murdered by Albanian highwaymen. These groups had a dual remit. They protected local Greeks from bandit gangs, while also cracking down on thieves and rustlers. Such activities made them particularly popular in their communities who elevated them to hero status.[41]

More organized forms of resistance began to appear in early 1942 when the left-wing National Liberation Front (*Ethniko Apeleftherotiko Metopo* – EAM) and its armed branch, the National Popular Liberation Army (*Ellinikos Laikos Apeleftherotikos Stratos* – ELAS) formed their first hub in Thesprotia. Several months later the rightist National Republican Greek League (*Ethnikos Dimokratikos Ellinikos Sindesmos* – EDES) also made its first appearance in the area.[42]

The two groups had different organizational structures and aims. The left-wing groups adopted a radical emancipatory agenda which entailed the enfranchisement of women, youths and minorities and relied on a well-functioning apparatus operated by political cadres, many of whom had experienced clandestine politics as members of the Communist Party of Greece. The EDES, on the other hand, was much more militarist. The nominal leader of the organization was Lieutenant General Nikolaos Plastiras; however, the real authority rested with Major Napoleon Zervas. The group lacked an organized political apparatus or the backing of a political party. Instead, it relied on the support of local notables who were tasked with forming and funding armed bands in their home districts.[43]

The first volunteers for ELAS and EDES came from the local home defence groups. Bolosis and his men enlisted in EDES, while Tsouknidas joined ELAS.[44] The decision about which group to enrol in was often shaped less by ideology and more by personal connections and kinship networks.[45] However, guerrilla numbers remained small until early 1943. The main reason for this was the severe lack of food and provisions. The area was desperately poor, and the resistance organizations lacked both the means and ability to sustain large bands in the field. The first groups were small in number and lived a peripatetic life. They relied on kinsmen and voluntary contributions for their supply of food and provisions. The harshness of guerrilla life led many volunteers to defect.[46]

The situation began to change after the establishment of the British Special Operations Executive (SOE) in the area. The SOE had already established a presence in central Greece during the winter of 1942–43. The aim of the organization was to bolster resistance activities, thereby keeping the Axis troops busy and diverting them from the main fronts. However, it did not appear in the area until April 1943. The presence of the SOE led to a dramatic shift in the fortunes of the resistance. The British showed a marked preference for the local EDES, which they saw as a useful counterweight to ELAS's growing influence.[47] The organization was provided with much-needed weapons, money and supplies, which they used to consolidate their rule and attract more recruits. The group also promised new recruits a monthly salary, along with a certain quantity of food for their families and a small sum of money upon enlisting.[48]

These offers appealed to the mass of impoverished and unemployed peasants in the area, who saw enlisting in the guerrilla bands of EDES as a means to relieve their financial plight and improve their situation. It was usually the youngest son or unemployed members of a family who were sent to the guerrilla bands with the understanding that half of their salary and any loot they seized would be sent back to their families. Giannis Haliasos, a stonemason from the village of Vereniki, recalled, 'Since I was the youngest son it fell on me to take the risk and join EDES. This way, every month, I could send my family part of my salary and also whatever food I could get, my older brother would stay home and take care of our parents and do a little barter on the side.'[49] Men like Haliasos were far from unique. A local EDES officer complained in his diary, 'Volunteers from these parts are never motivated by ideology. … They join us to put food in their belly, clothes on their back and shoes on their feet.'[50]

These tactics allowed EDES to dominate the local resistance. The number of EDES guerrillas increased from a mere 100 to over 800 between April and June 1943. The ELAS, on the other hand, lagged behind and was unable to deploy or sustain any forces outside the Mourgana mountains where several small bands operated. However, these tactics also had a series of adverse effects. This form of recruitment meant that attachment to EDES ideals and aims was only skin deep. Guerrilla bands retained a localist character and often refused to fight outside their home turf or to obey non-local officers and accept them as leaders. Moreover, this approach politicized food supply and the control of food resources by using it as a means to induce loyalty and sanction non-compliance. Families who refused to join EDES were punished by having their produce and crops destroyed or confiscated by the organization.[51] Despite these problems the guerrillas posed a major challenge to the Italian authorities who lacked the means and manpower to control the countryside. By April 1943, the entire upland area of Souli 'was in a state of revolt', as the resistance groups forbade armed Italians and Albanians from entering their territory on pain of death.[52]

Violence escalates

These developments alarmed the Italian authorities, which began to seek the direct assistance of Albanian communities who they armed and used as auxiliary troops. The Italians had previously toyed with the idea of incorporating Thesprotia and parts of Epirus into a 'Greater Albanian' state. However, such considerations had been abandoned by early 1942, as they presented almost insurmountable political and economic challenges.[53] That said, the Italian authorities did not reject the Albanian entreaties altogether. Many local Albanians openly bore arms in the presence of Italian troops, while Albanian communities were allowed to form local self-government institutions which were known as *keshilla*, or councils, and established their own home guard-type units. At the same time, the Italian authorities tried to avoid 'granting excessive power to such committees', for fear of alienating the Greek communities and state.[54]

This policy changed from the spring of 1943 when the Italians began actively arming and collaborating with these bands against the Greek resistance. The use of ethnically defined auxiliaries was not a local aberration. Similar units were used in parts of Thessaly and western Macedonia where Italian troops also engaged in counter-insurgency operations.[55] The Italian tactics focused on destroying the guerrillas' basis of support by targeting infrastructure, crops and food supplies in the context of a 'scorched earth strategy' the aim of which was to 'strangle the resistance by devastating its living environment'.[56] The control and regulation of food routes and supply were central to this strategy. Food was increasingly transformed, by both the resistance and its opponents, from a commodity and provider of nutrition to a means of exercising political power and drumming up support.

The Italian operations did not stall the activities of the resistance. In fact, recruitment was further accelerated after the Italian capitulation in September 1943. The fall of Italy convinced many local peasants that the liberation was imminent and that a brief stint in the resistance would give them an opportunity to get their hands on some loot and valuables. Such feelings were no less widespread among members of the Albanian minority, many of whom entered into talks with EDES and British military officers.[57] EDES leaders tried to convince a number of pro-Italian militia leaders to defect to their ranks by promising them guns, ammunition and a thousand golden sovereigns each. Some militia leaders from the area of Filiates found this offer appealing and made a provisional deal to defect to EDES.[58]

However, these efforts backfired as the *Wehrmacht* swept into the area. The German army arrested several Albanian clan leaders and prepared to face the growing Partisan threat. The *Wehrmacht* formed small mobile groups of 'hunters' (*Jäger*) composed of soldiers and Albanian militiamen whose purpose was to locate and destroy the guerrilla groups. At the same time, they targeted the rural communities that provided the resistance with food and recruits. This move had a twofold rationale. First, like the Italian command, they hoped it would undermine support for the resistance and drive a wedge between peasants and Partisans. Second, it would make the provisioning and sustenance of the guerrilla groups impossible, thus driving the guerrillas to desertion and causing their groups to collapse.[59]

The purview and ambitions of the German counter-insurgency plan exceeded those of their Italian counterparts. The operations began with the assault of the rich Fanari plain, an area that was famed as the granary of western Epirus and the Ionian islands. The onslaught of the *Wehrmacht* under the codename *Augustus* took place in the first two weeks of August 1943. The 'hunter' groups surprised and scattered a large ELAS band near the village of Gliki. Other groups pursued EDES and ELAS bands deep into the mountains.[60] Such operations were accompanied by massive reprisals against civilians. Over 300 civilians were executed and an additional 15,000 were rendered homeless, while 34 villages were put to the torch. The operations destroyed the existing food stocks and prevented the harvest, which traditionally took place in

September, thus depriving the local population and the resistance of a crucial source of food. The devastation was completed with the killing and confiscation of the animals (oxen, horses) used in agricultural labour, which precluded any chances of planting corn in the coming spring. The *Wehrmacht* operations resumed in September 1943, when German troops and Albanian auxiliaries crushed the last vestiges of the resistance in the area of Mourgana. By October 1943, the bulk of the guerrilla groups had been scattered from the area. Large units broke into smaller groups and took shelter in the more inaccessible areas, while others crossed the Olytsikas and Mourgana mountains into the interior of Epirus to attempt to brave the storm.[61]

The first phase of the anti-guerrilla operations in the area was completed by early October 1943. However, this was certainly not the end to the violence. The two groups had been at each other's throats for the best part of 1943. At the heart of the conflict between ELAS and EDES was the nature of postwar governance in Greece.[62] Sporadic violence had broken out between the two groups in the months leading up to 1943. The strain of counter-guerrilla operations, combined with the unfulfilled expectations of an Allied landing, radicalized the disagreement between the two groups, which finally erupted into an all-out civil war.

The first clashes took place in the area of Zagori in the nearby province of Ioannina but soon spread throughout Thesprotia. As the local ELAS lacked the strength or numbers to attack EDES, it was aided by the 24th and 15th ELAS regiments which were stationed in the nearby areas of Ioannina and Preveza. EDES troops assaulted ELAS positions in the area of Mourgana and engaged in guerrilla warfare against ELAS in the Souli mountains. Clashes spread to the lowlands where small bands engaged in acts of retributive violence against their enemies.[63]

Civil war and reprisals had a profound social and economic impact. By November 1943, more than 40 per cent of the rural population had been made homeless with one in three villages destroyed. 'Houses, barns, stables, schools and churches … have been burned … and there is no material left even to build a hut in order to shelter their families in the midst of winter.'[64] The loss of residences was not the only problem, however; food stocks and animals were almost completely depleted ('there is no fodder and no food left'), while crops, fruit and olive trees were systematically felled or burned.[65] This led to an over 80 per cent decrease in wheat and olive oil production. Food scarcity led to the outbreak of epidemics: 'Inadequate nutrition has led to an outbreak of malarial fevers … dysentery is an even greater enemy, the sight of men and women and children emaciated and half-naked, deathly pale, staring blankly and begging for mercy as if they were convicts is both disheartening and common.'[66] The housing and food situation further deteriorated because of the *Wehrmacht*'s policy of expressly forbidding the Red Cross from providing any kind of help to civilians living in areas and villages that were considered to be pro-guerrilla or in guerrilla-held areas.[67]

The situation was little better in German-held areas where Red Cross supplies were casually stolen by marauding militiamen and local collaborators. A Red Cross report admitted that the 'overwhelming' majority of provisions was claimed by Albanian militiamen 'who go about armed, threatening everyone', while Greek communities and individuals living in German-held areas had no recourse to justice or protection.

Civilians were murdered and robbed in broad daylight, while during the night people were gripped by fear, everyone stayed locked inside and no-one dared to venture out.[68] The reign of violence in the Axis-held lowlands led to a massive exodus of the Greek population. By November 1943, over one-third of the Greek population had abandoned their homes, seeking safety in guerrilla-held areas and towns further south. The influx of thousands of refugees and displaced persons further depleted the already-meagre local resources, exacerbating communal, political and social antagonisms and often resulting in violence.[69] A Red Cross official noted that

> anarchy and violence dominate everyday life, ... hunger has brutalized the people and narrowed their consciousness, banditry offers relief from hunger, and looting is used to quell their needs, the one village is afraid of the other, the one organization suspects the other, old passions are taking new shape and are brought to the surface and one brother sheds the blood of the other.[70]

This situation not only threatened the livelihoods of civilians but also put the survival of the resistance organizations into doubt. ELAS had suffered significant casualties, while EDES's leadership had, unbeknownst to their British backers, made a temporary informal truce with the *Wehrmacht*, hoping that this would provide them with respite and allow them to focus on their struggle against ELAS.[71] These hopes were dashed, however, as EDES experienced a number of defeats and was only saved from annihilation thanks to the intervention of the SOE which brokered a truce between EAM and EDES in February 1944.[72] The treaty allowed EDES to keep most of its territory in Thesprotia but was forced to sacrifice significant area further east, including the regions of Zagori, Tzoumerka and Radovizi. The group's forces, numbering several thousand guerrillas, were also ordered to evacuate these areas. In return, the accord limited ELAS's presence in Thesprotia to a small strip of land in the north of the district. Thesprotia, along with the nearby regions of Lakka, Xerovouni and Lakmos, thus became the mainstay of EDES.[73]

This decision saved EDES from total defeat but created a whole host of other problems. Over 10,000 guerrillas had to move to one of the poorest areas of Greece where they shared local resources with a civilian population over 100,000 strong as well as thousands of displaced persons. This posed serious logistical, social and military problems for EDES and the local society. Food shortages led many guerrillas to abandon their positions, while some resorted to robbery and black market trading to support their families. A small number of guerrillas even sold guns and ammunition to ELAS and the Albanian militias. There was also a massive increase in violence and crimes against property as local peasants and displaced persons vied over access to food and work.[74]

EDES adopted a twofold approach to deal with this problem. First, it militarized the local administration and placed the economy on a war footing. Exports of food and movement to and from the guerrilla-held areas were forbidden, pack animals were commandeered by EDES, while farmers were required to declare their production and contribute a monthly quota of food to the organization.[75] At the same time, EDES began offering a range of social services to the local population. Families of guerrillas, destitute refugees and the unemployed received a monthly stipend, free food and medical care in EDES's military hospitals. Funding for these activities was provided by the SOE. Besides these measures, EDES increased guerrilla salaries to two sovereigns per month and offered additional rations for the families of guerrilla fighters.[76]

However, such measures were not enough to alleviate the dire scarcity of food and material resources. *Wehrmacht* depredations had decimated agricultural production, resulting in rapid increases in the price of the food that was available. Moreover, EDES's decision to pay both the guerrillas and local peasants with golden sovereigns for their services had an inflationary effect. The proliferation of gold currency led to a sharp drop in the exchange rate and, by extension, in the purchasing power of local civilians.[77] As an EDES guerrilla noted, 'we were adequately paid but there was nothing left to buy, food was hard to come by and whatever was available was extremely expensive'.[78]

Moreover, the promises of free food and inflated salaries drew thousands of new recruits to EDES, thus depriving local communities of invaluable working hands, while increasing the size of the non-productive population. The total number of EDES guerrillas in the area increased from 800 to 3,000. This meant that one in three males aged between sixteen and fifty served in an EDES group. By early 1943, entire communities, numbering hundreds of inhabitants, had become dependent on EDES's monthly supply of food and money for their survival and thus abandoned any productive work to 'live by the gun'. This alarmed many EDES officers who brought it to the attention of their superiors that the organization's 'offers of money and supplies have led scores of peasants to turn away from productive work', thus 'dangerously' reducing the number of those involved in the production of food while at the same time also creating a culture of impunity, vigilantism and mercenaryism.[79]

Faced with another looming crisis, the local EDES command tried to appease its followers and guerrillas and provide peasants with food and materials by engaging in systematic raiding against Albanian and Greek communities deemed neutral or unfriendly. While previous EDES operations targeted the occupying forces and the Albanian militias, these operations almost exclusively targeted civilian communities and their structures.[80] The first raids took place in early January 1944 when hundreds of EDES guerrillas, accompanied by local civilians, stormed the Albanian towns of Gardiki and Dragoumi. Civilians returned to their mountain lairs in the Souli area carrying hundreds of animals (sheep, goats, cattle) and provisions. The raid was repeated a month later. This time every single Albanian who lived in the area was forced out, while food and provisions were distributed among guerrillas and their families who were resettled in Albanian properties. Raids continued over the next few weeks with guerrillas attacking several Albanian villages.[81]

The impact of the shift from productive activities to a 'war economy' sustained by predatory activities had profound social and political repercussions.[82] The extremities of violence undermined social hierarchies, the role of traditional elites and customary forms of conflict resolution. In the prewar period, violent conflict was mediated and controlled through practices such as blood brotherhood and hostage exchange brokered by local notables, professionals, affluent farmers, etc. The destruction of the productive basis of local societies and the concomitant inability of these notables to protect their communities and negotiate with the *Wehrmacht* undermined their social standing and prestige, thus leading to them being gradually supplanted by the various militia leaders, gang members and the EDES and Albanian warlords (*oplarhigoi*) who increasingly came to control local societies.[83]

Very few of these men came from affluent or prestigious backgrounds. Indeed, many hailed from the margins of society, such as Veip Hodo, an illiterate goatherd from the village of Grikohori; Liut Cane, a petty thief from the village of Mesovouni;[84] Zois Padazis, an illiterate shepherd from the village of Labanitsa who commanded a 100-strong EDES unit; and Thimios Tzimas, a rustler and EDES warlord who came to own significant property in the Souli area. The rise of these men shocked and angered political elites.[85] An Albanian notable angrily observed that 'the wastrels and the gangsters are all powerful and we men of property are completely powerless now'.[86] Such sentiments were echoed among local Greek elites who complained that the 'EDES bandits will become a new "ruling class"'; they will 'enter the offices of the political leaders and impose their own policies'.[87]

Yet, there was very little the elites could do to reverse this process. The displacement of the traditional elites and the concomitant militarization of society further radicalized violence. The 'new men' had a vested interest in the perpetuation and acceleration of violence since their social position relied on their ability to offer their followers food, resources and loot. As an EDES report noted, most guerrilla leaders 'believe that the primary purpose of fighting is first and foremost getting their hands on loot'.[88] EDES chieftains engaged in a wide range of profiteering activities, which went from smuggling to black market trading. Some of them amassed small fortunes through blackmail, appropriation of funds and raiding.[89] An EDES officer acerbically pointed out that for senior EDES members the war had become a means to generate wealth and prestige: 'Whenever I saw one of them, I began our conversation by asking them: how much?'[90]

Such attitudes were no less widespread among Albanian militia leaders. By early 1944, the *Wehrmacht* had trained and equipped over 1,500 Albanian militiamen. This increase allowed the German army to limit its commitment in the area and divert troops to other regions. Albanian militia leaders thus became the de facto authority in a number of communities,[91] with many of them taking advantage of *Wehrmacht* patronage and weapons to exploit local economic resources. Ethnic violence and anti-guerrilla operations often became a pretext for looting and profiteering. Albanian militia leaders had standing arrangements with black market peddlers in Ioannina and Corfu, whom they provided with a steady supply of stolen goods, food and valuables. Many of them had become fixtures in the Ioannina night-club scene where they spent 'huge' amounts of money on prostitutes, luxury goods and various forms of entertainment. Village raids conducted by both sides merely served as an excuse to appropriate goods that would later be sold on the black market.[92]

Such attitudes gradually resulted in a situation where there was no longer a distinction between civilians and combatants or between military resistance and outright robbery. The removal of these distinctions criminalized the conduct of war, as different groups reverted to violence to acquire resources, food and prestige. Guerrillas and militiamen broke into homes and executed their inhabitants so as to rob them;

they engaged in black market trading, highway robbery and extortion. An EDES guerrilla stated at the time: 'You were sorry about the bullet not the man, bullets were expensive, a life had no value.'[93]

These developments further radicalized the way warfare was conducted as well as the attitudes and policies of EDES towards the Albanian minority. Emboldened by their newly found prestige and support, guerrilla leaders lobbied the EDES leadership to adopt a more aggressive approach, while also engaging in increasingly radical behaviours against all groups perceived as enemies, often targeting entire communities. In June 1944, EDES troops from Thesprotia crossed into the nearby district of Preveza where they attacked and ransacked several EAM-backed villages in the neighbouring areas of Pogoni and Preveza. Guerrillas belonging to EDES demonstrated extreme brutality, looting, raping and even torturing civilians to extract valuables.[94] Albanian villages were treated equally harshly, with EDES raiders casually attacking and murdering shepherds, farmers and mill owners, stealing their produce and property.[95]

Such attitudes alarmed the British Liaison Officers seconded to EDES who believed that these activities were distracting the organization from their primary task – fighting against the Axis troops. Pressured by the British, the EDES command attempted to curb such attitudes by threatening and occasionally punishing guerrillas who engaged in looting and/or indiscriminate violence against civilians. However, such policies did not bear fruit. The EDES leadership was wary of alienating its support base, while local guerrillas threatened to defect to ELAS or even create their own independent organizations if EDES intervened in their activities. These were not empty threats. In August 1944, Padazis and his group declared their village and the nearby communities of Plakoti and Ozdina an independent state, which they used to launch raids against all and sundry. EDES threatened Padazis with retaliation but was initially forced to take him back and reward him with a promotion as they were terrified that he would eventually defect to ELAS.[96] Padazis was far from an exception as EDES groups often showed no regard for their leadership and its policies. In the same period, local EDES groups refused to follow orders and invaded Albanian territory in the hope of getting hold of additional loot.[97]

Gradually such operations took on the form of ethnic cleansing. Emboldened by the passivity of the EDES leadership and the looming withdrawal of the German troops from the area, guerrillas began to systematically target Albanian communities, forcing them to flee their homes, which were subsequently occupied and divided up between EDES supporters. An EAM activist noted that for EDES band leaders, 'killing a Turk' (a pejorative term used for Albanian Muslims) was a 'badge of honour …. They made no distinction between the guilty and the innocent … they were all the same to them'.[98] In the summer of 1944, Padazis's group engaged in small-scale ethnic cleansing in the area near the Thyamis River, where his men attacked and displaced Albanian peasants.[99] Such operations were not merely the work of opportunists looking for short-term gains. The experiences of displacement, extreme scarcity and ethnic violence led many EDES local leaders, functionaries and intellectuals to believe that the chronic poverty and land scarcity issue could only be solved through the mass displacement of Albanians. These views were popular both among the 'new elite' of guerrilla leaders who anticipated that an Albanian exodus would allow them to claim the lion's share of the Albanians' property, and ordinary guerrillas who hoped to solve the issue of chronic food poverty through violent expropriation.[100]

These groups lobbied the EDES leadership for a 'definitive solution' to the Albanian issue, which they believed could only be solved through mass displacement.[101] Such pressures and suggestions bore fruit in July/August 1944 when EDES liberated the Axis-held towns of Paramythia, Margariti and Parga. Fierce fighting was followed by mass reprisals against Albanian civilians and the looting of their property. Between 400 and 500 civilians were killed in Paramythia alone, while an additional 100–150 civilians were killed in other areas and their property was rapidly distributed among the guerrilla leaders.[102] Violence forced thousands of Albanian peasants to flee. Hundreds of them died either en route or succumbed to the awful conditions in refugee camps. The flight of the Albanian civilians was followed by the mass occupation of their homes and properties by Greek mountain villagers.

Conclusion

In late 1943, an EDES resister noted in his diary that 'peasants have become so brutalized … they would kill a person solely for amusement'.[103] Violence was nothing exceptional in this area, which had a long tradition of banditry and feuding. Yet, the occupation introduced a whole new level of brutalization which surpassed anything the local population had experienced before. Studies explain the violence which the area was subjected to through the prism of nationalist competition. This chapter revises that approach by exploring how food and economic insecurity and the concomitant transformation of social and economic networks facilitated conflict and led civilians and ordinary combatants to support and engage in acts of violence against their immediate neighbours.

Food and economic scarcity were not new phenomena. However, in the prewar period, these conditions were alleviated both with the state's help and through the use of the time-tested coping techniques and networks traditionally used by the peasants. The war and the onset of armed resistance and Axis reprisals recalibrated the role and salience of food and coping mechanisms. The peasantry tried to deal with this situation by employing a variety of methods, ranging from intensive cultivation to barter and black market trading. Others sought to relieve their plight by enlisting in the EDES bands.

These dynamics shifted after the collapse of Italy and the arrival of the *Wehrmacht* in the area. The *Wehrmacht* tried to control and eventually destroy the resistance movements by adopting a strategy of pacification through terror. The Axis forces systematically destroyed villages and homes, confiscated food and slaughtered animals in the hope of starving out the resistance groups and setting the civilian population against the guerrillas. German reprisals undermined the role of the local organs of administration, altered social differences and shifted the value of assets and skills in rural societies. The collapse of the rural economy rendered violence the primary means of attaining and controlling resources, leading to a rapid militarization of society as scores of civilians sought relief from poverty and a means of making profit and acquiring prestige by serving in the various military groups operating in the area.

This shift eroded the value of peacetime skills such as mediation and technical competence, while putting a premium on the willingness and ability to wield violence, thus leading to the supplanting of traditional elites by new local leaders recruited from among the ranks of the nationalist resistance. This change set in motion a process of cumulative radicalization among local groups. Nationalist guerrillas increasingly employed techniques of collective targeting, crop destruction and food deprivation against their opponents. The use of such methods legitimized the deliberate targeting of civilians by armed groups, thus setting the stage for the collective punishment and expulsion of the minority. Consequently, a mobilization that was initially focused on material claims turned into a nationalist one.

Thesprotia was no exception in this respect. As Nicholas Stargardt noted, collective anti-Partisan actions and the deliberate use of food as a weapon of war against the occupied populations served to radicalize ethnic and political violence across the East and Southeast European border areas. Economic collapse and food deprivation hastened the 'destruction of state structures and socio-economic pillars during the occupation … [and] whole regions of the countryside into civil war'. The 'tearing apart' of 'the structures of state and society' radicalized ethnic and political violence and encouraged the adoption of the *Wehrmacht*'s methods by local resistance movements, militias and other armed actors which sought to bring about a 'definitive solution' to the social and ethnic cleavages set in motion by the occupation and the subsequent collapse of the state.[104] The vicious circle of violence and counter-violence did not abate after the war. Instead, in Greece and in large tracts of Eastern Europe, violence continued almost unimpeded in the postwar period, as states and armed groups employed the same methods of extreme violence against their own citizens and opponents in an effort to 'reconstruct' and 'cleanse' contested territories.[105]

Notes

1 On food policies and the rise of resistance, see Giorgos Margaritis, *Apo tin itta stin exegersi: Ellada anoixi 1941–fthinoporo 1942* (Athens: Politis, 1993); on famine, see Violetta Hionidou, *Famine and Death in Occupied Greece, 1941–1944* (Cambridge: Cambridge University Press, 2006).

2 Polymeris Voglis and Ioannis Nioutsikos, 'The Greek Historiography of the 1940s. A Reassessment', *Südosteuropa* 65, no. 2 (2017): 316–33; Nikos Marantzidis and Georgios Antoniou, 'The Axis Occupation and Civil War: Changing Trends in Greek Historiography, 1941–2002', *Journal of Peace Research* 41, no. 2 (2004): 223–31.

3 Lizzie Collingham, *The Taste for War: World War Two and the Battle for Food* (London: Penguin, 2012); Tatjana Tönsmeyer, Peter Haslinger and Agnes Laba, eds, *Coping with Hunger and Shortage under German Occupation in World War II* (London: Palgrave, 2018); Ingrid de Zwarte, *The Hunger Winter. Fighting Famine in the Occupied Netherlands, 1944–1945* (Cambridge: Cambridge University Press, 2020).

4 Kostas Vlahos, *I antistasi stin Lakka Souli 1943–1944* (unpublished, Zosimaia Library Ioannina), 10.

5 Giorgos Margaritis, *Anepithymitoi sympatriotes* (Athens: Vivliorama, 2005); Eleftheria Manta, *Oi Mousoulmanoi Tsamides tis Ipeirou* (Thessaloniki: IMXA, 2004); Mark Mazower, 'Three Forms of Political Justice: Greece 1944–1945', in *After the War Was Over: Reconstructing the Family, Nation, and State in Greece, 1943–1960*, ed. Mark Mazower (Princeton: Princeton University Press, 2000), 24–42; Lambros Baltsiotis, 'The Muslim Chams of Northwestern Greece: The Grounds for the Expulsion of a "Non-Existent" Minority Community', *European Journal of Turkish Studies* 12 (2011): 1–31.

6 This discussion draws on the work of Fotini Christia, *Alliance Formation in Civil Wars* (Cambridge: Cambridge University Press, 2012), 5–9.

7 Mihalis Kokolakis, *To istero Gianniotiko pasaliki: Horos, dioikisi, kai plythismos stin Tourkokratoumeni Ipeiro 1820–1913* (Athens: Ethniko Idryma Ereunon, 2003).

8 Marios Bikas, *Sta aposkia tou Korilla* (Thessaloniki: self-published, 1999), 56.

9 Stefanos Papamokos, *I Selliani xthes kai simera* (Athens: self-published, 1997), 23–7; Petros Apostolidis, *Osa Thymamai, 1900–1969*, volume 1 (Athens: Kedros, 1983), 128.

10 Apostolidis, *Osa Thymamai*, 138.

11 Elisabeth Kontogeorgi, *Population Exchange in Greek Macedonia: The Rural Settlement of Refugees 1922–1930* (Oxford: Oxford University Press, 2006).

12 'O thorivos peri ta ktimata Tsamourias Ipirou', 1 October 1930, Arheia Sighronis Koinonikis Istorias-Arheio Alexandrou Mylona, folder 1.

13 'Ekthesi shetika me tin katastasi tis Mousoulmanikis meionotitas stin Ellada', 15 October 1930, Istoriko Arheio Mouseiou Benaki-Arheio Eleftheriou Venizelous (henceforth: IAMBEV), folder 58/01.

14 Stefanos Evangelou, *Simioseis mias zois* (unpublished, personal collection), 45.

15 'Egklima eis Margariti' *Thesprotika nea*, 1 September 1935.

16 Eleftheria Manta, 'The Çams of Albania and the Greek State (1923–1945)', *Journal of Muslim Minority Affairs* 29 (2009): 4–5.

17 'Ekthesi pros to grafeio tupou tou politikou grafeiou tou prothypourgou', 29 March 1932, IAMBEV, file 111/9.

18 Petros Giourgas, *Martiries kai viomata* (Athens: Sbilias, 2000), 8–9.

19 Toula Stefanidou, *Margariti genethlia gi* (Athens: self-published, 2000), 8–11.

20 Hajredin Isufi, *Musa Demi dhe qëndresa çame 1800–1947* (Tirana: Botimet Dudaj, 2002).

21 'Ekthesi pros to grafeio tipou', 29 March 1932, IAMBEV, file 111/9.

22 Vasilis Krapsitis, *To imerologio mou* (Athens: self-published, 1991), 16.

23 Vasilis Pavlidis, *Oi Alvanotsamides tis periohes Paramythias* (Athens: self-published, 2009), 30.

24 Krapsitis, *To imerologio mou*, 38.

25 Davide Rodogno, *Fascism's European Empire: Italian Occupation during the Second World War* (Cambridge: Cambridge University Press, 2006), 107, 324.

26 Ilias Reggas, *Autoviografia: Agones, istorika gegonota, prosopikes apopseis kai sholia* (unpublished, personal collection), 91–4.

27 Reggas, *Autoviografia*, 95.

28 Sokrates Natsis, *Anamnises mias zois* (Volos: self-published, 1998), 24–8.

29 Grigoris Gkatzougiannis, *To Horio Zerma-Plagia Konitsas Ipeirou* (Athens: self-published, 1982), 54–5.

30 Hristodoulos Hristides, *Pournia, Konitsis-Ioanninon to Horio mou* (Athens: self-published, 1991), 109.

31 Kostas Safarikas, *Sto potami tis zois mou* (Ioannina: self-published, 2008), 38–9.

32 Vasilis Bogdanis, *Ap'osa ezisa: Gola, Mourgana, Souli, Grammos, Taskendi* (Athens: Kokkini Vivliothiki, 2021), 29.
33 'Ekthesis epi tis episitistikis katastaseos horion tinon tis Lakkas', 1 March 1942, Istoriko Arheio Mouseiou Benaki-Arheio Nikolaou Dea (henceforth: IAMBND), folder 262/4.
34 Vlahou, *I antistasi stin Lakka Souli*, 10.
35 'Peri apopeira dimiourgias tarahon en Filiates para ton Mousoulamnon eis varos tou Ellinikou plithysmou', 7 November 1941, Elliniko Logotehniko kai Istoriko Arheio-Arheio Voulgarikes Katohes, folder 2/2.3.
36 'Ekthesis epi tis katastaseos tis dimosias asfaleias en Thesprotia', 14 October 1943, Genika Arheia tou Kratous-Arheio Mesis Anatolis, folder 1.
37 Reggas, *Autoviografia*, 189.
38 Holy Metropolitis of Ioannina, 26 February 1943, IAMBND, folder 262/4.
39 Gerasimos Priftis, oral interview, n.d., Elliniko Logotehniko kai Istoriko Arheio-Arheio Proforikon Martyrion (henceforth: ELIAAPM).
40 Giorgos Koletsis, oral interview, ELIAAPM.
41 Hristos Dimitriadis, *Apeleftherotikoi agones Thesproton* (Athens: self-published, 1999), 105–7.
42 Reggas, *Autoviografia*, 182.
43 For more on EDES, see Vangelis Tzoukas, *Oi oplarhigoi tou EDES stin Ipeiro 1942–1944* (Athens: Estia, 2013); for a discussion of EAM, see Mark Mazower, *Inside Hitler's Greece: The Experience of the Occupation, 1941–1944* (New Haven, CT: Yale University Press, 1993).
44 Mihalis Ntousias, *EAM Zalogou, ELAS Souliou* (Athens: self-published, 1987), 39.
45 Major Paul Bathgate, 'The Andarte Movement in Epirus June 1943–February 1944', 1 March 1945, The National Archives-Foreign Office (henceforth: TNAFO), folder HS5/695.
46 Gerasimos Priftis, oral interview, ELIAAPM.
47 Procopis Papastratis, *British Policy towards Greece during the Second World War* (Cambridge: Cambridge University Press, 1984), 72–104; Richard Clogg, *Anglo-Greek Attitudes* (London: Palgrave, 2000), 78–108.
48 Lieutenant Colonel Thomas Barnes, 'Report on Zervas Andarte Movement', Epirus HQ, 14 August 1944, TNAFO, folder HS5/695.
49 Giannis Haliasos, oral interview, 5 October 2009, personal archive.
50 Giorgos Romanos, *Mia Athinaiki veggera tou 1944, imerologio apo tin Eleftheri Oreini Ellada* (Athens: Potamos, 2008), 144.
51 Vlahou, *I antistasi stin Lakka Souli*, 15.
52 Ibid., 12.
53 Paolo Fonzi, *Fame di guerra. L'occupazione italiana della Grecia 1941–1943* (Rome: Carocci, 2019), 86–9.
54 Ibid., 89.
55 Ibid., 173–80.
56 Ibid., 173.
57 Panagiotis Mitsis, *Thymamai ... apo ta paidika mou hronia, tin ethniki antistasi, tous diogmous, ton emfilio, tin politiki prosfygia, ton epanapatrismo* (Igoumenitsa: self-published, 2008), 76.
58 Theodoros Sarantis, 'Empisteftiki kai epeigousa anaphora', 15 July 1943, Diefthinsi Istorias Stratou, Arheio Theodorou Saranti (henceforth: DISATS), folder 2/1.

59 Ben H. Shepherd, 'Guerrillas and Counterinsurgency', in *The Cambridge History of the Second World War*, vol. II, ed. John Ferris and Evan Mawdsley (Cambridge: Cambridge University Press, 2015), 700.
60 Nikos Ziagos, *Agglikos imperialismos kai ethniki antistasi 1940–1945*, volume 4 (Athens: self-published, 1980), 68.
61 'Ekthesi tis kyrias Ellis Adosidou kai ton kyrion Hr. Vasmatzidou kai Th. Papadimitriou epi tis katastaseos ton pyropathon perioxon Ipeirou kai Aitoloakarnanias', January 1944, IAMBND, folder 262/4.
62 John Louis Hondros, *Occupation and Resistance: The Greek Agony* (New York: Pella, 1983), 171–82; C. M. Woodhouse, *The Struggle for Greece 1941–1949* (Chicago: Ivan R. Dee, 2002), 60–1.
63 Ntousias, *EAM Zalogou, ELAS Souliou*, 185.
64 'Ekthesi tis kirias Ellis Adosidou', January 1944, IAMBND, Folder 262/4.
65 Ibid.
66 Ibid.
67 Ibid.
68 'Activité de la commission de gestion pour l'approvisionnement de l'Épire pendant les mois de janvier et de février 1944', March 1944, IAMBND, folder 262/4.
69 'Rapport comparatif de la situation en Épire d'une part et de celle de la région d'Aegionpatras et Kalavryta en Péloponèse de l'autre', November 1943, IAMBND, folder 262/4.
70 'Ekthesi tis kyrias Ellis Adosidou', January 1944, IAMBND, folder 262/4.
71 Hondros, *Occupation and Resistance*, 171–82.
72 Woodhouse, *The Struggle for Greece 1941–1949*, 67–71.
73 Richard Clogg, *Greece 1940–1949, Occupation, Resistance, Civil War: A Documentary History* (London: Palgrave, 2002), 169–70.
74 'Dioikitika kai oikonomika EDES, Eisigitiki ekthesis peri diefthetiseos tou oikonomikou provlimatos eis tin Elefthera Oreini Ellada', January 1944, Elliniko Logotehniko kai Istoriko Arheio-Arheio Zerva, folder 2.
75 'Appreciation of the military situation of Zervas' forces vis-à-vis EAM/ELAS and the Germans', 25 November 1943, Istoriko Arheio Mouseiou Benaki-Arheio Ioanni Pelteki (henceforth: IAMBAIP), folder 259/6.
76 'Brief Note on the General Situation and Present and Future Problems in Greece', March 1944, IAMBAIP, folder 259/6.
77 Ibid.
78 Giorgos Dimitriou, oral interview, Ledeza, 25 October 2009, personal archive.
79 'Diatagi genikou arhigeiou peri oikogeneion antarton', 2 August 1944, Diefthinsi Istorias Stratou-Arheio Kostantinou Mavroskoti (henceforth: DISAKM), folder 1/702.
80 Bikas, *Sta aposkia tou Korilla*, 217.
81 Pavlidis, *Oi Alvanotsamides*, 128.
82 For a discussion of war economies in irregular conflicts, see Jenny H. Peterson, *Building a Peace Economy: Liberal Peacebuilding and the Development-Security Industry* (Manchester: Manchester University Press, 2014), 3–9.
83 Theodoros Sarantis, 'Anafora pros to Ypourgion Exoterikon', 19 July 1946, DISATS, folder B/63/4.
84 Ibid.
85 'Peri tis emfanisthiseis symmorias', 23 May 1944, DISAKM, folder 1/468.
86 Evangelou, *Simioseis*, 52.

87 Romanos, *Mia Athinaiki veggera*, 189.
88 *Arheia Ethnikis Antistases (1941–1944) Antartikes Organoseis EOEA-EDES*, volume 1 (Athens: Diefthinsi Istorias Stratou, 1998), 196–7.
89 Romanos, *Mia Athinaiki veggera*, 205.
90 Ibid., 78.
91 Circular/Tsamouria Command, 'Direction of Operations', 1 June 1944, TNAFO, folder 371/48094.
92 Krapsitis, *To imerologio mou*, 35; Harilaos Vagias, *I Arta tis katohis* (Arta: Skoufas, 2004), 137–8.
93 Oral testimony, Georgios Daskas, 30 October 2009, personal archive.
94 Thanasis Pantoulas, *Flogismena hronia 1940–1945* (Athens: self-published, 1982), 204.
95 'Peri tis emfanisthiseis symmorias', 23 May 1944, DISAKM, folder 1/468.
96 Ibid.
97 'A Note on the Chams', 16 October 1945, TNAFO, folder 371/48094.
98 Nikos Ziaggos, *Agglikos Imperialismos kai Ethniki Antistasi 1940–5*, volume 1 (Athens: self-published, 1978), 375.
99 'Peri tis emfanisthiseis symmorias', 23 May 1944, DISAKM, folder 1/468.
100 Giourgas, *Martiries*, 185.
101 Pavlidis, *Oi Alvanotsamides*, 140.
102 'Note on Conversation with Lieutenant Colonel Palmer British Military Mission Albania', 13 April 1945, TNAFO, folder /371/48094.
103 Romanos, *Mia Athinaiki veggera*, 78.
104 Nicholas Stargardt, 'Wartime occupation by Germany, Food and Sex', in *The Cambridge History of the Second World War*, volume 2, ed. Richard Bosworth and Joseph Maiolo (Cambridge: Cambridge University Press, 2015), 400.
105 Norman M. Naimark, *Fires of Hatred: Ethnic Cleansing in Twentieth Century Europe* (Cambridge, MA: Harvard University Press, 2001); Timothy Snyder, *The Reconstruction of Nations: Poland, Ukraine, Lithuania, Belarus* (New Haven, CT: Yale University Press, 2004); Jessica Reinisch and Elizabeth While, *The Disentanglement of Populations: Migration, Expulsion and Displacement in Post-War Europe, 1944–49* (London: Palgrave, 2011).

Part Five

Liberated territories: Feeding the Partisans

9

Survival and equity: The moral economy of the liberated territories of Western Bosnia (1941–45)

Xavier Bougarel

There are many books devoted to the Yugoslav Partisan movement, but few deal with economic issues. Yet, for the Partisans, these issues were essential and they dedicated a substantial amount of energy and attention to them. The economy established in the liberated territories was crucial, not only for the material survival of the army and the population, but also, to a large extent, for the Partisans' own political legitimacy. To show this, I have chosen to focus on the case of Western Bosnia, also called Bosanska Krajina, which was incorporated into the Independent State of Croatia (*Nezavisna Država Hrvatska* – NDH) between 1941 and 1945 (see Map 2). During the Second World War, this region was the largest and most stable liberated territory in Yugoslavia. In this stronghold, the Partisans developed their own economic institutions and practices very early on, and these reached a level of sophistication not found in other regions. This choice of geographical subject is also motivated by more pragmatic considerations, namely, that Bosanska Krajina is the only region of Bosnia-Herzegovina for which substantial and easily accessible archives still exist today – in the Archives of Bosnia-Herzegovina and the Historical Museum of Bosnia and Herzegovina, in Sarajevo, as well as in the Archives of Republika Srpska, in Banja Luka. Based on these various archives, I will first describe the main features of the economy established by the Partisans, centred on the production, collection and redistribution of food. I will then turn to the practical difficulties the Partisans faced in this endeavour. Finally, I will try to identify the 'moral economy' that their relations with the population rested upon, referring to James Scott's classic work *The Moral Economy of the Peasant. Rebellion and Subsistence in Southeast Asia.*[1]

The central role of the People's Liberation Committees

The beginning of the People's Liberation Struggle (*Narodnooslobodilačka borba* – NOB) in Bosanska Krajina was marked by the capture of the town of Drvar on 27 July 1941. From then on, the first Partisan units appointed delegates or commissioners to organize their food supplies, and set up the first political institutions responsible for the administration of local life in the liberated territories. Yet in the early months of the People's Liberation Struggle, the food supply for combatants still came largely from their families and home villages, and the local institutions created by the Partisans varied widely from one place to another. The need for more uniform organization in the liberated territories and a more sophisticated supply system therefore quickly became apparent, as the Partisan units became larger and more mobile, and moved away from the villages which provided them with the bulk of their subsistence. As early as September 1941, at the Stolice conference in Serbia, the leadership of the Communist Party of Yugoslavia (*Komunistička partija Jugoslavije* – KPJ) decided to set up new civilian institutions in the liberated territories, namely the People's Liberation Committees (*Narodnooslobodilački odbori* – NOO). Five months later, in February 1942, the Supreme Staff of the People's Liberation Army adopted what were known as the Foča Regulations (*fočanski propisi*), which defined, for the first time, the exact composition, functioning and tasks of the NOOs.[2] The committees were to be elected by all members of the population over the age of eighteen, including women, and they were to bring together 'honest patriots', regardless of political opinion, religion or ethnicity. Two of their main tasks were to organize supplies for the army and to provide material support for certain categories of the population, such as the poor, refugees and the families of combatants in need. They controlled every aspect of local economic life and were to create People's Liberation Funds (*Narodnooslobodilački fondovi* – NOF) to pool available resources including money, food, clothing and other necessities. To replenish these funds, the NOOs relied primarily on voluntary contributions from the population, but could also carry out forced requisitions of foodstuffs or confiscate the entire property of the 'enemies of the people', starting with the local collaborators.

The Partisans formed the first NOOs at village and municipal level in 1941, and their members dealt with various issues related to local life. In the years that followed, however, the tasks of the committees increased in number and complexity, and their operation became more institutionalized. First of all, their relationship with the People's Liberation Army was redefined in September 1942 with the appointment of local and sector commands (*komanda mjesta* and *komanda područja*), whose area of responsibility corresponded to municipalities (*opština*) and counties (*okrug*). These structures, which were responsible for the organization of the rear, served as intermediaries between the NOOs and the army, transmitting to the NOOs the requests of the units present on their territory and then handing over the resources collected by the NOOs to the quartermasters of these units. The NOOs thus always had the same contact person, despite the numerous troop movements, and the army's combat units were, to a large extent, relieved of the worry about where their supplies were coming from. More generally, the NOO network was becoming denser and more hierarchical. In Bosanska Krajina, the first general election of village NOOs was organized on 27 December 1942, and that of municipal NOOs ten days later. In 1943, NOOs were appointed at the level of districts (*srez*) and counties (*okrug*). Finally, in September 1943, an NOO was formed for the entire region of Bosanska Krajina. At the local and regional levels, the NOOs became increasingly specialized, with the creation of commissions or departments for food, the economy, social affairs, justice, education and health.

In less than three years, the NOOs thus became the key stakeholders in the economic life of the liberated territories and the institutional foundation on which the new Yugoslav state would be based. In Bosnia-Herzegovina, this took the form of the Provincial Anti-Fascist Council for People's Liberation of Bosnia-Herzegovina (*Zemaljsko antifašističko vijeće narodnog oslobođenja Bosne i Hercegovine* – ZAVNOBiH), created on 25 November 1943 in Mrkonjić Grad. At the Yugoslav level, the Partisan movement formed an Anti-Fascist Council for the People's Liberation of Yugoslavia (*Antifašističko v(ij)eće narodnog oslobođenja Jugoslavije* – AVNOJ) on 26 November 1942 in Bihać, as well as a National Committee for the Liberation of Yugoslavia (*Nacionalni komitet oslobođenja Jugoslavije* – NKOJ), a quasi-government chaired by Josip Broz Tito, on 30 November 1943 in Jajce. The newly emerging Yugoslav state denied that it wanted to transform the country's economy and, in a widely circulated communiqué dated 8 February 1943, the presidency of the AVNOJ and the Supreme Staff of the People's Liberation Army affirmed that the People's Liberation Movement respected the inviolability of private property and the freedom of enterprise in industry, craftwork and agriculture. It renounced any radical changes in economic and social life, except for the replacement of the old local administrations by the NOOs, and postponed the democratic resolution of all questions concerning the organization of social life and the state until after the war.[3] The reality was, however, more complicated.

The organization of agricultural production

For obvious reasons, the NOOs' first task was to organize agricultural production: in the rural areas under their control, the vast majority of inhabitants lived from agriculture, and the supply of food for the army and the population was a constant source of concern. Despite the so-called 'leftist deviations' (*lijeva skretanja*) in the early years of the war, during which some Partisans denounced the power of the 'kulaks' or tried to create 'kolkhozes', the Partisan movement generally respected private ownership of land and each family was expected to work its own plots. But there were many exceptions to this general rule. For example, land confiscated from 'enemies of the people' became the property of the People's Liberation Funds and was allocated to poor families, families of refugees or families of combatants, who repaid the NOOs with part of their harvest. Similarly, there were many abandoned lands in the liberated territories: these may have belonged to Serbian families who perished or fled during the Ustasha massacres of 1941, or to Muslim and Croat families who fled to the city when their villages came under the Partisans' control. If these families were considered to no longer exist, their land also became the property of the People's Liberation Funds. In most cases, however, this land was only temporarily managed by the NOOs, pending the return of their owners. In order to cultivate as much farmland as possible and to ensure that everyone could provide for themselves, the NOOs also entrusted the abandoned land to poor families, families of combatants or refugees in need of land. Therefore, already during the war, they had de facto collectivized or redistributed a portion of the available arable land. A report written in the last months of the war mentions 200,000 *dulums* (20,000 hectares) of abandoned land in Kozara county, 35,000 *dulums* in Podgrmeč county and 28,000 *dulums* in Drvar county.[4]

Although most of the land remained under the control of its prewar owners, the NOOs profoundly transformed the organization of agriculture work. Indeed, they supervised the main stages of agricultural production, creating special committees for sowing, harvesting or threshing, depending on the season, and insisting on the pooling of labour and scarce resources such as tools, draught animals or seeds. This collective organization of agricultural work was based on certain traditional forms of community harvesting work, called '*moba*' in Bosnia-Herzegovina. However, it was more militarized, as illustrated by the creation of work units known as companies (*četa*), battalions (*bataljon*) or brigades (*brigada*), depending on their size, and made up mainly of young women, as most young men had been drafted into the army. Other labour units were involved in transporting goods across the liberated territories, either on people's (especially women's) backs or, depending on the routes taken, with mules or ox carts. Finally, the NOOs set up labour units to repair roads, collective infrastructures or houses destroyed by the enemy. This type of practice was reminiscent of the *kuluk*, a form of compulsory unpaid labour imposed on peasants since the Ottoman era. As far as agricultural work is concerned, the use of brigades of young people, as well as poor peasants or refugees, aimed at maximizing agricultural production by moving these workers from one region to another according to needs and priorities. Labourers were fed by the villages where they worked, and sometimes they received payment in kind. This system therefore also provided some relief to regions facing grain shortages or affected by wartime destruction by moving part of their population to wealthier or less damaged regions. Through these various forms of collective work, the NOOs reallocated resources such as labour, draught animals, agricultural tools and food products. This benefitted local families in need and, more broadly, the poorest regions.

While endeavouring to maximize agricultural production, the Partisans sought to encourage various forms of redistribution and solidarity. In March 1945, reviewing the mutual aid practices developed during the war, the NOO for Kozara county stated that 'this organization appeared during the People's Liberation Struggle and is in keeping with its spirit, it represents something new in the life of the people and is a great achievement of popular power. … We must develop the idea of mutual aid not only from neighbour to neighbour, from village to village, from town to town, but also from district to district, and thus everywhere and on all levels'.[5] This emphasis on the principles of solidarity and mutual aid also explains why the Partisan movement claimed to base the sustenance of the army and needy families on voluntary contributions from the population. The Foča Regulations adopted in February 1942 stated that the population was to feed the army through the People's Liberation Funds. Everyone was therefore called upon to make a contribution, if only symbolic, and every donation was duly recorded and, as far as possible, made public.[6] In practice, the NOOs and anti-fascist mass organizations arranged regular campaigns to collect food, clothing, shoes and other necessities. The NOOs usually kept 30 per cent of the donations for their own needy families and gave the rest to the People's Liberation Army. In January 1944, the NOO for Drvar county noted the failure of an earlier voluntary contribution drive, as the local councillors had neglected to set an example and the army representatives had not been invited to participate in the conferences organized for the occasion. It therefore decided to launch a new campaign from 16 to 26 January, which would see greater involvement of local NOOs, mass organizations and military authorities, and which would measure 'how much our people love their army'.[7]

No matter how persuasive the NOOs were or how much the population loved the People's Liberation Army, the continuous increase in the military personnel and the gradual depletion of local economic resources meant that voluntary contributions were increasingly insufficient and gradually gave way to forced requisitions. As a result, the notions of giving and volunteering dissipated. The Foča Regulations described the requisitions as a form of forced and deferred purchase: in exchange for seized goods, the NOOs would issue a 'receipt' (*priznanica*) redeemable at the end of the war.[8] In July 1944, Dušan Ivezić, in charge of economic matters for the ZAVNOBiH presidency, announced that in the liberated territories of Bosnia-Herzegovina, the army now needed 140 wagons (1,400 tonnes) of food per month. In this context, requisitions became the rule, especially in regions facing shortages.[9] NOOs and military authorities formed commissions to spread the burden of requisitions among regions, villages and families, first taking the surplus from wealthy farmers or those who had not participated much in the collection of voluntary contributions. The line between voluntary contributions and forced requisitions was therefore blurred, and I will return to this point later on. The same applies to the line between requisitions and confiscations. According to the Foča Regulations, only the property of 'enemies of the people' convicted by military tribunals could be confiscated, leaving their families with the bare minimum to survive.[10] In practice, however, the confiscation of the property of 'enemies of the people' could go hand in hand with the deportation of their families to the occupied territories, or be enforced without prior trial for any political opponents of the Partisans. In such cases, confiscation was actually just a particularly harsh form of requisition based on political rather than economic and social criteria.

The organization of other sectors of the economy

The control of the People's Liberation Committees was not limited to agriculture, but extended to all sectors of the economy. In the liberated territories, craftsmen were either called up for the army where they were assigned to military workshops or placed under the control of the NOOs. They were thus integrated into a 'subsistence economy' with rules that were very different from the prewar period: in most cases, they did not charge the population for their services, but received a lump-sum payment in kind from the NOOs (mainly food and clothing). This ensured that the various craft activities essential to economic life were provided, from the repair of agricultural tools by blacksmiths to the rebuilding of houses or the construction of makeshift shelters by carpenters and masons, not to mention the making of sandals by cobblers or the shoeing of horses by farriers. In December 1944, the NOO for the Drvar district stated that seventeen forges were operating on its territory, despite the shortage of tools and raw materials, and that they 'work as much for the needs of the population as for the needs of the military and civilian authorities. The blacksmiths have not yet been paid and they have not asked to be paid, except when one of them is destitute [in which case] he is given some food aid, and some have been provided with equivalent labour for ploughing their fields or something along those lines'.[11] Artisans thus donated free labour and free services in exchange for the voluntary contributions provided by the peasants or the tasks carried out free of charge by the labour brigades, and this was all part of the new equilibrium of the economy of gifts and counter-gifts established by the Partisan movement.

Did trade and money play any role in this subsistence economy? Due to the war, the interruption of communication routes and the general impoverishment of the population, commercial activities were considerably reduced in the liberated territories. In September 1944, the NOO for Podgrmeč noted that 'trade in our county is not developed at all and only in the town of Sana is there a market every eight days, in the workshops there is nothing and the reason for this is that the Ustashas looted all the workshops in the first days after the arrival of the NDH and for the last three years the population has not sold anything for or used cash, except for some of the outlying villages, which have been able to obtain salt, petrol and the like by smuggling, but there is a need to resurrect the trade through which the people could obtain the products and articles they need'.[12] The exchange of goods had to be organized on a local level, for example, between people who had food and those who had tools or other necessities, or on a larger scale, for example, between a grain-growing region such as Podgrmeč and a cattle-raising region such as Drvar. To this end, the NOOs set up exchange cooperatives and agricultural markets, registered goods sold or exchanged and set prices in order to limit speculation and the black market.

Among the products sold or exchanged in the cooperatives, salt was especially important as it was essential for human and animal nutrition but hard to find in the liberated territories. Throughout the war, trade developed between Bosanska Krajina and Dalmatia, a region traditionally lacking in grains but close to the sea and therefore able to obtain salt more easily. Whether it was the work of enterprising individuals, established traders or the NOOs themselves, the salt-for-wheat trade that developed between these two regions was essential to their food supply, but sometimes threatened the fragile economic balance of Bosanska Krajina. In January 1945, the ZAVNOBiH food department was alarmed that the arrival of numerous 'speculators' from Dalmatia was causing a sharp rise in food prices in Bosanska Krajina, and called for stricter supervision of inter-regional trade.[13] Moreover, salt was one of the products traditionally under state monopoly, and the Partisans confiscated large quantities of the commodity in the warehouses of the towns that they occupied for a few days or weeks. The quantities of salt thus obtained were partly distributed free of charge to the general population or merely to needy families, and partly sold or exchanged in the cooperatives, with the money or wheat obtained in exchange being used to cover the operating costs of the NOOs. Other monopolized products were treated similarly, including petrol, tobacco, matches and cigarette paper. The free distribution of these products was another component of the virtuous circle of gifts and counter-gifts and attested to the fact that the new authorities were more concerned about the population than the predatory prewar state had been.

This distribution of monopolized products was only possible insofar as they could be collected and shipped clandestinely by the resistance organizations present in the occupied towns, or seized as spoils of war when the Partisans managed to temporarily take control of a town. In some cases, the capture of towns brought about full-scale plundering. In November 1942, the KPJ committee for Bosanska Krajina was indignant, for example, that 'when Bihać was liberated, practically all our military units which participated in this action, and many people from the rear took part in shameful looting. This looting turned our great military victory in Bihać into a political defeat'.[14] The cadres of the Partisan movement struggled to prevent such actions, which occurred again when other towns were liberated in the years that followed. The capture of towns was also an opportunity for some combatants or peasants who had come from neighbouring villages to recover the livestock that had been looted from them a few weeks or months earlier, and the Partisans had to set up special arbitration commissions to ensure that these face-to-face situations did not degenerate into fights between the old and the new owners, or even clashes between ethnic communities.

These looting and counter-looting practices show that the economic circuits of the liberated and occupied territories were not totally separate. The same held true for trade. Although the Partisans forbade all trade with the occupied territories in principle, in reality, monopolized products and other essential goods such as acetylene could only be obtained in the occupied towns, and the NOOs often preferred to regulate trade with them than leave it to black market dealers or villagers living near the front-line. In March 1944, for example, the NOO for Drvar county authorized those who were able to travel to the occupied territory to buy salt and seeds there. The price was to be fixed in advance and buyers were entitled to a profit of half a kilogram of wheat per kilogram of salt or seed. Those who, on their return, did not hand over their goods to the NOOs would be prosecuted.[15] As Dušan Ivezić, who was responsible for economic issues in the ZAVNOBiH presidency, acknowledged in July 1944, 'under the current conditions, trafficking can only be prevented if the NOOs organize the trade of goods between the liberated and non-liberated regions'.[16]

Trade with the occupied territories was one of the few areas in which currency continued to play a central role. For transactions within the liberated territories, barter was much more frequent. Speaking to the ZAVNOBiH members, Dušan Ivezić noted that 'trade based on money has been transformed into ordinary barter'.[17] This partial demonetization of the economy also applied to the nascent people's state, since according to Dušan Ivezić, 'we have no cash income or expenditure ... Our main income is in kind, and comes from voluntary contributions and requisitions. Cash income is quite rare, and mainly comes from voluntary monetary contributions and money seized from the enemy'.[18] This does not mean that money was absent from the liberated territories. In fact, various currencies circulated there (Croatian kuna, Italian lire, old Yugoslav dinar, etc.), and the leading bodies of the Partisan movement sometimes had large sums of cash at their disposal, looted from tax offices and banks, or collected during the 'People's Liberation Loan' campaigns organized in towns on a more or less voluntary basis. However, in the daily life of the liberated territories, cash played only a secondary role compared to payments in kind or various forms of gifts and counter-gifts. The NOOs decreed a moratorium on debts and rents in the first months of the war, and even paid in kind the salaries of workers and civil servants and the pensions of pensioners. This situation was clearly temporary, and from 1943, remonetization of the economy began in the liberated territories. Yet this gradual remonetization brought its share of difficulties and tensions. Thus, when in December 1944 the ZAVNOBiH authorized craftsmen to start charging for their services again (exonerating only the poorest families), the NOO for the Sanski Most district noted that 'this situation resonated rather negatively with the population, and particularly among working people, because they pointed out that they, too, had been working for free and without any salary for the past three and a half years and that they were also helping the People's Liberation Struggle'.[19] The subsistence economy set up by the Partisan movement was by definition temporary, but it still had a coherent structure and rules, which could not be broken with impunity.

Harsh material conditions

To understand the difficulties faced by the NOOs in organizing the economy, we must delve more deeply into the wartime circumstances. In Bosanska Krajina, as elsewhere, the Partisan movement's strongholds were mainly in mountainous regions, which suffered from grain shortages. Specifically, while Podgrmeč and Kozara county were fairly fertile, Drvar and those counties in Central Bosnia attached to the NOO for Bosanska Krajina faced serious shortages. This initial situation was made worse by the occupying forces, which were determined to destroy the region's economic potential during their major offensives and through daily harassment in the liberated territories. In June 1944, the NOO for Bosanska Krajina noted: 'After a bloody and unequal three-year struggle, our people are physically exhausted and materially devastated, they are left today without the strength to work, without shelter, without clothes and shoes, without draught animals and without agricultural tools. The enemy has systematically worked to annihilate the population in every offensive, large or small, and has done so again this week. Our people endure all this proudly and fight heroically for their physical and economic survival. The coming harvest and haymaking will be a new struggle because, on the eve of its collapse, the enemy will again try to steal or destroy part of our harvest.'[20] In this already difficult context, the NOOs had to provide not only for their own population, but also for the soldiers and refugees on their territories.

It is therefore unsurprising that economic circumstances deteriorated as the war went on: while the army's needs increased day after day, local resources were inexorably exhausted. In September 1944, wheat production in Bosnia-Herzegovina had fallen by 35 per cent and livestock had been reduced by 70–75 per cent compared to their prewar levels.[21] This depletion of the economy is a recurring theme in the documents produced by the Partisan movement, and the ZAVNOBiH presidency wrote in March 1944 that 'throughout the liberated territory of Bosanska Krajina, the issue of feeding both the army and the civilian population is becoming more difficult every day. … The problem of feeding the civilian population has recently been further aggravated by the difficulties of feeding the civilian population in the liberated cities, where the majority of the population has no means of subsistence'.[22] This economic depletion of the liberated territories raised the spectre of famine: in May 1944, the NOO for the Bosanska Krupa district reported that some inhabitants were forced to eat grass,[23] and two months later, the NOO for Drvar county wrote that 'a large majority of families have not had bread in their homes for a long time. Their food consists of a little milk, vegetables and various plants. There have been no cases of death [from starvation] but there has been severe suffering'.[24]

In reality, despite all the hardships, there was no famine in Bosanska Krajina. However, the constant search for food took its toll on morale, and while an NOO councillor from Podgrmeč was pleased that 'the people are living in incredible misery, but they are all for our struggle',[25] the League of Communist Youth of Yugoslavia (*Savez komunističke omladine Jugoslavije* – SKOJ) in the Livno district was concerned that 'there is no momentum and goodwill among the people and it is useless to talk to them [about political issues] when they are oppressed by misery'.[26] These material conditions not only threatened the morale of the civilian population, but also that of the combatants. In February 1943, for example, the KPJ committee for Bosanska Krajina warned: 'We cannot leave the army without bread, because then we risk not only that the army will become demoralized but also that it will break down – a starving soldier is prone to theft and looting, and we cannot permit this.'[27]

Arbitrary army requisitions and ordinary injustices of the NOOs

In this context of widespread shortages, tensions often arose between the NOOs and the military authorities. Whenever necessary, army units, as well as sector and local commands, did not hesitate to make their own requisitions and, more generally, to impose their will on the NOOs and the civilian population. These arbitrary requisitions by the army were a source of great tension, not only because they sometimes threatened the survival of the civilian population, but also because they did not take into account the economic or political criteria that the NOOs endeavoured to enforce. Thus, in October 1944, the NOO for Podgrmeč county complained that the 13th Krajina Brigade had seized cattle in the village of Dabar without considering the material situation of those whose property had been requisitioned, and without handing over receipts, which caused great discontent among the population.[28]

These arbitrary army requisitions were also indicative of fierce competition between the military and the NOOs for control of scarce resources, and they greatly hampered the NOOs' efforts. In February 1944, the KPJ committee for Drvar county wrote that 'many difficulties and misunderstandings [with the NOOs] stem from the inappropriate attitude of unit leaders and military institutions towards them, … as a result of which the NOOs cannot properly organize the distribution of the workforce and means of transport'.[29] More generally, the brutality of the military weakened the legitimacy of the People's Liberation Committees. In July 1944, the NOO for Drvar county warned that 'the sector and local commands that look down on the forums of the people's power make no effort to strengthen the authority of the latter, but on the contrary, undermine its authority through their inappropriate actions and attitudes'.[30]

In so doing, the military upset the economic and social compromises reached between the Partisans and the population of the liberated territories, and as a result also threatened to rekindle rivalries between villages and between ethnic communities, and even to send the population into the arms of the enemy.

These arbitrary requisitions show that, when necessary, the army would willingly break the unwritten rules of the subsistence economy established by the Partisan movement. However, this was not the only difficulty the People's Liberation Committees faced. Because they were better known or more familiar with the economic situation in their villages, wealthy farmers were strongly represented in the NOOs. In February 1942, for example, the KPJ committee for Jajce county wrote: 'In the majority of cases, these [People's Liberation] Committees were elected to meet the economic needs of our army, and more care was taken to ensure that the wealthier farmers were also included in them than to secure the political importance of these committees from an ideological point of view. Consequently, today, there are elements in them on which our army can scarcely rely politically. This has become apparent in some places, where precisely these wealthier councillors remain passive in the struggle and consider only their own material interests.'[31]

The issue of the role of wealthy farmers in the economic practices of the NOOs remained undecided throughout the war, and higher authorities or KPJ organizations often criticized the local NOOs for the way they distributed the burden of requisitions. In November 1944, the NOO for the Bosanski Petrovac district reported, for example, that 'in many villages, the [forced] sale of meat and wheat was carried out according to the instructions given, i.e. to take from those who have [the most], but there are cases in some villages where this was not done, and the population was left to decide. Then the wealthier people organized themselves and argued strongly that it was right for everyone to give the same amount of whatever it was, and the majority of the poor population agreed with that'.[32] Two months later, the NOO for the Sanski Most district noted that 'mistakes have been made by some committees and individual councillors towards the population, which could be seen in some villages during the collection of food for the army, when the councillors unfairly distributed [the burden of requisitions] among the peasants, so that they sometimes burdened the poor and protected the wealthiest'.[33] The arbitrary army requisitions and the ordinary injustices of the NOOs alike raised questions about the criteria of fairness on which requisitioning should be based, and thus the very nature of the economic and social compromises reached between the Partisans and the population of the liberated territories. In the longer term, the Partisan movement's ability to establish itself as a new state was also at stake. I will now explore this topic in more detail.

What moral economy was at work in the liberated territories?

In their respective scholarly works on the agrarian question in Communist Yugoslavia, Melissa Bokovoy and Katherine MacCarthy both separate the war, during which an unwritten compromise between the Yugoslav communists and the peasantry prevailed, from the postwar period, where policies of forced purchase of crops and attempts at land collectivization challenged this tacit agreement.[34] However, contrary to what the aforementioned authors suggest, the wartime compromise was not a continuation of the *status quo ante*: formally, land remained the property of the peasants, but its uses and produce were controlled by the People's Liberation Committees. From this point of view, Radomir Bulatović is right to describe the economy of the liberated territories in Bosnia-Herzegovina as 'war communism', in which 'no one openly challenges the principle of private property, but all property becomes de facto social property, because individuals can only survive by fighting, feeding themselves and dying with the community'.[35]

However it is referred to, the main source of legitimacy for the economy established by the Partisan movement was its capacity to ensure, as best it could, the survival of the majority. Not only were there no famines in the liberated territories, but food conditions were not necessarily worse than in the occupied territories, where the NDH authorities also enforced a harsh regime of requisitions in the countryside, and where the population of the towns suffered from hyperinflation and increasing shortages.[36] In any case, the possibility of surviving in the liberated territories was the first criterion of the moral economy of the peasants, of their perception of what was fair and legitimate, but it was by no means the sole criterion. The subsistence economy established by the Partisan movement was characterized by a massive redistribution of economic resources to the benefit of poor peasants and the groups most affected by the war, such as refugees, the homeless, or war widows and orphans. This redistribution was itself a condition for the survival of all, but it was also motivated by a concern for equity and reciprocity shared by the cadres of the Partisan movement and the population of the liberated territories. Within the NOOs and the KPJ, there were endless discussions about which criteria of justice should be applied, and these referred as much to the collection of food and other basic goods as to their subsequent redistribution. In February 1945, for example, the councillors of the NOO for Podgrmeč spoke at length about the errors and injustices committed during the previous requisitioning campaign, to which a representative of the NOO for Bosanska Krajina responded with the following lecture:

> The food department's report and the [present] discussion show that food is our most sensitive issue. The quarterly purchase [of wheat] was not carried out as it should have been, and this is a source of complaints from the population, as no one had an overview of the economic situation by district and by municipality. In some municipalities, all the surplus was taken and in others it was not. This is politically damaging for us, because it means that the people's government is not pursuing a popular and fair policy. Currently, economic policy is the most sensitive issue, because through wheat and livestock, the people judge federal Bosnia-Herzegovina, federal Yugoslavia and the people's government. … The people know that they must give, but they want to know why. The people will give everything if they see that everyone is contributing equally.[37]

The equitable collection and redistribution of goods were therefore the second criterion of the moral economy at work in the liberated territories. Whenever this equity was violated, it did not take long for the population to complain. Thus, in February 1945, during a meeting of agronomists from Bosanska Krajina to prepare for the sowing season, the participants stressed that 'it is necessary to distribute the draught animals and the workforce as fairly as possible so that there is no discontent among the population'.[38] More generally, a criticism often levelled at the NOOs was that 'they always ask for something but never give anything',[39] thus violating the rule of gift and counter-gift that was supposed to regulate relations between the Partisan movement and the population of the liberated territories. This demand for reciprocity even extended to the army: in October 1944, the population of Ključ-Mrkonjić county criticized the local Partisan detachment for its passive attitude and wondered 'why we are feeding them for free if they do not want to fight'.[40] The civil and military authorities were aware of this unspoken bargain, and when in September 1943, the NOO for the Drvar district sent the municipality of Prekaja 350 kilograms of salt, it was careful to point out that the army had paid for this salt with its blood.[41] Indeed, in the moral economy of the liberated territories, the donations to the People's Liberation Army were only meaningful if its combatants were, in turn, ready to give up their lives.

Regardless of its willingness to fight, the army represented a major challenge to the moral economy of the liberated territories. Not only – as we have seen – did it not hesitate to brutally seize the food it needed, but it also gave rise to a group of people that enjoyed special benefits, namely the families of soldiers, war widows and war invalids. In March 1945, the ZAVNOBiH social policy department reported 1,790 war invalids, 5,834 families of dead soldiers and 2,795 other families of combatants in need in Bosanska Krajina.[42] At the same time, the finance department reported that it had distributed 7,000,000 kuna to soldiers' families and poor families in the region.[43] The KPJ regularly criticized the NOOs for neglecting this population group. In fact, the assistance allocated to them was relatively modest and apparently considered legitimate by the general population, but their *raison d'être* was sometimes misunderstood. Towards the end of the war, the NOO for the Bosanska Dubica district stated for example that following the distribution of the first cash benefits, the population believed that these were due to all those who had participated in the war, and not only to those who were no longer able to provide for themselves.[44] From this time onwards, a new social group began to form around the army, whose material status was linked to its military and political commitment, and whose emergence was all the more significant as, at the same time, the families of the 'enemies of the people' had their property confiscated.

Taken as a whole, the moral economy established in the liberated territories was surprisingly similar to that observed in the 1970s by James Scott in Southeast Asia, based on a 'right to subsistence' whereby 'all members of a community have a presumptive right to a living so far as local resources will allow', and on a 'principle of reciprocity', according to which 'a gift or service received creates, for the recipient, a reciprocal obligation to return a gift or service of at least comparable value at some future date'.[45] The main difference is that the moral economy observed by James Scott took shape over the long term, whereas that of the liberated territories of Bosanska Krajina, while certainly based on some traditional practices, experienced major changes dictated by urgency. Elsewhere, James Scott presents another difference that, in the context of the wars of national liberation in Southeast Asia, contrasts 'the ideas [of the radical intelligentsia] which may justify the label "nationalist" or "communist"' from 'a popular revolt [of the peasants] with quite divergent visions of order and justice which threatens to usurp the rebellion for its parochial ends'.[46] A similar difference could easily be identified in the Yugoslav case, but this would risk masking the way in which the cadres of the Partisan movement and the population of the liberated territories were involved in a constant process of negotiation and reciprocal adaptation, as revealed by a closer examination of the actual or supposed differences between voluntary contributions and forced requisitions.

Were voluntary contributions actually voluntary?

As we have seen, a distinction was made in as early as 1942 between voluntary contributions, forced requisitions and confiscations. This distinction is apparent in the documents of the People's Liberation Committees, and the NOO for Bosanska Krajina distinguished, for example in October 1943, between voluntary contributions, which had to be made on a 'purely voluntary' basis and which would bind the population to the People's Liberation Struggle, voluntary purchases with the provision of a receipt payable at the end of the war, and compulsory purchases or requisitions, also with a receipt, in the event that the two previous forms of supply were insufficient.[47] In practice, however, the line between voluntary contributions and forced requisitions often appeared blurred and porous. This was particularly the case when NOOs set quantitative targets for the collection of voluntary contributions from the outset, or when insufficient contributions led directly to forced requisitions. However, it would be a mistake to think that voluntary contributions were merely requisitions in disguise. Until 1944 at least, the leaders of the Partisan movement seemed very reluctant to resort to forced requisitions. During a regional meeting on food issues held on 8 and 9 May 1944, they even seemed frightened by this prospect: Đuro Bakonja, head of the economic department of the military region, believed that 'in the event of [compulsory] wheat purchases, the people will revolt', and Đuro Pucar, secretary of the KPJ committee for Bosanska Krajina, also feared that 'a revolt will take shape because the requisitions are not carried out uniformly'.[48]

On a less dramatic note, the requisitions carried out by NOOs were often criticized for their poor implementation and negative political impact. In this context, the NOOs attempted to find solutions that would allow them to avoid the use of requisitions. In May 1944, the NOO for Kozara county insisted that 'the taking [of surplus wheat] must be done fairly, in a political way [*na politički način*]. Summon the households from which there is something to be taken, explain the situation of the army and the population of the passive regions to them, and try to convince them to voluntarily give the extra wheat they have, and if that does not work, then carry out a requisition with the legal receipt'.[49] When they nevertheless had to resort to requisitions, the NOOs often limited them to villages whose support for the People's Liberation Struggle was the strongest or, on the contrary, to those considered definitively hostile. In May 1943, the KPJ committee for Bosanska Krajina thus recommended that requisitions should only be carried out in cases of extreme necessity, and in this case, 'the requisition should take place in the villages that are furthest from us, in other words those that are hostile to us'.[50] On the other hand, the NOOs sought to avoid upsetting the villages that had recently rallied the cause or whose support was still fragile. For instance, in November 1944, the KPJ committee for Bosanska Krajina told the committee for Glamoč-Livno county not to proceed with requisitions of livestock or food in the Croat villages around Livno, as these were beginning to side with the Partisans and a number of Croats had joined the local detachment of the People's Liberation Army.[51]

In short, we can say that the system of voluntary contributions was part-way between the direct and spontaneous donations of the early months of the war, when the Partisans were fed by their families or villages, and the forced requisitions that became increasingly important towards the end of the conflict. The 'voluntary' nature of voluntary contributions is therefore debatable, but they differ from forced requisitions in one essential respect: the former were based above all on moral pressure, whereas the latter relied, at least potentially, on physical force. This difference is illustrated by the way in which the NOOs organized village conferences during which the amount of each family's voluntary contributions was read out[52] or the names of the best contributors and the 'saboteurs' were listed.[53] However, as long as they were primarily a moral obligation, voluntary contributions continued to represent a form of giving that was part of a wider system of gifts and counter-gifts. Even if it was only symbolic, this form of gift-giving via voluntary contributions would be important in defining the relationship between the Partisan movement and the population of the liberated territories. Yet it also had practical implications: it left room for negotiation, at a time when the Partisans had not yet established their military and political hegemony, and when the population still had the option of remaining passive or defecting to the enemy.

It is therefore unsurprising that the Partisan movement gave up voluntary contributions in favour of forced requisitions at the very moment when it accelerated its transformation into a state, successfully claiming the monopoly of legitimate force on the territory it controlled. On 31 August 1944, the KPJ committee for Bosanska Krajina neatly summarized this transformation when it explained to the county committees:

> On the issue of the burden [of supplying the army] and how to bear this burden, the People's Liberation Committees must now gradually change their attitude and gradually adopt another guideline, shifting from voluntary contributions to get the masses used to constant obligations to the state. In terms of propaganda, this is the way to go, and not according to the widespread theory that you have to hold out for a few more months and then all obligations will fall away. … We must pursue such a policy and present ourselves to the masses today in such a way that they no longer perceive us as a movement, but as a state, as a power towards which they shall have certain obligations.[54]

This shift coincided with the period during which the new Yugoslav state definitively asserted itself at home and abroad, as evidenced by Tito's arrival in liberated Belgrade on 27 October 1944 and his appointment seven days later as prime minister of a government created from the merger of the National Committee for the Liberation of Yugoslavia and the royal government in exile headed by Ivan Šubašić. The liberated territories of Bosanska Krajina remained a separate enclave for several more months, and the Partisan movement fought against the German troops and those of the Independent State of Croatia until the end of the war in May 1945. It is therefore logical that some of the economic practices established in the early years of the war should continue there for longer. But in Bosanska Krajina, too, the Partisans' growing hegemony was accompanied by the gradual emergence of the confiscatory practices that would characterize the postwar period, and the disappearance of the economic and social compromises on which the relations between the Partisan movement and the population of the liberated territories had been based during the war.

Conclusion

Between 1941 and 1945, under extremely difficult material conditions, the Partisan movement established a 'subsistence economy' in Bosanska Krajina, giving rise to unique economic and social practices. Centred on the production, collection and redistribution of food, this economy involved the de facto collectivization or redistribution of part of the land, the collective organization of agricultural activities and material assistance for the most vulnerable groups such as poor peasants, refugees or the needy families of combatants. It established a largely non-cash system of gifts and counter-gifts in which voluntary contributions in kind played a central role, and which corresponded to a moral economy based on the survival of the greatest possible number, on the one hand, and scrupulous equity in the collection and redistribution of goods, on the other. This moral economy implemented day after day by the People's Liberation Committees (NOOs) was consistent with a political context in which the population still held significant bargaining power, insofar as it could, at any time, take a passive stance or defect to the enemy. This balance was regularly challenged by the army's arbitrary and harsh requisitions, which thus threatened the political legitimacy of the Partisan movement. Above all, as the Partisan movement moved towards the construction of a new state, it replaced the voluntary contributions of the early years of the war with forced requisitions, heralding the start of the confiscatory policies that would characterize the postwar period and lead to a rupture between the communist state and the peasantry.

Notes

1 James Scott, *The Moral Economy of the Peasant. Rebellion and Subsistence in Southeast Asia* (New Haven: Yale University Press, 1976).

2 *Fočanski propisi*, ed. Ahmed Salihćehajić (Sarajevo: Oslobođenje, 1981).

3 'Izjava Vrhovnog štaba NOV i POJ i AVNOJ-a o karakteru Narodnooslobodilačkog pokreta u Jugoslaviji', 8 February 1943, in *Prvo i drugo zasedanje antifašističkog veća narodnog oslobođenja Jugoslavije*, ed. Đorđe Lazović (Belgrade: Prosveta, 1983), 162–3.

4 'Za bolju proljetnu sjetvu', n. d., Arhiv Bosne i Hercegovine (henceforth: ABiH), NOR fonds, box Referati, rezolucije i izvještaji 1941–45.
5 Narodnooslobodilački odbor Kozara, 3 March 1945, Historijski muzej Bosne i Hercegovine (henceforth: HMBiH), NOB fonds, box 21.
6 *Fočanski propisi*, 19–20.
7 Narodnooslobodilački odbor Drvar, 14 January 1944, HMBiH, NOB fonds, box 9.
8 *Fočanski propisi*, 23.
9 Report by Dušan Ivezić to the second session of ZAVNOBiH, 1 July 1944, in *ZAVNOBiH - Dokumenti 1943–1944*, ed. Enver Redžić (Sarajevo: Veselin Masleša, 1968), 242–52, here 245–6.
10 *Fočanski propisi*, 24–8.
11 Narodnooslobodilački odbor Drvar, 7 January 1944, Arhiv Republike Srpske (henceforth: ARS), NOO Drvar fonds, box 1 (1944).
12 Narodnooslobodilački odbor Podgrmeč, 3 September 1944, HMBiH, NOB fonds, box 15.
13 Zemaljsko antifašističko vijeće narodnog oslobođenja Bosne i Hercegovine, Department for Food, 7 January 1945, ABiH, ZAVNOBiH fonds, box 3 (predsjedništvo 1944–45).
14 Komunistička partija Jugoslavije Bosanska Krajina, 22 November 1942, HMBiH, NOB fonds, box 5.
15 Narodnooslobodilački odbor Drvar, 1 March 1944, HMBiH, NOB fonds, box 10.
16 Report by Dušan Ivezić to the second session of the ZAVNOBiH, 1 July 1944, 248.
17 Ibid.
18 Ibid., 249.
19 Narodnooslobodilački odbor Sanski Most, 5 January 1945, HMBiH, NOB fonds, box 19.
20 Narodnooslobodilački odbor Bosanska Krajina, 23 June 1944, ARS, NOO BK fonds, box 1.
21 Zemaljsko antifašističko vijeće narodnog oslobođenja Bosne i Hercegovine, 6 September 1944, in *ZAVNOBiH - Dokumenti 1943–1944*, ed. Enver Redžić, 369.
22 Zemaljsko antifašističko vijeće narodnog oslobođenja Bosne i Hercegovine, 3 March 1944, in ibid., 97–9.
23 Narodnooslobodilački odbor Bosanska Krupa, n. d. [May 1944], HMBiH, NOB fonds, box 12.
24 Narodnooslobodilački odbor Drvar, 21 July 1944, ARS, NOO Drvar fonds, box 1 (1944).
25 Narodnooslobodilački odbor Podgrmeč, 10 January 1944, HMBiH, NOB fonds, box 9.
26 Savez komunističke omladine Jugoslavije Livno, 25 October 1944, ABiH, NOR fonds, box Obl. komitet SKOJ BK 1944 (3).
27 Komunistička partija Jugoslavije Bosanska Krajina, 14 February 1943, ABiH, NOR fonds, box Obl. komitet KPJ BK 1943 (1).
28 Narodnooslobodilački odbor Podgrmeč, 13 October 1944, HMBiH, NOB fonds, box 16.
29 Komunistička partija Jugoslavije Drvar, 1 February 1944, ABiH, NOR fonds, box Obl. komitet KPJ BK 1944 (1).
30 Narodnooslobodilački odbor Drvar, 21 July 1944, ARS, NOO Drvar fonds, box 1 (1944).
31 Komunistička partija Jugoslavije Jajce, 20 February 1942, HMBiH, NOB fonds, box 2.

32 Narodnooslobodilački odbor Bosanski Petrovac, 5 November 1944, ARS, NOO Drvar fonds, box 1 (1944).
33 Narodnooslobodilački odbor Sanski Most, 4 January 1945, HMBiH, NOB fonds, box 19.
34 Melissa Bokovoy, *Peasants and Communists. Politics and Ideology in the Yugoslav Countryside 1941–1953* (Pittsburgh: University of Pittsburgh Press, 1998); Katherine MacCarthy, Peasant Revolutionaries and Partisan Power: Rural Resistance to Communist Policies in Croatia 1941–1953 (PhD Diss., University of Pittsburgh, 1996).
35 Radomir Bulatović, *Narodna privreda Bosne i Hercegovine u oslobodilačkom ratu* (Belgrade: Narodna knjiga, 1984), 82 and 281.
36 On the food situation in the NDH, see Holm Sundhaussen, *Wirtschaftsgeschichte Kroatiens im nationalsozialistischen Grossraum 1941–1945* (Stuttgart: DVA, 1983), 263–76.
37 Narodnooslobodilački odbor Podgrmeč, 15 February 1945, HMBiH, NOB fonds, box 20.
38 Narodnooslobodilački odbor Bosanska Krajina, 19 February 1945, HMBiH, NOB fonds, box 20.
39 See, for example, Narodnooslobodilački odbor Dubovik, 28 August 1944, HMBiH, NOB fonds, box 14; Narodnooslobodilački odbor Kozara, 2 September 1944, HMBiH, NOB fonds, box 15.
40 Komunistička partija Jugoslavije Ključ-Mrkonjić, 20 October 1944, ABiH, NOR fonds, box Obl. komitet KPJ BK 1944 (3).
41 Narodnooslobodilački odbor Prekaja, 11 October 1943, HMBiH, NOB fonds, box 7.
42 Zemaljsko antifašističko vijeće narodnog oslobođenja Bosne i Hercegovine, Department for Social Policy, n. d. [March 1945], ABiH, ZAVNOBiH fonds, box 9 (razna odjeljenja).
43 Zemaljsko antifašističko vijeće narodnog oslobođenja Bosne i Hercegovine, Department for Finance, 26 February 1945, ABiH, ZAVNOBiH fonds, box 9 (razna odjeljenja).
44 Narodnooslobodilački odbor Bosanska Dubica, n. d. [1945], HMBiH, NOB fonds, box 22.
45 Scott, *The Moral Economy of the Peasant*, 167, 176.
46 James Scott, 'Revolution in the Revolution: Peasants and Commissars', *Theory and Society* 7, no. 1–2 (January 1979): 97–134, here 97.
47 Narodnooslobodilački odbor Bosanska Krajina, 31 October 1943, HMBiH, NOB fonds, box 7.
48 Narodnooslobodilački odbor Bosanska Krajina, 9 May 1944, ABiH, ZAVNOBiH fonds, box 2 (predsjedništvo 1944).
49 Narodnooslobodilački odbor Kozara, 28 May 1944, ARS, NOO Kozara fonds, box 2 (1944).
50 Komunistička partija Jugoslavije Bosanska Krajina, 26 May 1943, ABiH, NOR fonds, box Okr. komitet KPJ Podgrmeč 1942–45.
51 Komunistička partija Jugoslavije Bosanska Krajina, 19 November 1944, ABiH, NOR fonds, box Obl. komitet KPJ Bosanska Krajina 1944 (5).
52 Narodnooslobodilački odbor Podgrmeč, 2 April 1944, HMBiH, NOB fonds, box 11.
53 Narodnooslobodilački odbor Sanski Most, 3 September 1943, HMBiH, NOB fonds, box 7.
54 Komunistička partija Jugoslavije Bosanska Krajina, 31 August 1944, ABiH, NOR fonds, box Obl. komitet KPJ BK 1944 (3).

10

The National Liberation Movement and food policies in the liberated inland territories of southern Albania (1942–44)

Markenc Lorenci

For decades the official historiography of the Albanian Communist regime celebrated the Partisan war as a war of the people, enslaved and threatened by starvation, against the fascist occupation forces.[1] Although there has been no lack of studies on the economic difficulties brought about by the occupation, research on and analysis of the food policies pursued by the Albanian Partisan movement or National Liberation Movement (*Lëvizja Nacional-Çlirimtare*) in the territories it liberated, also known as 'free zones' (*zonat e lira*), is much more scarce.[2] This also applies to the works of both Albanian and foreign historians following the collapse of the Communist regime, which focused more on narrating political and military events.[3]

The aim of this chapter is therefore to reconstruct and examine the food policies pursued by the National Liberation Movement, with the General National Liberation Council (*Këshilli i Përgjithshëm Nacional-Çlirimtar* – KPNÇ) at its head, and its local National Liberation Councils (*Këshillat Nacional-Çlirimtar* – KNÇs) in the liberated territories. In order to do so, the chapter focuses on the hinterland of southern Albania, taking as case studies the Skrapar district in Berat prefecture and the Përmet district in Gjirokastër prefecture, both considered strongholds of the Partisan movement (see Map 5). The chapter covers the period from 1942, when the National Liberation Movement was founded and the first 'free zones' created, to the end of the war in the final months of 1944.[4]

In terms of chapter structure, I will begin by reconstructing the economic situation and local food conditions, the pre-existing heterogeneities and those that developed during the war. I will then address the way the National Liberation Movement set out and implemented its food policies in the liberated territories. The ultimate aim of the chapter is to analyse how and to what extent these food policies contributed to its establishment in these areas and to the recruitment for the Partisan formations during the war years.

From the interwar period to the fascist occupation: The changing economic situation

On the eve of the Second World War, and more precisely of the Italian occupation that preceded it in April 1939, Albania faced a difficult economic situation. The industrial sector was almost non-existent, and the primary sources of income throughout the interwar period remained agriculture, on which 80 per cent of the population depended, and pastoralism.[5] These sectors were also quite under-developed, however. The conditions in animal breeding and the techniques used produced small, fragile animals, while in the agricultural sector, despite the fertile land in the western plain, in the great lakes regions and even in certain inland plateaus, the percentage of cultivated land was very low, still amounting to only 9 per cent of the entire territory of Albania in 1938.[6]

The unfavourable situation in agriculture stemmed from a number of factors, including the fact that much of this land was marshy and unevenly divided.[7] Thus, while in northern Albania, where there was less arable land, land ownership was shared – albeit more in some places than others – by all the families, in central and southern Albania, it was concentrated in the hands of large landowners (the beys) and the state.[8] Neither the beys, with a few exceptions, nor the state managed their properties directly but merely rented out parts of their plots to landless peasants, often leaving huge segments uncultivated.[9] The tenants had no incentive to increase productivity, contented to simply meet the needs of their families, owing the landowner one-third of the harvest and the state the agricultural tithe.[10]

The largest number of landless peasants, who bore the highest tax burden, lived in the central and especially southern part of the country, but the economic situation did not differ significantly among Albania's rural regions, all of which were characterized by a poor subsistence economy. Within this economy, however, a new element had appeared in the villages of the south: namely, migrant remittances. In fact, the peasants from the south, unlike the rest of the country, which had remained very static, were the first to emigrate to the United States, France and Greece.[11] As a result, the rural regions of the south showed slight economic 'dynamism' compared to those in the rest of the country. It must be borne in mind, however, that it was the southern peasants who felt social injustices most keenly due to land being concentrated in the hands of the beys and the state.

Later, at the start of the fascist occupation and for at least the first year, there was an initial improvement in the living conditions of the Albanian population thanks to the large sums of money the country received both in the form of direct subsidies and through the construction of important public works, as well as to the abundance of foodstuffs that came to Albania from Italy.[12] However, this situation soon gave way to a gradual deterioration, mainly due to the Italian military campaign against Greece from October 1940 to April 1941, and its aftermath. This military action was poorly prepared and as such, after an initial Italian offensive on Greek territory, resulted in a Greek counter-offensive and the retreat of Italian and Albanian troops into the hinterland of southern Albania. It was here that fighting continued for months.[13] This had a whole series of negative consequences for the population of the southern hinterland and in particular for the peasants, who suffered not only the destruction or at least the looting of their homes by one or the other army in the field, but also great losses in livestock and enormous damage to agriculture.[14] After the end of the Italo-Greek War and the victory of the Axis forces, however, the fascist authorities did not take any decisive action to restore the economic and social conditions of the many villages and centres in the hinterland of the south that had been so severely damaged. In fact, it turns out that many of the war-affected areas never received reparations for the damage they suffered, despite multiple entreaties from local authorities.[15]

In addition to the damage suffered due to wartime actions, for many peasants in the southern hinterland, the outbreak of the Second World War meant an almost complete stop to the remittances sent by their emigrant relatives. To make matters worse, in particular during the Italo-Greek War, there was a major increase in prices throughout the country, accompanied by a general shortage of food in the markets. The rise in prices was due both to inflation brought about by the huge expenditures to finance the war effort and to keep the local population calm, and to the rampant speculation on consumer goods to which many Albanian and Italian traders had turned.[16] In fact, many of these traders resorted to hoarding entire warehouses of goods for speculation purposes, primarily to the detriment of troops stationed or in transit. This situation had also been fuelled and exacerbated by the fascist Lieutenancy issuing import permits to a small group of notables and high-ranking state officials, who could block and unblock large quantities of goods, greatly influencing price trends. Added to this was the transportation problem resulting from the lack of fuel and tyres.[17] A month after the end of the Italo-Greek War, for example, the Commandant of the *Carabinieri* in Albania reported that the prefecture of Gjirokastër was unable to provide transportation even for the meagre quantities of flour and corn sent by the Supply and Consumption Authority (*Ente Approvvigionamenti e Consumi*) to the other centres in the prefecture and especially to the mountain municipalities, 'due to the lack of means and convenient equipment'.[18]

All this led to a very difficult situation for the hinterland of the south, which only worsened over the course of the Second World War. As a consequence, on 19 October 1942, there was a protest over the bread shortage in front of the municipality and prefecture buildings in Gjirokastër, which the security forces dispersed.[19] In Berat, on the other hand, the poor supply of maize flour and the complete lack of salt had been reported as early as May 1942.[20] Also in Berat, despite the fact that the Central Committee of the Supply and Consumption Authority had set a quota of 250 grams of sugar and 750 grams of beans per person per month, the Regional Council for the Economy (*Këshilli Krahinor për Ekonomin*) was, in December 1942, forced to reduce that quota to 200 grams of sugar and just 200 grams of beans per person.[21]

The situation described also led to the development of an economic and food gap between this region and the rest of the country, which during this period was not exposed to wartime events of the same magnitude as those suffered by the southern hinterland. As a result, the fascist occupation and the Italo-Greek War had a decidedly negative impact on the perceptions of much of the population of the southern hinterland, thus creating a fertile terrain for the resistance.

Organization of the Partisan resistance: Formation of the first liberated territories and establishment of the KNÇs

Partisan resistance in Albania, as indeed in other countries in Eastern Europe and beyond, originated in the activities of the local Communist Party, in this case the Albanian Communist Party (*Partia Komuniste Shqiptare* – PKSh), which promoted and directed the Partisan resistance throughout the Second World War. When the PKSh was founded in November 1941,[22] its members immediately faced the need to form an armed front that would upgrade the anti-fascist resistance from the small urban guerrilla warfare animated by the members of the PKSh, and the isolated actions of a few apolitical armed groups operating in the rural hinterland, to a broader resistance, which in addition to its purely military functions would also perform civilian functions. Thus in September 1942, following an appeal by members of the PKSh to a number of nationalists and men-at-arms, a conference was held in the village of Peza, a few kilometres from Tirana, resulting in the formation of the General National Liberation Council (KPNÇ).[23] This, in turn, led to the creation of the National Liberation Movement, that is, the Partisan movement, which was the first actual Albanian resistance organization.

At the end of the Peza Conference, the participants passed a resolution prepared earlier by the members of the PKSh, which also specified the tasks of the local organs of the KPNÇ, namely the local National Liberation Councils (KNÇs) that would be formed throughout the country, distinguishing between actions to be carried out in the occupied territories and those to be conducted in the territories that would be liberated.[24] In the occupied territories, the KNÇs constituted organs of war, had the task of making propaganda, mobilizing the masses for the liberation struggle, procuring arms for Partisans and volunteers and supplying them with provisions. On top of this, in the occupied territories, the KNÇs were also to organize the sabotage of the harvest destined for the central authorities, the tithe and all other actions conducted by the occupying forces, such as those carried out through agricultural societies and banks.[25] In the liberated territories, however, they were to carry out executive rather than military tasks, enforcing law and order, fighting crime and theft. They were also in charge of the economy and responsible for feeding the population, and, like the KNÇs in the occupied territories, had to provide food and other supplies for the Partisan units.[26]

With the Peza Conference concluded, the first Partisan units formed and their actions coordinated, the first liberated territories in the southern hinterland, which the Italo-Greek War had hit hardest, also started to be established. Thus, from the autumn of 1942, the Partisan units began to conduct a series of continuous actions against small military garrisons in the villages of Skrapar (Berat) and Përmet (Gjirokastër) districts, leading on more than one occasion to the ousting of the latter, the overthrowing of the local government authorities and the establishment of the National Liberation Movement authority with the formation of the first local KNÇs.[27] Following the liberation of the first villages, in January 1943, the Partisans also liberated the capital of Skrapar district, Çorovodë, and with it the entire district,[28] thus creating the first sizeable liberated territory with a number of KNÇs founded throughout. However, the freedom of these areas was very fragile. In the absence of a front line, the occupying troops, although no longer stationed there, were, on several occasions, able to penetrate the areas and carry out reprisals, as had happened in the liberated territories under Partisan control in Yugoslavia.[29]

Simultaneously with the formation of these 'free zones' and the establishment of local councils, the Partisans immediately devoted themselves to the fight against banditry, a phenomenon that was particularly pronounced in the south because of the weakness and, in some cases even complicity, of the forces of law and order. In the Skrapar district, in particular, where the episodes of brigandage had become very frequent, the Partisan unit of Xhelal Staravecka was especially active in the armed struggle. In November 1942, Staravecka and his men captured three brigands who had stolen cattle. They then arranged for two of the brigands to be killed and buried at a crossroads where a plaque was erected indicating the crime they had committed to serve as a warning to anyone who might contemplate committing similar acts.[30]

The first Partisan formations also devoted themselves to combating the collection of the agricultural tithe and other taxes from the local population. In December 1942, the Finance Office of Gjirokastër informed that it was no longer possible to send their officials to villages to collect taxes due to the presence of armed resistance units.[31] Indeed, in all areas where Partisan units operated, tax collectors were at immediate risk of being killed. In March 1943, the political commissar of the Skrapar unit, Ramiz Aranitasi, wrote to tax collector Mihal Sallabanda with the following warning: 'If you go to the peasants to register or collect taxes, which by your hand will help the enemy, ... the bullet or the donkey rope will be waiting for you, therefore, if you love your children, step aside.'[32]

Parallel to the direct actions undertaken by the Partisans, the KNÇs in the liberated territories also gradually began to carry out their functions. However, it should be pointed out here that at least in the first months of their existence, these organs were weak, often only serving as a façade in their operations.[33] In addition to their initial structural weakness, the lack of centralization, i.e. of directives from above and links between the KPNÇ at the top and the provincial KNÇs, represented one of the main causes of the KNÇs' problems.[34]

Another problem had been the establishment in November 1942, i.e. shortly after the foundation of the National Liberation Movement, of the National Front (*Balli Kombëtar* – BK), an autonomous resistance body composed of intellectuals and landowners united by republicanism, nationalism and anti-communism.[35] Thanks to the power and influence its members had over the population, the BK was able to establish its own local councils, succeeding in quite a few cases in sabotaging the National Liberation Movement's KNÇs and drawing members of certain villages into its local bodies.

Indeed, at first, the peasants did not always welcome the Partisan units. In June 1943, the KNÇ of the Gjirokastër prefecture informed the few villages that had not shown commitment to providing food and lodging to Partisans that henceforth they were expected to be much more helpful.[36] The presence of the Partisan units was not solely a burden on the local population of the areas where they operated. Thanks to the various cash receipts and especially to the golden coins received from the British liaison officers which had initially infiltrated southern Albania at the beginning of spring 1943, the Partisan forces were able to make purchases from the local population and become part of the local economy in the areas in which they were operating. As British officer David Smiley recalls, Sundays in Shtyllë near Korçë, where the British mission had established its headquarters and where the Partisan forces also operated, had become market days. These markets attracted many peasants who would come to sell their mules, essential to the Partisan struggle for transportation.[37] For the supply of the First Partisan Brigade, Enver Hoxha, who had been the political secretary of the PKSh since March 1943, ordered the PKSh committee in Skrapar in August 1943 to buy 80 quintals of wheat, 20 quintals of beans and 4 quintals of oil with the £200 (gold) received from the British.[38]

Repression and deterioration of the economic situation

The actions carried out by the Partisan groups in terms of liberating territories, as well as those undertaken directly against enemy columns across almost the entire southern hinterland were followed by a series of reprisals by the occupation forces and the collaborationist government militaries, which in many cases also had a significant impact on the civilian population.

Thus, following the Partisan actions for the liberation of Çorovodë in December 1942, the High Command of the Italian Armed Forces in Albania had given orders to carry out a series of aerial bombardments on the settlements of Çorovodë and other surrounding villages where Partisan units were located.[39] Writing about this episode in his memoirs, Xhelal Staravecka claimed that the bombing and machine-gunning had deliberately targeted not only the inhabitants but also the livestock in the pastures, with the clear aim of creating terror.[40] As a result, the Italian forces injured a substantial number of people and seriously damaged property and livestock.[41] The fact that the Skrapar district then came under the control of the Partisans and that there was no longer any government authority there also resulted in supplies of primary foodstuffs to the region from the central authorities coming to a complete halt.

After the Partisan actions conducted in early July 1943 for the liberation of Përmet, the second-largest territory liberated after Skrapar, the Italian army had meted out harsh repressive measures. On 6 July, some Italian units sent to defend the city went on, after burning all the houses and the market in the small town of Këlcyrë and other surrounding villages, to enter Përmet where they destroyed 172 homes and burned seventy-seven shops.[42] A report by the Partisan unit 'Musa Fratari' estimated that as a result of these repressions about 3,000 people were left without housing and bread.[43] Consequently, the food conditions for the population of the first liberated territories, i.e. Skrapar district and especially Përmet district, immediately became critical.

Following the fascist capitulation in September 1943 and the establishment of the Nazi occupation, the situation for the entire inland south and the liberated territories became even more difficult. Unlike the Italians who had been sustaining their troops with supplies from Italy, the Germans hoped to feed theirs with local food resources. In addition to the failure to provide the necessary food supplies, the government authorities also complained to the Germans about the failure to provide transportation for these goods.[44]

In November, the Germans began a series of operations against Partisan forces known as the 'winter offensive', which was followed by another major offensive during the summer of 1944. Open confrontation between Partisan and BK forces also began in November, resulting in the BK ceasing its resistance activities and joining the government collaborationist forces. During the two anti-Partisan offensives, not only did the Partisan movement suffer major losses, but the German and collaborationist troops, along with the BK, also sought to damage the economy of their rearguard, i.e. the territories under their control. Organized in small units, the Nazi and collaborationist forces carried out frequent raids on liberated territories, seizing foodstuffs and animals and destroying fields.[45] The occupying forces also severely hampered maize cultivation in the plains, leading many farmers to resort to growing crops in the mountains.[46] In Berat, the BK prohibited the transfer of foodstuffs outside the city, thus depriving many peasants in the liberated territories of the possibility of buying food.[47] It should be added here, however, that unlike the Italian authorities, who were intent on destroying the Partisan forces, the German authorities' objective was to weaken the Partisans so they no longer posed a threat rather than eliminating them altogether. In fact, besides never providing the collaborationist forces with the required quantities of armaments and supplies, the Germans always left control of the mountains to the Partisans. In their view, the survival of the Partisan movement would keep the communist danger alive in Albania, thus tying anti-communist nationalist forces to the Germans.[48] The Italian repression, being followed by a similar action by the Germans, thus led to a further deterioration of the food conditions in the liberated territories and consequently also accentuated the disparity between these areas and the rest of the country, which experienced significantly less wartime violence.

That said, despite the serious food situation in the liberated territories, the local population never experienced dramatic levels of famine. This was, however, the fate suffered by many of the Italian soldiers who, following capitulation and after refusing to surrender to German forces, wandered the Albanian countryside in the hope of being repatriated. The initial disbandment and requisitioning of their food stores by Nazi and resistance forces meant many of them, especially during the first weeks, were completely deprived of food and in many cases perished from starvation on the edge of the road.[49] In this complex situation that had arisen in the liberated territories, it was up to the National Liberation Movement and its local organs to undertake the difficult task of managing economic life with a particular focus on food resources.

Strengthening the KNÇs and drafting economic and food policies

Although during the first year of their existence the role of the KNÇs in the liberated territories had been weak and in many cases they had served as no more than a façade, a gradual strengthening of the Councils took place from the summer of 1943 onwards. This happened for a number of reasons. The first was the formation in July

1943 of the General Staff of the Albanian National Liberation Army (*Ushtria Nacional-Çlirimtare Shqiptare* – UNÇSh), the aim of which was to organize the Partisan units into a proper army composed of brigades and divisions.[50] As part of this structuring work, the UNÇSh divided Albanian territory into large operational zones, while in the liberated territories, it organized military power on the basis of provincial and local commands, the latter being equipped with their own volunteer Partisan guards.[51] The improved military structuring of the Partisan movement and in particular the establishment of military power with related local commands, which were to operate in cooperation with the KNÇs and work to implement their resolutions, consequently also implied the strengthening of the KNÇs' authority in the liberated territories.

From the same period onwards, the KNÇs also gradually began to assume a more hierarchical and centralized structure, with village KNÇs at the base, moving up to municipal, provincial, district or sub-prefecture KNÇs, and then prefecture KNÇs, with the latter answerable only to the KPNÇ at the top of the hierarchy. At the same time, in order to better organize work from the top down, the higher councils also created specialized sections, such as the administrative, propaganda, education, economic, health and social welfare section.[52]

In addition to these internal factors, the incorporation of the BK into the government forces and the cessation of its resistance action also strengthened the KNÇs. The BK neglected its local councils, which had no way to consolidate and strengthen themselves and thus to continue to compete, in the south of the country, with the KNÇs of the National Liberation Movement. These remained the only properly structured resistance bodies.

If all this contributed to strengthening the KNÇs, the approval, during the Second KPNÇ Conference in September 1943, of the Statute and Regulations of the KNÇs (*Statuti dhe Rregullorja e Këshillavet Nacional Çlirimtar*)[53] sought to provide order and draw up the guidelines that all KNÇs were to follow from then on.[54] According to this Statute and Regulations, once again, while the function of the KNÇs in the territories that had not yet been liberated was to materially and morally support the UNÇSh and to organize and coordinate the people's fight against the occupier, in the liberated territories, the KNÇs were to assume all administrative, executive and judicial functions, except those considered to be of a military nature, as organs of the people's power.[55] Yet, although the KNÇs in the liberated territories were in charge of organizing and coordinating food supplies both for the local population in their own districts and for the Partisan forces, even in these territories priority had to be given to the war, which meant supplying the UNÇSh. In fact, a careful reading of the KNÇs Statute and Regulations reveals that the main function even of the KNÇs in the liberated territories was to support the UNÇSh by all means. In this regard, one of the first points of the Statute and Regulations stated as follows: 'The National Liberation Councils, in close cooperation with the National Liberation Army Commands, shall take all measures to supply the army with food, clothing and other necessities. For these reasons, they shall prepare the people to make the necessary sacrifices for their National Liberation Army.'[56]

For the supply of the UNÇSh, the Statute and Regulations stipulated that the KNÇs set up so-called National Liberation Funds (*Fonde Nacional-Çlirimtare*), which comprised warehouses and chests where aid supplies were to be collected from the people (albeit not exclusively), including food, clothing, money and other items. At least once a month, the village councils had to transfer all their income to the National Liberation Funds of the municipal councils. The municipal councils then had the right to keep 30 per cent of the funds for their own needs, such as for aid to be given to the families of refugees and poor Partisans, while paying the rest into the National Liberation Funds of the sub-prefectural councils on which the municipal councils depended, with the latter being the largest funds for technical purposes. The sub-prefecture councils then had to communicate the amount of funds to the prefecture councils, which in turn had to pass this information to the KPNÇ.[57]

Again, for the supply of the army, the KNÇs or military intendants were also to purchase food and other essentials. The same regulations specified that, where there was surplus, it was either to be donated to the National Liberation Funds or sold to the KNÇs or UNÇSh. If this surplus was not sold, the KNÇs and the military intendants – who also had the right to set the price of these goods – could forcibly purchase them. In cases of urgent need or monetary shortage, the KNÇs and military organs, always and exclusively at the request and on behalf of the military commands, could also carry out requisitions of food and animals, both for consumption and transport, primarily from the surplus of peasants or wealthy citizens. Such requisitions were understood as purchases that were not paid for immediately, and for each requisition a receipt had to be issued with which those concerned could demand payment for the requisitioned goods at a later date.[58] This established, it was nevertheless recommended that the KNÇs ensure that these measures were enforced on a voluntary basis, and that force only be used as a last resort.[59]

The National Liberation Movement also confiscated the properties of all those declared 'enemies of the people' and added them to its list of revenues. However, it was stipulated that if these people had family dependents, they should be left with a minimum share for their subsistence. The rest went to the funds of the municipality or sub-prefecture KNÇs or, if real estate was involved, placed under the latter's direct control.[60]

On the other hand, regarding the organization of food supplies for the local population of the liberated territories, again the link to the ongoing war and in many respects to military interests was quite clear. According to the Statute and Regulations of the KNÇs, the organization of food supplies for the population of their district was to help first and foremost the children of Partisans and volunteers, and in particular the children of those who had fallen in the war, of prisoners and internees, and of those whose homes had been destroyed by the occupying forces.[61] Indeed, as mentioned earlier, the municipal KNÇs were entitled to retain 30 per cent of their funds, which could be allocated to the families of refugees from other villages and the families of poor soldiers. In addition to food resources, real estate, i.e. the housing and land confiscated from the 'enemies of the people', was to be distributed primarily to families affected by the war and to families of the combatants in the ranks of the Partisan movement.[62] The same applied to real estate belonging to those families who had chosen to move away from the liberated territories. In this case, however, the Statute and Regulations specified that the allocation of these properties to the peasants was to be considered a temporary arrangement, until the actual owners returned. Finally, the fight against theft, profiteering and any form of taxation imposed by the government authorities was reaffirmed.

From paper to reality: The application of food policies in the liberated territories (September 1943–November 1944)

Now that the KNÇs followed well-established directives, the next step was their implementation at the local level. With regard to the collection of aid intended for the UNÇSh, the KNÇs of the prefectures informed the KNÇs below them of the urgent need to collect grain and other aid from the farmers. On 16 November 1943, the KNÇ of the Gjirokastër prefecture sent a circular letter to the KNÇ in Përmet with the following instruction: 'Considering the extent of the war and the increased size of the army … do what you can to ensure that in each village grain aid is provided according to each person's available resources, without imposing any additional hardship.'[63] While in this particular circular, the KNÇ of Gjirokastër had called for voluntary aid to be donated according to the available resources of each individual, in another letter addressed to all its provincial KNÇs, undated but most probably from the same period, it established the provision of grain aid at harvest time as compulsory for all and also fixed the quotas for this contribution: 5 per cent for those who produced very small quantities, 6 per cent for those who produced medium quantities and 7 per cent and upwards for those who produced quantities in excess of their family's needs.[64] The harvesting of this grain was considered so important that each village appointed an individual responsible for the grain harvest, as well as a controller for every two villages. In this way, the KNÇs imposed a form of progressive taxation on agricultural production, much like what was happening in the liberated territories under the control of the National Liberation Front (*Ethniko Apeleftherotiko Metopo* – EAM) in Greece.[65] In order to acquire a complete overview of the economic circumstances of the families living in these areas, the KNÇ of Gjirokastër also asked the provincial KNÇs to compile lists for each village, indicating the name of the head of the family, the number of family members, the number of transport animals and the family's economic circumstances.[66]

Unfortunately, there are no exact figures on the amount of food the National Liberation Movement received from the liberated territories. However, if we consider the fact that municipal councils got only 30 per cent of the National Liberation Funds and that another small part went to social welfare funds, the largest part of the aid obtained from the population, both in kind and in cash, went to supplying the UNÇSh. Having accumulated these foodstuffs in the funds of the municipal and sub-prefectural KNÇs, the supply of Partisan forces was the responsibility of the military authorities, which could draw on these funds. It was therefore the task of the Partisan and volunteer guards of the liberated territories to provide any passing Partisan units with food. The transport of food supplies to the various KNÇs and those destined directly for the Partisan forces was largely carried out with mules or, if available, horses. The army either bought or temporarily requisitioned the transport animals it needed.

Despite the priority given to supplying the army, the National Liberation Movement still took a number of civil measures to meet the needs of the population. And although, here too, the families of the Partisans and those affected by the war were prioritized, measures were also taken to help poor families and the population at large without discrimination. Thus, in order to maximize the availability of foodstuffs and to try to offset the shortage suffered by the local population, the KNÇ of the prefecture of Gjirokastër, in cooperation with the High Command of the First Operational Zone Gjirokastër-Vlorë, banned the export of all foodstuffs from its area as early as October 1943.[67] The KNÇ also extended this ban to exports to Greece, but stipulated that a form of exchange was allowed with EAM, subject to prior authorization.[68] To effectively enforce this ban and control the transit of any goods, the KNÇ in Përmet appointed Partisan and voluntary custom guards, who were to arrest anyone caught exporting prohibited goods and confiscate those goods. Instead, in order to combat the speculation on foodstuffs that had also affected the liberated territories, in March 1944, the same KNÇ fixed the prices of some of the most important foodstuffs.[69]

Another important initiative taken to improve the population's access to foodstuffs was the creation of inland markets in the liberated territories, as markets were generally held in the towns that were now largely under the control of enemy forces. The KNÇs of sub-prefectures and provinces were in charge of creating these markets, which were to supply the population with necessities at a modest price – equal to the purchase price plus expenses – and of setting prices for private traders who wanted to sell there. As products were in short supply, the provincial KNÇs had to constantly communicate with each other to exchange any surplus goods.[70] Within these markets, there were also some cases of the local military commands themselves selling foodstuffs at low prices.[71]

To cope with the deteriorating nutritional status of many families as a result of the Nazi repressions, the National Liberation Movement also established a 'social assistance' campaign in all liberated provinces to help the poorest families, under the slogan: 'No one should die of hunger' (*asnjë të mos vdesë urije*). As part of this campaign, in April 1944, the provincial KNÇ in Cerie, Përmet, appealed to those in a better economic situation to help their brothers and sisters who were in danger of starvation, even setting a quota for donations, which, it was hoped, people would pay voluntarily.[72] In addition to this, the social welfare sections set up in the prefecture councils allocated some aid to families in need, upon the village councils issuing declarations attesting to the families' poverty. In an attempt to remedy the difficult situation that had arisen, the National Liberation Movement also resorted to the assets of religious institutions. The sub-prefecture council of Përmet, for instance, in requesting precise information on all their goods and annual income in its district, also decided that, after deducting the expenses required to maintain the religious institutions and their employees, local parishes would distribute the rest to the poor people of the villages in cooperation with the village KNÇs.[73]

Considering that the liberated territories also became the main source of new Partisan recruits, thus removing them from work in the fields, it was also decided to organize 'work squads' for each liberated village. These were made up of men and women, mostly young or unfit for the front, who among other things – setting up temporary shelters for all displaced families, repairing the roads and bridges necessary for village life – were also to work the fields of the families whose men had enlisted as Partisans.[74] Following the fascist capitulation, many Italian soldiers also provided help in cultivating the fields. In fact, of the approximately 15,000 soldiers who decided not to surrender to the Nazis and instead to take the mountain route and join the Partisan forces, just a few hundred decided to join the Partisans in the armed fight.[75] Although their presence was a cause of concern for the National Liberation Movement, because sustaining them could aggravate the already-difficult food situation in the liberated territories, the UNÇSh military authorities deployed these men to various villages where they worked in exchange for food.[76]

Tilling the land in the liberated territories was indeed a priority on the National Liberation Movement's agenda. To this end, and to overcome the problem of the lack of working animals, either killed during the war or seized by the occupying forces, it was decided that villages with more animals should help those with few or no animals. Military commands themselves were no longer to slaughter or unnecessarily detain confiscated working animals, but were to hand them over to the councils of the most heavily damaged and deprived villages.[77]

The question that arises, however, is how the local populations reacted to the implementation of these food policies. It is important to emphasize at the outset that while the attitude of the population of the liberated territories had initially fluctuated, with a shift from one faction to another not an uncommon occurrence, the establishment of local commands and the strengthening of the KNÇs increasingly placed the people under the authority of the National Liberation Movement. As for the population's willingness to deliver aid as requested, although there were some very generous villages, others donated less and often reluctantly. In this regard, a report on Përmet's KNÇs stated that while the entire province of Dëshnicë, which was in good economic shape and had 700 men in the Partisan ranks, had contributed a great deal to supplying the Partisan forces with food, the village of Topovë in the province of Zagori, which faced a difficult economic situation and only had a few men in the Partisan ranks, had not provided aid particularly willingly, distinguishing itself as a village that was rather inhospitable.[78] In fact, the economic situation in which a village or province found itself when liberated and, above all, the personal connection with the Partisan movement were very important factors in the degree of benevolence or acceptance of the policies established by the National Liberation Movement through its councils. It is no coincidence that in October 1944, with the aim of collecting aid in the form of grape derivatives and clothes, the military intendancy of the Seventh UNÇSh Brigade informed the KNÇ of the sub-prefecture of Skrapar of the need to organize a campaign among the anti-fascist women of that district to obtain this aid, which was intended for the children of the Berat prefecture and in particular those of Skrapar who were members of that brigade.[79]

The attitude of the councils and Partisan forces towards the population was almost always very cautious. When it came to obtaining aid for the army, it was always advised to organize large gatherings with the population explaining the importance of the Partisan war, presented as a people's war. Indeed, there were cases of the participants present at a council meeting opposing the attempt to impose a form of taxation. Thus, for example, during a meeting of the Përmet sub-prefecture council held on 22 March 1944, delegates from the lower councils and other representatives of the population opposed the proposal for a mill tax.[80]

In their everyday conduct towards the population, too, the Partisan forces proved to be more disciplined than the other armed factions in the field, including the government forces, which on several occasions engaged in plundering at the expense of the population. The respect for private property, at least of those not declared 'enemies of the people', was a very important aspect for the National Liberation Movement. That said, Partisans sometimes violated these principles. Towards the end of the war, the High Command of the First Operational Zone Gjirokastër-Vlorë criticized a series of unjust and brutal acts perpetrated by local commanders, including confiscations which did not adhere to any criteria, requisitions made by ordinary Partisans over which compensation disputes arose, and violent behaviour of Partisan guards towards peasants. The same body reprimanded the village KNÇs for distributing the food aid and work animals intended for poor families on the basis of personal sympathies and acquaintances, or without applying any criteria, so much so that many of those who had obtained the aid and animals then sold or traded them. Such behaviour was strongly condemned as it did nothing but alienate the population, and the High Command specified that local commands, their staff and councils were to set an example for the population.[81]

Having said this, in all the territories under the control of the Partisan forces where the National Liberation Movement had established its military power, it is highly likely to have been difficult to oppose the established directives, even the food directives. While the presence of the local commands and their potential coercive power facilitated the implementation of the directives, the heavy and continuous patriotic propaganda conducted by all National Liberation Movement organs sought to justify and legitimize them. As the municipal KNÇ of Therepel (Skrapar) warned in a communiqué sent to all its village KNÇs, failure to comply with the established provisions in terms of donations and aid would put a burden on the latter and would also be considered sabotage.[82]

At least until the end of the war in November 1944, despite the violations committed by both the Partisan forces and the KNÇs, the National Liberation Movement in the liberated territories always preferred to use a mixed approach of voluntary donations, requisitions and confiscations, as well as the compulsory tax on grain at harvest time. In maintaining a balance between these forms of revenue, the National Liberation Movement sought not to exceed the limits that were acceptable to the local population.

Conclusion

When it came to the exercise of power by the National Liberation Movement and its local bodies in the liberated territories in Albania, the food issue played a crucial role, given that the countryside and the liberated territories were a very important source of sustenance for the Partisan forces from the very beginning. Once the National Liberation Movement had exempted the population of the liberated territories from the payment of all taxes, it gradually, through its local bodies, began to make its own demands, ranging from free donations to compulsory grain payment, thus assuming the functions of a parallel government. The two questions posed at the beginning of this chapter remain relevant: To what extent did the food policies pursued by the National Liberation Movement influence its establishment within the liberated territories? And to what extent did these policies swell the ranks of the Partisan units?

The Partisan actions and the National Liberation Movement taking control of the liberated territories triggered a series of reprisals by the occupying forces, leading to a deterioration of the food situation in these areas and the resentment of the local population. However, in taking over public life, the National Liberation Movement showed, or at least endeavoured to show that it was more present and less oppressive than both the prewar state and later collaborationist regimes. Even when it applied the compulsory grain tax, the National Liberation Movement implemented, for the first time, a tax based on the size of the harvest, which was an innovation that took into account the different resources of the peasantry. In the harsh wartime conditions that these populations endured, despite privileging certain categories, the National Liberation Movement managed to establish an economic system aimed at enabling the survival of the entire population, while promoting solidarity at the same time. Ultimately, in a context where the only local authority left was that of the National Liberation Movement, all these aspects led, over time, to a certain rapprochement of the population and in particular those affected by the occupying forces.

When it comes to the contribution made by these food policies to swelling the Partisan ranks, which occurred in particular from the autumn of 1943 onwards, it can be stated that here, too, the policies carried substantial weight. It is true that a number of other factors also played a role in increasing the UNÇSh forces, such as the Partisans' hoarding of a large part of Italian armaments, British supplies and the now clearly imminent end of the war in favour of the Allied forces. In addition to these aspects, however, the fact that food policies responded primarily to military needs allowed the UNÇSh to have access to the necessary resources to take in new recruits. For many of the inhabitants of the liberated territories, who constituted a large part of the new recruits, enrolment in the Partisan forces not only guaranteed a livelihood, albeit a modest one, but also provided reassurance that, during this particularly difficult period, their families would have priority when it came to receiving the assistance provided by the KNÇs.

Notes

1 Ndreçi Plasari and Shyqri Ballvora, *Historia e Luftës Antifashiste Nacional Çlirimtare të popullit shqiptar: prill 1939 – nëntor 1944* (Tirana: 8 Nëntori, 1975); Ndreçi Plasari and Shyqri Ballvora, *Histoire de la lutte antifasciste de liberation nationale du peuple albanaise 1939–1944* (Tirana: 8 Nëntori, 1976).

2 See, for example, Xhemil Frashëri, *Pushteti popullor në vitet e Luftës Antifashiste Nacionalçlirimtare* (Tirana: Akademia e Shkencave e RPS të Shqipërisë, Instituti i Historisë, 1983); Muharrem Dezhgiu, *Veprimtaria e shtetit të ri të demokracisë*

popullore (maj – nëntor 1944) (Tirana: Akademia e Shkencave e RPS të Shqipërisë, Instituti i Historisë, 1982); Muharrem Dezhgiu, 'Veprimtaria politike e shoqërore e Këshillave Nacionalçlirimtar (maj – nëntor 1944)', *Studime historike* 32, no. 2 (1978): 91–127.

3 See Muharrem Dezhgiu, *Shqipëria nën pushtimin italian 1939–1943* (Tirana: ENEAS, 2015); Paskal Milo, *Shqiptarët në luftën e Dytë Botërore I (1939–1943)* (Tirana: Toena, 2014); Hubert Neuwirth, *Qëndresë dhe bashkëpunim në Shqipëri 1939–1944* (Tirana: Instituti i Dialogut & Komunikimit, 2006); Bernd J. Fischer, *Shqipëria gjatë Luftës, 1939–1945* (Tirana: Cabej, 2004).

4 The realization of this chapter has been partly supported by a grant from the Italian Society for the Study of Contemporary History (SISSCO).

5 Stavro Skendi, *Albania* (New York: Praeger, 1956), 58; Mario Michelangeli, *Il problema forestale albanese* (Rome: Reale Accademia d'Italia, 1940), 18–20.

6 Michelangeli, *Il problema forestale albanese*, 14–18.

7 Joseph S. Roucek, 'Economic Conditions in Albania', *Economic Geography* 9, no. 3 (1933): 256–64, here 259.

8 'Çashtja agrare në Shqypni', *Hylli i Dritës* 3, no. 8 (1922): 345–54, here 347; Giovanni Lorenzoni, *La questione agraria albanese: studi, inchieste e proposte per una riforma agraria in Albania* (Bari: Laterza, 1930), 14.

9 Roucek, *Economic Conditions in Albania*, 260.

10 Lorenzoni, *La questione agraria albanese*, 15 and 21.

11 Nadège Ragaru and Amilda Dymi, 'The Albanian-American Community in the United States', *Canadian Review of Studies in Nationalism* 31, no. 1–2 (2004): 45–63; Mickaël Wilmart, 'La "colonie albanaise" de Paris dans l'entre-deux-guerres', *Mémoires Paris et Ile-de-France* 61 (2010): 179–93; Petro Marko, *Intervistë me vetveten* (Tirana: Omsca, 2000), 117–30.

12 Fischer, *Shqipëria gjatë Luftës*, 101–6.

13 Paolo Fonzi, *Fame di guerra. L'occupazione italiana della Grecia (1941–43)* (Rome: Carocci editore, 2019), 20–3.

14 Francesco Jacomoni, 27 May 1941, Archivio Storico Diplomatico del Ministero degli Affari Esteri (henceforth: ASDMAE), fond Gabinetto Albania 1938–54, box 107.

15 It is not surprising that in April 1943, towards the end of the Italian occupation, the new Lieutenant in Albania, Alberto Pariani, listed, in a report sent to Mussolini, the repair of war damage as one of the primary objectives. See Alberto Pariani, 1 April 1943, ASDMAE, fond Gabinetto Albania, box 180.

16 Gian Paolo Caselli and Grid Thoma, 'La storia economica albanese 1912–1950: lo stabilirsi dell'egemonia italiana e il primo tentativo di pianificazione', *Rivista di storia economica* 19, no. 1 (2003): 67–107, here 99; 'Lucio', 12 April 1943, Archivio Centrale di Stato (henceforth: ACS), Ministero degli Interni (MI), Pubblica Sicurezza (PS), fond Ispettorato Generale presso la Luogotenenza del Re a Tirana (IGLRT), box 5.

17 Alberto Basciani, *L'impero nei Balcani. L'occupazione italiana dell'Albania (1939–1943)* (Rome: Viella, 2022), 219.

18 Comando Superiore Carabinieri Reali d'Albania, 28 May 1941, Archivio Museo Storico dell'Arma dei Carabinieri, box 859.

19 Comando Superiore Carabinieri Reali Albania, 19 October 1942, Arkivi Qëndror i Shtetit Shqipëtar (henceforth: AQSh), fond 154, box 23.

20 Milizia Fascista Albanese, 11 May 1942, AQSh, fond 165, box 16.

21 Minutes of the Regional Council for the Economy in Berat, 15 December 1942, AQSh, fond 204, box 22.

22 On the events of the founding of the PKSh, see Markenc Lorenci, 'Comunisti senza proletariato: il Partito comunista albanese dalla fondazione alla presa del potere (1941–1944)' (PhD Diss., Università degli Studi Roma Tre, Rome, 2021), 44–78.
23 Minutes of the Peza Conference, 16 September 1942, AQSh, Arkivi i Partisë - Lufta (henceforth: APL), fond 40, box 1.
24 Enver Hoxha, *Kur u hodhën themelet e Shqipërisë së re* (Tirana: 8 Nëntori, 1984), 87.
25 Resolution of the Peza Conference, September 1942, AQSh, APL, fond 40, box 1, 7–8.
26 Ibid., 8–9.
27 Minutes of the Second Conference of the KPNÇ, 4–8 September 1943, AQSh, APL, fond 40, box 4.
28 Vlash Papa, Memories, AQSh, APL, fond Kujtime, box V/11, 4–5.
29 Vojislav G. Pavlović, 'Stalinism without Stalin. The Soviet Origins of Tito's Yugoslavia 1937–1948', in *The Balkans in the Cold War*, ed. Vojislav G. Pavlović (Belgrade: Institute for Balkan Studies, 2011), 38.
30 Xhelal Staravecka, *Përpara gjyqit të historisë* (Tirana: Naimi, 2012), 189–90.
31 Dezhgiu, *Shqipëria nën pushtimin italian,* 167.
32 Ramiz Aranitasi, 26 March 1943, AQSh, APL, fond 19, box 1/2–6.
33 On this subject, see Minutes of the First National Conference of the PKSh, March 1943, AQSh, APL, fond 14, box 10, 32.
34 Minutes of the KPNÇ meeting held in Labinot, 4–10 July 1943, AQSh, APL, fond 40, box 3, 12.
35 Sonila Boçi, 'Le formazioni di vario orientamento nel panorama della resistenza albanese (1941–1944) e intreccio della lotta di liberazione con la lotta civile', in *Caro Nemico. Soldati pistoiesi e toscani nella Resistenza in Albania e Montenegro 1943–1945*, ed. Lia Tosi (Pisa: Edizione ETS, 2018), 335.
36 Këshilli Nacional-Çlirimtar Gjirokastër, 23 June 1943, AQSh, APL, fond 222, box 3.
37 Major Smiley's Diary, April–November 1943, 1 August 1943, The National Archives, HS 5/143.
38 Shpati (Enver Hoxha), 17 August 1943, AQSh, APL, fond 14, box 11.
39 Comando Superiore Forze Armate Albania, 10 December 1942, Archivio dell'Ufficio Storico dello Stato Maggiore dell'Esercito (henceforth: AUSSME), fond N.1-11, box 970.
40 Staravecka, *Përpara gjyqit të historisë,* 204–5.
41 Plasari and Ballvora, *Histoire de la lutte antifasciste,* 300.
42 Nuri Dragoj, 'Treva e Përmetit në periudhën e viteve 1912–1944' (PhD Diss., Universiteti i Tiranës, Tirana, 2013), 236–7; Notiziario, 14 July 1943, ACS, MI, PS, fond IGLRT, box 5.
43 Dragoj, 'Treva e Përmetit', 238.
44 Fischer, *Shqipëria gjatë Luftës*, 264.
45 Ushtria Nacional-Çlirimtare Shqiptare Deshnicë, 8 July 1944, AQSh, APL, fond 96, box 4.
46 Ushtria Nacional-Çlirimtare Shqiptare Deshnicë, 6 July 1944, AQSh, APL, fond 96, box 4.
47 Ushtria Nacional-Çlirimtare Shqiptare Deshnicë, 19 March 1944, AQSh, APL, fond 96, box 4.
48 Fischer, *Shqipëria gjatë Luftës*, 257–8.
49 David Smiley, *Albanian Assignment* (London: Sapere Books, 2020), 120–1; Franco Benanti, *La guerra più lunga. Albania 1943–1948* (Milan: Mursia, 1966), 95.

50 Minutes of the KPNÇ meeting held in Labinot, 4–10 July 1943, AQSh, APL, fond 40, box 3, 17–18; Fischer, *Shqipëria gjatë Luftës*, 190.
51 UNÇSh General Staff, 5–10 July 1943, AQSh, APL, fond 41, box 1; UNÇSh General Staff, August 1943, AQSh, APL, fond 41, box 7.
52 Minutes of the Second Conference of the KPNÇ, 4–8 September 1943, AQSh, APL, fond 40, box 4.
53 'Statuti dhe Rregullorja e Këshillavet Nacional Çlirimtar', September 1943, AQSh, APL, fond 40, box 5.
54 In many points, the Statute and Regulations of the KNÇs seem to reproduce the 'Foča Regulations' (*fočanski propisi*) approved in February 1942 by the General Staff of the Yugoslav People's Liberation Army, which the PKSh was in close contact with during the war years. On the 'Foča Regulations' and its directives, see the chapter by Xavier Bougarel in this volume.
55 'Statuti dhe Rregullorja e Këshillavet Nacional Çlirimtar', September 1943, AQSh, APL, fond 40, box 5, 9–10.
56 Ibid., 11.
57 Ibid., 16–17.
58 Ibid., 18–20.
59 Ibid., 14.
60 Ibid., 23–7.
61 Ibid., 13.
62 Ibid., 25–6.
63 Këshilli Nacional-Çlirimtar Gjirokastër, 16 November 1943, AQSh, APL, fond 222, box 3.
64 Këshilli Nacional-Çlirimtar Gjirokastër, n.d., AQSh, APL, fond 222, box 3.
65 Yannis Skalidakis, 'From Resistance to Counterstate: The Making of Revolutionary Power in the Liberated Zones of Occupied Greece, 1943–1944', *Journal of Modern Greek Studies* 33, no. 1 (2015): 155–84, here 167 and 172.
66 Këshilli Nacional-Çlirimtar Gjirokastër, 29 December 1943, AQSh, APL, fond 222, box 3.
67 Këshilli Nacional-Çlirimtar Gjirokastër, 15 October 1943, AQSh, APL, fond 222, box 3.
68 Këshilli Nacional-Çlirimtar Përmet, 9 August 1944, AQSh, APL, fond 231, box 1.
69 Këshilli Nacional-Çlirimtar Përmet, 7 March 1944, AQSh, APL, fond 228, box 7.
70 Ushtria Nacional-Çlirimtare Shqiptare Deshnicë, 29 April 1944, AQSh, APL, fond 96, box 4.
71 Ibid.
72 Këshilli Nacional-Çlirimtar Cerie, 10 April 1944, AQSh, APL, fond 230, box 2.
73 Këshilli Nacional-Çlirimtar Përmet, 9 August 1944, AQSh, APL, fond 231, box 1.
74 Këshilli Nacional-Çlirimtar Gjirokastër, 20 June 1944, AQSh, APL, fond 230, box 3.
75 Elena Aga Rossi and Maria Teresa Giusti, *Una guerra a parte. I militari italiani nei Balcani 1940–1945* (Bologna: Il Mulino, 2011), 313–17.
76 Letter without sender sent to Dali (Dali Ndreu, UNÇSh officer), 30 September 1943, AQSh, APL, fond 41, box 9; UNÇSh General Staff Command, 1 October 1943, AQSh, APL, fond 41, box 9.
77 Këshilli Nacional-Çlirimtar Gjirokastër, 12 August 1944, AQSh, APL, fond 230, box 3.
78 Siri Shapllo, 22 March 1944, AQSh, APL, fond 222, box 16.

79 Këshilli Nacional-Çlirimtar Skrapar, 6 October 1944, AQSh, APL, fond 239, box 1.
80 Siri Shapllo, 22 March 1944, AQSh, APL, fond 222, box 16.
81 High Command of the First Operational Zone Gjirokastër-Vlorë, 24 August 1944, AQSh, APL, fond 96, box 1.
82 Këshilli Nacional-Çlirimtar Therepel, 30 July 1944, AQSh, APL, fond 239, box 1.

Conclusion: The power of food in wartime

Paolo Fonzi, Sabine Rutar and Xavier Bougarel

As a basic component of human reproduction and impacting all aspects of social life, food is a 'social total phenomenon'.[1] In this book, the authors address the topic of food in Albania, Greece and Yugoslavia during the Second World War and investigate how changes in the production, distribution and consumption of food produced multiple social and societal effects. Exploring the interconnections between food, scarcity and power, they research how different historical actors developed strategies and policies to master the new situation that led to changed socio-economic patterns of access, and more often than not, a lack of food. The authors showcase how the changes in the production and distribution of food led to the creation of altered, sometimes even new power constellations, but also resulted in the disempowerment, and death, of many.

In the words of Derek Aldcroft, in the interwar period, Southeastern Europe was part of 'Europe's Third World', namely 'those countries which ... still had around one half or more of their population dependent on agriculture and with incomes per capita of less than 50 per cent of those of the advanced nations of Western Europe'.[2] Indeed, in 1930s Greece, Albania and Yugoslavia, the share of the population dependent on agriculture lay between 70 and 80 per cent. Productivity in the agricultural sector was low compared to Western European standards, with overpopulation in the countryside generally regarded as a major hindrance to economic development. The average number of calorie units produced per person employed in the agricultural sector for the years 1931–35 amounted to 22 units in Albania, 38 in Yugoslavia and 50 in Greece, a poor result even compared to Austria's 134 in the same period, which was the lowest of the more developed European economies.[3]

Due to the policies of import substitution practised by most Southeast European countries as well as inefficient agrarian reforms implemented after the First World War, the rural population grew, which increased the number of smallholdings and inhibited socio-economic development. In addition, in both Greece and Yugoslavia, the agrarian reforms had been politically motivated, as they aimed to create a large layer of smallholders of Greek and Serb ethnicity, loyal to the respective state (see the chapters by Tsoutsoumpis and Zakić). Yet, in neither country did these newly created strata of smallholders lead to increased agricultural productivity or modernization. In Albania, interwar development was different. The country's reform plan, devised under King Zog in 1930 with considerable involvement of Italian experts, remained on paper. Here, the structure of agrarian property continued to be characterized by large estates, owned by absentee landowners, especially in central and southern Albania, which proved no more conducive to any kind of economic advancement than the land fragmentation in Greece and Yugoslavia (Basciani and Lorenci).

The three countries at the centre of our book were largely exporters of primary products, while at the same time being far from self-sufficient in terms of food consumption. However, their economies were not homogeneous in this regard, as food deficit areas existed alongside surplus areas. While such regional inequalities are common to national economies everywhere and at all times, they acquired a specific significance in Yugoslavia where occupation fragmented the country and disrupted the national market. Mirna Zakić showcases this significance in her discussion of the detrimental effects the German occupation had in the Banat, traditionally a surplus region, and Nikica Barić does the same for the Great County of Cetina in the Italian-controlled part of the Independent State of Croatia (NDH), which had largely been dependent on the import of basic food items and on remittances from abroad.

The occupation of Albania in April 1939 and that of Greece and Yugoslavia in April 1941 brought a radical break with the countries' prevailing economic normalities. Food scarcity, already palpable before the war, reached the region and became a part of everyday life. Agricultural production decreased and imports dropped, partly due to the Allied blockade. Moreover, soon after the occupiers had taken over, various kinds of insurgencies – Partisans, other politically or ethnically motivated armed groups, bandits – further disrupted economic activity, especially in the countryside, the natural habitat of irregular armies. This was compounded by large flows of people, made up both of those deported by different political actors – the German authorities, the Ustashas, etc. – and of refugees spurred to move elsewhere by the harsh conditions imposed by new incumbent powers. This included, for example, the Greeks fleeing from Bulgarian-occupied Thrace, the Slovenes in the German-occupied territories of northern Yugoslavia who were persecuted for not being 'Germanizable' or for being politically undesirable, and the Serbs persecuted by the Ustashas in the NDH. This was the case for Jewish populations everywhere. These sudden demographic disruptions also shook up economies. Last but not least, the occupying armies placed an immense burden on the local economies. While in the Greek case, both Germany and Italy imported foodstuffs to meet, if only in part, their soldiers' needs, the occupying armies were generally expected to feed themselves off the local resources (Fonzi).

In addition to significantly reducing food availability, the occupation led to the complete collapse of internal supply chains. In both Yugoslavia and Greece, the Germans made sure to take control of those regions that were important for their war economy, at the expense of the Italians (Rutar, Zakić and Fonzi). The newly created Province of Ljubljana (*Provincia di Lubiana*), annexed by Italy in April 1941, for example, now bordered with German-occupied Carniola. The traditional sources of agricultural supply could now only reach the city via the black market, and eventually not at all (Šorn). Similarly, the Great County of Cetina in the Italian-controlled part of the NDH experienced severely disrupted supply from those parts of Dalmatia that had been annexed to Italy (Barić).

Yet, also in Greece, whose state borders remained unchanged, the existence of different occupying powers meant a sudden multiplication of internal boundaries. The occupation authorities established different types of military governance in their respective areas, with different legislation, and were unable to establish any systematic coordination. Agreements reached between the Italian and German governments with the aim of facilitating such coordination came to nothing, and the third player in Greece, Bulgaria, implemented a fully independent policy in Thrace and Eastern Macedonia (Fonzi).

Even in Albania, officially independent but ruled by Italy through a complex power architecture, the occupation led to a fragmentation of the national market. Both Alberto Basciani and Markenc Lorenci, in their respective chapters, reveal how the Italian policies contributed to the collapse of the national market and to food scarcity. Since Albania had been an informal Italian protectorate since the 1920s and had been largely integrated with the Italian economy, on the occupation of 1939 and the outbreak of war, the flow of food imports from Italy initially continued. Indeed, in the first year of occupation, the living conditions of the Albanian population even improved (Lorenci). However, after 1939, a large number of Italian soldiers and civilians arrived in Albania, bringing with them an inflow of capital intended for the financing of construction projects. These were sudden demographic changes of a different kind to those seen in Yugoslavia and Greece, but they still heavily disrupted the balance between production and consumption. The population influx included men who had decided to move from the countryside to the Italian-financed construction projects in search of a better income. Italy's attack on Greece further aggravated this situation, as the expenditures to finance the war effort and the ensuing rampant speculation on consumer goods led to a huge rise in prices (Basciani). Moreover, the Italo-Greek war heavily affected southern Albania, as Italy invaded Greece from here, devastating the countryside (Lorenci).

Transport infrastructures were controlled by the occupiers and often interrupted due to the lack of coal or fuel or the acts of sabotage committed by the Partisans, who sought to interrupt railway lines or the transport of coal from the mines (Barić, Rutar and Lorenci). This further segmented the markets. Last but not least, while food rationing, that is state regulation of production and distribution, was strengthened on paper, in reality it became less effective. The Ustasha government in the NDH and the collaborationist government established in German-occupied Serbia were weak, as were the governing authorities in the Italian and German occupational zones of both Greece and (Greater) Albania. They relied on inefficient administration, which largely limited their control over the countryside. With his focus on Thesprotia/Chameria, the Greek region bordering with Albania, Spyros Tsoutsoumpis offers a vivid example of a multi-ethnic border area that drifted into a power void, with state power collapsing well before the Partisan movement took hold. Contrary to what previous scholarship has maintained, ethnic cleavages were not the cause of the formation of armed groups which then fought against each other. Rather, the radicalization of ethnic differences was prompted by the collapse of the state and the food crisis that came with it.

Inefficient administration also meant inefficient or no collection of data. Governments' efforts to curb the black market led peasants to hide their produce. It is very difficult to gain a clear picture of which areas suffered extreme scarcity, and which managed to maintain a viable, if informal, food economy. To at least partially compensate for the lack of official statistics, a consistent assortment of grey data can be extracted from the various available sources. Moreover, as theories of famine indicate, structures of entitlement in times of famine are much more complex than a simple deficit versus surplus configuration. Among other aspects, these structures include new forms of social stratification within local societies deriving from different opportunities to access food. Miners, for example, like other workers performing tasks that were important for the war economy, had privileged access to food (Rutar).

In the course of the war, the occupying powers and the collaborationist governments failed to maintain viable systems of food production and distribution. In Albania, even though Mussolini's Italy had nurtured ambitious ideas of agricultural modernization since the 1920s, it had to contend with the beys (the large landowners) and its plans to modernize the country never took off before the war (Basciani). In Greece, the Italian army tried to increase agricultural produce by importing seeds for sowing, but did not manage to successfully alleviate food scarcity (Fonzi). In German-occupied Serbia, the interwar land reform was partly repealed in favour of the ethnic Germans, who received more land. However, such redistribution, while racially motivated, had the primary aim of extracting the Banat's resources for the Reich's benefit (Zakić). The Yugoslav Partisan army, in the territories it liberated in Bosnia, understood that any attempt to redistribute land while the war was still ongoing would have endangered production at a time when it was most needed (Bougarel). In Thesprotia/Chameria in Greece, the Muslim population tried to exploit their status as collaborators of the occupiers to seize back the land that had been taken from them during the interwar period and given to Greek Orthodox peasants (Tsoutsoumpis). There were similar attempts to repossess land that had been forcefully transferred as an instrument of ethnic homogenization in Kosovo and in Bačka, which generally had a negative impact on agricultural production.[4]

Against the backdrop of the circumstances described thus far, the central activity of both the occupiers and the occupied was the acquisition and distribution of food. The governing authorities instrumentalized food, or rather its scarcity, for political ends, feeding first and foremost their staff, attempting to increase their legitimacy through food distributions, and denying food to those who they persecuted. While it proved impossible to introduce structural improvements in the agricultural sector, state actors found it similarly difficult to even maintain control over the distribution of agricultural output (Zakić, Barić, Basciani, Fonzi and Šorn). This was not least due to the fact that the occupiers generally had insufficient personnel at their disposal and relied on the collaborationist governments. These were representatives of states that had already been weak before the war, and the upheaval caused by the occupation was certainly not conducive to administrative efficiency, nor political legitimacy. Political measures such as mandatory crop collection, introduced in all three countries, partly on behalf of the occupiers, were difficult, sometimes even impossible, to implement. In Greece, in the summer of 1942, the Italian occupation army and the Greek state authorities tried to enforce the collection of public crops by all available means, including harsh measures against hoarding and incentives for the peasants, but failed completely. A major factor in this was the devaluation of the national currency, the drachma, which had spurred the peasants to sell their crops on the black market rather than at the regulated prices of the official economy. State weakness was both the cause and the consequence of the ineffective enforcement of crop collection, leading to further power voids. Underfed state officials were also largely dependent on the inflated black markets if they wanted to eat, and were less and less inclined to perform their duties. As a result, corruption was rampant (Fonzi and Tsoutsoumpis).

Although the occupiers resorted to the black market themselves, it was the Partisans who were in a better position to profit from this situation. Inhabiting areas that the state did not reach and by definition acting outside the law, they could use force in a more effective way than state officials. In southern Albania, the first acts of violence undertaken by the Partisans in the areas they had liberated were directed against tax collectors who had enforced the payment of the agricultural tithe by the peasants. The Partisans could also purchase large amounts of foodstuffs with the gold coins provided by British liaison officers, thus clearly profiting from the collapse of the official economy and the peasants' refusal to accept the devalued state currency. Gradually, the Partisans geared their administration of the liberated territories towards collecting the harvest from the peasants. However, by this point at the latest, the Partisans found that their counter-state building faced problems that were quite similar to those encountered by the Albanian state, as the peasants were not willing to feed the Partisans either (Lorenci).

In western Bosnia, part of the Independent State of Croatia, the Partisans were more successful in co-opting the peasants. Had they resorted to sheer force, they would have risked alienating them, the very backbone of their resistance army, from their cause. Instead, they adopted an approach that valued the moral economy on which the peasant society was built. In this way, in particular in the first phase of the war, they were able to channel the agricultural produce to themselves. Only towards the end of the war, once they had established their hegemony in the liberated territories, did they resort to a more compulsory approach (Bougarel). Both in Yugoslavia and Albania, the Partisans' governance created a new order in regions where, due to the collapse of the state, a power void had emerged. For example, in the liberated areas of southern Albania, they went to great lengths to put a stop to banditry: protecting property against arbitrary acts of seizure was part of their attempt to establish their monopoly on violence here (Lorenci).

Indeed, war and occupation meant not only altered legislation and political systems as well as the emergence of violence as a salient feature, they also (re-)created allegiances and enforced, sometimes shifted, patterns of loyalty, including moral economy regimes. This included the Holocaust. Marija Vulesica showcases how in Zagreb, the capital of the Independent State of Croatia, the food relief organization created by key actors within the Jewish Community relied heavily on material concessions by the Ustasha authorities, in other words the very same institutions that starved, harassed and murdered them. They knew that, if they wanted to succeed in providing food to those who had been deported to camps, they needed to involve, even rely on, the regime's institutions as well as individuals among the Ustashas. In describing the ways in which food got to those systemically condemned to death, Vulesica underlines the importance of agency in assessing war, occupation and the Holocaust. In his investigation of Italy's food deliveries to Greece, Paolo Fonzi echoes Vulesica's emphasis on what were, in a manner of speaking, interconnections between those in power and those attempting to help the prisoners facing death. Focusing on the perpetrators rather than on the victims, Fonzi asserts that assistance needs to be seen against the backdrop of political agendas: while the Italians did import food to Greece in order to prevent the spread of economic chaos, at the same time they instrumentalized these food deliveries in their imperialist policy.

Linked to both Vulesica's and Fonzi's arguments, Sabine Rutar and Mirna Zakić also investigate how racist ideology and imperialist mindsets were intertwined. Their focus is not on the Holocaust, however, but on German racism against Slavs. The occupying powers installed labour regimes that included determining what and how much workers ate. Miners were of central importance to the German war effort and were privileged both in terms of food rations and in terms of racial profiling. In the Slovenian mining industries, qualified miners that had been labelled 'non-Germanizable' often continued to work, rather than being deported, which increased their chances of survival. In the Bor copper mine in Serbia, racially motivated mistreatment was mingled with the oppression of forced and slave labourers, including thousands of Italian military internees (after September 1943) and Hungarian Jews (since 1944). Instrumentalizing food was part and parcel of these violent labour regimes in Yugoslavia, much as they differed in terms of their occupational logic and importance for the war economy (Rutar).

In the 'breadbasket' (*Kornkammer*) that was the Banat, it was the sense of belonging to the *Volksgemeinschaft* which increased the ethnic Germans' willingness to provide food to the German Reich. However, as they would soon come to understand, the German occupiers had created an agricultural labour regime that exploited this willingness at the ethnic Germans' expense, treating them as lesser Germans than those living in the Reich. Compared to the region's other ethnicities, especially the Serbs and other Slavs, the ethnic Germans were privileged; and yet, their loyalty to the Nazis was still not enough for them to be regarded as Germans of equal value (Zakić).

Ephemeral, pragmatic allegiances and loyalty shifts were in fact a core feature of seeking access to food, be these ethnically or politically motivated (often both). Thesprotia/Chameria in northwestern Greece and the Dalmatian Great County of Cetina in the NDH, both deficit regions, suffered a dire food crisis as a consequence of occupation (Tsoutsoumpis and Barić). In Thesprotia/Chameria, the occupation destroyed the rural economy, and food became the main issue that the various actors in the region fought over. For the peasants, joining one of the ethnically motivated armed factions was a way to access a larger share of the available food (Tsoutsoumpis). Similarly, in Cetina, allegiances to the three main political actors – the Ustashas, the Italians and the Partisans – were volatile, as they strongly depended on who was able to provide more food. The Ustashas' inability to feed the region undermined their political power, just as the Italians' tendency to destroy economic resources in their attempts to starve the Partisans alienated a large share of the population. The Partisans in Cetina, on the other hand, engaged in establishing a moral economy of sorts similar to that in western Bosnia (Bougarel), combined with targeted violent acts of food requisition (Barić).

As has become evident, and connecting Yugoslavia, Albania and Greece to the larger historiography on the Holocaust, forced labour, and national socialist and fascist schemes of economic exploitation, as well as on how occupying armies have dealt with counter-insurgencies, deliberate withholding of food was as important a policy factor as distributing food. For example, in December 1942, the Italian army conducted a large-scale operation against the settlements of Çorovodë in southern Albania, recently liberated by the Partisans, targeting not only people but also the livestock in the pastures (Lorenci). Similarly, in the Great County of Cetina in Dalmatia, the Italians sought to quell the resistance through the plunder and destruction of agricultural goods (Barić). In Greece, the Italians gave their food distribution schemes a 'humanitarian' gloss, while at the same time hindering the International Committee of the Red Cross from delivering food, so as to prevent their own efforts from being compromised (Fonzi).

Those who were devoid of any power to influence the distribution – and withholding – of food on a large scale were forced to adapt to scarcity and to develop strategies of survival. Like the Nazis, the Ustashas used starvation as one of the means to annihilate the Jews, and those who attempted to counter this genocidal policy faced a Sisyphean battle (Vulesica). After the Italians erected a barbed wire fence around the city of Ljubljana in an attempt to stop the strong underground urban resistance in its tracks, the city's inhabitants transformed the parks into vegetable gardens and engaged in small animal husbandry, activities previously quite unknown to urban dwellers. Smuggling also became a feature of everyday life, but eventually the black market flows from German-occupied Carniola started to dry out. Despite the considerable efforts to avert it, by the end of the winter 1944–45 Ljubljana was on the verge of a famine, and it was only the end of the war that prevented larger-scale losses among the starving population (Šorn).

Given that they were now fenced in, the citizens of Ljubljana could not get to the countryside to search for food, as people had done in other regions. From Thesprotia/Chameria, for example, people undertook long journeys to surplus regions in order to bring home some provisions. In doing so, they often ran the risk of losing their property and also their lives as the countryside was awash with bandits (Tsoutsoumpis). Food deliveries from the countryside to industrial sites faced similar problems, as carriages as well as railways were targeted as much by starving bands of people as by the Partisans who knew that workers who did not eat could not work and would be more prone to sabotaging their workplace, or defecting to the Partisans in the hope of finding more food there. 'Working for the enemy', whether by choice or by force, could be averted by preventing food supplies from reaching the company (Rutar).

While scholars interested in the topic of food during the Second World War have largely focused either on the occupiers and their policies of exploitation, on the Partisans and their relations with the peasants, or on the way people coped with or succumbed to shortages, this book significantly shifts the focus to the implementation and effect of food policies in local settings, showcasing the importance of the local dimensions of the war as well as linking these to broader patterns of interpretation and understanding. It does this by adopting a comprehensively interconnected approach, binding together various analytical and geographical tropes as well as the core actors that characterized the occupied societies of Yugoslavia, Greece and Albania. Such an endeavour can only be achieved by bringing together the expertise of a collective of scholars. This Conclusion sheds light on the many threads that bind the research of our authors together, both in terms of methodology and in terms of establishing commonalities and differences in the experiences of war and occupation.

While our book substantially adds to the existing literature on nutrition and hunger during the war with perspectives on a hitherto neglected European region that lived through multiple occupations, we also see it as a benchmark for much-needed further research. Our book charts the field and there are several issues about which we still know very little. For instance, how did collaborationist governments, such as the Ustashas and the government of Milan Nedić in German-occupied Serbia, design and implement food policies? How did they try to regulate agriculture and the distribution of agricultural output? Which food rationing schemes did they use, and how were these geared towards the construction of new social, and especially racial, hierarchies? The absence of such studies needs to be seen in the context of the general lack of research into the economic aspects of occupation.

Industrial workplaces which contributed to the war efforts of the occupiers would merit further research, especially taking an entangled and comparative approach that transcends the political boundaries created by the occupying forces – what continuities in production and in labour relations existed, and in what ways were they disrupted? This question not only concerns racist reshuffling of the workforce, but crucially also aspects of everyday life. Access to food was key in shaping people's decisions on whether or not to work for the enemy.

Similarly, questions concerning economic relations between surplus and deficit areas would merit a more comprehensive examination. Deficit regions were cut off from traditional food sources and were marked by informal attempts to maintain or re-establish such connections in order to prevent starvation. It is generally difficult to assess the flows of goods on the black market; yet, the black market is a key feature of the war years and the dearth of research is glaring. Several chapters in this book refer to the Banat as the 'granary' which supplied food to such an extent that it seems that this region, generally perceived as feeding the Reich, in fact fed the whole of Southeastern Europe. It would be a kind of 'demystification' of the 'granary' trope to write the transnational socio-economic history of who the Banat's grain actually fed during the war, including what part of this process went through the official nutrition schemes and what was in fact a part of the black market.

Generally, historiography has been marked by national frameworks as well as linguistic limitations. This is not only true for Greek scholars studying Greece, Albanian scholars studying Albania, and those in the successor states of Yugoslavia who have nationalized and thereby considerably scaled down their research horizons. International scholars, too, have largely adhered to this pattern. Almost equally importantly however, researchers have divided their focus on the occupying forces, concentrating on either the Italian (1939–43) or the German occupiers (1941–45). In regions that experienced both occupations, scholars have a tendency to either study the Italian phase (1941–43) or the subsequent German one (1943–45). Our book makes a strong argument for designing research agendas that ask both transnational and trans-occupational questions. As a part of this, a comparative and transnational approach that brings together the food policies of the various resistance movements would make for a fascinating and insightful research angle on the resistance against national socialism and fascism.

And last but by no means least, linking food, hunger and scarcity to violence, atrocities and genocide opens the door towards interconnecting the Holocaust with other schemes underpinned by racist ideology, targeting Slavs of all colours and the Roma. The occupiers' racism also links to their deliberate instrumentalization of the ethnic differences that characterized the region. Connecting questions around the socio-ethnic upheavals that the land reforms of the interwar years triggered with how these upheavals were exacerbated during the war makes for a very important research field, but only if not carried out under national(ist) auspices. A transnational and comparative analysis of the continuities and breaks in patterns of agricultural production would show the parallel experiences of the Southeast European societies, counteracting the nationalist narratives about territory that continue to predominate to this day.

Scarcity of the key resource of human reproduction, food, inevitably creates tectonic shifts in the balance of power and destroys whatever social cohesion existed. Violence is always part and parcel of this, but the war and occupation of the 1930s and 1940s exacerbated this link to the extreme. Charting hitherto scarcely explored territory, both in the methodological and the geographical sense, this book paves the way for further research.

Notes

1 A good introduction to this topic is Jeffrey M. Pilcher, ed., *The Oxford Handbook of Food History* (Oxford: Oxford University Press, 2012).

2 Derek Aldcroft, *Europe's Third World: The European Periphery in the Interwar Years* (Ashgate: Routledge, 2006), 3.

3 Ibid., 6.

4 For more on this, see Paolo Fonzi, *Oltre i confini. Le occupazioni italiane durante la Seconda guerra mondiale* (1939–43) (Florence: Le Monnier università – Mondadori education, 2020), 106–9; also Franziska Anna Zaugg, *Rekrutierungen für die Waffen-SS in Südosteuropa. Ideen, Ideale und Realitäten einer Vielvölkerarmee* (Berlin, Boston: De Gruyter Oldenbourg, 2021).

Index

www.ingramcontent.com/pod-product-compliance
Ingram Content Group UK Ltd.
Pitfield, Milton Keynes, MK11 3LW, UK
UKHW020808290926
15470UKWH00003B/1032

9 781350 333918